AMERICA'S WAR ON TERR

M000312188

With this updated version, the authors have made a significant contribution to the scholarly understanding of the complexities of the US-led war on terrorism. America's War on Terror, Second Edition *supplies experts with a number of different yet essential vantage points into the foreign policymaking process and issue areas that characterize and define US counterterrorism policy.*

Chris J. Dolan, Lebanon Valley College, USA

... presents a timely and comprehensive analysis of the background, consequences and challenges of the war on terror. It addresses such diverse and complementary topics as budgetary priorities, military power, homeland security and presidential leadership. The interdisciplinary approach, careful research and clear writing recommend this text highly to students and scholars alike.

Meena Bose, Hofstra University, USA

For Claudia, Gina, and Tracy

America's War on Terror, Second Edition

Edited by

TOM LANSFORD
University of Southern Mississippi, USA

ROBERT P. WATSON
Lynn University, USA

JACK COVARRUBIAS
University of Southern Mississippi, USA

ASHGATE

Published by
Ashgate Publishing Limited
Wey Court East
Union Road
Farnham
Surrey, GU9 7PT
England

Ashgate Publishing Company
Suite 420
101 Cherry Street
Burlington
VT 05401-4405
USA

www.ashgate.com

British Library Cataloguing in Publication Data
America's war on terror. -- 2nd ed.
   1. Bush, George W. (George Walker), 1946- 2. War on
   Terrorism, 2001- 3. United States--Foreign relations--2001-
   I. Lansford, Tom. II. Watson, Robert P., 1962-
   III. Covarrubias, Jack.
   327.7'3'09051-dc22

Library of Congress Cataloging-in-Publication Data
America's war on terror / by Tom Lansford, Robert P. Watson and Jack Covarrubias. -- 2nd ed.
   p. cm.
   Includes bibliographical references and index.
   ISBN 978-0-7546-7785-7 (hardback) -- ISBN 978-0-7546-7787-1 (pbk) --
   ISBN 978-0-7546-9533-2 (ebook) 1. Bush, George W. (George Walker), 1946- 2. Obama,
   Barack. 3. War on Terrorism, 2001- 4. United States--Foreign relations--2001- I. Lansford,
   Tom. II. Watson, Robert P., 1962- III. Covarrubias, Jack.
   HV6432.A526 2009
   973.931--dc22
                                                                              2009016977
   ISBN 978-0-7546-7785-7 (hbk)
   ISBN 978-0-7546-7787-1 (pbk)
   ISBN 978-0-7546-9533-2 (ebk)

Mixed Sources
Product group from well-managed
forests and other controlled sources
www.fsc.org Cert no. SA-COC-1565
© 1996 Forest Stewardship Council
FSC

Printed and bound in Great Britain by
MPG Books Group, UK

Contents

PART 3 FOREIGN POLICY IMPLICATIONS

PART 4 FUTURE CHALLENGES

List of Figure and Tables

Notes on Contributors

Neal Allen is an Assistant Professor of Political Science with the College of St. Benedict and Saint John's University since 2006. His research interests include the American Supreme Court, the Presidency, and American political development.

Kristin Andrews is an Associate Professor in the Department of Philosophy and Cognitive Science Program at York University, in Toronto, Canada.

Jack Covarrubias is an Assistant Professor of Political Science at the University of Southern Mississippi Gulf Coast. He is also a member of the governing board of the National Social Science Association. He has published numerous works, most recently including the co-authored book *To Protect and Defend: Homeland Security Policy* (2006); *Strategic Interests in the Middle East: Opposition or Support for US Foreign Policy* (2007); and the co-authored chapter, "The Best Defense? Iraq and Beyond," in the edited volume *The Second Term of George W. Bush: Prospects and Perils* (2006).

John Davis teaches at Howard University. His articles include "The Evolution of American Grand Strategy and the War on Terrorism: Clinton-Bush Perspectives"; "The Evolution of the Doctrine of Preemption"; and "The History of The War on Terrorism." Davis was a researcher with the National Defense University at Fort McNair in Washington, DC.

Michael G. Dziubinski is a retired military officer with expertise in nuclear command and control, national intelligence, information operations, and joint operations. He holds a PhD from Old Dominion University and researches joint warfighting. He currently works with United States Joint Forces Command.

Mark Evans is Senior Lecturer in the Department of Politics and International Relations, Swansea University. He is the editor of *The Edinburgh Companion to Contemporary Liberalism* (Edinburgh University Press, 2001); *Just War Theory: A Reappraisal* (Edinburgh University Press, 2005); and has authored numerous articles and chapters on liberal political theory, human rights, and international relations. He is currently working on the concept of *jus post bellum*.

Patrick Hayden is Reader in the School of International Relations at the University of St. Andrews, Scotland. He is the author of *Political Evil in a Global Age: Hannah Arendt and International Theory* (Routledge, 2009); *Critical Theories* *of Globalization* (Palgrave, 2006, with Chamsy el-Ojeili); *Cosmopolitan Global Politics* (Ashgate, 2005); and *John Rawls: Towards a Just World Order* (University of Wales Press, 2002).

Tom Lansford is the Academic Dean and a Professor of Political Science, International Development & Affairs at the University of Southern Mississippi Gulf Coast. He is a member of the governing board of the National Social Science Association and the author/co-author of numerous books, including: *All for One: NATO, Terrorism and the United States* (2002); *A Bitter Harvest: U.S. Foreign Policy and Afghanistan* (2003); *Strategic Preemption: US Foreign Policy and the Second War in Iraq* (2004); and co-editor of several collections including: *George W. Bush: A Political and Ethical Assessment at Midterm* (2004); *Transatlantic Security Dilemmas: Old Europe, New Europe and the US* (2005); and *Strategic Interests in the Middle East: Opposition or Support for US Foreign Policy* (2007).

Justin Miller is a graduate student at the University of Southern Mississippi Gulf Coast and is currently researching US homeland security in the post-9/11 world.

Shahdad Naghshpour is a Professor of Political Science, International Development and Affairs at the University of Southern Mississippi Gulf Coast. Dr Naghshpour is active in research and consulting in regional and environmental economics. He has published in *International Journal of Technology Management*; *Southern Economic Review*; and *Journal of Interdisciplinary Business Research*. His articles include "Globalization Discontent: The Effects of Globalization on Ethnic Protest" (*Peace Economics, Peace Science and Public Policy*, 2008) with Dr J.J. St. Marie; and "Global Shift: Is there a Link between Economic Growth and Globalization?" (*International Journal of Trade and Global Markets*, 2008, also with Dr St. Marie).

Robert J. Pauly, Jr. is an Assistant Professor of Political Science and Director of the International Policy and Development PhD program at the University of Southern Mississippi Gulf Coast. His principal research interests are US foreign policy toward the states of the Greater Middle East and the conduct of the Global War on Terrorism. His most recent books are *To Protect and Defend: US Homeland Security Policy*, with Jack Covarrubias and Tom Lansford (2006); and *US Foreign Policy and the Persian Gulf: Safeguarding American Interests through Selective Multilateralism* (2005).

Dirk C. van Raemdonck holds a PhD from the University of Georgia and is Graduate Coordinator for the Department of Education Reform at the University of Arkansas. He has written on topics of European unification and political development, security policy, international conflict, political parties, and education systems. Publications include book chapters and articles in scholarly journals including *Global Policy*; *Journal of Peace Research*; and *Southeastern Political Review*.

Neil Reedy holds Bachelor's degrees in History and Political Science and a Master's degree in Political Science from Villanova University. He has contributed to a UK-based Intelligence journal and most recently co-authored a chapter on Presidential leadership. He is currently an Intelligence Analyst for the US Government.

Vaughn P. Shannon is an Assistant Professor of Political Science at Wright State University in Dayton, Ohio. He is the author of *Balancing Act: US Foreign Policy and the Arab–Israeli Conflict* (2003), and his work has appeared in numerous journals, including *International Organization*; *International Studies Quarterly*; *European Journal of International Relations*; *Security Studies*; and *Foreign Policy Analysis*. Dr Shannon received his PhD from Ohio State University in 2001.

J.J. St. Marie is an Assistant Professor of Political Science, International Development and Affairs at the University of Southern Mississippi Gulf Coast. He holds a PhD from Texas Tech University. His publications include, "Labor Mobility in Asian Countries: An Empirical Investigation" (*Journal of Business, Industry and Economics*, Summer 2004, with T. Parker), and "Veto Players and the Asian Economic Crisis: Crisis and Recovery" (*International Relations of the Asia-Pacific*).

Robert P. Watson is the Director of American Studies at Lynn University in Florida. He is the author/editor of over 25 books and has published hundreds of scholarly articles, book chapters, reference essays, and newspaper columns on various topics in American politics and history. Dr Watson has convened or co-convened several national conferences on the American Presidency, regularly hosts community town hall programs throughout south Florida on current issues, and is frequently interviewed by television, print, and radio outlets in south Florida and around the country.

Matthew A. Williams is a graduate student in Political Science at the University of Southern Mississippi Gulf Coast. His research interests include international relations theory, international security, and globalization.

Steve A. Yetiv is a Professor of Political Science at Old Dominion University. Dr Yetiv's research explores American foreign policy toward the Middle East, global energy, interdependence, and theories of decision-making, foreign policy and international relations. His recent book is *The Absence of Grand Strategy: The United States and the Persian Gulf (1975–2005)* (Johns Hopkins University Press, 2008). His recent articles have appeared in *Security Studies*; *The British Journal of Political Science*; and *The Middle East Journal*.

Preface

America's War on Terror is designed to serve several goals and several audiences. Of course, it is never an easy undertaking to produce a book suitable for a wide readership, but this focus was never far from the minds of the editors and contributors. The book should serve scholars of US foreign policy, security policy, Middle East studies, and terrorism. At the same time, because we believe the book is highly readable and approachable for non-experts, it is suitable for university students, college classrooms and the general public interested in an introduction to the theoretical and historical underpinnings of terrorism and America's War on Terror.

Every effort was made to produce a balanced and fair account of the war. Terrorism and war bring out emotions in everyone, especially when the incidents are still happening, and care was paid to provide an array of perspectives on the topic while treating it with objectivity and thoroughness. Likewise, recognizing the challenge in producing the first edition of this book at the relative outset of the war, the second edition was put together over several years after the 9/11 attacks. This proved to be a challenge as well because of the uniqueness of this war and the ongoing and fundamental transformations that define many terrorist organizations and the conduct of the war. This war is unlike any other and, in our effort to produce a timely assessment of the reasons for and consequences of the war against terrorism, we tried to encompass the broadest possible views.

The second edition features a new introductory chapter to place the war in its proper historical context. New chapters have been added on homeland security and the conflicts in Iraq and Afghanistan as well as on the importance to the war of states like Pakistan. Readers will also find chapters from the first edition updated to 2009 and updated and expanded appendices with useful information on terrorist groups and incidents.

This research and writing effort would have been impossible were it not for the enthusiasm of the contributing authors. The contributors represent a wide array of perspectives in their writings and come from equally diverse scholarly backgrounds. This diversity is a real strength of the book. We also acknowledge the staff of professionals at Ashgate and thank them for their support of the project and interest in a second edition. Any mistakes in the book are entirely those of the editors. Lastly, we offer our wives and families our gratitude for the time spent away from them to produce this book.

It is difficult to know how the international war against terrorism will progress and perhaps ultimately end, if it ever does. It is certain only that the war will experience both further successes and failures; that serious challenges will remain and new threats will arise; and casualties on all sides will occur. It is our hope that this book will help readers understand some of the fundamental forces shaping international terrorism and American efforts to combat it. It is our sincere hope too that, as much as is possible, a peaceful and timely resolution to some of the most pressing threats of international terror will result.

Tom Lansford
Long Beach, Mississippi

Robert P. Watson
Boca Raton, Florida

Jack Covarrubias
Long Beach, Mississippi

Chapter 1
The Politics and History of Terror

Robert P. Watson

Introduction

On the morning of September 11, 2001, four US commercial aircraft were hijacked and used as weapons of mass destruction by 19 terrorists of the radical Islamist terror network, al-Qaeda.[1] After seizing control of the planes, terrorists crashed two of them into the twin towers of the World Trade Center in New York City, while another plane was flown into the Pentagon in the US capital city. After learning of the fate of the other three aircraft from loved ones by cell phone, passengers of the fourth plane struggled for control of the aircraft and succeeded in diverting it from its intended target. The plane crashed into the ground in western Pennsylvania, killing all aboard but not a single individual beyond those on the flight. These tragic events produced a death toll reaching into the thousands and marked the start of America's War on Terror.[2]

As horrific as the events of September 11 were, the sad reality is that they were merely the latest in a long history of terrorism.[3] Even though the 9/11 tragedy prompted America's War on Terror and were the first acts of foreign aggression of considerable magnitude on US soil since the War of 1812, or on a US territory since the Japanese strike on Pearl Harbor in 1941, numerous terror incidents have been directed against US targets and citizens.[4]

Terrorist attacks again the United States also predate the attacks of September 11. In April of 1983, for example, the US Embassy in Beirut, Lebanon was bombed, killing 63. Later that same year, in October, the US Marine Corps barracks in Beirut were attacked, killing 299. Some years later, another US military complex, this time in Riyadh, Saudi Arabia, was bombed and 19 were killed. Other US embassies in Nairobi, Kenya and Dar-es-Salaam, Tanzania were bombed in August

---

1   The terrorist group, al-Qaeda, is spelled various ways around the world, including Al-Qaeda, al-Qaida, and al-Qa'ida, but the present form will be used in this text.

2   The total death toll of the attacks on September 11, 2001 was 2,976 plus 19 hijackers.

3   Terror attacks have been happening for as long as recorded human history. Appendix B contains a list of worldwide terrorist acts since 1990.

4   The Japanese attack on the naval base at Pearl Harbor in Hawaii in December of 1941 was an act of war, but Hawaii was not yet a state. Until 1959 it was a territory.

of 1998, resulting in 223 deaths. Almost one year before the 9/11 attack, 17 were killed when the *USS Cole* was bombed while in port in Aden, Yemen in October of 2000.

Throughout human history there have been threats to safety and security, losses of life and property, large scale displacements of populations and the spread of illness and disease as tools of terror. Perhaps the first use of the word terror to define what is now understood to be terrorism occurred during France's Reign of Terror from 1793 to 1794, when revolutionary forces tried to identify and kill those deemed to be traitors to the cause. In the ensuing years, the word would be synonymous with state violence such as torture, imprisonment and the dreaded guillotine.[5]

The start of modern international terrorism is widely seen as occurring on July 22, 1968, when three terrorists of the Popular Front for the Liberation of Palestine (PFLP) hijacked an El Al airliner en route from Rome, Italy to Tel Aviv, Israel.[6] The plane was carrying 38 passengers plus 10 crew members and was commandeered to Algiers by the terrorists. Unlike the trend it started and so many recent terrorist events, this hijacking did not end in tragedy, as negotiators were eventually able to obtain the release of the passengers and crew. The hijacking did, however, usher in a new approach and a new element to international terrorism, especially by Islamic extremists; that being dramatic mass attacks designed to generate publicity (and intense coverage by the international media) and employing modern instruments (such as aircraft).

One of the most infamous incidents of terrorism before the 9/11 tragedy occurred during the 1972 Munich Olympics when Palestinian terrorists—in front of a worldwide audience—infiltrated the Olympic compound and killed Israeli athletes. Such terror incidents strike bloody and symbolic blows against not only the foes of terrorists, but also the international community of nations, using violence, publicity and the lives of innocent people to achieve their objectives.

Defining Terrorism

Terrorism is a worldwide plague that knows no state borders. In the modern era of international terror, starting with the El Al hijacking in 1968, terrorism has frequently involved airline hijackings and bombings. For instance, terrorists were

---

5   See, for example, Fife, G. (2006), *The Terror: The Shadow of the Guillotine: France, 1792–1794*, New York: St. Martin's Press; and Brooman, J. (1986), *The Reign of Terror in France: Jean-Baptiste Carrier and the Drownings at Nantes*, New York: Longman Publishers.

6   Good sources on the history and start of contemporary terrorist attacks are: Carr, M. (2008), *The Infernal Machine: A History of Terrorism*, New York: New Press; and Chaliand, G. and Blin, A. (2007), *The History of Terrorism: From Antiquity to al Qaeda*, Berkeley: University of California Press.

responsible for an Air India wreck in June of 1985 over the Irish Sea that killed 329, a Pan Am flight that crashed over Lockerbie, Scotland in December 1988 killing 270, the Union des Transports Aériens (UTA) flight over Chad in September 1989 which resulted in 170 deaths, and many others.

Indeed, many international terrorists have attempted commercial airline hijackings. But the 9/11 tragedy might have marked yet another historic turning point just as the El Al hijacking by Palestinian terrorists did. Both involved an aircraft and a radical Islamic group seeking to make a statement and inflict terror. Yet this time the aircraft was used not just as the means for drawing attention but also as a weapon. As such, 9/11 can be seen as the perversely inevitable outgrowth of the suicide bombing trend.

The aircraft remains a powerful symbol of modernity, a source of publicity and a mechanism not bound by geography (like terrorism itself). As was mentioned in the opening paragraphs, international terrorism is undergoing a metamorphosis even though some of the old practices and causes remain. New technologies aid terrorists in spreading destruction and fear while at the same time helping law enforcement bodies in fighting them.

There are many types and forms of terror, from camouflaged guerrilla combatants in the jungles of Colombia and Peru, to the Irish Republican Army (IRA) in the streets of Northern Ireland, to right-wing militia groups in rural parts of the United States. As the US learned so tragically in April of 1995, terrorism can be "homegrown." Timothy McVeigh, a military veteran who was also an adherent of the ultra right-wing militia movement, detonated a bomb in front of the Alfred P. Murrah Federal Building in Oklahoma City killing 168. Likewise, a hermit with a PhD nicknamed the "Unabomber" by the press, terrorized the country by mailing explosive devices to his victims. It should also be said that the ugly history of slavery and the actions of white supremacists in the American South in the years before and after abolition, and during the Civil Rights Movement, mark a long history of acts that meet the definition of terrorism.

There is no universally accepted definition of terrorism, in part because there are so many varieties of terror incidents, such as assassinations, bombings, hijackings, kidnappings, and new trends involving biological, chemical, or radiological weapons and even cyber attacks against computing systems and telecommunications.[7] Moreover and politically, one person's terrorist might be another person's freedom fighter.

Accordingly, diplomats and governments often disagree on how to define terrorism and on which incidents fit the definition. There are, however, some basic tenets that are central to defining and understanding the phenomenon.

---

7   For a discussion of the definitional problems see, for example, Saul, B. (2008), *Defining Terrorism in International Law*, New York: Oxford University Press; and White, J.R. (2008), *Terrorism and Homeland Security: An Introduction*, Florence, KY: Wadsworth Publishing.

4 America's War on Terror, Second Edition

Most dictionaries and reference books offer standard definitions that describe terrorism as:

> The unlawful use or threatened use of force or violence by a person or an organized group against people or property with the intention of intimidating or coercing societies or governments, often for ideological purposes.[8]

Key to any definition are concepts such as civilians being targeted by violence during times of peace or when the party attacked is not engaged in war. Yet, terrorism can occur during times of war if it targets civilians or noncombatants. This definitional threshold can be extended to include military personnel if they are unarmed or not on duty, or if attacks on military facilities or personnel are performed when the nation is not at war or engaged in hostilities. One view of terrorism is offered by the US Federal Emergency Management Agency (FEMA), which considers terrorist acts as involving three characteristics:

1. to create fear;
2. to try and convince citizens that their government is unable to protect them or prevent terror attacks; and
3. to gain publicity.[9]

US federal statute offers another helpful definition of terrorism:

> The term "terrorism" means premeditated, politically motivated violence perpetrated against non-combatant targets by sub-national groups or clandestine agents, usually intended to influence an audience ... and involving citizens or the territory of more than one country.[10]

The United States also classifies a terrorist group as "... any group practicing, or that has significant subgroups that practice, international terrorism." The US Immigration and Nationality Act offers a definition of terrorist activity that includes a number of examples. This is listed in Table 1.1.[11]

---

8   This definition comes from Yahoo's online dictionary, which is available online at http://education.yahoo.com/reference/dictionary/entry/terrorism.
9   FEMA's description of terrorism is available online at http://www.fema.gov/hazard/terrorism/info.shtm.
10   The appropriate statute is: 22 USC. 2656f (d).
11   The Immigration and Nationality Act that defines terrorism is: Section 212 (a)(3)(B).

Table 1.1 Operational definition of terrorism

- The hijacking or sabotage of any conveyance (including aircraft, vessel, or vehicle);
- the seizing or detaining, and threatening to kill, injure, or continue to detain, another individual in order to compel a third person (including a governmental organization) to do or abstain from doing any act as an explicit or implicit condition for the release of the individual seized or detained;
- a violent attack upon an internationally protected person of the United States;
- an assassination;
- the use of any: biological agent, chemical agent, or nuclear weapon or device; explosive or firearm (other than for mere personal monetary gain), with intent to endanger, directly or indirectly, the safety of one or more individuals or to cause substantial damage to property;
- a threat, attempt, or conspiracy to do any of the foregoing: the term "engage in terrorist activity" means to commit, in an individual capacity or as a member of an organization, an act of terrorist activity or an act which the actor knows, or reasonably should know, affords material support to any individual, organization, or government in conducting a terrorist activity at any time, including any of the following acts:

     a. the preparation or planning of a terrorist activity;
     b. the gathering of information on potential targets for terrorist activity;
     c. the providing of any type of material support, including a safe house, transportation, communications, funds, false documentation or identification, weapons, explosives, or training, to any individual the actor knows or has reason to believe has committed or plans to commit a terrorist activity;
     d. the soliciting of funds or other things of value for terrorist activity or for any terrorist organization;
     e. the solicitation of any individual for membership in a terrorist organization, terrorist government, or to engage in a terrorist activity.

Types of Terrorism

Increasingly, terrorists since the El Al hijacking in 1968 have been motivated by one of two general—and at times a hybrid of both—factors: religious extremism and ethnic nationalism. Both are important factors in understanding contemporary terrorism. The perpetrators of the hijacking in 1968, as is the case of those attacking the United States on 9/11 and the other incidents mentioned in the opening of this chapter, were Islamic extremists of Arabic or Middle Eastern identity. As shall be discussed below, there are many forms of terrorism and equally as many types of terrorists. It is important that any assessment of terrorism does not make the mistake of ignoring other forms and perpetrators of terrorism. It is equally important that students of terrorism—as well as policymakers—do not equate Islam with terrorism, as the religion is far from monolithic in practice and interpretation.

Even within the profile of radical Islamic terrorism, it is inaccurate to describe the phenomenon as monolithic. For instance, Sunni terrorists are more likely to be individual, militant Islamicists acting apart from the state, while Shiite terrorists are at times more collective in their actions and have supported regimes such as the Iranian government. Indeed, states do sponsor terrorism, with governments in Libya, Sudan, Syria, and elsewhere having connections to terrorists through fundraising, offering safe havens, and so forth.

It would appear that, among the mistakes made by the Bush Administration in prosecuting the War on Terror, were such decisions as focusing almost singly on Islamic fanaticism to the neglect of other types of terror and alienating much of the Muslim world because of insensitive and, at times, sweeping statements and actions.[12]

There are several identifiable characteristics and forms of terrorism which makes contemporary threats especially dangerous (and effective). These elements are listed in Table 1.2.

Table 1.2　Elements of radical Islamic terrorism

- Islamic extremists have many supporters worldwide and a global reach to their terror network.
- They are marked by the fanaticism of their members with a willingness to go to great lengths—including suicide bombing and the killing of innocent civilians—to achieve their objectives.
- They generally exhibit little or no allegiance to nations or any organization beyond their terror network.
- They ignore international agreements, civil law and even the most rudimentary codes of humanity and civility, along with basic notions of innocence, cause and effect, and "just causes" of war.
- They act in ways opposed to modern notions of rationality.
- They are sub-state actors.
- They resort to violence without efforts to engage in peaceful resolution of grievances.

Many terrorists of this brand are raised in a culture of violence, oppression and despair, one whereby suicide terrorists are seen as glorious martyrs by even family members. This is seen in the suicide bombings that have increased in frequency against Israel in recent years, for example. The terrorists themselves are younger and younger, now sometimes female, and increasingly aggressive, using explosives such as grenades and pipe bombs. Many of the more high profile and deadly terrorist attacks against the United States and Europe have been committed by radical Muslim terrorists—the mujahadeen (those declaring Jihad—a holy war)—and such religious extremist groups have become the main focus of America's War on Terror.

12　Isikoff, M. (2007), *Hubris: The Inside Story of Spin, Scandal, and the Selling of the Iraq War*, New York: Three Rivers Press.

Terror training camps are appearing with increased frequency, while terrorists are more skillful in weaponry, false documentation and explosives. Osama bin Laden, the founding force behind al-Qaeda and mastermind of the 9/11 attacks, with his vast wealth and organizational prowess, offers a good example of the changing dynamic of terrorism. The world is faced with a new variety of suicide bombers and terrorists seeking and using weapons of mass destruction. More sophisticated methods and targets—high profile, crowded public places, government offices, and tourist destinations—designed to inflict maximum terror to innocent civilians, are replacing random, isolated and low-tech attacks. Nerve agents were used by the Aum Shinri Kyo cult in Japan in 1995, while al-Qaeda resorted to commercial airliners in the 2001 attacks on the United States. Both these incidents, as is the current trend, are orchestrated and meticulously planned by terror cells and networks.

In addition to religious extremism, ethnic nationalism often factors into modern international terrorism. The world has witnessed the devastating effects of an array of nationalist and ethnic disputes, including long-running hostilities by the Palestinians, Basques, Kurds, Timorese, and the IRA in Northern Ireland. Such groups fight for separatism, the right of self-governance or out of sheer hatred. Ideology is at times used as a rationale to guide such movements. This occurs in both left-wing and right-wing movements. Examples include the Shining Path (Peruvian Sendero Luminoso) guerrillas and Turkish Revolutionary People's Liberation Front found around the world on the political left, or the Ku Klux Klan and Christian Identity movements which operated on the political right in the United States.

On that note, it is possible to study terrorism as occurring within one or more of five basic categories of terrorist activity. These are listed in Table 1.3.

Table 1.3 Categories of terrorism

Nationalist or Separatist Terrorism

Such terrorist activity is committed by individuals or groups seeking separate status as a nation or ethnic group. Examples include the Basque Homeland and Liberty (ETA), Irish Republican Army (IRA), and the Kurdish Workers Party (PKK).

Religious Terrorism

This category is defined by violence committed because of the belief in a divine commandment or in the name of religious doctrine. Examples include al-Qaeda, Hamas, and Hezbollah.

Racial or Ethnic Terrorism

Terrorist acts are sometimes directly against an individual because of his or her identification with a certain ethnic or racial group. Examples include the Sunni-Shiite violence in Iraq, the tensions between the Kurds and Turks, and Ku Klux Klan violence against Blacks in the American South.

Left-Wing Terrorism

This category of violence aims to undermine capitalist systems and includes the German Red Brigade and the Weather Underground.

Right-Wing Terrorism

This category of violence aims to overthrow liberal democracies and institutions of democratic government. An example includes Timothy McVeigh and various white supremacist and militia movements in the United States.

Terrorist Groups

The US Department of State develops a list of international terrorist groups. The "Foreign Terrorist Organizations" list is updated and revised periodically and terrorist group designations must be reclassified in subsequent reports, typically completed every one or two years.[13] The first list appeared in October of 1997 during the Presidency of Bill Clinton and was overseen by Secretary of State Madeleine Albright. In it, Albright identified 30 groups. In 1999, Secretary Albright recertified 27 groups, removed three from the list, and added a new group (which happened to be al-Qaeda). Another group was added in 2000. The Administration of George W. Bush continued the list, with Secretary of State Colin Powell recertifying 26 of the groups in Albright's list in his 2001 report. A few additional groups were added over the course of the Bush years.

The significance of such a designation is that it becomes illegal for a person in the United States to provide funding or support for a group or member of any

---

13 A list of terrorist groups appears in Appendix A.

group designated as a Foreign Terrorist Organization. Members of these groups can be denied travel visas and can be excluded from entering the United States, and the list also raises awareness internationally about such groups, with the goal of isolating any support for the group in the international community. Along with the terrorist listing, the US Department of State also publishes a listing of terrorist attacks. Concern was thus raised when the Bush Administration announced that it would stop publishing the list. Critics alleged that the Administration was trying to downplay the fact that incidents of terror attacks worldwide spiked during their watch, which countered their claim that the War on Terror was reducing terrorism.[14]

Three simple criteria are used in developing the list (see Appendix A for the official list), as is indicated in Table 1.4.

Table 1.4 US Government's criteria for listing terrorist groups

- The organization must be foreign.
- The organization must engage in terrorist activity as defined by the US federal code (Section 212 (a)(3)(B) of the Immigration and Naturalization Act).
- The organization's activities must threaten the security of US nationals or national security.

Arguably the most visible terrorist group—and the focus of much of the Bush Administration's War on Terror—was and is al-Qaeda. One of the founding forces of al-Qaeda was Osama bin Laden, a wealthy Saudi adherent to radical jihadi Islam. The terror group was responsible for the 1998 bombings of US embassies in Kenya and Tanzania, the 2000 bombing of the *USS Cole* in Yemen, and the 9/11 attacks, among other terror strikes. According to the *9/11 Commission Report*, prior to 9/11 al-Qaeda was dedicated to uniting Muslims to overthrow non-Muslim regimes in the Middle East and to purging from Middle Eastern nations any Westerners and Western influences, and was believed to have an annual operating budget of roughly $30 million and thousands of trained fighters.[15]

A 2001 report issued by the US Department of State, for example, described al-Qaeda as serving as an umbrella organization for many other terror groups, especially other Sunni extremists. In the Islamist world and among terrorists, al-Qaeda was viewed by some as a source of inspiration. The organization also sent money and trained fighters to terrorist causes around the world, from Chechnya to Kashmir and throughout Africa, Asia, the Middle East, and Europe.[16]

---

14 Isikoff op. cit. fn. 12.
15 The 9/11 Commission Report, July 22, 2004.
16 Patterns of Global Terrorism, a report by the US Department of State, 2001, online at www.state.gov/s/ct/rls/crt/2001/html.

However, the terror group was weakened by US efforts under the Bush Administration in that many of the leaders were assassinated or captured, their financial base was seized or limited, and they could no longer operate with safety out of Afghanistan, as they did for years under the Taliban regime.[17] Accordingly, since the War on Terror commenced in 2001, al-Qaeda has changed and adapted to the circumstances out of necessity. In a way, it has "gone back to its roots," as one terrorism expert has described it. Al-Qaeda was forced to become more decentralized to the point where it is composed of "self-generating cells," each of which must rely on alternative sources of financing such as counterfeiting CDs and drug trafficking.[18] At the same time, any successes enjoyed by US forces in Iraq are balanced by the fertile recruiting ground that the country has turned out to be for al-Qaeda, whose cells have been discovered in cities such as Madrid (March 2004), London (July 2005), Los Angeles (July 2005), Toronto (June 2006), and elsewhere.

Components of America's War on Terror

Terrorism is a multifaceted problem and, accordingly, requires an aggressive, multifaceted and long-term solution. There are many sides to the American War on Terror, as it is being fought on the military, diplomatic, financial, homeland security and other fronts. The military attacks that routed the Taliban regime from power in Afghanistan in late 2001 and the war against Iraq in spring and summer of 2003 are only the most visible and newsworthy facets of the War on Terror. Table 1.5 lists several of the early efforts that defined the Bush Administration's War on Terror in the years following the 9/11 attacks.

Prosecution of the war has required new laws, new agencies, and a new political commitment. The US Congress has enacted numerous measures since the War on Terror began. Immediately after the 9/11 attacks, President Bush enjoyed considerable support among the American public and in Congress, as the nation "rallied around the flag." In the immediate period following the 9/11 attacks, Congress moved quickly to provide the President with support for the war. Although Bush's approval rating dropped gradually after the conclusion of the campaign to eliminate the Taliban's control over Afghanistan, at the outset of fighting in Iraq in 2003 the Congress again offered the President support for discharging the war. In addition to regular intelligence and national security authorizations—and considerable amounts of money for supplemental and emergency appropriations in the wake of 9/11 and after the Iraq war commenced—the Congress has played an active role in the effort. Countless symbolic measures from honoring those who lost their lives to the marking of the anniversary of the 9/11 attack to awarding

---

17   Kaplan, E. "The Rise of al-Qaedaism," report by the Council on Foreign Relations, July 18, 2007, online at www.cfr.org/publication/11033/rise_of_alqaedaism.html.
18   Ibid.

medals for the New York City fire and police officers were all passed, and a host of Bills enacted. This includes the following initial Bills, listed in Table 1.6, which formed the basis of the war effort.

Table 1.5 Examples of the US War on Terror

- President Bush signed the Anti-Terrorism Act on 26 October 2001, expanding the powers of and tools available to the nation's intelligence and law enforcement communities.
- The US Department of State, under the direction of the Secretary of State in consultation with the Attorney General and Secretary of Treasury, periodically develops a Foreign Terrorist List.
- Diplomatically, the United States works with other countries and international organizations to combat international terror. For instance, the United States sent a delegation to the Inter-American Committee Against Terrorism (part of the Organization of American States), which met in San Salvador in March of 2003, where efforts were made to improve technological measures to prevent terrorism. The United States also participated in the Conference on Combating Money Laundering and Terrorist Financing, which was held in Bali, Indonesia in December of 2002 and was sponsored by Australia and Indonesia.
- Presidential Executive Order 13224, signed on September 23, 2001, blocked the ability of people who commit terrorist acts or aid or support terrorist activities from conducting various financial and property transactions in the United States.
- The US Department of State submits an annual report entitled Patterns of Global Terrorism to Congress on the activities of terrorists and membership of terrorist organizations.
- Federal agencies promote awareness of terrorism and offer training programs for other countries. For example, the United States participated in a "Tri-border" terrorism conference in Argentina in December of 2002 focusing on cooperation among neighbors such as Argentine, Brazil and Paraguay that examined terrorist fundraising efforts and financial intelligence sharing.
- The Office of the Coordinator of Counter-terrorism has a Foreign Emergency Support Team, charged with helping to respond quickly to terrorist attacks and preparing officials to deal with terrorists and terrorism.
- Counter-terrorism policy workshops are convened for the purpose of bringing together US officials and their counterparts in other countries to discuss policy responses and cooperation in combating terrorism.

Table 1.6 Legislation for the War on Terror

- Victims of Terrorism Relief Act of 2001 (HR 2884; PL 107–134)
- Bioterrorism Response Act of 2001 (HR 3448; PL 107–188)
- Enhanced Border Security Act of 2002 (HR 3525; PL 107–173)
- Aviation and Transportation Security Act of 2001 (S 1447; PL 107–71)
- Authorizing Use of Force Joint Resolution of 2001 (S.J. Res. 23; PL 107–40)

Conclusion

Supporters of the Bush Administration claim that their policies have kept America safe, but critics note that, worldwide, terror attacks have spiked since 2001 and especially after the US invasion of Iraq. Highlights of the initial war include the capture of Iraqi strongman, Saddam Hussein, on December 13, 2003, and his subsequent execution on December 30, 2006 as well as the capture of Khalid Shaikh Mohammed on March 1, 2003 in Pakistan, the alleged mastermind of the 1993 World Trade Center attack and other notable incidents of terrorism including the nightclub bombings in Bali, Indonesia and the murder of kidnapped journalist, Daniel Pearl.

Because of its nature, any war against terror requires collaboration among governments worldwide, as well as collaboration among governmental units domestically. For instance, on January 21, 2003, a two-day Counter-terrorism Finance Workshop was hosted by Singapore and the United States and was held in Singapore for senior officials from over 20 countries in the Association of Southeast Asian Nations (ASEAN) and the Pacific Islands Forum (PIF). This is the case with America's War on Terror, although many suggest the campaign under the Bush Administration has lacked adequate efforts to enlist the international community,[19] and it remains to be seen as to whether the emphasis on intergovernmental cooperation within the US bureaucracy has truly been effective. Some intelligence and security agencies opposed consolidation within the new Department of Homeland Security, for instance, while many states complained of being shortchanged by the Bush Administration in terms of financial aid for the states to implement homeland security measures, and about the information flow from Washington to the states.

Tragically, the wars in Iraq and Afghanistan did not produce the intended results of stable, viable democracies and allies of the United States. Bush's war policies and ham-fisted statements often alienated many potential allies and a few traditional allies, which limited his ability to prosecute the war and conduct

---

19   See, for example, Ricks, T.E. (2007), *Fiasco: The American Military Adventure in Iraq, 2003–2005*, New York: Penguin Books.

other international affairs.[20] A chorus of critics also note that President Bush did not listen to alternative viewpoints, labeled any voice of dissent as unpatriotic, underestimated the Sunni–Shiite rift and opposition from average Iraqis to an occupying army, mistakenly disbanded the Iraqi military and Baath party apparatus, and failed to secure the border with Iran in the immediate aftermath of the war. The inability of America to get essential services like water or electricity up and running or to train Iraqi security forces in a timely manner also proved to be problematic as US forces tried to win the hearts and minds of Iraqis. In short, support for the President and the war dropped precipitously after the first three years of fighting, and numerous critics have labeled Bush's invasion of Iraq and the War on Terror as the worst planned war efforts in American history.[21]

By the end of the Bush years, the popularity enjoyed by the President and the support the American public demonstrated for both the War on Terror and the War in Iraq had eroded to the point of record lows in approval and a majority of Americans disapproving of the invasion and Bush's handling of the war. New disclosures further damaged any momentum enjoyed by the Bush Administration in the first two years of the war such as the discovery of secret prisons in Eastern Europe, the encroachment of civil liberties at home such as domestic wiretapping programs, and bogus claims made against large numbers of "terrorist" detainees at Guantánamo Bay military prison in Cuba. Court rulings also went against the President on many of the aforementioned issues, which undermined Bush's claims of executive privilege in implementing the war.[22] Nor did the Bush White House ever develop an effective "counter ideology" as a strategy to support military efforts in the Middle East. Ultimately, Bush's framing of the war through fear and placing ultimatums on friends and foes alike, undercut the long-term support for his war policies. For example, President Bush stated "Every nation in every region now has a decision to make. Either you are with us, or you are with the terrorists."[23] At the same time, his Secretary of State, Colin Powell, gave misleading testimony about the need for war before the world community at the United Nations.

So, too, has the price tag for the war been high. Three reports were released in 2008—by such respected organizations as the Center for Strategic and Budgetary Assessments, the Government Accountability Office, and the Congressional

---

20   A number of reliable sources have been produced offering criticisms of President Bush's handling of the War on Terror, including; Ricks, T.E. (2009), *The Gamble: General David Patraeus and the American Military Adventure in Iraq, 2006–2008*, New York: Penguin Books; Woodward, B. (2008), *The War Within: A Secret White House History, 2006–2008*, New York: Simon & Schuster; Woodward, B. (2007), *State of Denial: Bush at War III*, New York: Simon & Schuster.

21   Ibid.

22   Walsh, S.C., "Supreme Court Halts Guantánamo Bay Military Commissions, Applies Geneva Convention to War on Terror," Center for Defense Information report, July 6, 2006, online at www.cdi.org; the case in question was *Hamden v. Rumsfeld*.

23   Bush made the comments on September 20, 2001.

Research Service—concluding that, by 2009, the total cost to America for the War on Terror exceeded a whopping $1 trillion.[24] The cost from 2001 to 2009 for America's War on Terror was, even counting for inflation, four times the total of America's cost for World War I (WWI), ten times the cost of the first Persian Gulf War, and more than the total cost of the wars in Korea and Vietnam. At the end of George W. Bush's Presidency, he had spent over $904 billion on the War on Terror, not counting the long-term costs of healthcare for the thousands of wounded soldiers, the money borrowed by the federal government, or the interest on the national debt, which exceeded $11 trillion when Bush left office—the largest debt in the world.

It also appears that the Bush Administration was far less than open and honest about not only the conduct and success of the war, but also of the costs. During the time of the invasion of Iraq, the White House economic advisor, Larry Lindsey, suggested the war might cost $200 billion. Lindsey was sternly reprimanded by the White House, who refuted the numbers as excessively inaccurate and high. Secretary of Defense Donald Rumsfeld, for instance, countered that Americans would be greeted as liberators and that the war would pay for itself once the Iraqi oil flowed. Of the costs of the war, Secretary Rumsfeld rebuked the press, claiming "It's not knowable what a war or conflict like that would cost. You don't know if it's going to last two days or two weeks or two months. It certainly isn't going to last two years."[25] Such statements have been anything but accurate.

The conduct of the war will continue to evolve through the Administration of President Barack Obama, just as his election in 2008 also signified another change in the war. The wars in Iraq and Afghanistan, as well as the overall counterterrorism efforts, have been passed to a new Administration and one of a different political party. The war continues, just as terrorist tactics continue to mutate, America's efforts in response continually evolve, and scholarly debate on the success of the war remains heated and divided.

---

24   The three organizations making reports are the Center for Strategic and Budgetary Assessments, online at www.csbaonline.org; the Congressional Research Service, online at www.crs.gov; and the Government Accountability Office, online at www.gao.gov.

25   Donald Rumsfeld is quoted in Thompson, M. (2008), "The $1 Trillion Bill for Bush's War on Terror," *Time*, December 26.

PART 1
Origins of the War on Terror

Chapter 2

Osama bin Laden, Radical Islam and the United States

Tom Lansford and Jack Covarrubias

Introduction

On December 25, 1979, 100,000 Soviet troops crossed the border into Afghanistan and began an occupation of the country that would initiate 20 years of internal conflict and would profoundly affect the growing militancy of radical Islamic groups throughout the world. The Soviet invasion and occupation would set the stage for the rise of the Taliban in Afghanistan and the concurrent rise of the al-Qaeda terrorist network of Osama bin Laden. During the occupation, the United States provided a variety of overt and tacit assistance to the anti-Soviet rebels, or mujahadeen. Once the Soviets withdrew, US strategic interest in Afghanistan ended and the vacuum created by the disengagement of both superpowers created the conditions which produced the Taliban and al-Qaeda.

This essay examines the evolution of radical, militant Islamic groups in the context of US policies toward Afghanistan during the Soviet occupation and the period of Taliban rule. The work details the rise of Osama bin Laden and the al-Qaeda network. It further explores the broader patterns of Islamic fundamentalism within the region and the subsequent proliferation of anti-US and anti-Western sentiment. Specifically, the essay seeks to answer a variety of questions related to US foreign policy during the period from 1979 to the present day:

1. Did US actions and programs exacerbate the radicalization of Islamic fundamentalist groups in South Asia?
2. What events led the mujahadeen to turn against their former benefactors?
3. Where there steps that successive US Administrations could and should have taken to contain the growth of the Taliban and al-Qaeda? and
4. What polices can the US and Western powers now adopt to contain or ameliorate conflict within the region and to constrain the spread of radical Islam?

The Soviet Invasion and Occupation

In 1973, Mohammad Daoud Khan overthrew his cousin King Zahir Shah and established a republic in Afghanistan. Over the next few years, Daoud's increasingly repressive regime lost what little support it had among the Afghan people while Moscow increasingly signaled a willingness to back a revolt by Afghan communists. By 1977, the leadership of the Afghan Communist Party, the People's Democratic Party of Afghanistan (PDPA), began to develop concrete plans to overthrow Daoud and was actively recruiting among the Afghan military, many of whom had been trained in the Soviet Union. By 1978, the PDPA had expanded their support within the Army by 100 percent.[1] On April 26, 1978, Daoud ordered the arrest of top PDPA leaders which led the communists to launch a coup.

The next day, Afghan Army units loyal to the communists attacked the Presidential palace where Daoud and his family were killed. PDPA leader, Nur Mohammad Taraki, became President and Hafizullah Amin became Deputy Prime Minister. The PDPA coup was not a broad-based uprising; only about 600 troops took part in the main attack, and the new regime did not enjoy popular support. As the regime tried to consolidate its power, it engaged in ever-increasingly repressive measures, including widespread executions. By 1979, there were widespread revolts throughout the countryside which culminated in a major uprising in Herat in March of that year which left 5,000 dead, including 100 Soviet advisors and their families. On September 14, 1979, Amin overthrew Taraki as political chaos spread throughout Afghanistan. The increasing instability prompted Moscow to begin considerations about military intervention. Raymond Garthoff asserts that by the eve of the invasion:

> The real Soviet fear was that Amin was neither reliable as a partner nor subject to Soviet guidance, and at the same time was ineffective in controlling the growing resistance. In desperation Amin might turn to the United States as Egyptian President Sadat and Somali General Siad had done. Alternatively, he would likely be swept away by a populist Islamic national movement. In either case the Soviet Union would lose all its cumulative investment in Afghanistan.[2]

In response, the Kremlin ordered Soviet troops in Afghanistan put on alert and increased deployments along the border. On December 24, the invasion decision was made.[3] The following day Soviet troops crossed into Afghanistan. Resistance

---

1   Arnold, A. (1983), *Afghanistan's Two-Party Communism: Parcham and Khalq*, Stanford: Hoover Institution Press, 47.

2   Garthoff, R. (1984), *Detente and Confrontation: American Soviet Relations From Nixon to Reagan*, Washington, DC: Brookings Institute, 921.

3   Galeotti attributes much of the impetus behind the decision to invade to Yuri Andropov who was engaged in a campaign to succeed the increasingly ill and senile

was light and the invasion force suffered only 20–30 killed and approximately 300 wounded. Amin was killed on 27 December when Soviet forces stormed the Presidential palace and by the beginning of the New Year, the Soviets had control of all major Afghan cities.

The US Reaction

In the initial aftermath of the coup which deposed Daoud, the Administration of Jimmy Carter endeavored to retain ties with the Taraki government. The Administration was not even sure if the new regime was Communist.[4] Even once the true nature of the regime became apparent, US programs were continued and Zbigniew Brzezinski, Carter's National Security Advisor, even asserted that the Administration should strive to develop a "restrained" policy toward Taraki to keep the Afghans from growing closer to the Soviet Union.[5] US policy changed following the death of its Ambassador, Adolph Dubbs, who was killed during a rescue attempt after he had been kidnaped in February 1979. The Afghans refused to cooperate with the US investigation of the Ambassador's death. Carter then began to curtail US aid and authorized the CIA to use $500,000 to aid anti-government factions in Afghanistan.[6]

By December of 1979, there was increasing intelligence that the Soviets were preparing for an invasion of Afghanistan, however as was noted at the time, "private warnings to presidential aides last month that the neutralist regime in Afghanistan was 'ripe like a red apple' for a pro-Soviet communist takeover met official silence here, a non-response highlighting the Administration's dangerous inertia in meeting the current Soviet worldwide offensive."[7] Nonetheless, as the historian John Lewis Gaddis points out, Carter had the "misfortune to come to power at a time when the Soviet Union was launching a new series of challenges to the global balance of power" but the United States faced a "general decline in super-power authority" and the "effects of the post-Vietnam conviction" about the

---

Brezhnev. Andropov envisioned a success in Afghanistan as a means to secure his future while the other Soviet leaders present, including Foreign Minister Andrei Gromyko and Defense Minister Marshall Andrei Ustinov, envisioned that a quick victory and the restoration of order in their southern neighbor would allow the Kremlin to return its attention to more pressing global matters; Galeotti, M. (1995), *Afghanistan: The Soviet Union's Last War*, London: Frank Cass, 10–12.

4 Hammond, T.T. (1984), *Red Flag Over Afghanistan: The Communist Coup, the Soviet Invasion and the Consequences*, Boulder: Westview Press, 60.

5 Ibid., 62.

6 These funds were distributed over a six-week period by CIA officers based in Kabul; Gates, R. (1996), *The Ultimate Insider's Story of Five Presidents and How They Won the Cold War*, New York: Simon & Schuster, 142–9.

7 Evans, R. and Novak, R. (1978), "Ignoring the Dangers of the Afghan Coup," *The Washington Post*, May 8.

"use of force."[8] Carter had already faced the fall of pro-American regimes in Iran and Nicaragua and was constrained by domestic issues such as the struggling US economy.

Aid for the Mujahideen

The Soviet invasion united the hawks and doves within the Administration and Carter was personally angry with Moscow. The Soviet invasion marked a sea change in US policy toward the Soviet Union. At the heart of the new American attitude was the Carter Doctrine which was promulgated in the State of the Union Address on January 23, 1980. Carter stated that: "An attempt by any outside force to gain control of the Persian Gulf region will be regarded as an assault on the vital interests of the United States of America, and such an assault will be repelled by any means necessary, including military force."[9] The President further declared that "verbal condemnation is not enough. The Soviet Union must pay for its aggression."[10] Carter would impose economic sanctions on the Soviets, boycott the 1980 Moscow Olympics and authorize covert military assistance for the mujahadeen, including arms transfers.[11]

The election of Ronald Reagan in 1980 accelerated US aid for the mujahadeen, especially in the aftermath of the announcement of the Reagan Doctrine which promised US military support for "those risking their lives on every continent from Afghanistan to Nicaragua to defy Soviet-supported aggression."[12] In order to operationalize the Reagan Doctrine in Afghanistan, in March of 1985, the President signed National Security Decision Directive (NSDD) 166. This Directive authorized the CIA to help the mujahadeen with "all means available."[13]

---

8 Gaddis, J.L. (1982), *Strategies of Containment: A Critical Appraisal of Postwar American National Security Policy*, New York: Oxford University Press, 350–52.

9 US, White House, "The President's State of the Union Address," press release, January 23, 1980.

10 Ibid.; as a sign of Carter's anger, he asked the various US officials involved in relations with the Soviet Union to draw up lists of potential action. While the staffers assumed Carter would pick and choose from the various lists, he instead incorporated all of the suggested punitive actions in his response. This was a response that even Brzezinski thought too provocative at first; Skidmore, D. (1993–94), "Carter and the Failure of Foreign Policy Reform," *Political Science Quarterly* 108/4 (Winter), 723–4.

11 The first shipments consisted of "several thousand" World War II era Lee Enfield rifles which were already in common use by Afghan tribes. These would be followed by weapons made in Warsaw Pact countries, such as AK-47s, in order to provide "plausible deniability" to the US; Bearden, M. (2001), "Afghanistan, Graveyard of Empires," *Foreign Affairs* 80/6 (November/December).

12 Ronald Reagan, quoted in Krauthammer, C. (1986), "The Reagan Doctrine," *The New Republic*, February 17.

13 Quoted in Kuperman, A.J. (1999), "The Stinger Missile and US Intervention in Afghanistan," *Political Science Quarterly* 114/2, 227.

US military assistance to the mujahadeen rose from $122 million in 1984 to $250 million in 1985, and from $470 million in 1986 to $630 million by 1987.[14] The CIA provided the rebels with a range of military equipment, including Stinger missiles beginning in May of 1986,[15] and intelligence support such as satellite images and communications intercepts. The US also worked with its allies, including Saudi Arabia and other Gulf states to coordinate other financial aid. By the mid-1980s, non-US aid reached about $25 million per month or $300 million per year.

Still, by 1985, the groundwar had reached a stalemate. The Soviets had about 100,000 troops deployed while the mujahadeen fielded about 250,000. Military parity was achieved by the Soviets because of their aerial superiority.[16] However, the introduction of the Stinger missile dramatically changed the air war. Stingers were credited with destroying 279 Soviet aircraft from 1986 to 1989.[17] In addition, Afghan air force losses doubled from 1986 to 1989 with 17 planes and 12 helicopters shot down in 1986, 33 planes and 21 helicopters downed in 1987, and 44 planes and 24 helicopters destroyed in 1988.[18] The missiles forced the Soviets to change their tactics and utilize high-level bombing and eliminate some aerial missions. This, in turn, gave the mujahadeen greater operational freedom and resulted in increased operations.[19]

The Soviet Withdrawal

The introduction of the Stinger and growing casualties led Soviet leader Mikhail Gorbachev to begin negotiations with the United States over withdrawal. These talks culminated in the April 1988 Geneva Accords which called for a Soviet withdrawal in February 1989 and an end to military aid by both superpowers. On February 15, 1989 the last Soviet troops withdrew from Afghanistan and the period of superpower rivalry in the country came to an abrupt end. The Soviets

---

14   Roy, O. (1991), *The Lessons of the Soviet/Afghan War*, Adelphi Papers 259, London: Brassey's, 35. US support was generally matched dollar for dollar by the Saudis; Evans, K. (1992), *The Guardian*, January 2.

15   The US also approved the transfer of Stingers to anti-Soviet rebels in Angola. On September 25, 1986, the mujahadeen fired their first five Stingers and shot down three Soviet helicopters; ibid., 234–5.

16   McMichael, S.R. (1991), *Stumbling Bear: Soviet Military Performance in Afghanistan*, London: Brassey's, 84, 89.

17   The higher figures are contained in Karp, A. (1987), "Blowpipes and Stingers in Afghanistan: One Year Later," *Armed Forces Journal International*, September, 36–40; while the more conservative figures are cited in McManaway, W. (1990), "Stinger in Afghanistan," *Air Defense Artillery*, January-February, 3–8; and McManaway, W. (1989), "The Dragon is Dead!" *Air Defense Artillery*, July-August. Kuperman discusses controversy in great detail in Kuperman, op. cit. fn. 13, 244–7.

18   Cordovez, D. and Harrison, S.S. (1995), *Out of Afghanistan: The Inside Story of the Soviet Withdrawal*, New York: Oxford University Press, 199.

19   Ibid., 198–9.

officially lost 13,310 dead, 35,478 wounded and 310 missing during their eight-year occupation, a figure roughly proportional to American losses in Vietnam in terms of the number of troops deployed.[20] Meanwhile, the amount of US military aid during the period of the Soviet occupation was five times the dollar amount of total US assistance from 1947 to 1979.[21]

The United States and the Soviet Union continued to provide arms and supplies to their respective factions even after the withdrawal as a means of preventing the opposing sides from gaining ascendancy in Afghanistan.[22] This exacerbated the country's civil war and extended the fighting. In testimony before the US Congress, Deputy Assistant Secretary of State, Robert A. Peck described US policy in the following terms when asked why the United States did not stop unilateral arms shipments:

> The obligation which the United States would take as a "guarantor" would relate exclusively to our own policies. We would bear no responsibility for the actions of others, or for the successful implementation of the agreement as a whole. We and the Soviet Union would agree to the same basic commitment regarding noninterference and nonintervention. We would be prepared, if completely satisfied with the agreement, to prohibit US military assistance to the Afghan resistance. We would expect the Soviet Union to show reciprocal restraint under the Geneva accords in stopping its military support for the Kabul regime.[23]

The end of the Cold War expedited efforts to end external arms transfers, however, and by December 1990, the superpowers reached a tentative agreement to end their involvement in the conflict. The Gulf War further added impetus to the need to end arms shipments as militant Islamic groups supported Saddam Hussein, to the dismay of the Saudis and Pakistanis. A final agreement between the US, Russia, Pakistan and Saudi Arabia was reached in December 1991.[24] None of the major Afghan groups, including the pro-Soviet regime in Kabul, participated in the discussions. That their main supporters, including the US and Saudi Arabia

---

20   Dobbs, M. (1988), "Soviets Say 13,310 Soldiers Died in Afghan War," *Washington Post*, May 26.

21   From 1947 to 1979, the US provided a total of $532.87 million in aid to Afghanistan; US, Agency for International Development (AID) (1979), *US Overseas Loans and Grants, 1979*, Washington, DC: GPO.

22   See Khan, R.M. (1991), *Untying the Afghan Knot: Negotiating Soviet Withdrawal*, Durham, NC: Duke University Press; and Harrison, S.S. (1988), "Inside the Afghan Talks," *Foreign Policy* 72 (Fall), 31–60.

23   Quoted in Klass, R. (1988), "Afghanistan: The Accords," *Foreign Affairs* 66/5 (Summer), 933.

24   The framework agreement was originally reached in May 1991, but officials in Moscow resisted implementation until after the coup. For details of the original agreement see UN, Department of Public Information, "Statement by Secretary-General Javier Perez de Cuellar" (May 21, 1991).

would cut off their arms and supplies without significant consultations would infuriate many mujahadeen leaders and increase tensions with the West while it also reinforced the notions about the corruptness and shallowness of the Saudi regime.

While most observers expected the pro-Soviet regime to immediately collapse after the withdrawal, infighting among the mujahadeen groups allowed the regime to remain in place until 1992, when rebel forces captured Kabul. However, civil war and political fragmentation continued until 1996 when a relatively new group, the Taliban, was able to fill the political vacuum and ultimately gain control of approximately 90 percent of the country. The ethnic and religious differences of the mujahadeen which caused the lengthy post-Soviet civil war reflected the tensions and political infighting of both Afghan history and the more contemporary problems that emerged during the Soviet occupation.

The Mujahadeen

In 1979, Afghanistan remained a conservative Islamic country. The PDPA was determined to reform the country by minimizing the power of Islam. It introduced a variety of new programs to secularize the legal and educational systems and the new leaders even publicly disparaged Islam. For instance, the new President, Taraki, declared in an interview that "we want to clean Islam in Afghanistan of the ballast and dirt of bad traditions, superstition and erroneous belief."[25]

These efforts turned the overwhelming majority of Afghanistan against the regime. As R. Lincoln Keiser points out, "the introduction of communist ideology and the debunking of Muslim beliefs in the schools ... not only aroused the emotions of the tribes against the Taraki/Amin regime, but also destroyed the foundation of the central government's legitimacy."[26] The PDPA's policies "violated practically every Afghan cultural norm, and strayed far beyond the allowable bounds of deviance in the social, economic, and political institutions. It appears that they systematically planned to alienate every segment of the Afghan people."[27]

All of the main opposition groups that developed in response to the Communist government were Islamic in nature. Prior to the Soviet invasion there were already six Islamic insurgency groups working to overthrow the Taraki regime. Following the invasion, that number rose to 22 major groups based in Pakistan

---

25 Nur Mohammad Taraki, interview, *Die Zeit* (June 9, 1979) in US, Department of State, Foreign Broadcast Information Service/Western Europe (June 9, 1979), S4.

26 Keiser, R.L. (1980), "The Rebellion in Darra-I-Nur," paper presented at the meeting of the American Anthropological Association, Washington, DC (5 December), 8, cited in Hammond, op. cit. fn. 4, 72.

27 Dupree, L. (1980), *Red Flag Over the Hindu Kush, vol. III, Rhetoric and Reforms, or Promises! Promises!* Asia Report, no. 23, Hanover, NH: American Universities Field Staff Reports, 4.

with an additional 10 in Iran.[28] The majority of the mujahadeen tended to divide themselves along traditional ethnic divisions. Afghanistan's largest ethnic group is the Pashtuns who comprise about 51 percent of the population and who have dominated Afghan politics throughout the state's modern history. The Tajiks are the second largest groups and make up about 25 percent of the people. The Hazara form 10 percent of the population, the Uzbeks, 8 percent, while the Turkmen, Balochs and Aimaks comprise a combined total of 11 percent of the population.[29]

The main fundamentalist mujahadeen groups came together in a broad coalition known as the Islamic Alliance. The Alliance advocated the establishment of an Islamic republic along the lines of Iran and had substantial external support from states such as Iran, Saudi Arabia and Pakistan.[30] Within the coalition, there emerged an ethnic division that would lead to later conflict after the Soviet withdrawal. The Islamic Society was made up of mainly ethnic Tajiks and Uzbeks. The Society's political leader was Dr Burhanuddin Rabbani and its military commander was Ahmad Shah Massoud. In 1992, Rabbani would become the first post-Soviet President of Afghanistan. The Society's major rival, the mainly Pashtun Islamic Party, was led by Gulbuddin Hikmatyar who would ultimately challenge Rabbani's rule and help sow the seeds for the rise of the Taliban.

Local mujahadeen commanders often had little loyalty to the Afghan political leadership in Pakistan or to their nominal superiors. Barnett R. Rubin wrote that "the affiliation of commanders to parties is determined by a combination of patronage, traditional networks, reaction to local rivalries (a commander will join a different party from that of his traditional rival) and ideology."[31] In 1982, Amaury de Riencourt, a noted French scholar of the region, observed that the mujahadeen "seem to be more interested in fighting for the complete autonomy of their areas than in any common struggle against the Russian invaders—a vivid illustration of the fact that, up to now, Afghanistan never was a homogeneous nation-state."[32] One result was that the different ethnic mujahadeen often fought each other as much as they fought the Soviets. Successive efforts by both the United States and Pakistan to establish a broad-based political coalition to serve as a true government-in-exile never truly succeeded.

---

28   *Sovietskaya Rossiya* (July 10, 1980), 1 in US, Department of State, Federal Broadcast Information Service/Soviet Union and Eastern Europe (July 15, 1980), D1–2.

29   Population percentages are taken from US, Central Intelligence Agency, "Afghanistan," *CIA World Factbook, 2002*, Washington, DC: CIA, online at www.cia.gov/cia/publications/factbook/print/af.html.

30   Harrison, S.S. (1988), "So Far it Looks Like Another Win for the Islamic Fundamentalists," *The Washington Post*, April 17.

31   Rubin, B.R. (1989/1990), "The Fragmentation of Afghanistan," *Foreign Affairs* 68/5 (Winter), 153.

32   De Riencourt, A. (1982/1983), "India and Pakistan in the Shadow of Afghanistan," *Foreign Affairs* 61/2 (Winter), 430.

The Arabs and Fundamentalist Islam

Internal conflicts among the mujahadeen were exacerbated by the presence of non-Afghan, Arab volunteers. From 1982 through 1992, approximately 35,000 Muslims (including 25,000 Arabs) fought as mujahadeen against the Soviets.[33] Often "the Arabs that did travel to Afghanistan from Peshawar were generally considered nuisances by mujahadeen commanders, some of whom viewed them only slightly less bothersome than the Soviets."[34] These foreign-born mujahadeen usually did not appreciate or accept the goals of the local commanders. They were also mainly Shia while the overwhelming majority of Afghans were Sunni (among the Afghan people, only the Hazaras were predominately Shia). Before they were deployed, many of the Arabs spent time in Pakistani religious schools, or madrassas, which reinforced their fundamentalist beliefs.

These Arabs reflected the growing radicalization of Islam among certain groups. This religious militancy has been termed "Islamic fundamentalism," "radical Islam" or simply "militant Islam." All of these terms describe a transnational trend of the late twentieth century marked by an increasing opposition to what Samuel Huntington described as "Western ideas of individualism, liberalism, constitutionalism, human rights, equality, liberty, the rule of law [and] democracy."[35] This opposition is based on the fact that as a theology Islam "created a religion and a state at the same time."[36] Consequently, as Hilal Khashan notes:

> according to the fundamentalists, it is completely unacceptable for Muslims to be ruled by any system of government unless it is based on *Shari'a* [italics in original]. Western-inspired secular laws, now applies in most Islamic states contradict Islamic tenets, and most fundamentalists wholeheartedly reject the application of these laws. The fact that radical Islamic groups constitute mainly domestic movements operating against state authority within the boundaries drawn by Western colonial powers does not mean that they necessarily accept the existing Middle Eastern state order.[37]

Radical Islam has been increasingly manifested by an expansion of the use of political violence or terrorism, especially against non-military targets as a means to undermine that state order. Hence, as Hrair Dekmejian writes, "confrontation

---

33   Rashid, A. (2002), "Osama Bin Laden: How the US Helped Midwife A Terrorist," in Logevall, F. (ed.), *Terrorism and 9/11: A Reader*, Boston: Houghton Mifflin, 51.

34   Ibid., 24.

35   Huntington, S.P. (1993), "The Clash of Civilizations?" *Foreign Affairs* 72/3 (Summer), 40.

36   G. Hossein Razi (1990), "Legitimacy, Religion, and Nationalism in the Middle East," *The American Political Science Review* 84/1 (March), 76.

37   Khashan, H. (1997), "The New World Order and the Tempo of Militant Islam," *British Journal of Middle Eastern Studies* 24/1 (May), 12.

is an important part of the world view of Islamic fundamentalists and many conventional Muslims."[38] And, it is the duty of all true believers to participate in jihad, or holy war, against infidel.[39] This combination of factors has resulted in a notion of "historical determinism which considers the ultimate triumph of Islam as prescribed by God."[40]

The invasion of Afghanistan, a Muslim country, by an atheistic power, the Soviet Union, provided radical groups with a cause, and a variety of clerics responded with calls for a jihad against the invaders. This turned the insurrection into a holy war for both Afghans and Arab recruits. That the mujahadeen were able to defeat the Soviets elevated the status of the radical groups (who argued that their victory was based on God's will). Many of these groups would also assert that they played a major role in the downfall of the Soviet Union because of its defeat in Afghanistan.[41]

By the late 1980s, there were repeated clashes between the Afghan and Arab mujahadeen as more radical fighters joined the rebel side. Many of the foreign-born mujahadeen became convinced that if native Afghans did not join the call for jihad then they were apostates and could no longer be considered Muslim. As a result, these people were subject to the laws of futuhat, or conquest.[42] This led fundamentalist mujahadeen to engage in a variety of atrocities, including executing prisoners, rape, and the practice of selling women and children as slaves.[43] These actions angered local mujahadeen who were often related or ethnically linked to the populations. It also made it less likely that Afghan Army troops would desert or surrender.[44]

Islam is not a monolithic religion and is instead divided into a variety of sects and is influenced by scores of national cultures. In addition, Islamic fundamentalism developed in a region of the world that was previously known most for "both religious tolerance and the prevalence of traditional religious practices."[45] Still, as Graham Fuller and Ian Lesser point out "Islamic fundamentalism" (an imprecise

---

38   R. Hrair Dekmejian (1995), *Islam in Revolution: Fundamentalism in the Arab World*, 2nd edn, New York: Syracuse University Press, 22.

39   See Munson, H., Jr. (1988), *Islam and Revolution in the Middle East*, New Haven: Yale University Press; or Sivan, E. (1985), *Radical Islam*, New Haven: Yale University Press.

40   Khashan, op. cit. fn. 37, 10.

41   Fuller, G.E. and Lesser, I.O. (1995), *A Sense of Siege: The Geopolitics of Islam and the West*, Boulder: Westview Press, 153–54.

42   Under fundamentalist Islamic doctrine, the concept of futuhat, or wars of liberation, which result in the spread of Islam, allows for the confiscation of property of non-believers, the execution of males and the enslavement of women and children; see Akram Diya al 'Umari (1991), *Madinian Society At The Time of The Prophet*, Huda Khattab (trans.), Riyadh: International Islamic Publishing House.

43   Rubin, op. cit. fn. 31, 155, 158.

44   Hussain, Z. (1992), "Snub for Hard-Line Afghans," *The Times*, January 28.

45   Khashan, op. cit. fn. 37, 6.

and poor term for analytical purposes) has been the single most anti-Western force over the past two decades especially with the withering away of communism. Muslim states have, furthermore, provided the West with several dramatic "hate figures" unparalleled almost anywhere in the world: Gamal Abdel Nasser, Muammar al-Qadhafi, the Ayatollah Khomeini, and Saddam Hussein among the most arresting examples in Western demonology."[46] The latest of these figures is, of course, Osama bin Laden.

Osama bin Laden

From the ashes of the mujahadeen that formed to "liberate" Afghanistan from the Soviets, Osama bin Laden, or Usamah bin Mohammad bin Awad bin Laden, formed the core elements of what has become al-Qaeda. This organization has been responsible for many of the more prominent terrorist acts of the 1990s and 2000s. From his 1993 affiliation with the killing of US service personnel in Somalia to the subsequent destruction of the World Trade Center towers on September 11, 2001 the organization that he founded in 1988 has formed the nucleus of a world wide ring of terrorists bent on the forced realization of their minority views. The context of this alliance of terrorists lies within a narrow interpretation of the Quran that calls for the rise of Muslim culture via jihad.[47] This doctrine amounts to a concept of "total war" in which all means are acceptable, as documented through severe interpretation of the Quran, in order to achieve the desired goal of the indoctrination of Sharia into all cultures.[48]

Osama bin Laden was born in 1957 in Riyadh, Saudi Arabia into the wealthiest class of society, affording him the benefits that such wealth bestows.[49] Growing up as one of 57 children, he inherited millions when his father, Sheik Mohammed Awad bin Laden, died in a plane crash near San Antonio, Texas in 1968.[50] His education and early formation were a product of his father's death, his affiliation with the Muslim brotherhood, and a series of lessons with Islamic scholars.[51] He took these lessons with him to the King Abdul-Aziz University where he earned degrees in public administration and economics.[52] During his time at the University,

---

46   Fuller and Lesser, op. cit. fn. 41, 2.

47   Asfour, G. (1998), "Osama bin Laden: Financier of 'Desert' Islam," *New Perspectives Quarterly* 15/4 (Summer), 39–40.

48   Zeidan, D. (2001), "The Islamic Fundamentalist View of Life as a Perennial Battle," *Middle East Review of International Affairs* 5/4 (December).

49   Bellamy, P. "Osama bin Laden: High Priest of Terror," online at http://www. crimelirary.com/terrorists/binladen.

50   Ibid.

51   Ibid.; Asfour, G., online at http://www.fas.org/irp/world/para/mb.htm for an overview of the Muslim Brotherhood.

52   Bellamy, op. cit. fn. 49.

bin Laden used his free time to further his education with travel. The 1979 Soviet invasion of Afghanistan coincided with one of these trips giving bin Laden his first relationship with the United States.[53]

Bin Laden was one of the Arab Islamic warriors who traveled to Afghanistan, bent on defending their fellow Muslim brothers from the perils of the Soviet occupation. Bin Laden's immense personal wealth and his ties to the Middle Eastern social elite placed upon him a unique role. He became a conduit for funneling money from the Middle East into the resistance movement in Afghanistan.[54]

As the United States continually increased its involvement in the Afghan conflict, bin Laden was quickly becoming an important figure in the movement of money into the conflict and the training of volunteers in various camps he had set up throughout the region.[55] Through Maktab al-Khidamar (MAK), the organization with which bin Laden was affiliated, he became involved with Pakistan's state security services.[56] Pakistan's Interservice Intelligence agency (ISI) was heavily funded by the United States. Ahmed Rashid stated in 1999:

> With the active encouragement of the CIA and Pakistan's ISI, who wanted to turn the Afghan jihad into a global war waged by all Muslim states against the Soviet Union, some 35,000 Muslim radicals from 40 Islamic countries joined Afghanistan's fight between 1982 and 1992. Tens of thousands more came to study in Pakistani madrasahs. Eventually more than 100,000 foreign Muslim radicals were directly influenced by the Afghan jihad.[57]

The Afghan war served as a proving ground for Islamic fundamentalists throughout the Middle East. The system of bringing new volunteers and funding from around the world into the organization set up by bin Laden did not end with the Soviet withdrawal. Bin Laden had splintered from MAK by 1988 to form his al-Qaeda (The Base). This new organization was to utilize the talents he honed in organizing Muslim extremists in order to continue the fight of a Muslim Holy war. This new organization would act as a "holding company for globalized terror."[58]

Osama bin Laden, along with top lieutenants such as Dr. Ayman al-Zawahiri of the Egyptian al-Jihad and Muhammed Atef, who is thought to have been killed in the American air campaign over Afghanistan, formed the nucleus of the new

---

53   "The New Powder Keg in the Middle East," *Nida'ul Islam*, October-November 1996.

54   "The Myth, the Reality: The Mission and Method of Osama bin laden," *CNN*, online at http://www.cnn.com/CNN/Programs/people/shows/binladen/profile.html.

55   "Usama bin Laden: Islamic Extremist Financier," CIA assessment, 1996.

56   Moran, M. (1998), "Bin Laden Comes Home to Roost," *MSNBC News*, August 24, 1998.

57   Rashid, A. (1999), "The Taliban: Exporting Extremism," *Foreign Affairs* 78/6 (November/December), 22–35.

58   Wedgewood, R. (2002), "Al-Qaeda, Military Commissions, and American Self Defense," *Political Science Quarterly* 117/3 (Fall), 357–372.

al-Qaeda organization. Most of the members of the organization were the same Arab "freedom fighters" that had joined the mujahadeen to defeat the Soviets in Afghanistan.[59] These soldiers chose to expand the jihad against the West and bin Laden continued to provide the logistical support and leadership that they needed in such places as Kosovo and Chechnya.[60] Bin Laden noted that "I discovered it was not enough to fight in Afghanistan, but that we had to fight on all fronts against communism or western oppression. The urgent thing was communism, but the next target was America ..."[61]

Osama bin Laden is different than most other Islamic religious leaders. He does not focus on the individual sects of Islam as much as he encompasses the whole. His view is of a Pan-Islamic society in which all of Islam is marked by its devotion to the tenets of the Quran.[62] He views this society as having been shamed and humiliated by the Western nations, as led by the United States. Consequently, his focus is that of bringing back honor to Islam, as a whole, by shaming the west. He blames the West for all the ills that have befallen this great Muslim society, and most importantly, he blames the West for the failure of Muslim culture to live by the rules set out in the Quran. Consequently, the destruction of the West should "release" the hold it has taken upon Muslim nation's world wide for it is the West that chooses to go against the rule of Islam. Bin Laden summarized this notion in the following manner: "You are the nation who, rather than ruling by the Shariah of Allah in its Constitution and Laws, choose to invent your own laws as you will and desire. You separate religion from your policies, contradicting the pure nature which affirms Absolute Authority to the Lord and your Creator."[63] It is the driving need to "rescue" Islam that gives bin Laden and his followers their sense of purpose. It is the success of the mujahadeen in Afghanistan that makes them feel like they are truly acting with God's purpose.

Al-Qaeda has proven to be very dangerous indeed. Bin Laden's 1996 declaration of war against the United States, his 1998 fatwa to all Muslims and his 1998 announcement of the International Islamic Front as the unifying force behind the cooperation of terrorist organizations towards a "common cause" have served as media announcements in the continual struggle for the hearts and minds of

---

59   Wooten, J. (2002), "Beyond Bin Laden: From Surgeon to Terrorist: The Second Most Wanted Man in the World," *ABC News*, October 2.

60   Chossudovsky, M. (2001), "Osamagate: Role of the CIA in Supporting International Terrorist Organisations During the Cold War," *Centre for Research on Globalization*. "Hunting bin Laden: Who is Osama bin Laden and What Does He Want?" *PBS Frontline*, online at http://www.pbs.org/wgbh/pages/frontline/shows/binladen/who/edicts.html (interview from April 1995).

61   Ibid.

62   Zeiden, D. (2001), "The Islamic Fundamentalist View of Life as a Perennial Battle," *Middle East Review of International Affairs* 5/4 (December).

63   "Full Text: Bin Laden's 'Letter to America'," *The Observer* (2002) November 24.

young Muslims around the world.[64] The successes that al-Qaeda has achieved are one of purpose. This purpose is to make popular a dogma of religious extremism with bin Laden and al-Qaeda as symbols of resistance to Western influence.[65] His stated goal is to instigate an uprising of Muslims from around the world: "... If the instigation for jihad against the Jews and the Americans ... is considered a crime, then let history be a witness that I am a criminal. Our job is to instigate and, by the grace of God, we did that, and certain people responded to this instigation."[66]

The time period between the fall of the Soviet backed regime and the subsequent fall of the Taliban regime marks the integration point between these "foreign mujahadeen," as represented by Osama's al-Qaeda, and the local mujahadeen under the influence of the Taliban. This relationship served a duel purpose in providing a base for al-Qaeda operations and training, and legitimacy through show of arms for the Taliban regime.

The Taliban and al-Qaeda

A variety of anti-Western militant Islamic groups emerged during the 1980s and 1990s; however, what set al-Qaeda apart was the degree of independence from state influence. While many militant Islamic groups such as HAMAS, Hizballah and the Palestine Islamic Jihad are closely linked with a variety of state sponsors, including Cuba, Iran, Iraq, Libya, North Korea, Sudan and Syria,[67] al-Qaeda enjoyed a degree of financial independence that allowed it access to the resources obtained by groups with state sponsors, but it avoided the political control often exercised by state-based regimes. The eventual location of the al-Qaeda leadership within Afghanistan provided the organization with a base for training and operations and maximum political freedom.

While al-Qaeda developed from the Arab mujahadeen, the Taliban (which literally translates as "students") evolved from the Afghan refugee camps in Pakistan where many youths attended madrassas or Islamic schools run by Sunni Muslims of the Deobandi sect. Because of generous outside support, the majority of the Deobandi madrassas were outside the control of the Pakistani government.[68]

---

64 Doran, M. (2002), "Somebody Else's Civil War," *Foreign Affairs* 81/1 (January/February), 22–42.

65 Doran, M. (2002), "The Pragmatic Fanaticism of al Qaeda: An Anatomy of Extremism in Middle Eastern Politics," *Political Science Quarterly* 117/2 (Summer), 177–190.

66 Osama bin Laden interview, *ABC news* (1998), December 23.

67 See US, Department of State, Office of Counterterrorism (2002), *Patterns of Global Terrorism, 2001*, Washington, DC: GPO.

68 Deobandism is closely linked with the conservative Wahhabi creed of the Saudi Royal family and therefore, the madrassas received significant financial support from the Saudis during the Soviet occupation.

They formed the core of the 10 to 15 percent of the 45,000 Pakistani madrassas which advocated militant Islam of "jihadi" ideologies.[69] The Deobandi madrassas proved very popular since the sect combined the traditional, conservative tenets of Islam with the strict Pashtunwali code of personal honor which was practiced by most ethnic Pashtuns in both Afghanistan and Pakistan.[70]

The Taliban initially received widespread popular support from the Afghan population in the mid-1990s, since the organization seemed devoted to correcting the worst abuses of the mujahadeen warlords. The Taliban was able to bring peace and stability to regions that had been wracked by fifteen years of civil war. Since the group was predominately Pashtun, they enjoyed the support of the majority of Afghans opposed to rule by the ethnic Tajik Rabbani. The Taliban also initially disavowed any desire to rule Afghanistan until after they captured Kabul in 1996.[71] However, as they consolidated their control of Afghanistan, they imposed a strict interpretation of sharia and ruthlessly suppressed any dissent.

With the fall of Mazar-i-Sharif in 1998, the Taliban effectively controlled 90 percent of the country and its only serious rival for power, the United Front or Northern Alliance, a coalition of mainly ethnic Tajiks and Uzbeks, was effectively bottled-up in the north of Afghanistan. Bin Laden developed a number of contacts with militant Islamic leaders in Afghanistan during his experiences as a logistics planner during the Soviet occupation.[72] In fact, a number of Afghans joined bin Laden when he established a base of operations in Khartoum, Sudan in 1992. Under pressure from the United States and Saudi Arabia, Sudan expelled bin Laden in 1996, at which time he returned to Afghanistan, just as the Taliban came to power.

A Terrorist State

Although the Taliban's immediate concern in 1996 was the consolidation of power in Afghanistan, the regime, led by the reclusive one-eyed, Mullah Mohammad Omar, also began to extensively support militant Islamic groups around the world. In addition to providing a base for al-Qaeda, the Taliban regime provided both overt and tacit support to a variety of terrorist organizations. By 1998, there were

---

69   Echeverri-Gent, J. (2001), "Pakistan and the Taliban," *Miller Center Report* 17/4 (Fall), 26–30, reprinted in Logevall, F. (ed.), *Terrorism and 9/11: A Reader*, Boston: Houghton Mifflin Company, 107.

70   Rashid, A. (2001), "Afghanistan: Ending the Policy Quagmire," *Journal of International Affairs* 54/2, Spring, 398.

71   Rashid, A. (1999), "The Taliban: Exporting Extremism," *Foreign Affairs* 78/6, November/December, 24.

72   During the Afghan insurgency, bin Laden primarily served as a supply coordinator where he raised funds for the mujahadeen and oversaw supply efforts, tunneling and road construction operations. He did fight in several battles and was wounded during the siege of Jalalabad.

bases for groups involved in terrorist activities in Tajikistan, Uzbekistan, China, Bangladesh, Kashmir, Pakistan, Saudi Arabia and the Philippines.[73] The Taliban also provided training for soldiers who fought alongside Muslims in Chechnya and Kosovo. Meanwhile, bin Laden was able to recruit and train approximately 5,000 al-Qaeda members. Some of these recruits would be dispatched to undertake terrorist operations in the West (or form sleeper cells for future operations) while the al-Qaeda leader maintained a standing force of about 2,000 troops in Afghanistan as a sort of personal militia which supported the Taliban's military operations.[74]

Bin Laden remained quite popular with the Taliban leadership and took pains to ensure that he stayed in their good graces. He paid for the construction of houses for Mullah Omar's family and for those of other top Taliban leaders.[75] He also provided other funds that the Taliban used for military equipment or infrastructure construction, including road-building. Al-Qaeda troops also fought alongside the Taliban in their continuing campaign against the Northern Alliance and in offensives to suppress the Shiite Hazaras of Afghanistan.

When the United States demanded that the Taliban surrender bin Laden in the late 1990s, the Taliban initially used the terrorist leader as a "bargaining chip" and tried to negotiate diplomatic recognition and expanded US aid in return for bin Laden's surrender. When these discussions failed to come to fruition, the Taliban allowed bin Laden to quietly disappear from public view in Kandahar in an effort to shield him from covert action by the United States.

The Taliban received substantial support from the Pakistani intelligence service (the Inter-Services Intelligence agency or ISI) as the Islamabad government sought to use the Afghan regime as a tool to undermine Indian control of Kashmir. For instance, the Taliban provided a base for the Harkat ul-Mujahadeen, one of the main terrorist groups in Kashmir, and in return the Kabul regime received military and financial aid from Pakistan.[76] With Pakistani and continued Saudi support, the Taliban were able to expand their external operations and reinforce their internal control over the country.

The ISI provided the Taliban with intelligence, weapons and training. The Pakistanis also served as the main diplomatic conduit for the Taliban. Pakistani support for the regime, even in the light of Kabul's terrorist connections, further provided a sense of empowerment to the Taliban (especially as the regime faced a series of crises with both Iran and later the United States). One result of this confidence was that by 1998, as Ahmed Rashid points out, "Afghanistan was now

---

73 Khalilzad, Z. and Byman, D. (2000), "Afghanistan: The Consolidation of a Rogue State," *The Washington Quarterly* 32/1 (Winter), 72.

74 Rashid, op. cit. fn. 70, 399.

75 For a more extensive overview of the ties between bin Laden and the Taliban, see Rashid, A. (2000), *Taliban: Militant Islam, Oil and Fundamentalism in Central Asia*, New Haven: Yale University Press.

76 Ganguly, S. (2000), "Pakistan's Never-Ending Story: Why the October Coup Was No Surprise," *Foreign Affairs* 79/2 (March/April), 4.

truly a haven for Islamic internationalism and terrorism and the Americans and the West were at a loss as to how to handle it."[77]

US Policy

With the 1991 agreement to stop arms shipments and military supplies, the US policy toward Afghanistan shifted back to its more traditional benign neglect. The US supplied humanitarian aid, but did not provide substantial support for the Rabbani regime. After the Taliban seized power, the US continued to recognize Rabbani as the legitimate President of Afghanistan, but it also provided food and other humanitarian assistance to the Taliban regime. The US policy of avoidance ended with the August 7, 1998 terrorist attacks on the American embassies in Nairobi, Kenya and Dar-es-Salaam, Tanzania which were traced to al-Qaeda. The attacks led the Clinton Administration to redouble its anti-terrorist efforts and marked the beginnings of a shift away from the view that bin Laden and al-Qaeda were a criminal issue.[78] The Administration increasingly viewed Osama bin Laden as a hard security or military threat, instead of a law enforcement concern, and subsequently launched cruise missile attacks on three suspected al-Qaeda bases in Afghanistan and a facility in Sudan. The attacks, which killed 26 people in Afghanistan, infuriated the Taliban and reinforced their unwillingness to negotiate his handover to the Americans.[79]

The trend toward the growing recognition of the security threat posed by al-Qaeda accelerated with the attack on the *USS Cole* in October of 2000.[80] Within the Administration, Secretary of State Madeleine Albright and Secretary of Defense William Cohen pressed strongly for military action against bin Laden and his al-Qaeda terrorist network while Attorney General Janet Reno strongly dissented.[81] However, intelligence problems and a military coup in Pakistan in 1999 forestalled the implementation of most of the Administration's plans.[82]

---

77   Rashid, op. cit. fn. 75, 60.

78   US, White House (1998), *Combating Terrorism: Presidential Decision Directive 62*, Fact Sheet, May 22; US, White House, Press Briefing by Jake Siewart, January 5, 2001.

79   Gohari, M.J., *The Taliban: Ascent to Power*, London: Oxford University Press, 141.

80   For an overview of administration reaction to the *USS Cole* attack, see US, Department of Defense (2001), *USS Cole Commission Report*, January 9.

81   Albright and National Security Advisor Sandy Berger specifically advocated the use of special operations forces to kill or capture bin Laden.

82   In 1998, Clinton signed three Memoranda of Notification to allow the military to specifically target bin Laden, including shooting down civilian aircraft if bin Laden or his top aides were aboard. In addition, after the August 20, 1998 missile attack on Bin Laden's camp in Afghanistan, Clinton authorized three new attacks, but intelligence problems prevented verification of bin Laden's whereabouts. Meanwhile, arrangements with the government of Benazir Bhutto of Pakistan for the capture of bin Laden through CIA operations fell apart after the Prime Minister was toppled in a military coup; Gellman, B. (2001), "Broad Effort Launched After '98 Attacks," *Washington Post*, December 19, A1.

The unwillingness of the Clinton Administration to take strong action against al-Qaeda or to exert significant pressure on the Taliban regime emboldened bin Laden. It also led the Taliban to believe that they could defy the United States with few serious consequences. This combination of under appreciation would lead bin Laden to plan even more daring and powerful attacks on the United States, while it encouraged the Taliban to be dismissive and contemptuous of US threats in the aftermath of September 11.

Conclusion

The United States, in its efforts to control Soviet expansion, formed a policy of neglect once a client state was no longer in contention between the two superpowers. Afghanistan is no exception to this. The lack of strategic concern once the Soviets withdrew caused the United States to abandon Afghanistan. This, in turn, exacerbated a situation in which Islamic fundamentalism was already an historical part of the existing governmental structure. When millions of dollars of US supplied military aid is added to the equation, without an equal amount of economic and infrastructure support, it is no wonder that groups within Afghanistan that were formerly pro-Western turned decidedly anti-US This situation may have forced Afghanistan into Taliban rule and its subsequent support of the al-Qaeda organization, and weakened the stance of the elements within Afghanistan that held a more moderate world view. Once the lukewarm commitment by the United States and the Soviets dried up after the fall of the Berlin Wall, the different factions within the mujahadeen were left without the leadership necessary for any one of them to control what remained. This, in essence, allowed the Taliban to gain control.

On top of this local impetus towards anti-Western sentiment were the introduction of American and Saudi backed Islamic "Crusaders". The dependence upon these wholly militant Islamists and the subsequent "internationalizing" of their goals can be attributed to the international community's willingness to support their actions and needs in Afghanistan. The failure of American policy towards supporting these foreign mujahadeen was not a failure in the sense that the US should have recognized the threat. The US commitment to Afghanistan must be looked at from the bipolar view that shrouded the decision making apparatus at the time. What appeared to be a logical marriage then would have naturally been illogical without the Soviet threat. This was not a failure in American policy at all in terms of the goal being achieved. What failure there is derives in the inability to control the side affects that American support for these Muslim fighters caused. The cure should have been (1) the ability to separate their cause against communism from its implications of anti-Westernism; (2) the removal of the more militant leaders from the scene and; (3) a greater effort toward promoting positive compatible Western values.

With respect to the future of US interactions within Afghanistan, and other nations that are under the constraints of extremist Muslim dogma, the US and other Western powers need to reinvest in their commitment to support democratic capitalistic ideals. Long term commitments to economic development will eventually take away the overwhelming poverty of the region and, consequently, the attractiveness of a system of beliefs that blame hardship on the "hedonistic" success of the West. The failure of the United States to invest in a stable government within Afghanistan once the need to counter Soviet aggression was no longer an issue, can be directly related to the rise of the Taliban as the leading regime. If that investment had been made, a wholly different outcome could have been expected. This is truer now than it was then. The fledgling democracy that is currently forming in Afghanistan will not succeed without a direct investment in time and energy by Western powers. It is with this investment that a secure future can exist in this historically torn region.

Chapter 3

The Fight against Terrorism in Historical Context: George W. Bush and the Development of Presidential Foreign Policy Regimes

Neal Allen

Introduction

President George W. Bush responded to the events of September 11 by setting new priorities in foreign policy, and attempting to increase Presidential power within the American political system.[1] This response to crisis parallels previous changes in how the United States responds to the world, and how it formulates that response at home. The President articulated a new set of national commitments that have the potential of altering both the content of American foreign policy and the institutional arrangement and capacity of American government. This chapter discusses these new commitments in the historical context of Presidential foreign policymaking, elaborating on the connections between Bush's attempts to set lasting national goals, and those of other similarly situated Presidents. The War on Terror and the institutional change it set in motion may result in a significant transformation of the Presidency, and the American political system in general.

This chapter provides an assessment of the possible historical significance of the Bush War on Terror just after the end of his Presidency. While any first appraisal is tentative, historical comparison helps to identify the post-September 11 developments that could have long-term importance. I link Bush to the history of Presidents and foreign policymaking through a theory of Presidential foreign policy regimes, defined as the commitments, constraints and capabilities crafted by creative Presidents. My proposed regime structure takes much from the cyclical model Stephen Skowronek outlines in *The Politics Presidents Make*, but I outline a separate foreign policy regime cycle, existing alongside the domestic regime cycle Skowronek identifies. The foreign policy cycle is not directly tied to partisan affiliation, and has two regimes: the McKinley/Theodore Roosevelt

---

1   I would like to thank Peter Trubowitz, Bartholomew Sparrow and Peter Jenkins for comments on earlier drafts of this chapter.

regime establishing a substantial but limited American colonial commitment, and the Cold War regime crafted by Franklin Roosevelt and Harry Truman.

After September 11, George W. Bush began to construct a new Presidential foreign policy regime, setting new commitments for US overseas involvement. He created institutions to support his new regime commitments, and attempted to further increase the power of the President over national policy. I first set out my theory and historical analysis, and then discuss Bush as a possible regime-creating President in the area of foreign policy.

A Theory of Presidential Foreign Policy Regimes

If George W. Bush was successful in altering the long-term commitments and institutional structure of American politics, his War on Terror is the third Presidentially created foreign policy regime, becoming part of a cyclical pattern going back over a century. The connections between Bush and previous transformative Presidents can be understood through a punctuated equilibrium model. Stephen Skowronek puts forth such a model for the Presidency in *The Politics Presidents Make*,[2] placing the President at the core of the process of regime construction and breakdown. He argues that certain Presidents, like Andrew Jackson and Franklin Roosevelt, create a set of policy directions and institutional arrangements that endures as a stable equilibrium until the next transformative President is elected.

An extension of Skowronek's basic argument regarding foreign policy yields a different kind of regime cycle. Taking a regime to be a set of commitments that motivate and constrain politics and political behavior, a survey of Presidents from McKinley forward yields a regime analysis of the Presidency similar in many respects to Skowronek's, but following a different track through the twentieth century, and having different core characteristics. While Skowronek argues that Thomas Jefferson formed the first regime, and successor commitment structures were constructed by Jackson, Lincoln, FDR and Reagan, I argue that the foreign policy regime process did not begin until the 1890s, and only two regimes have motivated American foreign policy since then. The McKinley-Theodore Roosevelt regime of limited international engagement and economic expansionism, and its successor, the Franklin Roosevelt-Truman Cold War regime, originated and were maintained under different conditions and in different ways than concurrent domestic regimes. A Presidentially created foreign policy regime is not tied to a specific political party, unlike Skowronek's domestic policy regimes. Successors to regime-creating Presidents adhere to his commitments and institutional arrangements, regardless of partisan affiliation. Truman was instrumental in creating the Cold War regime, and his Democratic and Republican successors continued his policy of opposition

---

2   Skowronek, S. (1997), *The Politics Presidents Make: Leadership from John Adams to Bill Clinton*, Cambridge, MA: Belknap Press.

to international communism. If Bush was successful in creating an anti-terrorism regime, future Republican and Democratic Presidents will adhere to the policies and institutional arrangements he established in response to September 11. The foreign policy regime cycle differs from the domestic cycle because in foreign affairs Presidents have more flexibility to craft policy, and are less restrained by partisan arrangements. Aaron Wildavsky had the insight in his classic essay, "The Two Presidencies,"[3] that Presidential-congressional relations were of a different kind in foreign policy than domestic policy, with the President more powerful in foreign policy. I find a similar difference in the creation of regime commitments.

The two core components of any cycle of regimes are conflict and creative power. A change of regime occurs when a conflict arises which cannot be resolved within the current set of perceived received political commitments. An actor or group of actors in the political system is able to create a new regime structure with the ability to resolve conflict and set politics on new foundations. This particular regime creation sequence is not unique to Skowronek's analysis; it forms the core of other theories that view American politics as a punctuated equilibrium system. In analyzing electoral politics, Walter Dean Burnham[4] argues that realigning elections occur when a particular conflict is not resolvable within the existing party system and an activated electorate establishes a new equilibrium with the parties on a different footing than before. Bruce Ackerman applies a punctuated equilibrium analysis to constitutional politics, claiming that constitutional change occurred during the Founding, Reconstruction and New Deal because the existing constitutional arrangements were inadequate to resolve the conflicts of contemporary politics.[5]

Presidential foreign policy making also functions according to a punctuated equilibrium model, but in a markedly different manner. The divergence between domestic and foreign policy regimes in American politics occurs because of the varying nature of conflict and the different resources possessed by the President in each case. Scholars like Burnham, Ackerman and Skowronek show that in domestic politics, conflict arises within the domestic political system and is resolved through the transformation of that system. But in foreign policy, the chief opposition to the President comes from outside American politics and his resources are much greater owing to the nature of foreign policy-making and the lack of institutional constraints he faces.

This outward orientation in foreign policy enhances the President's symbolic role as a representative of the American nation-state. The head-of-state function

3   Wildavsky, A. (1975), "The Two Presidencies," in Wildavsky, A. (ed.), *Perspectives on the Presidency*, Boston: Little, Brown and Co.
4   See Burnham, W.D. (1970), *Critical Elections and the Mainsprings of American Politics*, New York: W.W. Norton.
5   See Ackerman, B. (1991), *We the People: Foundations*, Cambridge, MA: Belknap Press; and Ackerman, B. (1998), *We the People: Transformations*, Cambridge, MA: Belknap Press.

is more prominent in global politics than in domestic. Instead of acting as head of government, negotiating with Congress and other domestic political actors over the content of public policy, the President is representing America and American values to the world when structuring and implementing foreign policy. The symbolic and rhetorical resources emerging from this patriotic, outward-oriented Presidential role support the executive's greater capacity to create governing regimes in foreign policy. George W. Bush drew on the head-of-state role to recast himself as the personification of the War against Terrorism. The mass and elite support he gained from this role transformation enabled him to create a conception of terrorism and how it should be opposed, secure victories in Congressional elections for his party, and expand the institutional power of the Presidency. If these changes endure, he will have created a regime along similar lines of the two previous Presidentially created foreign policy regimes.

The McKinley/Roosevelt Regime

The Presidency of William McKinley (1897–1901) is the starting point of the Presidential foreign policy regime cycle. It marks the first time since the end of the wars with Great Britain that the United States committed itself to sustained involvement in international affairs. American foreign policy commitments in the nineteenth century, when they existed, were to protect the nation from European domination and gain additional contiguous territory for the United States. The transformation in American foreign policy that started with the Spanish-American War (1898) constituted the first national commitment to sustained foreign involvement. Begun and principally accomplished under McKinley and completed and solidified under Theodore Roosevelt, the new regime carried with it both substantive and institutional changes. The construction of this first regime established commitments of greater internationalism and enhanced Presidential power that would last until the next transformation in the 1940s.

William McKinley's mandate for Presidential leadership came about from the intersection of growing American economic power and the opportunities available for American expansion, both politically and economically. Under his leadership, and that of his successor, the United States became a player in international colonial politics as well as a staunch supporter of American economic interests overseas. Both strands of the new Presidential foreign policy regime had roots in earlier eras: the United States had taken on colonial responsibilities in Alaska and Hawaii over the previous decades, and had exerted influence on politics in Latin America. Promotion of American business interests overseas can be linked back to Jefferson's conflict with the Barbary pirates. But the McKinley/Roosevelt regime systematized and extended these commitments, expanding the power and authority of the Presidency in the process. By the end of Roosevelt's term in office, according to Fareed Zakaria's, *From Wealth to Power*, even though he exercised power of foreign policy previously considered congressional, "the expectations of congressional and Presidential behavior had changed so much that

Roosevelt's relationship with Congress, like McKinley's was generally cordial and productive."[6]

In the context of system-wide commitments, the actions against Spain stand not just as the entry of the United States into the international colonial system. The forcible acquisition of current colonies like Puerto Rico in the Caribbean and Guam in the South Pacific, along with controlling influence in Cuba and the Philippines, is the military manifestation of what Emily Rosenberg refers to as "the promotional state." In *Spreading the American Dream*, she identifies five components of the promotional state, deriving from "liberal-developmentalist" ideology:

1. Belief that other nations could and should replicate America's own developmental experience;
2. faith in private free enterprise;
3. support for free or open access for trade and investment;
4. promotion of free flow of information and culture; and
5. growing acceptance of governmental activity to protect private enterprise and to stimulate and regulate American participation in international and cultural exchange.[7]

America under McKinley, according to Zakaria, took "the most dramatic extension of its interests abroad since the annexation of Texas."[8] By fully committing the United States to systematic involvement abroad, McKinley constructed the first Presidential foreign policy regime. In order to forge such commitments, he and Theodore Roosevelt expanded the power and authority of the Presidency. In their drive to carve out a substantive leadership role for themselves in the fractured American political system, Presidents find new ways of gaining and using power.

In the case of William McKinley and Theodore Roosevelt, this expansion of Presidential power took two forms. First, they used the commander-in-chief power in ways not seen since the Civil War, and never seen in previous American history except when hostile forces occupied American soil. Responding to calls for the United States to come to the defense of Cuba and other Spanish colonies, McKinley committed American forces to actions in two hemispheres, gaining Congressional approval for his decisions.[9] Roosevelt later followed McKinley's lead by using troops in Latin America and exhibiting the new American Navy around the world.

---

6   Zakaria, F. (1998), *From Wealth to Power*, Princeton: Princeton University Press, 174.

7   Rosenberg, E.S. (1982), *Spreading the American Dream: American Economic and Cultural Expansion*, New York: Hill and Wang.

8   Zakaria, op. cit. fn. 6, 163.

9   Ibid., 158–60.

A related development was McKinley and Roosevelt's practice of making fundamental American foreign policy commitments without the specific Congressional approval needed in previous eras. Not only in the case of the Spanish-American War, but also in China and throughout the Western Hemisphere, the two regime-creating Presidents set the form of American international policy. A case in point is Theodore Roosevelt's direct defiance of previous deferential norms governing President-Congress relations with respect to acquiring the territory needed for the Panama Canal. "If I had followed the general consultative method I should have submitted an admirable state paper, occupying a couple of hundred pages detailing the facts to Congress and asking Congress consideration of it ... I took the Canal Zone and let Congress debate, and while the debate goes on the Canal does too."[10] Roosevelt's own characterization of his action concerning the canal shows an intentional expansion of Presidential capacity in furtherance of new policy goals.

The McKinley/Roosevelt regime, consisting of substantial but limited international involvement and promotion of American international interests, was the dominant idea in American foreign policy until the onset of the Second World War. Its most important test was Woodrow Wilson's attempt to take the United States into the League of Nations, which foundered in the Senate. In his failure, Wilson showed the limits of the Presidential foreign policy regime, demonstrating that the regime was not reconcilable with international obligations outside narrow conceptions of imperialism and economic promotion. This first foreign policy regime would continue in its limited form through the more isolationist years of Republican rule, until the Second World War when Franklin Roosevelt would create the conditions necessary for regime change.

The Roosevelt/Truman Regime

The best parallel to the Bush anti-terrorism regime is the Cold War regime created by Franklin Roosevelt and Harry Truman. After the Second World War ended, Truman was confronted by a communist adversary fundamentally opposed to the values and existence of the United States of America, just as Bush confronts an international terror network whose mission is to remake the world in a way antithetical to American and Western values. Truman drew on the public role and institutional resources built up by his predecessor to craft a foreign policy regime to oppose Soviet expansionism. The new regime had as its component parts all the familiar attributes of Cold War policy. Soviet expansionism was to be opposed in all conceivable forms, in all places across the world. The idea of containment, which defined the primary aim of United States foreign policy as the limitation of the spread of communism, became the motivating ideology.[11] A key step in the move

---

10   Quoted in Zakaria, op. cit. fn. 6.
11   Sparrow, B.H. (1995), "The Presidency and the World: Adjusting to the Post-Cold War Era," in Nelson, M. (ed.), *The Presidency and the Political System*, 4th edn, Washington, DC: Congressional Quarterly Press, 557.

toward containment was the later-famous telegram by George Kennan, American diplomat in Moscow, which crystallized in the minds of American government officials the image of the Soviet Union as a threat to national security.[12]

While the Cold War regime would have been impossible without the consensus among political elites and masses supporting it in the post-war years, Harry Truman's decisions and actions were vital in forming and solidifying the commitments that would define American foreign policy for the next four-and-a-half decades. Truman inherited a system left in flux by the end of the war and ambiguous agreements and understandings between Roosevelt and Stalin. By creating, with the Western European powers, the North Atlantic Treaty Organization (NATO), setting a precedent for action motivated by the domino theory by aiding Greece and Turkey to contain communism in the Balkans, and finally by committing the American troops to the defense of South Korea, Truman set American priorities in foreign relations. He supplemented these substantive actions with groundbreaking reorganization of the executive national security apparatus. In 1947, Congress granted Truman's request to combine the War and Navy departments, set up the National Security Council (NSC), and convert the nascent foreign intelligence-gathering apparatus into the Central Intelligence Agency (CIA). These reforms enlarged the resources available to Truman and his successors in their waging of the continuing conflict with the Soviet Union.[13]

After Truman, all American Presidents until George H.W. Bush governed under the Cold War regime in foreign policy, with its motivations and limitations. Presidential election contests were increasingly marked by agreement over US foreign policy goals, with the Kennedy-Nixon race particularly notable for the consonance of candidate positions, with both Democrat and Republican firmly within the Cold War consensus. While Cold War commitments usually ran parallel to and supported the New Deal regime in domestic politics, Johnson's Presidency stands as an example of what can happen when a President's domestic and foreign policy commitments come into conflict. Johnson's attempt to extend the social democratic ideals he inherited from the regime-builder FDR ran aground as his adherence to the Cold War regime drove him toward increasing personal and fiscal commitment to the war in Vietnam.

While post-Vietnam policy marked an easing of tensions with the Soviet Union, and Reagan rhetoric and arms buildup evidenced an increase in combativeness, Presidential Cold War politics always took place within the bounds established by the Truman Doctrine in the 1940s. According to LaFeber in *The American Age*:

> From Truman to Ronald Reagan, presidents repeatedly revived the Truman Doctrine's specific words to justify their polices in such places as Lebanon, Southeast Asia, and Central America. As Senator J. William Fulbright wrote

---

12   LaFeber, W. (1995), *The American Age: US Foreign Policy At Home and Abroad*, vol. 2, New York: W.W. Norton, 449–52.

13   Ibid., 458–59.

in the 1970s, "More by far than any other factor the anti-communism of the Truman Doctrine had been the guiding spirit of American foreign policy since World War II."[14]

While Franklin Roosevelt may have bequeathed to Harry Truman a fluid, uncertain international situation, he left his successor with a strong precedent for easier Presidential decision-making in international affairs. As Bruce Ackerman and David Golove have shown in *Is NAFTA Constitutional?*,[15] FDR and Truman recast the constitutional arrangements governing foreign policy formation in their successful attempt to transform American commitments after the Second World War. Overturning the precedent of the Senate's rejection of the League of Nations during Wilson's Presidency, FDR used the executive-legislative agreement to gain approval for a variety of measures defining post-war American commitments in foreign relations, culminating with the approval of membership of the World Bank and International Monetary Fund (IMF) with the ratification of the Bretton Woods agreement in 1945.[16] The vital difference between treaties and executive-legislative agreements is that treaties require a two-thirds vote of the Senate, while executive-legislative agreements only require a majority of both houses. The latter device frees the President from the difficulty of gaining 68 votes in the Senate, thus allowing results like the passage of the North American Free Trade Agreement (NAFTA) in 1993 by a vote of 61 to 38. Ackerman argues this change in constitutional process came about through FDR's "piecemeal presidentialism." By gaining approval for international commitments of increasing importance, "each time the Administration convinced a majority of the Senate to join the House in support of an executive agreement, it created a new precedent for further expansion."[17]

The Cold War regime continued through Republican and Democratic Administrations until the collapse of communism eliminated its reason for existence. Neither George H.W. Bush's New World Order nor Bill Clinton's limited humanitarian intervention rose to the level of regime commitments. The institutional capacities created to fight Soviet communism remained, however, and have been revitalized and expanded by George W. Bush in his response to terrorist threats.

---

14   Ibid., 455; quote from Fulbright, J. (1972), *The Crippled Giant*, New York: Random House, 6–24.
15   Ackerman, B. and Golove, D. (1995), *Is NAFTA Constitutional?* Cambridge, MA: Harvard University Press.
16   Ibid., 90–91.
17   Ibid., 93.

George W. Bush and the Creation of an Anti-terrorism Regime

Before September 11, George W. Bush continued the case-by-case foreign policy of his two immediate predecessors. He retained most Clinton Administration international commitments, with the exception of a withdrawal from direct intervention in the Middle East peace process. Bush began to move American foreign policy to a more unilateralist position, withdrawing from the Kyoto global warming talks and abrogating the Anti-Ballistic Missile treaty with Russia, but created no new alliances, institutional structures or commitments. Events on September 11 broke this continuity, and began a creative process led by the Presidency. The attacks on New York and Washington, DC certainly transformed American foreign policy, but transformation does not necessarily constitute a new regime in American foreign policy, or a Presidentially created one. It is, of course, too early to judge the lasting significance of Bush's War on Terror, but it fits the pattern of a Presidentially created foreign policy regime. His first term witnessed a transformation of American foreign policy commitments, and an expansion of Presidential capacity to set those commitments and carry out policy. This transformation was precipitated by the exogenous shock of the September 11 attacks, but President Bush was the dominant actor in responding to that crisis with new substantive commitments and institutional changes.

At least for the time being, the War on Terror has reoriented most American foreign policy commitments, much as the Cold War did in the post-war period. Bush outlined a policy of opposing terrorism with military force everywhere it exists, and also taking military action against foreign governments that harbor and support terrorists. This commitment, called for the time being the Bush Doctrine, also includes the assassination of terrorist and foreign leaders implicated in terrorism against Americans. This new commitment quickly came to fruition with the war in Afghanistan, an operation pursued under a broad grant of authority by Congress to the President, and at a time and place chosen in the White House, not the Congress.

The Bush Doctrine is much like the Truman Doctrine, pledging the United States to act anyplace in the globe to combat a particular enemy. What separates these regime-level commitments from less lasting ones is the broad, amorphous definition of the enemy. Terrorism, like communism, can stretch to include a variety of groups, movements and social phenomena. Additionally, al-Qaeda terrorism, like Soviet expansionism, is avowedly opposed to American interests and values, and directed at international expansion. Thus, the Bush and Truman Doctrines differ from regional commitments like the Monroe Doctrine and its imperial extension by McKinley and Roosevelt, and from commitments specific in time and place like the Gulf War and peacekeeping operations.

Many existing American operations have now been recast as anti-terrorism, and expanded to encompass the new priorities. The best example is Columbia, in which US support for the government in its civil war against the narcotic-financed rebels has morphed into a fight against terrorists opposed to American interests abroad. Bush also moved the US into conflicts that previously were not on the agenda for American involvement, like the ongoing Russian campaign against the Chechnyan rebels operating out of Georgia.

Bush elaborated the necessarily ambiguous concept of the War on Terror through a substantive expansion of new regime commitments beyond fighting terrorism narrowly defined. In his 2002 State of the Union address Bush characterized Iraq, Iran and North Korea as the "Axis of Evil," because of their attempts to acquire and develop nuclear, chemical and biological weapons. This shift in rhetoric, along with the move against Iraq, could mark another significant departure from previous American policy if it carries with it a commitment to act against such states outside of international organizations. The Administration's recent national security strategy document, at least on paper, commits the United States to multilateral and unilateral preemptive attack upon threatening nations. A move from containment to preemption could in the long term be as significant as the Cold War shift from cooperation with the Soviets to containment.

Also like the Cold War regime, the nascent anti-terrorism regime extends foreign policy priorities into the domestic arena. The War on Terror has immigration, public health, and local law enforcement connections. This new set of commitments, while sparked by the threat of international terrorism, has become a public safety regime as well. The institutional manifestation of this new public safety regime was the creation of the Department of Homeland Security (DHS), an aggregation of agencies from the Coastguard to the Secret Service to Aviation Security. This recent development is exactly the kind of institutional change that regime-creating Presidents bring about, with the executive now possessing enhanced powers over personnel and funding of the new department. When Presidents create foreign policy regimes they gain new powers and means of setting policy.

A particularly controversial expansion of Presidential authority, reversed through executive order by President Obama, was the creation of military tribunals at Guantánamo Bay. This process was created anew within the Department of Defense to try foreign terrorism suspects, along with the detention of citizens as unlawful combatants without constitutional protection. By superseding the congressionally-created civilian justice system, which in the past has tried terrorism suspects like the first World Trade Center attackers, Bush expanded the reach of the Presidency in foreign affairs to pursue the new priorities he set. Bush also expanded American public relations efforts abroad, and proposed sending thousands of Americans abroad as part of a new "USA Freedom Corps." The federalization of aviation security, with its attendant bureaucracy, is another result of the extension of foreign policy priorities into domestic affairs.

The September 11 attacks are often compared to the Japanese attack on Pearl Harbor, because both attacks caused enormous numbers of casualties and led the United States into war. But the War on Terror does not have a foreseeable endpoint like the German and Japanese surrenders. Bush is thus best understood in comparison to Presidents that led the nation into long-term foreign commitments. With the overthrow of the Taliban government in Afghanistan, the War on

Terror changed quickly from a traditional war with a foreign state to a long-term commitment to expansive foreign policy goals. Here, new commitments to resist terrorism are similar to the commitment to limited colonialism of McKinley and Theodore Roosevelt, and to the Cold War regime of FDR and Truman. Comparison between the current Bush Administration and these regime-creating predecessors yields three tests of the existence of a stable Presidentially created foreign policy regime. The 2003 invasion of Iraq speaks to all three of these tests.

First, the substantive commitments of the regime-creating President must become a bipartisan consensus, with later Presidents of the opposing party adhering to the regime. The Democrat Woodrow Wilson continued the colonial involvement of his republican predecessors, and Republicans Eisenhower, Nixon, Reagan and George W. Bush founded their Administrations on Cold War commitments. If a new regime was established after September 11, a core component of it is the "Bush Doctrine," a commitment to treat a foreign government that sponsors terrorism as an enemy that must be destroyed. Bush extended this doctrine to include countries like Iraq that could have potentially provided chemical, biological and nuclear weapons to terrorists.

For a Presidential foreign policy regime to exist, elected officials across parties and institutions must also accept the conceptual framework that underlies regime commitments. Thus it is clear in retrospect that Truman created a Cold War regime because his contemporaries and predecessors in Washington accepted his conceptualization of international communism as Soviet expansionism, and that Soviet expansionism must be opposed in all its forms. Future developments in American policy toward Iraq and Iran will demonstrate how much latitude other political actors give President Bush in defining the necessarily ambiguous concept of terrorism. It is one thing for Democrats in Congress to have supported war against an Afghanistan that harbored and supported terrorist organizations whose members attacked the United States, and another for them to have supported war with Iraq because of the possibility that it might acquire and distribute weapons of mass destruction.

Second, the regime must support large-scale military actions, like the occupations of the Philippines in the first part of the twentieth century, and the Korean War (1950–1953). Iraq was the anti-terrorism counterpart to Korea. It marked a shift and expansion of the regime commitments, with the United States intervening abroad against a nation that had not yet attacked America. Also, the war against Iraq would test how transferable the broadened anti-terrorism regime was to other nations and international organizations. Like Korea, the manner in which the United States ends such a war and occupation will set a precedent for future US-led construction of governing arrangements for another country. President Obama campaigned on a pledge to withdraw American combat troops from Iraq within 16 months. The open-ended commitment of the Bush Administration, however, may constrain his freedom of action.

Third, the new institutional arrangements the President crafted to meet new challenges must remain after the initial crisis period. In the two previous

Presidential creations of foreign policy regimes, Presidents seized new authority to act abroad, with Theodore Roosevelt seizing the Panama Canal, and Truman committing America to the opposition of Communists in Greece. Obama has reversed some expansion of Presidential power with respect to the treatment of detainees, and maintained others in the area of warrantless wiretapping.

If Bush succeeded in transforming American foreign policy and governmental structure in response to terrorism, he reinvigorated the Presidency as the dominant order-creating actor in the political system. In an era where political parties lack the mass connections to stimulate domestic regime construction, foreign policy remains an issue area susceptible to the creative leadership of the President. But it is worth noting that regime-creating success in foreign policy does not always carry with it domestic and electoral success. Harry Truman set the commitments and institutional arrangements that would define American politics for over fifty years, but had mixed success at the polls. His election in 1948 was much like Bush's 2000 victory, with support drawn mainly from his party's core supporters. His second term fell victim to needs of the regime he created, with the Republicans gaining support from Cold War ideology after the communist takeover of China.

Thus far the Obama Administration has signaled a willingness to reverse some Bush Administration expansions of Presidential power, pledging to close the Guantánamo Bay detention center within a year of taking office. The new President has, at the time of this writing, held to his commitment to wind down the Iraq commitment but increase the number of troops in Afghanistan. Taken together, these policies are similar to the policies of the Bush Administration before the run-up to the Iraq War in 2002, albeit with limits on detention and interrogation methods. Possibly the Iraq War will turn out to be a temporary divergence from a more narrowly focused War on Terror foreign policy regime, even though that divergence was electorally disastrous for George W. Bush's Republican Party. One test of whether Bush was successful in creating a Presidential foreign policy regime may be the response of the Obama Administration to a major national defense crisis, and whether that response resembles the institutional transformation of Bush's response to September 11.

Chapter 4

The War on Terror and the Just Use of Military Force

Patrick Hayden

Introduction

In this chapter, I would like to sketch a framework for thinking about the United States Government's response to the terrorist attacks of September 11. Particularly, I would like to examine the moral and legal rules that apply to the US-led fight against terrorism, and articulate what I take to be the appropriate limits to waging the so-called "War on Terror." Following the violent attacks of September 11 by al-Qaeda operatives one of the fundamental questions faced by the Bush Administration, as well as by the broader international community, is how are we best to respond to the threat and reality of terrorism? The Bush Administration has assumed that the answer is obvious and uncontroversial: we may resort to war in order to strike back at terrorists, as well as those nations suspected of harboring them. Yet the Bush Administration has thus far failed to elaborate the normative judgments that led them to this answer, so that their justification for resorting to the use of armed force remains incomplete.

The complexity of the question concerning the just use of force—which brings together moral, legal, political and military issues—cannot be overstated, and its implications are profound with regard to the formulation of appropriate foreign policy. Debate surrounding the United States' response to the specter of international terrorism necessarily revolves around different conceptions of the national interest and how best to define and defend it. The willingness and the capacity of the United States, as well as other nations, to respond militarily to the form of "warfare" embodied in international terrorism are therefore open to critical assessment so that we may begin to develop an understanding of how the War on Terror and its underlying policy are shaping our world.[1] Towards that end,

---

1 For a discussion of how terrorism and modern forms of war differ see, for example, Detter, I. (2000), *The Laws of War*, 2nd edn, Cambridge: Cambridge University Press; Guelke, A. (1995), *The Age of Terrorism and the International Political System*, New York: St. Martin's Press; and Lackey, D. (1989), *The Ethics of War and Peace*, Englewood Cliffs, NJ: Prentice Hall. On the emergence of "new wars" between states and non-governmental militants see Kaldor, M. (1999), *New and Old Wars: Organized Violence in a Global Era*, Stanford: Stanford University Press.

I will set out the fundamental criteria of just war theory and the corresponding international laws of war, and apply these as the requirements that the US and its allies must meet in order to be justified in resorting to military force.[2] My aim will be to analyze whether the War on Terror is a justified use of military force or illegitimate aggression, and thus whether the war's pursuit is the result of good or bad foreign policy.

The Principles of Just War Theory

In traditional just war theory there are two basic categories of norms: *jus ad bellum*, the justice of the cause of resorting to war to begin with, and *jus in bello*, the justice of the means or conduct of war once it has begun.[3] Given these two categories, a comprehensive analysis of the just use of military force will consider whether warfare is justly begun as well as justly fought.

The structure of comprehensive just war theory also presupposes the priority of *jus ad bellum* to *jus in bello*. In other words, the two sets of norms are placed in serial or lexical order, with *jus ad bellum* lexically prior to *jus in bello*. This means that the just resort to military force must satisfy the norms of *jus ad bellum* before the norms of *jus in bello* come into play. The lexical order thereby ensures consistency between, and coherency throughout, the two just war categories to prohibit the trading off of norms. While a war may be justly begun it is conceivable that it will be unjustly fought. The justness of any given war therefore must be determined in light of both sets of norms, and the failure to satisfy one set of norms will preclude judging the war as a whole to be just.

Before considering each of the just war categories it should also be noted that the normative conditions specified in the theory are not taken to be subjective. Individual states are disallowed from simply asserting that they have satisfied the norms of both categories, and the rest of the international community is neither obligated nor expected to accept their claims as self-evident. The norms of just war theory instead function as universal moral principles against which state conduct can and ought to be publicly assessed according to transparent

---

2   The body of work on just war theory is vast, but the following works are of notable significance: Elshtain, J.B. (ed.) (1994), *Just War Theory*, New York: New York University Press; Holmes, R.L. (1989), *On War and Morality*, Princeton: Princeton University Press; Ramsey, P. (1968), *The Just War: Force and Political Responsibility*, Lanham, Boulder, New York, Oxford: Rowman and Littlefield Publishers; Regan, R.J. (1996), *Just War: Principles and Cases*, Washington, DC: Catholic University of America Press; Walzer, M. (1977), *Just and Unjust Wars*, New York: Basic Books.

3   Recent work in just war theory points to the need to consider a third category, *jus post bellum*, the justice of the cessation of hostilities and the subsequent transition from war to peace. See Orend, B. (2002), "Justice after War," *Ethics and International Affairs* 16/1, 43–56.

standards of evidence, reasonableness, integrity and relevance. In this way, just war theory serves as the underlying normative foundation for corresponding rules and obligations embodied in international humanitarian law and the laws of war. Just war theory thus constitutes a reasonable guide to foreign policy questions concerning the use of military force, in particular those pertaining to the aims that states are to have in mind when considering the use of force, and the means they may use or must avoid using in the conduct of war.

Jus ad bellum

In this section, I will discuss the six major principles governing the justice of resorting to war. These principles can be stated as follows:

1. Just cause: the war must be fought in a just cause.
2. Right intention: states must have the right reason and proper motivation for going to war, which excludes war for personal or national gain, or for some other hidden purpose.
3. Legitimate authority: the war must be declared publicly and waged exclusively by the competent authority having the right to do so.
4. Last resort: recourse to war must be a last resort.
5. Likelihood of success: those engaging in war must have a reasonable hope of success.
6. Proportionality of the ends of war: the damage and harm that the war ultimately entails must be judged proportionate to the injustice which occasions it.

It should be kept in mind that no single principle by itself offers sufficient justification for the use of military force. Following the general trend in the just war tradition, the criteria here will be taken as individually necessary and jointly sufficient for a war to count as just. For instance, while a just cause is a necessary condition for the resort to war, it is not itself a sufficient condition. A state may go to war justly only when all the remaining *jus ad bellum* conditions are met as well. Thus, simple failure to meet any particular one of the criteria may warrant a judgment that the resort to war is unjust; conversely, satisfying all of the criteria may warrant a judgment that the resort to war is just. Nevertheless, even if sufficient justification exists, the criteria ought to be understood primarily as negative constraints on the decision (or conduct) of war. This proviso means the decision to go to war does not become mandatory simply because all *jus ad bellum* conditions are met; it means only that going to war is permissible. The purpose of the criteria is not to justify war in the sense of fostering or promoting it, but only in the sense of defending morally what would otherwise be prohibited actions.

The first necessary *jus ad bellum* condition that must be satisfied, then, begins with the concept of just cause. Traditionally, this has meant that a state considering going to war must identify an injury received, most notably aggression directed at its territorial integrity and political sovereignty. Injury might also arise when the human rights of innocent citizens are violated in some systematic and severe way, even in another state. Acceptable just causes therefore include self-defense from aggression, reclaiming people and territory wrongly seized or threatened by an aggressor, and defending or rescuing the innocent from gross violations of their human rights. The second, and closely related, criterion that must be satisfied is that of right intention. Most fundamentally, the principle of right intention means that a state must not only have the right cause to resort to armed force, it must also have the proper motivation, which is to achieve the just cause. A state may not use the concept of a just cause to prosecute a war for some secret end(s) incompatible with the cause, such as for purposes of material gain derived from the capture of territory and resources, or to exact revenge based upon religious or ethnic hatred. In addition, right intention demands that a state must, prior to prosecuting war, commit itself to upholding all the other just war criteria.

The dual influence of just cause and right intention has led, since the end of the Second World War, to a general proscription of all first use of force or wars of aggression. Article 2(4) of the United Nations Charter, for instance, states that "All members shall refrain ... from the threat or use of force against the territorial integrity or political independence of any state." Thus under the Charter the threat or use of force is illegal except in circumstances of self-defense and the collective use of force by the organization itself, for the purpose of securing a just cause. Offensive aggression constitutes an illegal, immoral and unjustified use of force, which provides an acceptable rationale for resorting to defensive war against the aggressor. Notably, the proscription of offensive aggression also provides a constraint on the possible abuse of the principle of just cause. In other words, the actual presence or imminent threat of overt aggression is a prerequisite to the just use of armed force; a mere suspicion about the possible occurrence of violence is insufficient justification.[4]

The principle of the proportionality of the ends of war is supposed to ensure that the good or end intended by war outweighs both the evil that induced the war and the evil that will result from the war itself. This principle clearly requires a consequentialist assessment of the foreseeable harm that likely will be caused by resorting to armed force, insofar as states must consider how their actions will affect their own citizens as well as the citizens of other states. If serious doubts exist as to whether the good that is generated by the use of force will be greater than the harm caused, war should be avoided. Requiring a reasonable chance of success supports the principle of proportionality, insofar as the human costs of prosecuting a war should not be disproportional to the political objective being sought. A military campaign that has a high likelihood of failure will simply add additional misery to the harm caused by the initial aggression. The principle of last resort adds additional emphasis to the previous point. It stipulates that war may be undertaken only when all good-faith efforts to resolve the conflict

---

4   This point will be touched upon again in the final section of the chapter.

through diplomacy, arbitration and other means that fall short of armed force have failed. Together, these three criteria aim to limit the suffering and destruction that inevitably accompany war.

The final *jus ad bellum* condition to be mentioned is that only a legitimate, competent authority—typically the political figure or institution in a national Government holding sovereign power—is morally and legally entitled to declare war, and must express its intention to initiate war by means of a public declaration.

Jus in bello

There are two just war principles regulating the way in which war is conducted once it has begun, thereby providing minimum standards for what is morally permissible in fighting. These are:

1. Discrimination: combatants must distinguish between military targets and civilian populations, and non-combatants must be immune from attack.
2. Proportionality of the means of war: all military actions taken in war must be reasonably expected to produce benefits that outweigh the expected harms or costs.

The significance of the *in bello* principles is that they require continual adherence to the norms of just war theory. While a state may be justified in initiating war by satisfying the *ad bellum* criteria, it is quite possible that the same state could violate the norms of *jus in bello* during the course of war. If a state were to conduct war in violation of the *in bello* criteria, its claim to be prosecuting a just war would be discredited.

Consequently, a war must be fought justly in order to be just in a complete sense. During the conduct of war, the principle of discrimination (also known as the principle of noncombatant immunity) demands that no act of war may be intentionally directed at noncombatants. This condition is clearly intended to protect innocents from being targeted militarily either as direct ends or as indirect means to some further ends. The norm of noncombatant immunity was codified in Articles 22–28 of the Fourth Hague Convention of 1907, in the Fourth Geneva Convention of 1949 and in Articles 48–58 of the 1977 First Protocol to the Geneva Conventions.[5] The basis of the principle of discrimination is a moral distinction between combatants, whose activity purposefully contributes to aggression or the imminent threat of aggression, and noncombatants, who do not purposefully or actively contribute to aggression. Failure to draw this distinction implies that all persons, regardless of their guilt or innocence, are legitimate targets and, moreover, that there are no meaningful moral and legal constraints on the conduct of war.

---

5   The texts of these documents can be found in Roberts, A. and Guelff, R. (eds) (1999), *Documents on the Laws of War*, 3rd edn, Oxford: Oxford University Press.

If this were the case, however, there would then be no basis for distinguishing between just and unjust, or legal and illegal wars. The resultant moral vacuum would undermine any claim to justice by both sides in a conflict.

Nevertheless, given the nature of war it would be foolish to deny the possibility of noncombatant casualties. The doctrine of double effect has been developed to address this problem, in light of the requirements of discrimination. What this doctrine recognizes is that there is a relevant distinction between intended and unintended consequences. In particular, certain actions may be performed for the purpose of causing a good end, yet which have bad unintended consequences or "side effects". The side effects may be wholly accidental or they may be foreseen, but as long as they are unintended with regard to the action taken to achieve the good effect, the action itself is permissible. For example, it may happen that a person kills an attacker while engaged in self-defense, even though the intention was not to kill the attacker but simply to fend off the attack and save the person's life. The act of self-defense here thus has two effects, one good and one bad. Extending the argument, it can be said that a military operation which aims at legitimate targets or objectives, but has accidental or foreseeable bad consequences, is permissible provided it meets the following four conditions:[6]

1. The act is good in itself and its intended effect is morally acceptable.
2. The intention of the actor is good, that is, the actor aims narrowly at the acceptable effect, such that the bad effect is unintended, and not pursued as an end or as a means to the end.
3. Actions are taken to minimize any foreseeable bad effects as much as possible.
4. The good effect is achieved and sufficiently outweighs the bad effect.

The doctrine of double effect is defensible, then, only when the principle of discrimination is supplemented with the principle of proportionality. Actors are responsible for reducing or minimizing the unintended effect as much as possible, and there exists a threshold to the acceptable limit of the possible bad effect; the good effect must be proportional to the foreseeable bad effect. If the foreseeable bad effect is disproportionate to the value of the intended action or objective, then the intended action is not justified. For this reason, certain weapons or methods, such as rape, torture, genocide and chemical and biological weapons, are prohibited in all cases and therefore are not subject to legitimization by the doctrine of double effect. Unintended civilian casualties are likely in war, yet combatants have an obligation to minimize the risks and harm they impose on civilians, even if that means that a particular military operation cannot be undertaken. Conversely, while it is impermissible to deliberately target noncombatants, some unintended civilian casualties are excusable.

---

6   These conditions are slightly modified versions of those found in Walzer, op. cit. fn. 2, 153–55.

Responding to Terrorism: Two Options

Terrorism is a notoriously difficult term to define, and one which is open to competing interpretive and normative conceptualizations.[7] It is fraught with ethical, political, legal and military dilemmas. Nevertheless, I think it is possible to offer a workable definition that identifies the core meaning of the term, and it is necessary to do so in order that we might better understand what it is that is being responded to by the War on Terror. For purposes of this chapter, terrorism will be defined as seemingly random and unpredictable acts or threatened acts of violence aiming at political, religious or cultural objectives, which target both direct and indirect victims—including innocent individuals, groups, institutions and governments—causing immediate harm and the inducement of fear.[8] A crucial distinction between terrorism and legal acts of warfare, then, is that perpetrators of terrorist acts intentionally target innocent third parties. This is done as a means to provoke the shock and fear designed to coerce the opposing party into some desired course of action or to focus attention on some particular cause. In this way, terrorism involves the deliberate transgression of international norms governing legitimate forms of violence, including the laws of war as they apply to innocent noncombatants. We should also note that terrorism can be either domestic or international in scope. International terrorism consists of acts that transcend the national boundaries of the perpetrators or that are aimed at foreign nationals within the perpetrators' own country.

At present, the international law on terrorism consists of several disparate treaties concerning, for example, hijacking, kidnapping and hostage-taking, attacks against officials and diplomats, and bombing.[9] While various terrorist acts are regarded as illegal, a comprehensive framework capable of guiding the actions of states confronted with, or supporting and perpetrating, international terrorism

---

7   See the chapter by Mark Evans in this volume.

8   Based on Title 22 of the US Code, Section 2656f (d), the US State Department defines terrorism as "premeditated, politically motivated violence perpetrated against noncombatant targets by subnational groups or clandestine agents, usually intended to influence an audience." International terrorism is defined as "terrorism involving citizens or the territory of more than one country." See the State Department's annual report, *Patterns of Global Terrorism: 2000*, introduction, online at http://www.state.gov/s/ct/rls/pgtrpt/2000/2419.htm.

9   These include the 1963 Tokyo Convention (in-flight aviation safety), 1970 Hague Convention (aircraft hijackings), 1971 Montreal Convention (aviation sabotage), 1979 Hostages Convention, 1979 Convention on the Physical Protection of Nuclear Material (unlawful taking and using of nuclear material), 1988 Protocols to the Montreal Convention (extends the Convention to terrorist attacks on airports, ships, and fixed offshore platforms), 1997 Convention for the Suppression of Terrorist Bombings, and 1999 Convention for the Suppression of the Financing of Terrorism. Text of these and other related documents at the United Nations Treaty Collection, online at http://untreaty.un.org/English/Terrorism.asp.

is only now beginning to emerge.[10] Consequently, the burden of responding to terrorist acts has fallen for the most part on individual states.[11] Given this situation, the efforts of the United States to respond to the acts of international terrorism directed against it from September 11 onwards have assumed two broad forms, namely, antiterrorist and counterterrorist measures and strategies.

Antiterrorism refers to the employment by the Government of administrative, police, judicial, penal, political and security resources, tactics and equipment for the purpose of preventing terrorist attacks. Antiterrorist measures taken by the Government are also intended to apprehend and bring to justice suspected terrorists, and to punish convicted terrorists, thereby providing a deterrent effect. The creation of the new Department of Homeland Security (DHS) is a prominent example of the US Government's antiterrorist measures.[12] In conjunction with Government actions, security measures are also taken by the private sector at airports, train stations, industries and corporations in order to deter and prevent terrorism. Antiterrorist strategies can be characterized as nonviolent, since they operate through domestic and international regulative, legislative, juridical and security agencies rather than military forces.

In contrast, counterterrorism involves the overt and covert use of military force by the Government's regular military units and specialized state agencies, such as the Central Intelligence Agency (CIA). Counterterrorism focuses exclusively on the use of military resources, tactics and equipment for the purpose of targeting terrorists and eliminating their organizations. Counterterrorism can include assassinating suspected terrorists, raiding and bombing the hideouts and headquarters of suspected or known terrorists, abducting suspected or known terrorists and declaring War on Terrorist organizations, terrorist states or states that sponsor terrorist organizations. Thus, the US War on Terror can be properly understood as consisting of counterterrorist measures and strategies designed to combat international terrorism and prevent harm to innocent citizens.

However, because counterterrorism employs military force in pursuit of its objectives, it raises serious ethical, legal and political issues. Some of the covert activities that may be conducted by the Government's special operations and intelligence forces in combating terrorism, such as kidnapping, assassination and torture, are not only immoral but potentially illegal as well.[13] Yet the use of

---

10   The UN General Assembly approved the "Declaration on Measures to Eliminate International Terrorism" (UN Doc. A/RES/49/60) on December 9, 1994, which was the first formal call to implement a comprehensive antiterrorist treaty framework.

11   This does not, of course, preclude multiple states developing collective mechanisms for responding to terrorism.

12   The Department was established officially on November 25, 2002, when President Bush signed the "Homeland Security Act of 2002" into law; online at http://www.whitehouse.gov/homeland/.

13   For example, the US Government has stated that American citizens working abroad for al-Qaeda can be legally targeted and killed by the CIA. The Bush Administration

conventional military force in defense of the United States' territory and citizens may have justified claim to morality and legality. Thus, the counterterrorist measures and strategies of the US War on Terror, as a form of potentially justifiable national self-defense must now be examined.

Applying Just War Principles to the US War on Terror

Counterterrorism, as a critical foreign policy option, advocates the use of military operations against terrorists, states that harbor terrorists and terrorist-sponsoring states. The clearest example of US policy in this respect has been recourse to war in Afghanistan, commencing with Operation Enduring Freedom on October 7, 2001. However, the Bush Administration has made it clear that the War on Terror is open-ended, and may involve US military forces in numerous counterterrorist operations in other countries over an indeterminate period of time. President Bush, in his September 20, 2001 address to a joint session of Congress, articulated the view which has become the basis of US policy for the expansive nature of the War on Terror: "From this day forward, any nation that continues to harbor or support terrorism will be regarded as a hostile regime."[14] His State of the Union Address on January 29, 2002 later reinforced the US position on war as a means to achieve security: "Our War on Terror is well begun, but it is only begun ... I will not wait on events, while dangers gather. I will not stand by, as peril draws closer and closer. The United States of America will not permit the world's most dangerous regimes to threaten us with the world's most destructive weapons."[15] Given the broad and continuing operations of the War on Terror—including continuing operations in Iraq and Afghanistan—it is difficult to offer a comprehensive analysis of its legitimacy as a whole. Thus, the focus of this section will be on the war in Afghanistan, followed by some concluding observations about the characteristics and aims of the War on Terror as it has developed post-Operation Enduring Freedom.

Did the United States have just cause in resorting to war in Afghanistan? I believe the answer is yes. The attacks of September 11 involved the hijacking of civilian aircraft, kidnapping of their passengers, massive destruction of civilian and

---

claims that the authority to kill US citizens is granted under a secret directive signed by Bush after September 11, which orders the CIA to covertly attack al-Qaeda anywhere in the world, making no exception for Americans. See Lumpkin, J.J. (2002), "American al-Qaida Operatives Can Be Targeted for Strikes," *Shreveport Times*, December 4, A5. For an analysis of assassination as an instrument of foreign policy, its proscription, and its possible use as a counterterrorist measure, see Thomas, W. (2001), *The Ethics of Destruction: Arms and Force in International Relations*, Ithaca and London: Cornell University Press, Chapter 3.

14　"Address to a Joint Session of Congress and the American People," online at http://www.whitehouse.gov/news/releases/2001/09/20010920-8.html.

15　"The President's State of the Union Address," online at http://www.whitehouse. gov/news/releases/2002/01/20020129-11.html.

Government property, and the killing of several thousand persons. The al-Qaeda attacks clearly amounted to serious, human rights-violating aggression depriving innocent victims of their life and liberty. The attacks also struck at the territorial integrity and sovereignty of the United States. As we have seen, the principle of just cause can be vindicated in a most fundamental sense when military operations are undertaken for the purpose of national self-defense, as approved under Article 51 of the UN Charter.[16] Moreover, states are obligated to provide for the security of their citizens. Given that the Taliban regime had supported terrorism and harbored Osama bin Laden and large segments of the al-Qaeda network within Afghanistan, it seems reasonable to conclude that the US was justified in invading Afghanistan in order to prevent future acts of violence against its citizens and national integrity.

Did the US have the right intention in invading? The fact that the US has very few national interests in Afghanistan indicates a lack of incentive to intervene for motives other than self-defense and security, and this was the United States' avowed intent. Some critics have contended that the real motivation was to take focus off the possibility that the threat presented by the Taliban and al-Qaeda was merely the result of US policy in Afghanistan during the Cold War,[17] or perhaps to secure American control over strategic oil reserves in central Asia.[18] I doubt these latter claims are true, and in any event they seem much less plausible as manifestations of intent than the professed motivation of preventing future terrorist attacks. Nevertheless, one should acknowledge that purity of intention is probably illusory, and that there may be secondary motivations mixed with the primary, legitimate motivation. We can only require that the main motivation be appropriate in terms of just cause, so as to satisfy the condition of right intention.

The United States publicly declared its resort to force and initiated conflict according to the principle of legitimate authority. On September 12, 2001, President Bush declared the previous day's attacks to be acts of war against the United States. That same day, the North Atlantic Treaty Organization (NATO) invoked Article Five of the Washington Treaty for the first time, which provides that an attack on one member of the Alliance will be regarded as an attack on

---

16   Article 51 states: "Nothing in the present Charter shall impair the inherent right of individual or collective self-defence if an armed attack occurs against a Member of the United Nations, until the Security Council has taken measures necessary to maintain international peace and security. Measures taken by Members in the exercise of this right of self-defense shall be immediately reported to the Security Council and shall not in any way affect the authority and responsibility of the Security Council under the present Charter to take at any time such action as it deems necessary in order to maintain or restore international peace and security."

17   Popham, P. (2001), "Taliban is a 'Monster Hatched by the US'," *Independent*, September 17, A4.

18   Monbiot, G. (2001), "America's Pipe Dream: The War Against Terrorism is also a Struggle for Oil and Regional Control," *Guardian*, September 23.

every other member.[19] The Organization of American States (OAS), too, found the attacks triggered the Rio Treaty's provisions on collective self-defense,[20] as did the Australian Government, which invoked the collective defense clause in Article IV of the ANZUS Treaty.[21] In addition, the UN Security Council quickly enacted several resolutions that require all member states to pursue terrorists, dismantle financial support systems and prevent all forms of terrorism, and also created a Counterterrorism Committee to monitor implementation of the resolutions.[22] On September 14, the US Congress authorized the use of the armed forces against terrorists.[23] On September 12, the Secretary of Defense directed the preparation of "credible military options" to respond to international terrorism, under the guidance of General Tommy Franks. United States Central Command (USCENTCOM) recommended a military course of action that was approved by Secretary of Defense Donald Rumsfeld on October 1. President Bush was briefed on the course of action on October 2, and he directed combat operations to begin on October 7. United States and British military operations against Afghanistan commenced on October 7 using aircraft and cruise missiles, and Special Forces ground troops began operations in Afghanistan on October 19. Both the United States and the United Kingdom notified the UN Security Council in writing that Operation Enduring Freedom was an exercise of individual and collective self-defense in compliance with Article 51 of the UN Charter.[24]

Was the US initiation of war the last resort? Questions arise concerning the satisfaction of this criterion. In particular, there is reasonable doubt as to whether serious attempts were made at a negotiated settlement. In his address to the joint session of Congress on September 20, 2001, President Bush identified al-Qaeda as the suspected perpetrators of the September 11 attacks, and emphasized the mutual interdependence of the Taliban Government and al-Qaeda, with the former

---

19   For an analysis of this event see Lansford, T. (2002), *All for One: Terrorism, NATO and the United States*, Aldershot: Ashgate Publishing.

20   "OAS Resolution on Terrorist Threat to Americas" (September 21, 2001), online at http://www.oas.org/OASpage/crisis/RC.24e.htm.

21   "Application of ANZUS Treaty to Terrorist Attacks on the United States" (September 14, 2001), online at http://www.pm.gov.au/news/media_releases/2001/media_release1241.htm.

22   Resolution 1368 (September 12, 2001), Resolution 1373 (September 28, 2001), and Resolution 1377 (November 12, 2001).

23   US Congress, S.J. Res. 23 ("Joint Resolution to Authorize the Use of United States Armed Forces against those Responsible for the Recent Attacks Launched Against the United States"), online at http://www.whitehouse.gov/news/releases/2002/10/20021002-2.html.

24   Letter dated October 7, 2001 from the Permanent Representative of the United States of America to the United Nations addressed to the President of the Security Council, UN SCOR, 56th Sess., UN Doc. S/2001/946; letter dated October 7, 2001 from the Chargé d'affaires a.i. of the Permanent Mission of the United Kingdom of Great Britain and Northern Ireland to the United Nations addressed to the President of the Security Council, UN Doc. S/2001/947.

providing a safe haven for the latter and the latter helping to solidify the control of the former throughout much of Afghanistan. He also issued the following demands to the Taliban Government:

> Deliver to United States authorities all the leaders of al-Qaida who hide in your land. Release all foreign nationals—including American citizens—you have unjustly imprisoned, and protect foreign journalists, diplomats, and aid workers in your country. Close immediately and permanently every terrorist training camp in Afghanistan and hand over every terrorist, and every person in their support structure, to appropriate authorities. Give the United States full access to terrorist training camps, so we can make sure they are no longer operating. These demands are not open to negotiation or discussion. The Taliban must act and act immediately. They will hand over the terrorists, or they will share in their fate.[25]

Bush clearly indicated, then, that negotiation with the Taliban was not an option. Between September 20 and October 7, the launch date of the military campaign in Afghanistan, the US Government declined to pursue bilateral discussions directly with the Taliban Government, and opted instead to utilize the Government of Pakistan as an intermediary. The Taliban showed signs of a willingness to make compromises, even suggesting that Osama bin Laden could be handed over to a third country for possible trial. Because the Bush Administration clearly had little interest in pursuing a diplomatic solution, it may be reasonable to conclude that the resort to force of war was too hasty. A good faith effort to satisfy the condition of last resort—preferably through multilateral and international diplomatic, economic, legal and other pressures—was not made.

Even so, the presence of some extenuating circumstances may mitigate the severity of this conclusion. Examples of such extenuating circumstances include the fact that the Taliban had close diplomatic relations with only a very few countries, including Pakistan. Thus, it might have made sense to use the Pakistani Government as an intermediary rather than attempt to negotiate directly with the Taliban. In addition, the Taliban had demonstrated over time that they were not susceptible to the concerns of the international community, ignoring earlier pleas for changes to their regime, their treatment of women and their policy of destroying non-Islamic cultural artifacts. Furthermore, a condition of war already existed in Afghanistan, primarily between the Taliban and the Northern Alliance forces. Indeed, the UN Security Council had issued several declarations in the years between 1996 and 2001, addressing the ongoing conflict in Afghanistan and calling upon states to take action against the Taliban—including sanctions prohibiting the sale of arms and ammunition—for its support of terrorism and

---

25   "Address to a Joint Session of Congress and the American People," online at http://www.whitehouse.gov/news/releases/2001/09/20010920-8.html.

bin Laden.[26] All of this may lead to the alternative, plausible conclusion that any attempted negotiations with the Taliban were bound to fail in the end and thus would unduly delay critical defensive military operations.

Next, there are questions regarding the reasonable likelihood of success and proportionality. Applying the criterion of the likelihood of success requires assessment of the stated aims of the war in Afghanistan. In his October 7, 2001 Department of Defense news briefing, Secretary Rumsfeld explained that Operation Enduring Freedom had dual aims of carrying out both counterterrorism and humanitarian relief operations.[27] Several specific objectives of the military operation were stated explicitly: to make clear to Taliban leaders that the harboring of terrorists was unacceptable; to acquire intelligence on al-Qaeda and Taliban resources; to develop relations with groups in Afghanistan opposed to the Taliban; to prevent the use of Afghanistan as a safe haven for terrorists; and to destroy the Taliban military allowing opposition forces to succeed in their struggle. Requiring a reasonable prospect of success before going into a war is obviously an imprecise criterion, and is certainly one open to controversy since it depends upon predicting the likelihood of both success and failure under complex and variable conditions. However, given the overwhelming advantage of the US and coalition military forces over the Taliban and al-Qaeda forces, there would have been little reason to doubt the success of Operation Enduring Freedom in achieving its objectives. The outcome of the war and subsequent events supports the notion that US forces achieved initial success with military operations in Afghanistan.

The principle of proportionality injects evident consequentialist concerns into the analysis of US policy on the war in Afghanistan. Assuming that the war in Afghanistan satisfied the requirements outlined above, in order to be just it must also be the case that the harm and damage it occasioned was proportional to the ends sought. The ends identified by the Bush Administration would seem justifiable insofar as they sought to eliminate al-Qaeda camps and hideouts, apprehend and extradite suspected terrorists and end the Taliban sponsorship of international terrorism. While armed force was employed to achieve these goals, the war's aim was to produce overall good consequences by eliminating the immediate threat of al-Qaeda and Taliban-sponsored terrorism at its source. The proportionality of the ends of war in this case is consistent with the intention to remedy injustice and produce a net gain for the cause of justice.

We must also consider proportionality of the means of war and discrimination, both applicable to the actual conduct of hostilities. In prosecuting Operation Enduring Freedom, US policy incorporated humanitarian and political objectives intended to avoid the infliction of unnecessary suffering and to consolidate a just and

---

26   See, for instance, UN Security Council Resolutions 1193 (August 28, 1998), 1214 (December 8, 1998), 1267 (October 15, 1999), 1333 (December 19, 2000), and 1363 (July 30, 2001).

27   "Statement of the Secretary of Defense," online at http://www.defenselink.mil/news/Oct2001/b10072001_bt491-01.html.

favorable resolution to the conflict that existed in Afghanistan under the oppressive Taliban regime. Humanitarian relief efforts constituted a central component of US policy, in recognition of such factors as the onset of winter, poor infrastructure conditions in Afghanistan and the deterioration of those conditions caused by the escalation of conflict. In his televised address to the nation announcing the start of military strikes in Afghanistan, President Bush stated: "As we strike military targets, we will also drop food, medicine and supplies to the starving and suffering men and women and children of Afghanistan."[28]

Questions were raised about the efficacy of air-dropping humanitarian supplies at the same time as conducting a bombing campaign, as this may have led to foreseeable harm to Afghan civilians and refugees.[29] The ability to deliver humanitarian supplies more effectively and safely increased with the collapse of the Taliban regime in early December 2001 and the subsequent access to secure land routes. In the first six months of the war, US military forces delivered more than 2.5 million humanitarian daily rations, 1,700 tons of wheat and 328,200 blankets.[30] United States humanitarian assistance—totaling $588 million in the period between October 2001 and October 2002—was supplemented by the extensive involvement of United Nations agencies, humanitarian NGOs and international financial contributions to Afghan relief and reconstruction.[31]

Criticisms and concerns also were raised about the ability to satisfy the criterion of discrimination over the course of a widespread bombing campaign.[32] General Richard B. Myers, the Chair of the Joint Chiefs of Staff, addressed this concern in an ABC TV interview on October 21, 2001. Myers stated:

> The last thing we want are any civilian casualties. So we plan every military target with great care. We try to match the weapon to the target and the goal is, one, to destroy the target, and two, is to prevent any what we call "collateral damage" or damage to civilian structures or civilian population.[33]

---

28   "Presidential Address to the Nation," online at http://www.whitehouse.gov/news/releases/2001/10/20011007-8.html.

29   Neuffer, E.A. (2002), "Food Drops Found to do Little Good," *Boston Globe*, March 26, A1.

30   See the numerous transcripts published by the US State Department online at http://usinfo.state.gov/topical/pol/terror/humanit.htm.

31   See the websites online at http://www.whitehouse.gov/news/releases/2002/10/20021011-1.html; http://www.usaid.gov/afghanistan/factsheet.html; http://www.icrc.org/Web/eng/siteeng0.nsf/iwpList78/5AD8FF827923A9C5C1256BC90059EF15; and http://www.unhcr.ch/cgi-bin/texis/vtx/afghan.

32   See de Torrenté, N. (2002), "Challenges to Humanitarian Action," *Ethics and International Affairs* 16/2, 2–8.

33   Richard Myers, interview with *This Week* on ABC TV (October 21, 2001), online at http://www.defenselink.mil/news/Oct2001/briefings.html.

Despite the stated intent to avoid as much as possible the infliction of civilian casualties and damages, such casualties and damages did occur. There were widespread reports of civilian injuries and deaths in Jalalabad, Kandahar, Kabul and elsewhere. It is difficult to ascertain the exact number of civilian casualties caused by the bombing campaign, as well as the ground operations conducted by US, coalition and Northern Alliance forces. The highest reported estimate was nearly 4,000 civilian deaths, although this estimate has been convincingly critiqued.[34] Other reports estimate the number of civilian deaths to be in the range of 1,000–2,500.[35] Obviously, high altitude bombing, despite the use of "smart" bombs, is a far from accurate method of warfare. Still, the incidence of civilian deaths as a result of the bombing campaign must be weighed against the corollary doctrine of double effect. Civilian casualties and damage per se cannot be excused if the US had acted indiscriminately. Yet, the evidence suggests that civilian deaths in Operation Enduring Freedom were, for the most part at least, unintended. This is not to deny the life-destructive nature of the war or the tragedy of civilian deaths. However, given the intensity of war, deaths of innocents are to be expected; this fact points to the necessity of adhering to the stringent observance of the proportionality rule. What is important here is that the civilian casualties were unintended and regrettable, resulting from various errors such as misdirected bombs, and that all reasonable and appropriate measures were taken to minimize damage and casualties. In addition, we can point to US and international efforts to remedy the human and material damage caused by the war through their immediate and ongoing relief and reconstruction efforts.

Extending the War beyond Afghanistan: The New US Security Policy

The preceding discussion should make clear that I endorse the US war in Afghanistan as a morally and legally justifiable resort to force for purposes of self-defense and to combat injustice of al-Qaeda's terrorism. United States policy with respect to the war's justification and objectives was largely informed by and sensitive to the normative constraints of the just war tradition. Perhaps uncertainty surrounds the possibility that the US ran afoul of the condition of last resort. As I discussed above, though, the answer to that question can be reasonably divided. My own judgment is that, owing to the previous unresponsiveness of the Taliban regime

---

34   The high figure was given by Professor Marc H. Herold, online at http://www.cursor.org/stories/civilian_deaths.htm. The critique of Herold's report was made by Professor Jeffrey C. Isaac, online at http://www.indiana.edu/~iupolsci/docs/doc.htm.

35   See Connetta, C., "Operation Enduring Freedom: Why a Higher Rate of Civilian Bombing Casualties," Project on Defense Alternatives, online at http://www.comw.org/pda/0201oef.html; and Traynor, I. (2002), "Afghans are still dying as air strikes go on. But no one is counting," *The Guardian*, online, http://www.guardian.co.uk/world/2002/feb/12/afghanistan.iantraynor.

and the time-sensitive nature of attempting to apprehend al-Qaeda operatives and eliminate their camps, the US at least had an excuse, and probably a justification, for launching the military campaign in Afghanistan when it did.

This assessment, however, in no way alleviates the grave concerns that I have about US policy as it has developed post-Operation Enduring Freedom. My key concern arises from consideration of what has come to be the foundation of US foreign policy in the War on Terror. President Bush provided the first glimpse of the developing US position in a speech at West Point on June 1, 2002. There, Bush cautioned that the United States faced "a threat with no precedent" through the proliferation of weapons of mass destruction and the emergence of international terrorism. Given the nature of this new threat, Bush declared that the traditional strategies of deterrence and containment were no longer adequate and that "if we wait for threats to fully materialize, we will have waited too long."[36] The Office of the President then released, on September 17, 2002, a document titled "The National Security Strategy of the United States", which clearly sets forth the distinctive new statement of current US foreign policy. The document states that the US Government will defend:

... the United States, the American people, and our interests at home and abroad by identifying and destroying the threat before it reaches our borders. While the United States will constantly strive to enlist the support of the international community, we will not hesitate to act alone, if necessary, to exercise our right of self-defense by acting preemptively against such terrorists, to prevent them from doing harm against our people and our country.[37]

It also announces that, with regard to so-called "rogue states and their terrorist clients," the US must be prepared to stop them "before they are able to threaten or use weapons of mass destruction against the United States and our allies and friends." Thus, the US "must deter and defend against the threat before it is unleashed."[38] These words disclose a new policy of support for the presumed right of the United States to wage preemptive war against both terrorists and rogue states engaged in the production of weapons of mass destruction. This policy has come to be called the "Bush Doctrine."

Although the National Security Strategy document portrays the Bush Doctrine as a logical extension of the Cold War strategy of deterrence to the new threats of terrorism, it contains at least three significant and troubling developments. First, the Bush Doctrine states an offensive rather than defensive policy. While the doctrine expresses the US position as grounded in the legitimate right of national self-

36   "Remarks by the President at 2002 Graduation Exercise of the United States Military Academy," online at http://www.whitehouse.gov/news/releases/2002/06/20020601-3.html.

37   "The National Security Strategy of the United States," online at http://www.whitehouse.gov/nsc/nss.html. See Part III, online at http://www.whitehouse.gov/nsc/nss3.html.

38   Ibid., see Part V, online at http://www.whitehouse.gov/nsc/nss5.html.

defense, codified in Article 51 of the UN Charter, it declares rather casually that "our best defense is a good offense."[39] As long as the perceived threat to national security is deemed "sufficient" by the Administration, then a "compelling" case exists "for taking anticipatory action ... even if uncertainty remains as to the time and place of the enemy's attack."[40] Consequently, unilateral and preemptive war is now an officially acknowledged element of US foreign policy. Second, the policy of preemptive war is elevated to the position of a right of the United States, and indeed even a duty that the US is obligated to pursue. If the US were to "remain idle while dangers gather," the doctrine holds, it would fail to satisfy its "unparalleled responsibility" to "make the world not just safer but better."[41]

Third, the far-reaching license to engage in preemptive strikes against perceived threats asserted by the Bush Doctrine is granted almost exclusively to the United States. This is because the doctrine articulates a further aim of US policy, namely, to "build and maintain" US military strength "beyond challenge."[42] In essence, unassailable military strength is the foundation of the Bush Doctrine. The ability to wage unilateral preemptive war—at any time and any place deemed necessary— can be made operational only by maintaining permanent military superiority over every other nation in the world. As the doctrine puts it, "Our forces will be strong enough to dissuade potential adversaries from pursuing a military build-up in hopes of surpassing, or equaling, the power of the United States."[43] Given the fluid dynamics of global politics, the category of "potential adversary" could refer to any country whose military policies are considered by the Bush Administration to be at odds with US national interests.

Finally, the doctrine reinforces the belief in American exceptionalism and has already expressed this by noting that the US "will take the actions necessary to ensure that our efforts to meet our global security commitments and protect Americans are not impaired by the potential for investigations, inquiry or prosecution by the International Criminal Court (ICC), whose jurisdiction does not extend to Americans and which we do not accept."[44] The Bush Administration's position with regard to the ICC is shortsighted in that failure to prosecute grave breaches of the laws of war contributes to the perception of impunity which fuels resentment of the United States abroad and possibly encourages terrorism. It also ignores the principle of complementarity, according to which the ICC's jurisdiction is subordinate to the domestic jurisdiction of the state. In short, the

---

39   Ibid., Part III, online at http://www.whitehouse.gov/nsc/nss3.html.
40   Ibid., Part V, online at http://www.whitehouse.gov/nsc/nss5.html.
41   Ibid., Part V, online at http://www.whitehouse.gov/nsc/nss5.html, and Part I online at http://www.whitehouse.gov/nsc/nss1.html.
42   Ibid., Part IX, online at http://www.whitehouse.gov/nsc/nss9.html.
43   Ibid.
44   Ibid. After coming to power the Bush Administration moved quickly to withdraw US support for the ICC, and formally retracted the US as a signatory to the Rome Treaty on May 6, 2002.

doctrine declares that the US will proceed to consolidate with relative impunity its position as the world's only military superpower, and reserve for itself the right to strike preemptively at any perceived threat with or without UN endorsement and irrespective of international legal prohibitions.

My concerns about the Bush Doctrine are reducible to the probability that it is inconsistent with the norms of just war theory and the codification of those norms in contemporary international law. I do not think the appeal to preemptive war, made possible by unmitigated military expansionism, is a correct and justifiable response to the threat of terrorism, and I think it fails for several reasons. First, the doctrine renders meaningless the notion of defensive and therefore legal war. A state's right to self-defense is not unqualified; in other words, any perceived threat does not itself constitute sufficient reason to resort to armed force. If defense is the basis for the morality and legality of war, there is no justification for intentionally harming those who have not yet harmed, or attempted to harm, one's own state. There is of course some merit to the claim that an actor is justified in employing defensive force in the face of an imminent threat.[45] What constitutes an "imminent threat," however, is not entirely clear. Nevertheless, an imminent threat can be defined as an actual, immediate and identifiable danger to life and security. When such an imminent threat exists, that is, when it is clear that an attack is about to happen, the preemptive use of force is permissible. In such a situation, though, the burden of proof rests with the actor undertaking the preemptive action. A potential, hypothetical, distant or unidentifiable threat cannot count as imminent, and a state cannot properly be said to be defending itself against such generic threats.

Secondly, then, the Bush Doctrine collapses the distinction between preemptive strikes and preventive war.[46] Preventive war is the deliberate decision to resort to armed force simply because the actor perceives that it is to his advantage in maintaining his balance of power over potential adversaries. Here, no imminent threat exists, rather the actor's perception is that "striking first" will maintain a favorable balance of power before inevitable conflict occurs, and thus will also prevent the potential adversary from developing into an imminent threat.[47] Preventive war clearly is offensive rather than defensive and, as such, is illegal under international law. As mentioned above, the Bush Doctrine employs the vague category of "potential adversary" rather than actual adversary and also advocates the strategy that the "best defense is a good offense." Furthermore, the doctrine

---

45   For a useful analysis of the right of self-defense, with regard to individuals and political communities, see Norman, R. (1995), *Ethics, Killing and War*, Cambridge: Cambridge University Press, especially Chapters 4 and 5.

46   On preemptive strikes and preventive war see Baylis, J., Wirtz, J.J., Cohen, E. and Grey, C. (eds) (2002), *Strategy in the Contemporary World: An Introduction to Strategic Studies*, Oxford: Oxford University Press; Levy, J.S. (1987), "Declining Power and the Preventive Motivation for War," *World Politics* 40/1, October, 82–107; and Walzer, op. cit. fn. 2.

47   Ibid., 76.

admits that the US "must adapt the concept of imminent threat to the capabilities and objectives of today's adversaries", in other words, revise the condition of imminent threat to that of "sufficient threat."[48] However, a legitimate act of self-defense is not a preventive attack against a potential adversary. A just actor cannot have the intention to initiate military violence simply because the actor assumes that some harmful event *could* happen when the event is not imminent. Unfortunately the Bush Doctrine seems to embrace this very possibility.[49]

Finally, the Bush Doctrine jeopardizes the criteria of last resort, proportionality and civilian immunity. It will be recalled that the condition of last resort requires that the actor not use military force against an imminent or actual threat if there is some other nonviolent way to avoid the threat. Although the doctrine does make mention of developing cooperative and multilateral agreements, these are spoken of almost entirely within the context of using such agreements to help strengthen America's military and intelligence capabilities. Little, if any, mention is made of developing cooperative mechanisms and institutions aimed at understanding the root causes of terrorism—such as accumulated anti-colonial grievances and anti-American sentiments, along with the failure to resolve the Israeli-Palestinian conflict—and working towards political resolution of these precipitating factors. The Bush Doctrine conveys the impression that the Administration prefers to resort to war as the first rather than last resort.[50]

Moreover, the condition of proportionality requires that the actor use only the minimal (self-defensive) force necessary to terminate aggression or preempt a legitimately imminent attack. To be just, the force used to terminate or thwart an attack, if unavoidable, must be proportional to the actual or threatened violence used by the aggressors. Given the Bush Doctrine's emphasis on the deployment of an overwhelming US military presence across the globe,[51] the possibility is

---

48   "The National Security Strategy of the United States," Part V, online at http://www.whitehouse.gov/nsc/nss5.html.

49   The claimed right to preventive war contained in the Bush Doctrine would, if acted upon, also set a dangerous precedent for numerous states (for example, India, Pakistan, Russia, North Korea, Azerbaijan, and so on) to embark on their own "first strike" campaigns.

50   Nelson Mandela has argued that "the attitude of the United States of America is a threat to world peace … . [America] is saying … that if you are afraid of a veto in the Security Council, you can go outside and take action and violate the sovereignty of other countries. That is the message they are sending to the world. That must be condemned in the strongest terms." Interview published in *Newsweek* (September 10, 2002), online at http://stacks.msnbc.com/news/806174.asp. Former President Jimmy Carter, in his lecture for receiving the 2002 Nobel Peace Prize, stated "For powerful countries to adopt a principle of preventive war may well set an example that can have catastrophic consequences." The Nobel Lecture given by The Nobel Peace Prize Laureate 2002, Jimmy Carter (Oslo, December 10, 2002), online at http://www.nobel.no/eng_lect_2002b.html.

51   "The National Security Strategy of the United States," Part IX, online at http://www.whitehouse.gov/nsc/nss9.html.

raised that any application of armed force against perceived adversaries will not be measured or restrained. The overall cost in lives and property that could result from the use of overwhelming military force in preventive war may exceed the value or gains sought by the War on Terror's ultimate goal—achieving its just cause—and the probability is high that innocent persons would suffer foreseeable harm. All these factors constitute a serious risk to the recognized norms of restraint on when and how states may justifiably use force.

There is no question that in the twenty-first century, terrorism is a major moral, political, legal and military problem of global scope. As the attacks of September 11 clearly demonstrated, terrorism seeks deliberately and violently to harm innocents and damage the security of states and the international community. Consequently, terrorism is both morally wrong and illegal. While the United States was justified in responding to the attacks perpetrated by al-Qaeda and supported by the Taliban, the permissibility and justness of the war in Afghanistan rests upon its having satisfied the interconnected principles of just war theory and international laws of war. However, in pursuing its stated foreign policy goal of eradicating terrorism worldwide, on the basis of the neoconservative aims and strategies outlined in the Bush Doctrine—a peculiar blend of realism and idealism that Condoleezza Rice has termed "American realism"[52]—the United States is now undermining the legitimacy of its War on Terror.

Postscript

Much has happened with both the "War on Terror" in general and the war in Afghanistan in particular since this chapter was originally written. Most notably, of course, the US-led invasion of Iraq in 2003 has become emblematic not only of the tremendous difficulties that states face when attempting to employ conventional military force against transnational terrorist networks such as al-Qaeda, but also of the ease with which just war ideals may be compromised in theory and in practice. The optimism and triumphalism that followed in the immediate aftermath of the invasion—captured by Bush's controversial "Mission Accomplished" speech delivered on board the *USS Abraham Lincoln* on May 1, 2003—have been supplanted by widespread frustration, pessimism, and anger towards the US occupation, the Bush Administration's military and counterterrorism strategies, and the generalized insecurity that pervades daily life in post-invasion Iraq. On November 27, 2008, shortly before this postscript was written, the Iraqi Parliament ratified a bilateral status-of-forces agreement requiring the withdrawal of US combat troops by the end of 2011.[53] The Iraqi Parliament also has approved a

---

52   Rice, C. (2008), "Rethinking the National Interest: American Realism for a New World," *Foreign Affairs* 87/4, 2–27.

53   Samuels, L. (2008), "Iraqi Parliament Passes Status of Forces Pact," *Newsweek*, November 27, online at http://www.newsweek.com/id/171054. The text of the bilateral

plan for non-US troops to leave the country by the end of 2009, and the British Government intends to withdraw all of its troops by June 2009.[54] While this particular chapter of America's War on Terror is therefore being brought to a close, others surely wait to be written, in Iraq and elsewhere.

The war in Iraq can be assessed against just war criteria, in part because these criteria were selectively invoked by the Bush Administration itself. In his radio address of March 22, 2003 announcing the invasion of Iraq, President Bush declared that "[o]ur cause is just ... a fight for the security of our nation and the peace of the world." He insisted that "[o]ur nation entered this conflict reluctantly" and that "coalition forces will make every effort to spare innocent civilians from harm." In comparison, he suggested, "American and coalition forces face enemies who have no regard for the conventions of war or rules of morality."[55] From the start, then, the demands of *jus ad bellum* and *jus in bello* constraints were appealed to in order to provide legitimacy for the decision to initiate the war and for at least the implicit promise to conduct the war in a manner that demonstrated due regard for the conventions of war and "rules of morality." Subsequent events have raised serious doubts about the strength of US commitment to *ad bellum* and *in bello* constraints, and indeed to the justifiability of the war at all.

In the same radio address, Bush asserted that the war "will not be a campaign of half-measures" and that "we will accept no outcome but victory." Reading these claims in light of subsequent events, it seems that the radio address expresses, at the least, a certain dissonance or, more worryingly, a performative contradiction between the Administration's actions and their assertion that they accept the demands of just war criteria. In other words, the US appeared to claim that it would be both bound by and free to transgress *ad bellum* and *in bello* constraints simultaneously. If this is the case, we have good reason to be skeptical about the justifiability of the Bush Administration's position regarding the war in Iraq. The contention that the US entered the war "reluctantly," for instance, is belied by the Bush Administration's persistent attempts, immediately after September 11 until the start of the war, to link Iraq with al-Qaeda and the attacks on America.[56] The US and British Governments paraded what was purported to be evidence demonstrating Iraqi threats to peace—including assertions that Iraq had attempted to purchase uranium ore from Niger, that it possessed chemical and biological weapons, that al-Qaeda operatives had trained in Iraq, and that Iraq possessed missiles and unmanned aircraft capable of carrying out attacks against the US and its allies—all of which has since been discredited as either faulty or fabricated

---

agreement can be read online at http://www.whitehouse.gov/infocus/iraq/SE_SOFA.pdf.

54 "UK Troops to Leave Iraq by July," *BBC News* (December 17, 2008), online at http://news.bbc.co.uk/1/hi/uk_politics/7787103.stm.

55 "President Discusses Beginning of Operation Iraqi Freedom," online at http://www.whitehouse.gov/news/releases/2003/03/20030322.html.

56 "President Bush Outlines Iraqi Threat," online at http://www.whitehouse.gov/news/releases/2002/10/20021007-8.html.

intelligence.[57] When considered in light of the aggressively preemptive (or perhaps preventive) strategy endorsed by the Bush Doctrine, it is difficult to resist the conclusion that the US had little interest in strict tests of imminence and necessity, and even less interest in the criterion of last resort when it came to the decision to invade Iraq.

It is not necessary in this chapter to discuss at length the various other controversies that surround the war in Iraq. From the manipulation of intelligence in the run-up to the war, to the "systematic and illegal abuse of detainees" at the Abu Ghraib prison,[58] to the tens of thousands of non-combatants who have died as a result of the war,[59] the invasion and occupation of Iraq raises critical questions about whether the US failed to satisfy the principles of last resort, right intention, discrimination and proportionality. Similarly, many questions have been raised about the possible failures of coalition forces in Afghanistan. For example, it has been suggested that the aerial bombardment strategy adopted by the US throughout Operation Enduring Freedom was no longer appropriate after the Taliban were removed from power.[60] This is because it can lead to targeting facilities and infrastructure that are vital to the country's infrastructure and to the quality of life of Afghan civilians. Further, given the sheer scale of aerial bombardment in the continuing operations in Afghanistan, and the use of munitions such as "daisy cutters" and "cluster bombs," the intelligence mistakes and human error inherent in such operations have led to a large number of non-combatants killed by US and NATO forces. Afghan President Hamid Karzai has repeatedly expressed frustration at the continued killing of innocent civilians by coalition airstrikes.[61] While official figures of non-combatant deaths since the start of Operation Enduring Freedom

---

57   See Lord Butler (2004), *Review of Intelligence on Weapons of Mass Destruction*, London: The Stationery Office; and US Congress (2004), *The Congressional Commission Report on the Attacks of 9/11*, Washington, DC.

58   The Taguba Report, Article 15–16 Investigation of the 800th Military Police Brigade (March 2004), online at http://www.npr.org/iraq/2004/prison_abuse_report.pdf.

59   President Bush himself estimated, in December 2005, that "30,000, more or less" Iraqi citizens had died as a result of the war. See "President Discusses War on Terror and Upcoming Iraqi Elections," online at http://www.whitehouse.gov/news/releases/2005/12/20051212-4.html. In November 2006 the Iraqi Health Minister estimated that 100,000–150,000 Iraqis had been killed since the invasion. A formal survey conducted by the Iraqi Health Ministry for the World Health Organization concluded that 151,000 Iraqis were killed by violence between March 2003 and June 2006, out of a total of 400,000 "excess deaths" attributed to the war; see Alkhuzai, A.H., Ahmad, I.J., Hweel, M.J. and Ismail, T.W. (2008), "Violence-Related Mortality in Iraq from 2002 to 2006," *New England Journal of Medicine* 358/5, 484–93.

60   Cryer, R. (2002), "The Fine Art of Friendship: *Jus in Bello* in Afghanistan," *Journal of Conflict and Security Law* 7/1, 37–83.

61   "President Karzai Concerned About Civilian Casualties In Operations by Coalition Forces," Office of the Spokesperson to the President, Islamic Republic of Afghanistan, online at http://www.president.gov.af/english/statements_press_releases/May1pressrelease.

are not available, credible reports estimate that at least 6,000–7,000 civilians have been killed by US and NATO-led forces,[62] including nearly 600 civilians in the first eight months of 2008.[63] These figures arguably indicate not merely the effects of military targeting mistakes but rather indifference towards the due care constraints imposed by the principles of discrimination and proportionality. Such constraints are reflected in the 1977 Geneva Convention Protocol I, which obligates states to "at all times distinguish between the civilian population and combatants and between civilian objects and military objectives" (Article 48), and to "take all feasible precautions" (Article 57) to ensure that the "civilian population as such, as well as individual civilians, shall not be the object of attack" (Article 51).

The reality of war is, of course, that innocent lives will be lost and civilian infrastructure will be damaged or destroyed. But the just war theory holds that such injury and death should never be the result of unnecessary actions and merely expedient decisions and policies. The actions, decisions, and policies of the Bush Administration's uncompromising approach to the War on Terror—involving the overwhelming use of force, a rush to judgement about preemptive military action, "extraordinary rendition[s]," secret detention facilities, and torture—raise serious doubts about the Administration's actual commitment to the ethical and legal requirements of the just war tradition and international law, and thus about the legitimacy of the war to this point. Perhaps these doubts will be eased if not erased by the policies and actions of the Barack Obama Administration. It may be the case, however, that the War on Terror has exposed the illusion underlying the just war idea that at least some wars are justifiable "lesser evils."[64] As Hannah Arendt observed more than fifty years ago, "… far from protecting us against the greater ones, the lesser evils have invariably led us into them." The moral and political danger of the lesser evil illusion, she cautions, is that of "becoming blind to the numerous small and not so small evils with which the road to hell is paved."[65]

---

mspx; "Karzai Decries Civilian Deaths," online at http://www.washingtonpost.com/wp-dyn/content/article/2007/06/23/AR2007062300355.html.

62   "Over 1,000 Afghan Civilians Said Killed in 2006," online at http://www.msnbc.msn.com/id/16883222/; "UN Eyes US in Afghan Civilian Deaths," online at http://www.cbsnews.com/stories/2008/08/26/world/main4386496.shtml?source=RSSattr=World_4386496; M.W. Herold, "Dossier on Civilian Victims of United States' Aerial Bombing," online at http://pubpages.unh.edu/~mwherold/.

63   Report of the Secretary-General to the UN Security Council on the Situation in Afghanistan and its Implications for International Peace and Security, September 23, 2008, online at http://www.unama-afg.org/docs/_UN-Docs/_repots-SG/2008/08sep23-SG-report-SC-situation-in-afghanistan.pdf.

64   See Ignatieff, M. (2004), *The Lesser Evil: Political Ethics in an Age of Terror*, Edinburgh: Edinburgh University Press.

65   Arendt, H. (1994), *Essays in Understanding: 1930–1954*, New York: Schocken Books, 271–2.

Chapter 5

Identifying and Confronting the "Axis of Evil": A Critical Retrospective

Robert J. Pauly, Jr.

Introduction

In his State of the Union address in January 2002, then American President George W. Bush characterized Iraq, Iran and North Korea as members of an "axis of evil, arming to threaten the peace of the world" through the development and proliferation of nuclear, biological and chemical weapons of mass destruction (WMD) and the direct and indirect state sponsorship of terrorist organizations. More pointedly, he pledged that the United States would take the requisite action—ideally multilaterally, but also unilaterally if necessary—to reduce, if not eliminate, the dangers those adversaries pose to its interests at home and abroad, emphasizing that "all nations should know [that] America will do what is necessary to ensure our nation's security."[1]

The overarching points Bush raised in promulgating his nascent "axis of evil" approach—and the reiteration of those points over the subsequent weeks and months by the President and senior Administration officials such as Vice President Richard Cheney, Secretary of State Colin Powell, National Security Advisor Condoleezza Rice and Secretary of Defense Donald Rumsfeld—beg two related questions, ones that were as relevant then as they are now, seven years later, as Bush's successor, President Barack H. Obama faces significant, although by no means identical, challenges emanating from the same three states.[2] First, how accurate was it to identify Iraq, Iran and North Korea as the principal focal points

---

1 Bush, G.W., "State of the Union Address," *White House Office of the Press Secretary*, January 29, 2002.

2 For examples, see Cheney, R., "Speech to Veterans of the Korean War," *White House Office of the Press Secretary*, August 29, 2002; Cheney, "Speech to Veterans of Foreign Wars 103rd National Convention," *White House Office of the Press Secretary*, August 26, 2002; "Secretary Rumsfeld Interview with Newt Gingrich," *US Department of Defense*, July 13, 2002; Rice, C., "Remarks on Terrorism and Foreign Policy at Paul H. Nitze School of Advanced International Relations," *White House Office of the Press Secretary*, April 29, 2002; "Colin Powell, Interview on NBC's 'Meet the Press'," *US Department of State*, February 17, 2002; "Colin Powell, Interview on CNN's 'Late Edition'," *US Department of State*, February 17, 2002.

of a collective "axis of evil" and then confront those states over their behavior at the time? Second, what foreign policy implications did that connection carry for the United States and its allies, particularly those situated in Europe, the Middle East and Asia—in January 2002, over Bush's ensuing seven years in office, and for the Obama Administration at present? This essay addresses each of these critical questions generally before providing deeper analyses of the cases of Iraq, Iran and North Korea.

As to the first question, there were both strengths and weaknesses in Bush's identification of Iraq, Iran and North Korea as members of an "axis of evil," then as well as now, the latter of which have grown progressively more pronounced and significant since 2002. Positively, regarding the veracity of the "axis of evil" classification, Iran, Iraq and North Korea exhibited three fundamental similarities at that historical juncture. First, all three were governed by autocratic regimes: an Islamic theocracy with a multi-party but largely powerless parliament in Iran, and one-man military dictatorships administered by Saddam Hussein[3] and Kim Jong Il in Iraq and North Korea, respectively. As Rumsfeld argued then, the "one thing that is common is the viciousness of those regimes, the way they are repressing their people."[4] Since then, little has changed in terms of the fundamental character of the Iranian and North Korean autocracies. However, the United States eliminated Saddam's regime through the prosecution of Operation Iraqi Freedom (OIF) in the spring of 2003, a campaign that left Iraq as a failing state that America and some of its allies (the United Kingdom in particular) continue to attempt to build into a stable, enduring democracy today. The results in that ongoing nation/state-building project have been mixed. Second, militarily, Iran, Iraq and North Korea had long pursued the acquisition and proliferation of WMD and missile systems to deliver those munitions, and each was characterized by the US Department of State at that juncture as a state sponsor of terrorism (Iran and North Korea have since been removed from that list). Third, they possessed the military and political capacity to undermine regional and global stability generally and threaten the national interests of the United States and its allies specifically.[5]

However, both then and now, all three states exhibited many distinctive characteristics, most notably in the economic and cultural/religious contexts. Economically, for instance, Iran was the wealthiest member of the trio by a considerable margin, both then and now, possessing a per capita gross domestic product (GDP) of $6,300 ($13.100 in 2009) as opposed to $2,500 in Iraq ($4,000 in 2009) and $1,000 in North Korea ($1,800 in 2009). Additionally, its military expenditures were then and still are markedly lower as a proportion of GDP than

---

3 Saddam Hussein will be referred to as Saddam in all subsequent references in this essay, as has been the norm in scholarly publications since the 1990–91 Persian Gulf War.

4 "Secretary Rumsfeld Interview with Newt Gingrich," op. cit. fn. 2.

5 "Iran"; and "Korea, North," *CIA World Factbook*, online at www.cia.com, 2002, 2009; US Department of State, "State Sponsors of Terrorism," 2002, 2009; "Know Thine Enemy," *Economist*, January 31, 2002.

is true of the regimes in Baghdad and Pyongyang, both of which continue to pour billions of dollars into their armed forces annually. Furthermore, with respect to religion, Shia Islam is central to the theocratic governance of the Iranian society, whereas Saddam's Baath Party-dominated state was secular in orientation and North Korea is an atheistic dictatorship. The characteristics of the Iranian and North Korean regimes remain the same; Iraq, by contrast, is now a parliamentary democracy, with control of the national government in the hands of the majority Shi'ites rather than the Sunnis, and considerable autonomy for the Kurds in the north of Iraq.[6]

Given their similarities, especially with respect to the threats posed by the volatile combination of autocratic—and thus domestically unaccountable—political systems, and WMD and missile developmental programs, Bush's "axis of evil" characterization appeared prudent in January 2002, but also extraordinarily challenging in terms of its foreign policy implications. For instance, Bush placed emphasis on the long-term nature and global scope of the War on Terror declared by the United States (rhetorically, albeit not formally), while linking that struggle explicitly to the dangers presented by states that have signed, but consistently violated, the provisions of the Nuclear Non-Proliferation Treaty (NPT). Further, he left room for diplomatic engagement with Iraq, Iran and North Korea, but stressed that absent progress on that front, the United States would not hesitate to take military action against any of the three. Finally, by putting Baghdad, Tehran and Pyongyang explicitly on notice, he also implied an openness to take similar measures against other suspected state sponsors of terrorism such as Cuba, Libya, Sudan and Syria—and thus encouraged those actors to alter their behavior voluntarily or suffer whatever consequences Washington deemed appropriate.[7]

Conversely, Bush's warnings also carried three potentially negative implications, all of which have indeed had grave consequences in the years that have elapsed. First, the threat—and subsequent conduct—of a second Iraq War alienated American allies across Europe and the Greater Middle East and has since complicated nation/state-building efforts in Iraq and increased the economic, military and political costs to the United States. Second, the prosecution of Operation Iraqi Freedom created one of the most serious ruptures of the transatlantic relationship in its history. France and Germany in particular opposed the war and continue to favor a more diplomatic approach in attempting to prevent Iran from acquiring nuclear weapons. The same was true in the Far Eastern context, where Japan and South Korea were understandably reluctant to further exacerbate relations with North Korea.[8] Those reservations remain particularly pronounced in the case of Japan. Third, by raising these issues, Bush created the expectation that the United States

---

6   "Iran"; and "Korea, North," op. cit. fn. 5; "Know Thine Enemy," op. cit. fn. 5.

7   Bush, op. cit. fn. 1.

8   Colin Powell, op. cit. fn. 2. In an interview with CNN's Wolf Blitzer, Powell acknowledged that "there is a bit of a stir in Europe [over President Bush's 'axis of evil' approach] but it is a stir I think we will be able to manage with consultations, with contacts

would act forcefully. It did so in the case of Iraq in 2003, but no such action was taken against either Iran or North Korea, undermining the credibility of its rhetorical threats against those two pariahs.

These general observations serve as a useful point of departure for deeper analyses of the implications of Bush's "axis of evil" approach vis-à-vis Iraq, Iran and North Korea in the context of this essay. In order to achieve that objective, incisive sections focusing on Iraq, Iran, and North Korea are presented below. Each section addresses the following four questions. First, why did Bush single out and threaten to confront the members of the "axis of evil" in 2002? Second, what options were prudent for the United States at that historical juncture? Third, what economic, military and political costs and benefits have the measures the Administration did take entailed in the years since then? Following these state-by-state analyses, the essay will conclude with an assessment of the utility of the Bush Administration's "axis of evil" approach and a set of recommendations for the Obama Administration moving forward.

Iraq

Given the circumstances and available intelligence on the situation in Iraq in 2002, there were four interconnected reasons why the United States chose to confront Baghdad then rather than later. First—and most significantly—Iraq had demonstrated in the past both the technical and logistical capacity to acquire, and the political will to utilize, WMD. Saddam's regime spent $10 billion on its nuclear program in the 1980s and was within months of constructing a fission bomb prior to the start of the Persian Gulf War in January 1991.[9] Additionally, United Nations (UN) weapons inspectors uncovered evidence of vast Iraqi chemical and biological weapons programs prior to their expulsion in December 1998—some of the elements of which were deployed against both Iranian soldiers and Iraqi dissidents during the 1980s.[10] Second, there was reason to believe that, if allowed to maintain its pursuit of WMD procurement unhindered, Iraq's potential to threaten the stability of the Persian Gulf region and American access to the oil supplies therein would only increase. As Cheney asserted in making the case for the use of force against Saddam in an August 2002 speech, the "Iraqi regime has in fact been very busy enhancing its [WMD] capabilities … These are not weapons for the purpose of defending Iraq; these are offensive weapons for the purpose of inflicting death on a massive scale, developed so Saddam can hold the threat over

---

of the kind I have almost everyday with my European colleagues. And we will find a way to move forward that will gather the support we need."

9   "Secretary Rumsfeld Interview with Newt Gingrich," op. cit. fn. 2; "Know Thine Enemy," op. cit. fn. 5.

10   "Phoney War," *Economist*, August 3, 2002; Cheney, op. cit. fn. 2.

the head of anyone he choose, in his own region or beyond."[11] Third, a Central Intelligence Agency (CIA) estimate at that juncture suggested that Baghdad had the potential to develop missiles with the range to strike targets in the continental United States by 2015 if not forced to abandon its path then. Fourth, Iraq was on the US Department of State's list of state sponsors of terrorism, which only added to the range of possible threats it was thought to pose to American security interests at home and abroad.[12]

Taking each of these points into account, given what the White House knew at the time, it was critical for the United States to take action to eliminate Iraq's WMD development programs before it acquired the capacity to produce a nuclear weapon. Time was necessarily of the essence, particularly given the level of concern among policymakers and the American public in general in the aftermath of al-Qaeda's attacks against the United States on September 11. However, notwithstanding the convenience of confronting Saddam as part of the ongoing war against terror, the Bush Administration would have been wise to plan and pursue its action against Baghdad more pragmatically than was ultimately the case. The Administration took that action through a three-stage approach. Bush opened the first stage with his verbal warning to Iraq. In addition, the United States demonstrated a willingness to try to cultivate a measure of political support among its allies in the Greater Middle East and Europe—North Atlantic Treaty Organization partners Britain, France, Germany and Turkey, and Persian Gulf power brokers Saudi Arabia and Egypt in particular—for military action against Baghdad, assuming Saddam continued to ignore, if not openly violate, UN sanctions. To that end, Cheney traveled to the Middle East in March 2002 for consultations with regional leaders in order to determine the extent of support Washington was likely to receive and thus the logistical hurdles it would have to clear—bases of operations for air and ground forces, for instance—if forced to act unilaterally.[13]

The second stage of the above approach included diplomatic as well as military measures. Initially, the United States set a deadline for compliance on Iraq's behalf that, if not met, would trigger military action. The time allotted prior to that deadline, in turn, had to be sufficient to allow for the buildup of a substantial American military presence in the region. Those diplomatic and military buildup processes, which unfolded in the fall of 2002 and winter of 2002–03, were designed to force Iraq to allow a resumption of UN weapons inspectors, reveal the extent of its WMD capabilities and eliminate those capabilities. These demands were mandated by UN Security Council Resolution 4112, which was passed, by a vote of 15–0, in November 2002. Iraq denied the WMD allegations and issued a 12,000-page report to that effect, which was rejected by Washington and London in particular. The United States and its allies subsequently launched

---

11   Cheney, op. cit. fn. 2.

12   "Phoney War," op. cit. fn. 10; "Know Thine Enemy," op. cit. fn. 5.

13   "America and the Arabs," *Economist*, March 23, 2002; "Unwilling Allies Against Saddam," *Economist*, March 16, 2002.

OIF in March 2003, which resulted in the elimination of Saddam's regime within a month's time.[14] The United States had since led nation/state-building efforts in Iraq, which have produced mixed results in the economic, judicial, political and security issue areas, which will be examined in the assessment of the costs and benefits of American intervention in Iraq that follows.

It was evident in 2002–03 that any action the Bush Administration took against Iraq would have both costs and benefits. The most significant of those costs were twofold. First, American threats—let alone military action—designed to remove Saddam from power caused a serious break in Washington's relations with many of its allies in Europe and the Middle East. Many Arab and European states—most notably Egypt, Saudi Arabia, France and Germany—discouraged US strikes on Baghdad, which Egyptian President Hosni Mubarak warned would trigger "chaos ... in the region."[15] And, although US plans for Iraq drew steadfast support from the United Kingdom, the French and Germans refused to endorse Bush's call to arms.[16] That rupture in the transatlantic relationship has still not been fully repaired.

Second, the concern at the time was that an operation of the scope necessary to topple Saddam's regime was likely to result in substantial US military casualties that dwarf those sustained in toppling the Taliban in Afghanistan. Powell, who served as Chairman of the Joint Chiefs of Staff during the 1990–91 Persian Gulf War, has assumed a cautionary stance relative to Administration hawks such as Cheney and Rumsfeld regarding the potential military costs of a large-scale war against Iraq. In a February 2002 interview, for example, he noted that there "... are lots of options, [but] I don't want to single out specific ones such as a full-scale Desert Storm type attack ... I think I will let the United States military leadership determine what kind of an operation it would be and let them, rather than journalists and pundits determine what will be a cakewalk or not a cakewalk."[17] Ultimately, the casualties during the conduct of OIF were minimal. However, the violence complicating nation/state-building operations in Iraq in the years since has resulted in the deaths of more than 4,200 US servicemen and women and serious injuries to more than 32,000 more. It has also led to the deaths of tens of thousands of Iraqi civilians.[18]

---

14   Pauly, R.J., Jr. (2005) *US Foreign Policy and the Persian Gulf: Safeguarding American Interests through Selective Multilateralism*, Aldershot: Ashgate Publishing, 98–101; Lansford, T. and Pauly, R.J., Jr. (2004), *Strategic Preemption: US Foreign Policy and the Second Iraq War*, Aldershot: Ashgate Publishing, 71–78.

15   Quoted in "Putting your Cards on the Table," *Economist*, August 29, 2002.

16   Pauly, op. cit. fn. 14, 98–101; Lansford and Pauly, op. cit. fn. 14, 71–78.

17   Powell, C., op. cit. fn. 2.

18   O'Hanlon, M. and Campbell, J.H. (eds) (2009), "Iraq Index: Tracking Reconstruction and Security in Post-Saddam Iraq," *Brookings Institution* (April), online at http://www.brookings.edu/saban/~/media/Files/Centers/Saban/Iraq%20Index/index.pdf.

The probable benefits when the United States intervened in Iraq in March 2003 appeared to be threefold. First, by harnessing (through diplomacy) if not eliminating (via military force) Iraq's WMD programs, Washington could reduce the threats Baghdad posed to regional stability and ensure maintenance of the indispensable access to Persian Gulf oil that the United States and its European and Asian allies then enjoyed. Regrettably, the United States did not uncover any significant evidence of the WMD it thought Iraq possessed.[19] In addition, the lack of security in Iraq between 2003 and early 2007 proved more destabilizing than stabilizing—both within Iraq and in the broader Persian Gulf region. Second, the Bush Administration felt that the liquidation of Saddam's regime—provided it was followed by the development of an enduring democratic government—would ameliorate the living conditions of ordinary Iraqis substantially and perhaps improve the standing of the United States in the eyes of other repressed lower-class Muslims across the region. While Iraq does have a democratically elected government, the costs to America have been substantial. In addition to the loss of life denoted previously, the United States has spent more than $610 billion in Iraq to date[20] and the standard of living for Iraqis is not substantially better than was the case under Saddam. Third, if achieved, it was felt that those outcomes would bolster US credibility and render any opposition expressed by its transatlantic allies (or, for that matter, the Russians or Chinese) insignificant over the long term. That has not been the case. The economic and physical expenses of the war in particular have led to a downward spiral in the standing of the United States among the general populations of states around the world, allies as well as adversaries. Put simply, at present, the costs have exceeded the benefits. Whether or not that assessment changes moving forward will depend on the evolving situation in Iraq.

Iran

There were four compelling reasons why the Bush Administration chose to confront Iran in 2002. All four reasons are still relevant, at least to an extent, today, and are likely to remain so in the future. First, Tehran was (and remains) in the process of acquiring and refining WMD and the means to use them to strike targets within and beyond the Greater Middle East. Notwithstanding its status as a signatory to the NPT, Iran is currently developing a series of nominal civilian reactors (with Russian help) that could provide the fissile materials necessary to construct atomic weaponry. In addition, Washington suspects Iran has broken its

---

19   Duelfer, C. (2004), "DCI Special Envoy Report on Iraq's WMD," *Central Intelligence Agency* (October), online at https://www.cia.gov/library/reports/general-reports-1/iraq_wmd_2004/index.html.

20   "The War in Iraq Costs ..." *National Priorities Project* (April 2009), online at http://costofwar.com/.

obligations under the provisions of the Chemical Weapons Convention (CWC) and Biological Weapons Convention (BWC) and may have the capacity (again thanks to Moscow's collusion) to deliver missiles armed with WMD to the continental United States by 2015.[21] Second, while Iran has never been linked to the events of 9/11, it remains on the Department of State's list of sponsors of terrorism and is under suspicion for complicity in the June 1996 bombing of the Khobar Towers US military housing complex in Saudi Arabia.[22] Third, and relatedly, Tehran continues to undermine what little is left of the fleeting Israeli–Palestinian peace process by providing economic, military and political support to terrorist organizations such as Hamas, Hezbollah and Islamic Jihad.[23] Fourth—and most significantly—in each of these ways, Iran presents a clear and present danger to American interests. As Rice concluded in 2002, "Iranian behavior puts it squarely in the 'axis of evil'—whether it is weapons of mass destruction or terrorism or any of those things. It's a complicated situation, but I think the behavior speaks for itself."[24]

In light of these observations, it was prudent for the United States to confront Iran sooner rather than later. The war against terrorism served as a useful vehicle to employ in challenging an autocratic Iranian regime that (fortuitously for Washington's purposes) was struggling to repress the democratic ambitions of political reformers who gained a parliamentary majority—albeit in a largely powerless body (the *Majlis*)—in February 2000.[25] Rumsfeld, for example, argued in 2002 that the "thought that [reform-minded members of the *Majlis*] should be under the thumb of the extremists that govern [Iran,] is just a crime, it's a shame for those people … I'm not going to be naïve and hold my breath, but I think that is not beyond the possibility that the Iranian people could throw off that regime."[26] Regrettably, a profoundly anti-American Iranian President, Mahmoud Ahmadinejad, was elected in June 2005; the reformists have struggled to increase their power since then and the prospects for political change in the June 2009 Iranian national elections are unclear as this chapter goes to press. Ultimately, in order to help foster that type of governmental change from within, the Bush Administration was right to act pragmatically rather than rashly through political and economic means during its time in office and a comparable approach, albeit

---

21   Blair, D.C. (2009), "Annual Threat Assessment of the Intelligence Community for the Senate Select Committee on Intelligence," *Office of the Director of National Intelligence* (February 12), online at http://www.dni.gov/testimonies/20090212_testimony.pdf; "Blowing your Chances"; "Know Thine Enemy," op. cit. fn. 5.

22   US Department of State, op. cit. fn. 5; "Background Note: Iran," *US Department of State*, December 2001.

23   Blair, op. cit. fn. 21; "The Spectre of being Next in Line," *Economist*, April 11, 2002.

24   Rice, op. cit. fn. 2.

25   "Background Note: Iran," op. cit. fn. 22.

26   "Secretary Rumsfeld Interview with Newt Gingrich," op. cit. fn. 2.

one with greater potential for US–Iranian political engagement, would be prudent for the Obama Administration as well.

Politically, Bush's warning was designed to put the Iranians and American allies in and beyond the Middle East alike on notice as to the seriousness of his concerns over Tehran's development of WMD and sponsorship of regional and transnational terrorist organizations. Under Bush, the United States also focused on the reduction of transatlantic differences vis-à-vis relations with Iran. One useful way Washington could proceed on this front moving forward, for example, would be by linking a de-emphasis of the 1996 Iran–Libya Sanctions Act with concrete improvements in the mullahs' treatment of advocates for domestic political reform as judged directly by Western European diplomats in Tehran. Those diplomats, in turn, would act as intermediaries to enable Washington to better express its support—rhetorical as well as financial—for parliamentary representatives struggling to increase their influence relative to that of the all-powerful clerical Iranian executive branch.

Economically, sanctions emanating from Washington must continue to reflect Iranian behavior (both positively and negatively), particularly with respect to WMD threats and the confrontation of transnational terrorist organizations such as al-Qaeda and its myriad affiliates. Instead of concentrating exclusively on punitive measures, the United States should also impress upon Tehran the fact that American investment is possible if the mullahs alter their present train of thought regarding the development of WMD and sponsorship of terrorist groups. One way the mullahs could demonstrate that kind of a shift would be by allowing the reformers more influence in domestic and foreign affairs. This type of change—albeit unlikely to occur in the short term—could help to clear the path for cooperative ventures (the piping of Caspian Sea oil and gas reserves through Iran to the West, for instance) over the long term.

Militarily, the United States should remain circumspect regarding the use of force against Tehran, particularly given the extent to which American forces are already stretched in nation/state-building operations in Afghanistan and Iraq. The potential for democratic change from within is greater in Iran—as evidenced by the reformers' aforementioned electoral gains—than is the case for North Korea. In addition, Iran's considerably larger relative geographic size and population would be sure to present more daunting logistical challenges for US forces in the case that they are eventually deployed there. Thus, it is clear that, as was true for the Bush Administration as soon as it had invaded Iran, the Obama Administration should not consider military action any more robust than launching air strikes against WMD developmental threats, if clearly identified, and conducting special operations to liquidate terrorist groups supported by the mullahs.

As is true of the Iraqi case, each of these recommended courses of action had for the Bush Administration (and also for the Obama Administration) potential costs and benefits, of which the latter exceed the former markedly. The costs are threefold. First, strident US rhetoric, as put forward at times by Bush and his foreign policy team, always had the potential to strengthen the mullahs' resolve, rendering any easing of economic sanctions less probable and thus reducing the potential for US firms to profit from future investment in Iran. Second, European emphasis on a strictly diplomatic approach to address concerns over Tehran's WMD transgressions and sponsorship of those terrorist groups that claim their fight is a just one for Palestinian sovereignty as opposed to an illegitimate and indiscriminate war against the West at large will only further complicate a transatlantic relationship still recovering from the rift over US-led intervention in Iraq. Third, if the United States, or, more likely, Israel, eventually resort to military action, an attack on Iran would be substantially more challenging than OIF, or, for that matter, the 1991 Persian Gulf War.

By contrast, there were for Bush—and remain for Obama—three potential benefits to the above policy prescriptions. First, intransigence by the mullahs may eventually mitigate their own influence, especially among members of Iran's growing middle class—and perhaps to a greater extent if bolstered by overt and covert American and Western European political and economic assistance. Second, and more significantly in terms of national security, any reductions in Iran's capacity to develop and deliver WMD over increasingly greater distances and its willingness to support terrorism—no matter how small—will reduce threats to the United States itself and its forces stationed abroad, regardless of the means through which any such reductions are achieved. Third, any progress Washington achieves in moderating Tehran's behavior is likely to increase US credibility— among allies, adversaries and neutral observers alike—to back its rhetoric with concrete and effective action.

North Korea

The Bush Administration's choice to confront Pyongyang in 2002 was both just and sensible for the following four reasons, all of which are just as valid in 2009. First, North Korea has demonstrated the technical capability and political will to develop WMD, and also to acquire and profit from the sale of missiles capable of delivering those munitions over progressively longer distances. Most notably, Pyongyang was caught producing more plutonium than allowed under the auspices of the NPT, prompting the negotiation of a 1994 Framework Agreement with the United States, South Korea and Japan to install less proliferation-friendly reactors in North Korea, the implementation of which has since stalled. Additionally, Kim's regime has not signed the CWC and is suspected of possessing stockpiles of sarin and VX gases and experimenting with anthrax, plague, cholera and smallpox despite signing the BWC in 1987. And, perhaps most significantly, North Korea has assisted pariah states such as Iran and Syria with their WMD and missile development programs. Despite US engagement with Pyongyang through the multilateral Six Party Talks, which included America and Pyongyang as well as China, Japan, Russia and South Korea, in an attempt to convince the Kim regime to abandon its nuclear weapons development program, the regime tested an atomic weapon in October 2006 and has yet to agree to shut down its reactors in a verifiable fashion.[27]

Second, despite his own deteriorating health, Kim still runs a de facto one-man dictatorship that has watched hundreds of thousands of his state's citizens struggle to feed themselves, while he spends nearly one-quarter of its GDP maintaining a one-million-man army—one necessarily countered by the stationing of a robust American military presence along the border of the demilitarized zone (DMZ) established as a result of the 1950–53 Korean War.[28] Third, Kim's intransigence and his actions—including a 2009 missile test designed to intimidate Japan—present threats to Far Eastern regional stability generally and the security of American allies in particular.[29] And fourth, North Korea is on the Department of State's list of sponsors of terrorism, which—conveniently for Washington's purposes, albeit justly in light of the proliferation dangers its WMD programs present—leaves it as an adversary in the context of the War on Terror.[30]

Given these points, it is essential that the United States impress upon Kim Jong Il that it will not stand idly by while North Korea threatens American interests. However, Washington should take care to do so pragmatically through political, economic and—as a last resort—limited military means. Politically, two interconnected measures are necessary to achieve this end. The first was Bush's initial rhetorical warning, bolstered by subsequent diplomatic efforts, which intentionally served notice to American allies and adversaries within and beyond the Far East that Washington would not tolerate unmitigated North Korean development and proliferation of WMD and missile systems. Second, the Obama Administration must follow up on the Bush Administration's efforts in the context of the Six Party Talks by continually striving to convince the Japanese and South Korean governments (and, to the extent possible, the Chinese and Russians) of the indispensability of the cultivation and maintenance of a united front in relations with Pyongyang.

Economically, the United States must stress to both Pyongyang and Seoul that requests by North Korea for financial inducements will not be answered positively without the prior creation of credible behavioral verification mechanisms. The Bush Administration should also consider conditioning trade relations with the Chinese on the extent to which Beijing nudges North Korea toward compliance with American demands. Militarily, the Administration must act circumspectly, perhaps bolstering its presence on the DMZ, but ruling out the use of force against Pyongyang unless Washington acquires unequivocal evidence that Kim's regime is close to acquiring missiles with the capacity to deliver WMD to targets in Hawaii, Alaska or the continental United States.

---

27 Blair, op. cit. fn. 21.
28 Ibid.
29 Ibid.
30 US Department of State, op. cit. fn. 5.

There are potential costs and benefits associated with each of these courses of action. The costs are twofold. First, maintaining a robust—albeit essential—deployment of forces on the DMZ while concurrently prosecuting the war against terrorism may strain the American military, especially if the latter undertaking includes large-scale operations against Iraq. Second, pressuring North Korea could undermine Washington's alliance with South Korea and further exacerbate already tenuous Sino-American relations. On the other hand, these suggested courses of action are also likely to generate four significant benefits. First, if pursued unequivocally, the prescribed political and economic measures may very well induce Kim Jong Il to negotiate before the use of force becomes unavoidable. Second, singling out North Korea provides balance in the context of the War on Terror, demonstrating that America's focus on the elimination of WMD threats to American security is truly global and not directed universally toward any distinctive ethnic, national or religious group. Third, Washington's willingness to act decisively to mitigate if not eliminate these threats is, in turn, sure to bolster its international credibility. Fourth, the development and implementation of initiatives to identify and confront pariah states generally and North Korea in particular will sharpen the strategic clarity of US foreign policy while enhancing the security of American citizens at home and abroad.

Conclusions

In order to determine the extent to which Bush's initiative was helpful or detrimental to the conduct of the war against terrorism over both the short and long terms, an incisive assessment is instructive, one best handled contextually in terms of economic, military and political concerns. That assessment pertains to the past, but will also prove helpful to the Obama Administration in drawing insights on how best to proceed moving forward. Economically, the United States is—and will almost certainly remain—dependent on Middle Eastern oil, the flow of which could be staunched by leaving regimes left unchecked to develop WMD and the means to deliver them at a regional if not intercontinental range. Iraq no longer presents such a threat (if it ever did given the lack of the discovery of WMD there); Iran most certainly does. On the basis of the results of the Second Iraq War, engaging in a military conflict against either Iran or North Korea singly and on a small scale—let alone collectively and concurrently—will entail unacceptable costs. Politically, in order to justify the physical consequences and ensure that American credibility remains intact among allies as well as adversaries, the United States should emphasize a multilateral approach to any action it does take. Further, the United States must demonstrate a long-term commitment to cultivate friendly, democratic governments in those formerly despotic states it defeats, one manifested in the deployment of peacekeeping troops and provision of economic assistance commensurate to its GDP relative to that of its regional allies.

In theory and in terms of its rhetoric, the Bush Administration's unambiguous challenge to pariah states and transnational terrorist groups was packaged in an interest-based blueprint comparable to President Ronald Reagan's masterful rollback of the Soviet empire in the final act of the Cold War. However, in practice, it proved considerably more costly and challenging than the Administration anticipated. Because it was not carried out prudentially—with diplomacy as the first option, followed by military action only if absolutely necessary and adequate planning for the nation/state-building efforts that followed—President Bush's initiative did not reduce markedly the threats posed by terrorists groups and their state sponsors. Ultimately, to date, the potential benefits of the Bush "axis of evil" approach have outweighed the costs. However, that is not to suggest that de-emphasizing, or ignoring altogether, the present threats to American interests posed by either Iran or North Korea is an acceptable course of action for the Obama Administration.

PART 2
Domestic Implications

Chapter 6

Presidential Priorities and Budgetary Realities: How Critical is the President as an Individual in Shaping the National Budget?

Michael G. Dziubinski and Steve A. Yetiv

Introduction

Major crises that pose a national security threat tend to focus attention on the role of the President of the United States. This was certainly true of the terrorist attacks of September 11 which focused attention on the leadership potential of President George W. Bush. Some of his detractors had questioned whether he had the acumen to lead the United States, but the President scored high marks among the public for how he handled the crisis—marks that would contrast sharply with his public approval ratings later in his Presidency.

While some observers praised Bush's individual role in shepherding the United States through a difficult period and stressed his individual role in shaping budgetary priorities thereafter, we could ask a deeper question about his performance. Under a contrarian view, we could say that budgetary priorities and funding, especially in the defense arena, were shaped not so much by Bush the individual, or by his key advisors, but by a plethora of other factors, including government politics,[1] organizational culture,[2] the military–industrial complex, external threats, and domestic politics and pressures.[3] Consideration of such factors places the role of the individual in contradistinction to that of the state, its government and internal

---

1   The government politics model stresses bureaucratic politics as predominant over the influence of particular individuals. See Yetiv, S.A. (2001/2002), "Developing a Theory of Government Politics: The Case of the Persian Gulf Crisis," *Security Studies* 11 (Winter).

2   The organizational process model stresses the role, culture, and routine of organizations and their resistance to change, and subordinates individuals to the machinery of organizations. See Allison, G. and Zelikow, P. (1999), *Essence of Decision*, 2nd edn, New York: Longman.

3   On the importance of domestic politics and the discussion of this literature, see Rearden Farnham, B. (1997), *Roosevelt And The Munich Crisis: A Study Of Political Decision-Making*, Princeton: Princeton University Press, especially Chapter 2. Also see Tetlock, P.E. (1985), "Accountability: The Neglected Social Content of Judgment and Choice," *Research in Organizational Behavior* 7, 295–332.

processes, and that of the system of inter-nation relations and global processes—a classic set of competing variables.[4]

In the present study, exploration of these classic variables takes the form of a core question: how important is the President in general as an actor?[5] In particular, how important is the President in shaping the budget? In the past two decades, scholars of the Presidency have argued predominantly that Presidents have limited power. Different arguments have been put forth for this conclusion, including the effects of the increasing complexity of world affairs, fragmented and loosely defined political parties that create democratic gridlock, fragmented government, checks and balances writ large, an uncooperative bureaucracy, a challenging media, poor public relations skills, and poor information and advice.[6] At the same time, the popular imagination is fired by the notion that Presidents matter, that they are quite powerful.[7] Indeed, it is not uncommon to hear political pundits say that the President of the United States is the most powerful individual in the world, quite capable of bringing about desired outcomes. Understanding the role of the President against a range of constraints is vital for explaining, understanding, and even predicting outcomes involving Presidential behavior and it also can lend some insight into the broader question of the role of individuals in political contexts.[8]

In this chapter, we seek to explore the question of how critical George W. Bush was, first as candidate and then as President, in shaping the national budget and subsequent funding. The analysis not only examines the early period of the Bush Administration but also draws on new budget data which allow for an exploration

---

4   In modern times, this analysis was elevated in importance in Waltz, K. (1957), *Man, the State, and War*, New York: W.W. Norton. Also see Harold and Margaret Sprout (1956), *Man-Milieu Relationship Hypotheses in the Context of International Politics*, Princeton: Princeton University Press.

5   On the importance of the President relative to other actors and factors in shaping foreign policy, see Yetiv, S.A. (2004), *Explaining Foreign Policy: The United States and the Persian Gulf War*, Baltimore: Johns Hopkins University Press.

6   On this broad literature, see Whicker, M.L. (1993), "The Case AGAINST the War," in Whicker, M.L., Pfiffner, J.P. and Moore, R.A. (eds), *The Presidency and the Persian Gulf War*, Westport, CT: Praeger, 114–116.

7   And scholars no less prominent than Richard Neustadt, as well as more recent thinkers, argued several decades ago that Presidents can be very powerful, especially if they know how to persuade. For references, see Smith, C.A. and Smith, K.B. (1994), *The White House Speaks: Presidential Leadership as Persuasion*, Westport, CT: Praeger, especially 16.

8   On how individuals can shape foreign policy decisions, see Hermann, M.G. (ed.) (1977), *A Psychological Examination of Political Leaders*, New York: The Free Press; and Falkowski, L.S. (ed.) (1979), *Psychological Models in International Politics*, Boulder: Westview Press. For a good synopsis of case studies of individual leaders, see Winter, D.C. (1992), "Personality and Foreign Policy: Historical Overview of Research," in Singer, E. and Hudson, V. (eds), *Political Psychology and Foreign Policy*, Boulder: Westview Press, especially 85–86.

of nearly his full Presidency. In the following sections, we first discuss how we intend to study this subject, and then execute the work in the body of the study. From this analysis, we also draw some insights about the extent to which President Barack Obama will be able to generate the change that is reflected in his stated goals.

The Approach of this Study

Merely examining budget dollars, and attributing increases or decreases in dollars to either an individual leader or other factors is unlikely to be informative. Rather, it is more useful to examine and compare the language used by President Bush with the budget proposals that followed. This "language versus dollars" approach can indicate whether language is matched by a plan to allocate resources in the manner specified. This would tend to support the idea of individual leadership as a potent force in shaping the budget. Alternatively, it can indicate situations where language was not matched with budget proposals. This would tend to support the idea that conditions outside an individual leader's control were stronger determinants of state behavior.

In the case of George W. Bush, it is useful to examine two language/budget figure pairs. The first is Bush's pre-election language regarding the budget, and then the national defense portion of his first federal budget proposal. The second is his language which accompanied his first federal budget proposal, and then the resource allocation in the second proposal. In this fashion, the research will be able to uncover if publicly announced policies survive and reflect substantive environment changes. The first would be a change from candidate to elected official; the second, a change from peace- to war-time President. If previously enunciated policies can survive these changes, and if the changes themselves do not cause significant alterations in the individual's preference, then this would tend to support the position that individual leadership can be a substantive force.

Candidate Bush

The first case involves George W. Bush as a candidate for President. Candidate Bush put forth a well-crafted and forceful message on defense issues in his campaign against the incumbent Vice President Al Gore. His message, articulated in multiple fora, provided both rational arguments on how to manage defense, and in some areas, dollar figures needed to accomplish the stated goals.[9] This

---

9   "Gov. George W. Bush on the Economy and Taxes," in C-Span.ORG Public Affairs on the Web, online at http://cspanrm.fplive.net:554/ramgen/cspan/ldrive/ c2k090600_5.rm, September 6, 2000; Bush, G.W. (1999), "Issues – Defense," in *United States Special*

specificity will allow some direct comparison of the period before and after the campaign. We will also offer comparison through qualitative discussion.

Candidate Bush's message on defense provided a vision of the purpose and importance of the military, and three broad ways to achieve that purpose. His vision was "that a strong, capable and modern military is essential to defend our nation, advance US interests, and extend our peace."[10] But his vision also encompassed a perception at the time regarding the condition of the Department of Defense. He characterized US defense capabilities to be in a debilitated condition, because of over-commitment and decreases in funding. He stated that the US military undertook an average of one new deployment every nine weeks, during the Clinton-Gore Administration. Further, he stated that US defense spending had declined by nearly 40 percent in the same period.[11] He characterized US Forces as overused and under-funded precisely at a time when they were confronted with a host of new threats and challenges, resulting in a military force unprepared to deal with the threats of a new century. To overcome this condition and meet his vision of the US military, Candidate Bush outlined three goals.

Renewal

The first goal was to "Renew the bond of trust between the President and the Military."[12] Within the discussion of this goal, he highlighted a range of personnel issues. The first along these issues was low pay, indicating that military pay is an average of 13 percent lower than comparable civilian pay. He also highlighted military housing, claiming that over 200,000 military families reside in substandard quarters. Further, he introduced military personnel shortages in terms of the missed reenlistment goals, an Air Force pilot shortfall of 2,000 and Navy personnel shortfalls of 18,000 sailors, among other examples.[13]

As a part of addressing these problems, Candidate Bush identified some fairly specific, but potentially costly steps. To help narrow the overall difference in compensation between the armed forces and the civilian sector, he stated that he would increase a planned military pay raise by $1 billion. Without specifying amounts, he also indicated that he would increase targeted reenlistment bonuses and special pay for critical specialties to reduce the pay gap for individuals with skills that are in high demand, such as pilots, computer programmers, and engineers. Again, without specifying amounts, he indicated he would improve military housing by renovation or construction of barracks or family housing units, or in other cases, increase basic housing allowances, especially in high cost areas.

Weapons Nuclear, Biological, Chemical and Missile Proliferation News, online at http://www.fas.org/news/usa/1999/09/990923-bush-dod.htm.

10   Ibid., 1.
11   Ibid., 2.
12   Ibid., 3.
13   Ibid., 3.

Finally, in the area of improving military training: he promised to correct funding shortfalls in training center facilities, equipment and operations to reverse the decline in the quality and level of training for our men and women in uniform.[14]

Returning to the central question of this study, if individual leadership is a significant factor, we should expect a minimum increase of $1 billion in personnel funds over what was already programmed. We would also expect additional funds to address the 200,000 substandard housing units, some of which could be in construction, some in additional housing allowances, and additional funding for training centers and programs.

Protect

The second goal was to "protect America itself from attack."[15] Bush highlighted that over two dozen countries have ballistic missiles, a number of which—including North Korea, Iran, and at the time, Iraq—may ultimately reach intercontinental range. He also noted that arms control agreements needed to be addressed. Further, he contended that the US is vulnerable to a state or a terrorist group using nuclear, chemical, and biological weapons that have proliferated around the world.

To protect the nation, Candidate Bush stated that he would deter terrorist attacks against the US by ensuring that every group or nation understands that if it sponsors such attacks, America's response will be devastating. In order to directly counter the missile threat he would accelerate research on, and deployment of, both national and theater missile defenses, as soon as possible. Further, he would either amend the 1972 Anti-Ballistic Missile Treaty to permit deployment of effective national and theater missile defenses, or withdraw from it. To get the most accurate threat information, he stated that he would make it a priority to strengthen US intelligence resources, focusing on human intelligence and the early detection of threats.[16]

Candidate Bush stated his desire to build and deploy a missile defense system to protect the homeland against missiles fired accidentally, by rogue nations, or in future conflicts. He highlighted the need to improve cooperation with US allies as they face many of the same threats, and should share in the burden of defense. Although Candidate Bush does not provide a hard dollar figure in this goal area, he does assert unequivocal support to a national and theater missile defense and to increased intelligence capability. This leadership position creates the expectation for substantive increases in defense budget for missile defense programs; however, intelligence funding is perennially difficult to ascertain, so may not be as visible in the defense budget.

---

14   Ibid., 4.
15   Ibid., 4.
16   Ibid., 5.

A New Military

Candidate Bush characterized the US military as organized more for Cold War threats than for the challenges of a new century. He called for a new architecture of American defense to permit the US to project power swiftly under new conditions, requiring very different kinds of forces from those in the past. These forces would be required to combat adversaries with access to ballistic and cruise missiles, weapons of mass destruction, and other technologies that may deny the US its forward bases and logistics capabilities. These adversaries would likely target airfields and ports critical to the flow of American forces and material, and would choose environments in which to fight where American forces, dependant on large amounts of logistical support, would be disadvantaged. To meet such future challenges, Candidate Bush outlined a review of US military force structure, strategy, and procurement to be conducted under the future Secretary of Defense. He would be tasked with creating the military of the future—lethal, agile, and easier to deploy. This future military would be equipped with modernized existing weapons, but would seek to replace existing systems with new technologies. To enable this action, Bush noted that he would earmark at least 20 percent of the procurement budget to address future challenges, and increase defense R&D spending by at least $20 billion from FY 2002 to FY 2006.[17]

Returning to the central question of this work, we should expect to see, if we are to conclude that Bush played a vital individual role, some evidence that these goals were reflected in budgetary priorities. It would be even more definitive if we observed, for instance, a planned increase of $20 billion in R&D across five years.

Bush's First Tally

Did Bush's platform translate into real budgetary action? To recapitulate, if individual leadership had a major impact, it would be sensible to expect to see:

1. a minimum increase of $1 billion in personnel funds for a pay raise;
2. additional funds to address 200,000 substandard housing units;
3. funds to accelerate research on, and deployment of, both national and theater missile defenses;
4. earmark(s) for at least 20 percent of the procurement budget to address future challenges, and
5. an increase in defense R&D spending by at least $20 billion from FY 2002 to FY 2006 in the budget proposal for FY 2002.

The proposed 2002 budget increase for the Department of Defense was $14.2 billion over 2001. In fact, we can easily detect a $1.4 billion increase for military pay

---

17   Ibid., 5–7.

and allowance. However, the other evidence is less clear-cut. The budget proposal has provisions for an increase of $400 million to improve the quality of housing and decrease out-of-pocket housing-related expenses for military personnel and their families. Given Candidate Bush's statement that more than 200,000 housing units were substandard, this equates to less that $2,000 per unit to upgrade housing or to ameliorate expenses.[18] The budget does propose a total increase of $3.567 billion in R&D for the Department of Defense (DoD)[19] with a $2.6 billion initiative in research and development for missile defense.[20] It also contains proposed specific focus areas of leap-ahead technologies and cost reduction for new weapons and intelligence systems; improvements to the laboratory and test range infrastructure; and efforts focused on countering unconventional threats to national security.[21] However, the original budget document does not provide a projection for the outyears that could substantiate the previously mentioned $20 billion over five years in R&D. Interestingly, the DoD portion of the budget allocates $3.9 billion for better retirement benefits for military personnel. This proposal appears to be in response to Congressional actions[22] as it was not in evidence in previous goal statements from Candidate Bush.

Overall, the scorecard based on our comparison is mixed. The proposed budget meets the test on the military personnel pay issue, does not seem to adequately address the housing issue, provides for a robust R&D effort in terms of missile defense, identifies focus areas, but does not provide outyear figures for $20 billion in R&D. The $3.9 billion for retirement benefits is not part of the Bush campaign initiatives. A $3.6 billion decrement to the Navy shipbuilding program also appears in the budget.[23] Although Candidate Bush indicated the need to choose weapon systems carefully, he had not previously identified the Navy shipbuilding program as the target for reductions.

President Bush

The policies embedded in President Bush's first budget appear to be crafted with a long-term perspective. Highlighting a new budgeting approach, the budget calls for a moderation of recent rapid growth in spending, paying down the debt, and providing tax relief. The largest percentage increase in the budget is in the

---

18   *A Blueprint for New Beginnings: A Responsible Budget for America's Priorities* (2001), Washington, DC: Government Printing Office, online at http://w3.access.gpo.gov/usbudget/fy2002/pdf/blueprnt.pdf.

19   *Fiscal Year 2002: Analytic Perspectives* (2001), Washington, DC: Government Printing Office, online at http://w3.access.gpo.gov/usbudget/fy2002/pdf/spec.pdf.

20   *A Blueprint for New Beginnings*, op. cit. fn. 18, 86.

21   Ibid., 86.

22   Ibid.

23   *Fiscal Year 2002: Analytic Perspectives*, op. cit. fn. 19, 505.

Education Department (11.5 percent). It also focuses on Social Security, saving a surplus, and directing modernization of the system. Other social services such as Medicare receive attention in an effort to modernize and reform programs. Last in the list of significant efforts is President Bush's attempt to restore the commitment to military personnel and begin transitioning to a twenty-first century force structure. In fact, defense comes next to last on a list of initiative highlights, just above increasing embassy security and, preceded by social service improvements and tax relief.[24]

Governing Principles

In a discussion of the governing principles of the budget, the budget document highlights the conviction that the Government should play a role that is both activist and limited. It notes that the important role of the Government is to foster an environment in which all Americans have the opportunity to better themselves and their families. This is operationalized in the budget language as: providing good educational opportunities for all youths; allowing families to keep more of their incomes; keeping commitments to the elderly and future generations; keeping the peace; and ensuring that communities have the ability to minister to their local needs.[25] Once again, the reader can note the order of these imperatives, domestic oriented aspects both predominate in order and number. The budget language then provides a set of limiting ideas. It highlights the need "not to overstep," and to ensure that it keeps the commitments it makes. Additionally, it indicates that the Government must take lessons from the private sector, finding ways to increase efficiency and customer satisfaction, stating the intent to make the Government more accountable, thereby increasing American citizen's confidence in a Government/private sector partnership that would raise everyone's standard of living.[26] By ascertaining if President Bush's individual leadership was predominant over external forces, we should be able to see the same principles, albeit with some slight adjustment, repeated in the language of the next budget, all the while accounting and adjusting for the changes in Bush's own budgetary views that were engendered by the September 11 attacks. Overall, as the President outlines the budget as a ten-year plan, the principles should not vary substantially within that time period. However, if we believe that the external environment shapes the policies, we would expect to see a different set of principles enunciated, with the possibility of some minor portions being a continuation of the previous principles.

---

24 *A Blueprint for New Beginnings*, op. cit. fn. 18, 9.
25 Ibid., 11.
26 Ibid.

Allocating the Taxpayers' Dollars

The Fiscal Year 2002 budget contains an extensive discussion of how a surplus is generated and proposes a way to disburse that surplus. It indicates that over the next 10 years, the federal Government projects it will collect $28 trillion in revenues from American taxpayers. The President's budget estimated that it would cost roughly $22.4 trillion to continue the Government in existence today, including new initiatives outlined previously. This leaves a $5.6 trillion surplus. The budget allocates the entire Social Security surplus for Social Security and debt retirement. It partially justifies the expenditure on debt retirement, as a further cost savings measure in the long term, paying off $2 trillion in debt that matures at and before 2011 over the next 10 years. The budget language estimates that by 2011, federal debt will have fallen to 7 percent of Gross Domestic Product (GDP), its lowest level in more than 80 years. It claims that net interest payments on this debt will be less than 0.5 percent of GDP, less than one quarter of the 2009 share and only three percent of the budget. A portion of the surplus is proposed to fund a return of $1.6 trillion tax dollars to the taxpayers.[27] Whether the arguments above are correct or not, it is important to note that the focus of the discussion is on domestic issues of debt retirement, Social Security, and tax refunds. The budget allocation discussion further reinforces the domestic, economic focus. The budget language continues to address issues beyond Social Security, paying off the debt, and tax refunds, by highlighting Medicare reform, and establishing a true financial reserve for future priorities and unexpected contingencies. This financial reserve is noted to be $1 trillion. In the discussion of this reserve, the issue set is broadened slightly beyond purely domestic concerns, adding a mention of the potential for increased defense spending almost in parallel with farm conditions that could require additional resources for agriculture, and additional debt retirement.[28]

The principles go on to highlight the need to examine existing programs, looking for ways to redirect resources to their most productive end and the potential of freeing resources to address emerging needs. Ideas such as flattening the federal hierarchy, moving the Government toward performance-based contracting, opening Government functions to competition, reducing erroneous payments by federal agencies, expanding electronic Government (e-government), including procurement, were claimed to have the potential for savings to exceed $100 billion over 10 years.[29]

The budget document recognizes that, like any long-term plan, it is subject to alteration due to unanticipated needs. It claims that by using cautious, estimating assumptions, reserving the Social Security surplus for debt retirement and Social Security reform, and preserving an additional large reserve beyond the Social Security surplus, the Administration will be able to adjust the budget in the future

---

27   Ibid., 11–12.
28   Ibid., 13.
29   Ibid., 18.

to meet new requirements as they arise.[30] This coda implies that President Bush's principles would remain as the guiding factors despite trillion dollar emergencies, as an adjustment to the budget would suffice to address the issue.

If we believe that President Bush's leadership shapes the agenda, this allocation discussion builds the expectation that the priorities outlined here will remain much like this in the budget for a number of years. The importance of retiring debt, protecting Social Security and other social services should remain highly regarded. Even an emergency should not substantially change the inherent importance of the domestic economic well-being. However, if environmental factors are determinant, we would expect wholesale changes to funding priorities outlined here.

Bush's Second Tally

To recapitulate, continued stability in principles and funding would tend to support the premise of leadership as the key contributor to policy, with the adjustment that the events feed back into the leader's views. Meanwhile, substantial shifts in policy and funding would tend to indicate non-individual factors as important, either because they shape individual views or because of an independent set of effects on policy.

The Fiscal Year 2003 budget document highlights the following priorities:

1. Protecting the Homeland;
2. Winning the War on Terrorism Abroad;
3. Returning to Economic Vitality;
4. Governing with Accountability; and
5. other Priority Initiatives.

The first category includes funding for equipping and training first responders, enhancements to hospitals, medical research, information nets for detection for biological issues, better border control, and aviation security issues. The second category supports a defense budget increase, and military aid to other allied countries. The third category contains economic stimulus to assist the unemployed, moderates the growth of spending, with the exception of national security and homeland issues to 2 percent, and balances the budget by 2005 without raising taxes. The fourth category incorporates a set of five management reforms into agencies' budgets and plans, shifting the budget's focus to what is being accomplished, beginning with the integration of performance measures in the budget process, and seeks reprogramming and reorganization authority to better align programs and resources. The final category includes Education, National Institutes of Health, Community Health Centers, Medicare Prescription

---

30   Ibid.

Drugs, Health Insurance, Breast and Cervical Cancer Screening, Compassion and Faith-Based Initiatives and many other social service initiatives.[31]

President Bush's previous theme of moderating growth in spending survived the change in environment, albeit in a weak form, as evidenced by his attempt to keep spending growth, aside from defense and homeland security, at 2 percent.[32] His goal of paying down the debt appeared to have been excised from the budget, as the phrase "debt retirement" does not appear, even once, in the 431-page document. The importance of providing tax relief had taken on the crucial role of helping to regain economic vitality, versus acting purely as a moral imperative of returning the taxpayers money. The priority focus on education had not been entirely lost but was falling to be the first element in the last category of "Other Priority Initiatives." Other social programs such as Medicare received attention short of the previous year's effort to modernize and reform, and would theoretically benefit from an approach that looks to incrementally improve and reengineer the program.[33] We also observe issues that were last in the list of significant efforts in 2002, increased in importance in 2003. Chiefly, the President's attempt to restore the commitment to military personnel and to begin the transition to a twenty-first century force structure assumed both a near-term focus as well as a more important longer term focus on military transformation, with a 12 percent increase in budget authority.[34]

Overall, we find as we did in the analysis of the previous figure pairs that the scorecard is mixed. However, it appears that most of the previous principles survived the transition in circumstance, with some variation in priority. Funding, however, suffered a substantial shift. For example, the Education Department benefited from the highest increase in 2002 at 11.5 percent, but in 2003 would be held within a 2 percent increase for all but defense and homeland security programs. The plan to retire substantial amounts of debt and sustain any emergency through the use of a reserve fund did not survive either.

President Bush (FY 2003–2007) and the Obama Factor

The election of President Obama highlights the importance in the question of the extent to which an individual President can truly drive an agenda. There is not yet sufficient information on President Obama's performance to provide a fair analysis, but much is expected of him as an individual. Much data, however, has accumulated for President Bush, and understanding the case of Bush may offer some insights into President Obama's potential for change. To gain that

31   US, White House (2002), *Fiscal Year 2003 Budget of the US Government*, Washington, DC: Government Printing Office, 11–13.
32   Ibid., 8.
33   Ibid., 8–9.
34   Ibid., 29.

perspective, two key set of data were examined in early 2009; the language of the President's budget message and the actual expenditures by the Government in FY 2003 through FY 2007.

The President provides a budget message as the first part of each fiscal year (FY) budget proposal to Congress. The budget message sketches priorities regarding where federal dollars should be focused, and if the President's influence on the Congressional process is great enough, his priorities will be reflected in the final budget.

The priorities expressed by President Bush for FY 2003 through FY 2007 are strikingly consistent. Starting in FY 2003, the President identified his top three priorities: homeland defense; improvements to America's military to "find, pursue, and destroy our enemies"; and restoring economic health. The next year he identified the top three national priorities to be the global war on terror, securing the homeland and generating economic growth. For FY 2005, the three were prevailing in the War on Terror, strengthening homeland defense, and building on our economic recovery. For FY 2006, the idea of winning the war on terror was expanded to address both overseas and domestic goals, subsuming homeland defense and the military aspects into a single idea, and the other idea which remained was the goal of promoting economic growth and opportunity. In FY 2007, President Bush expressed the same priorities as he did for FY 2006. Despite some wording variations, the same three ideas were at the top of budget priorities for the period in question. But does consistency of language result in actual success in driving expenditures?

Because of our ability to look back at federal expenditure with perfect hindsight for these years (FY 2003–2007), we will be able to determine if the priorities indentified by President Bush actually received the level of funding he intended. The first two priorities are relatively easy to understand, as the war against terror and the homeland security have departments that are the main proponent for those activities. Examining their proposed and actual budget authority figures provides a barometer for the entire activity.

Although the Department of Homeland Security (DHS) did not exist when the FY 2003 budget was drafted, the President's budget proposal provided an FY 2003 "Homeland Security" dollar figure on page 15 of the budget. This proposed amount was a composite of costs across multiple agencies that were to become the DHS.

In examining this data, it seems clear that the President's intent, at least in the area of homeland security and national defense, was influential in setting funding levels. In fact, all of the actual expenditures, with the exception of the FY 2003 future DHS situation, were well above the proposed figures. Some of the amounts over the proposed figures were generated from subsequent supplemental funding by Congress designed to support operations in Iraq.

The third priority, increasing economic health/growth/opportunity, is a little harder to explore as there is no single Government agency that holds sway in this area. To understand the intent and result of this priority, a closer look at the wording of the budget proposals is required. A set of economic themes becomes apparent in reviewing the area of Presidential budget proposals in the period FY 2003–2007 that deal with "Returning to Economic Vitality," "For Everyone Willing to Work, A Job," "Promoting Prosperity, Expanding Opportunity," "Promoting Economic Opportunity and Ownership," and "Expanding Economic Opportunity." These themes are: lower tax burdens and increased private savings through credits and tax rate reductions; reduced Government regulation; tort reforms, both general and specifically for medical cases; increased spending on research and development; and lastly, fiscal constraint on spending other than defense and homeland security.

The President's budget results in the area of economics are more of a mixture than appeared to be the case in the areas of defense and homeland security. Despite multiple calls for permanent tax relief, temporary tax changes were made. Further, these measures did not adopt the entire range of the President's proposals. Likewise, in the area of tort reform, Congress took some action, such as in the Class Action Fairness Act of 2005, but did not fully adopt the President's agenda. In the area of research and development, examining the category of general science and basic research discretionary funding, actual outlays were more than the budget proposal in three of the five years and below the proposed budget two of those years. Finally, the idea of fiscal constraint in areas other than defense and security was largely rejected. Indeed, the actual outlays were $30 to $87 billion more than the President's budget proposal in four out of the five years.

This analysis (FY 2003–2007) also suggests, like the earlier analysis in this chapter, that the President's influence—even a President with depressed approval ratings—seems to be considerable in key areas of defense and homeland security but less so in economic areas. In turn, we may infer from these findings that President Obama will likely have to overcome many challenges outside direct expenditures on defense and homeland security to be successful in the global war on terror. Given the above results, it will likely be difficult over the long term for President Obama to routinely deliver the federal budgets and programs that he believes are required for economic prosperity necessary to pursue the Global War on Terror.

Conclusion

This study has sought to assess the importance of the role of Candidate and President Bush in shaping the national budget. This research task, no doubt, is complicated by the ever present challenge of attempting to assess causality when numerous different variables are at play. Doing so with enhanced rigor would require greater attention to isolating different variables that could explain budgetary priorities and shifts. But that is a task more sensibly handled in one or more volumes, and not in a short foray of this kind.

Rather, while we do not want to present our findings as definitive, we do believe that they are suggestive and useful. What we would argue is that in the present case, neither the individual nor the non-individual factors were pre-eminent. Rather, the results appear to indicate an interaction between both factors. When Candidate Bush became President his intention to bolster defense was moderated by the need to understand better how to transform US armed forces in order to make them more effective against the emergent adversary. The global environment in which Bush would have to operate post-9/11 included an unmistakable transnational element since al-Qaeda represented at its core a transnational terrorist threat. The war on terrorism in this new environment shaped the budget both independently and partly by shaping Bush's views—views that also had their own inertia and continuity.

Moreover, when the principles in the first budget were challenged by an emergent adversary, the second budget provided funding for current counter-terrorist operations, while retaining force transformation principles and funding. There was by no means a serious break with previous budgetary imperatives, but the September 11 realities accelerated some priorities that were already in motion, while generating their own independent effects. Although funding for education dropped in importance, education did maintain its relative priority within the social services arena.

Evidence on the FY 2003–2007 period also suggests that the President's influence is uneven. As with the analysis of the earlier part of the Bush Presidency, this analysis suggests that the President's influence is much higher in the areas of defense and homeland security than in economic areas. If so, President Obama may run into some challenges executing his full economic agenda in the coming years. That prediction, however, should be tempered by the fact that the level of economic crisis as of 2009 is so high that Obama is likely to be given more leverage in dealing with the economy than otherwise would be the case under less difficult and pressing economic conditions.

As a note for future study, it would be interesting to conduct additional case studies that explore the extent to which the languages of candidates and Presidents about budgetary priorities matches the actual outcome that results once the process takes its course. This can help illuminate the budgetary process and yield greater insights into the extent to which individuals as candidates and Presidents are really crucial. We should expect their central platforms to be reflected in interim and final budgets, if we are to conclude that they are influential. Assessing the extent of their influence, however, will also require developing a baseline of what we should expect. The more case studies we conduct, the better we will be able to assess what we can expect in terms of the match between their platforms and budgetary outcomes.

Ultimately, what may be most interesting is the combination of factors, individual and non-individual, that produce outcomes. It may be that we find the most sensible answers as to how budgets are shaped and what factors are most germane in shaping them, in the complex mix of factors. But even so, that leaves a more difficult and interesting question: what are the conditions under which some factors or combination of factors will be more important than others in this process? That is a question more suitably tackled in future work.

Chapter 7

President Bush and the War on Terrorism: Historic Opportunity Lost to Complete his Father's Legacy and Define his Own Place in History

John Davis

Introduction

Long after the Bush Presidency is concluded, the anticipated "legacy" cottage industry continues to assume shape. As one of the most unpopular American Presidents in history, scholars have not rushed to publish or to have open and prolonged discourse on the success or failure of the Bush Presidency. The reason is fundamental: all too many assume, in the absence of professional scholarship, that his legacy is one characterized by failure. This study represents an effort to provide an examination of a critical component of the Bush legacy: its conspicuous connection with that of his father.

In considering President George W. Bush's foreign policy legacy one cannot escape the fact that inexplicably three components of the younger Bush's policies are directly connected to initiatives explored by his father. Employing three case studies—the search for stability in the international system, confronting Iraq, and the war on terrorism—this study represents an effort to explore this linkage and its impact on the legacy of George W. Bush. Similarly, the author asserts that the results of this examination offer significant information about Bush's stewardship of US foreign policy. Of equal significance, the research illustrates that Bush had an opportunity to redefine aspects of his father's legacies, and second, as a by-product, to define his own place in history. At issue in this chapter is whether Bush excelled or failed in this historic opportunity.

The First Linkage: The Search for Stability in the International System

The "new world order" defined represents an attempt to stabilize the international system following a period of upheaval characterized by a period of major war. Similarly, it is important to evaluate the efforts of the "ordained great power" to reorder the new system under new auspices.[1] The great power endeavor to reorder the new system is a critical component to understanding the postwar development of any international system. With respect to the United States, beginning with Woodrow Wilson, US Presidents endeavored to create an international system based on democratic values. Under the direction of President George H.W. Bush, the Administration articulated a vision of world order that was very much consistent with Wilsonian-Idealism where collective security and the rule of law were paramount instruments of global security.[2] The resulting confrontation with Iraq offered the elder Bush two significant opportunities: 1) to define a post-Cold War vision; and 2) Iraq represented a test case for the evolving security arrangements that would be critical for the establishment of a successful new world order.

In a joint address to congress on March 6, 1991, President George H.W. Bush ushered in a period of *Triumphalism*. In fleshing out the vision, Bush spoke of "guaranteeing an era of perpetual peace." He also noted that, in the absence of rules to guide postwar stability, and in the wake of our victory over Iraq, an era symbolized by an "enduring peace must be our mission." On the second point, the President offered the following elaboration and goals: "A world where the United Nations, freed from Cold War stalemate, is poised to fulfill the historic mission of its founders ... a world in which freedom and respect for human rights find a home among all nations."[3] The Gulf War, according to the President, "put this new world to its first test" adding, "and my fellow Americans we passed that test."[4]

According to Brent Scowcroft, former national security advisor to President Bush, and the architect of the postwar strategy, the new world order as envisioned by the President had a supplementary objective: to prevent interstate conflict.[5] For Scowcroft, the Administration's postwar strategy fulfilled its purpose. However, in the months immediately after the celebratory environment that swept the United States after the Gulf War, the President's vision lost its luster and became a source of discontent and disillusionment among scholars, who incessantly argued that postwar recommendations were problematic.[6] That is, while the Administration strategy proved successful in precluding interstate war, the vision did not address

---

1   This definition was employed in my doctoral dissertation *Unfilled Promises: American Foreign Policy and the New World Order* (unpublished August 2000).

2   Some authors assert that the vision represented a reversal of the Reagan doctrine. Under Reagan, the Administration concluded that the UN personified a weak institution and was thus unable to assist with US policy objectives: mainly the rollback of communism. For more on this point and a comparison of the Wilsonian and Bush visions of a new order, see Tucker, R.W. and Hendrickson, D. (1992), *The Imperial Temptation: The New World Order and America's Purpose*, New York: Council on Foreign Relations Press, 54–59.

3   Bush, G.H.W. (1991), Joint Address to Congress (6 March), reprinted in *The New York Times* (March 7, 1991).

4   Ibid.

5   Interview with Brent Scowcroft (February 2000).

6   Schwartz, B. (1994/1995), "The Vision Thing: Sustaining the Unsustainable," *World Policy Journal* (Winter), 101–21.

the burgeoning ethnic civil wars that simmered throughout the postwar period. Moreover, the President's postwar strategy offered no solutions to the increasing threat of transnational terrorism.

Having allowed these conflicts to fester, and in the absence of counterterrorist strategy, one pundit opined that "for the country and the world, was that the new world order had no content."[7] Within the Administration, with the campaign season approaching, and hounded by queries about the details of the new world order which were overwhelming the Bush White House staff, several senior members informed the President that it was time to distance the Administration from this vision. David Gergen, the former Director of Communications, offered the following account:

> In his frequent incantations of a "new world order," President Bush seemed on the verge of setting forth a new set of doctrines for US policy, and the White House even announced that he would give four commencement addresses in the spring of 1991 fleshing out his vision. Because his staff felt that a public debate over a new order was spinning beyond control, however, the President gave only one of the addresses and then pulled back, returning to a more comfortable, day-to-day management of foreign affairs ... the new world order seemed destined to become no more than a campaign slogan for 1992. A rare moment of opportunity had passed ... Few outside the White House talk anymore of creating a "new world order," except in jest.[8]

Once a productive component of Bush's impending legacy, the construction of a new world order emerged as a failure for the self-described foreign policy President. In an effort to escape this reality, the President turned inward to confront the ailing American economy as the 1992 Presidential Campaign approached. In the wake of this shift in the Administration's strategy, the grand coalition that was successful during the Gulf War (and a symbol of Administration multilateralism) withered as a neo-isolationist impulse gripped the United States. As a result, disorder became the phrase employed to describe the international system.[9]

The War on Terror provided the younger Bush with an opportunity to revive discourse on the new world order, and second, September 11 presented the President with something equally significant, an opportunity to learn from the mistakes of his father. For George W. Bush, the War on Terror was couched in verbiage that was consistent with language employed by the elder Bush. In making the case against Iraq, the elder Bush argued the time had arrived to confront "the darker

---

7   Graubard, S.R. (1992), *Mr. Bush's War: Adventures in the Politics of Illusion*, New York: Hill and Wang, 164–67.

8   Gergen, D. (1991/1992), "America's Missed Opportunities," *Foreign Affairs* 71/1 (Winter), 12 and 1.

9   Freedman, L. (1991/1992), "Order and Disorder in the New World Order," *Foreign Affairs*, America and the World Edition, 20–37.

side of human nature" and "forge a future" for the expansion of democracy and the rule of law throughout the world. Following the tragic events of September 11, the younger Bush offered his prescription for a new order during a joint address to the Congress on September 21, 2001:

> Some speak of an age of terror. I know where there are struggles ahead, and dangers to face. As long as the United States of America is determined and strong, this will not be an age of terror; this will be an age of liberty, here and across the world ... Our nation—this generation—will lift a dark threat of violence from our people and future. We will rally the world to this cause by our efforts, by our courage. We will not tire, we will not falter, and we will not fail.[10]

As with the elder Bush, in making the case for the campaign on terror, "W" employed the same "good versus evil" imagery. For the younger Bush, "The course of the conflict is not yet known, yet its outcome is certain. Freedom and fear, justice and cruelty, have always been at war and we know that God is not neutral between them."[11]

This statement notwithstanding, there is an irony awaiting public discourse. In an effort to confront post-Cold War stability, George H.W. Bush spoke of ending interstate aggression, but failed to provide solutions for ethnic conflicts and transnational terrorism. The magnitude associated with this failure is clear: the inability of the elder Bush to deal with intrastate conflict sealed the fate of the vision of the new world order. Interestingly, in the campaign against terror, George W. Bush proposed the eradication of terrorism. In opting for this approach, unknowingly, the President confronted an element of intrastate aggression (transnational terrorism which functioned within and between states) that contributed to the withdrawal of his father's vision. Finally, if Bush's post-September 11 vision offered an opportunity to revive the father's idea of a different world, the strategy would invariably open the Administration up to a series of questions. Unfortunately there were dilemmas associated with this opportunity. For example, will Bush complete the eradication of terrorism and pave the way for the survival and the expansion of American values? Similarly, did the younger Bush repeat a critical error of his father? That is, in the midst of questions regarding the parameters of the post September 11 world, will the President provide answers or withdraw from the vision? In the end, the outcome of the War on Terror will be the defining moment for the legacies of both Presidents.

---

10   Bush, G.W. (2001a), *Joint Address to Congress* (September 21), reprinted in *The New York Times* (September 22, 2001).

11   Bush, G.W. (2001b), *Joint Address to Congress and the American People*, US Capital, Washington, DC (September 20).

The Second Linkage: Iraq and the Search for Regional Stability

The younger Bush and his father found their Presidencies intertwined again on the subject of Iraq. For the elder Bush, Iraq emerged as a potent foreign policy issue following Saddam Hussein's invasion of Kuwait. In the case of the younger Bush, Iraq developed as a corollary to the war on terrorism: as a member of the "axis of evil." This section explores George W. Bush's effort at regime change in Iraq and how this strategy carried an unspoken objective: the revival and completion of George H.W. Bush's legacy.

For the senior Bush, the objectives were rudimentary: the removal of Iraqi forces from Kuwait and the destruction of Saddam's "offensive military capabilities," thereby limiting Iraq's ability to attack neighboring states. Throughout Operation Desert Shield and Operation Desert Storm the Administration acknowledged that the removal of the Saddam Hussein carried with it consequences that were beyond the parameters of US national security. Similarly, the UN Security Council did not approve of the removal of Hussein, and the Administration maintained that toppling the Iraqi leader would force Arab coalition partners to end their participation and association with President Bush's multilateral strategy. Finally, the Administration argued that without a unified Iraqi opposition the elimination of Hussein could lead to "Lebanonization of Iraq."[12]

Although these were the stated war aims, President Bush and members of his staff quietly articulated that there were indeed efforts at regime change. Initially, the Administration viewed efforts to topple Hussein as "nonsensical" and counterproductive. This public face aside, the Administration never expected Hussein to survive the war, and second, Bush privately authorized several plans to remove the Iraqi leader. With respect to the first point, Secretary of State James Baker offered this statement: "It's important to recall that, while it would have been welcome Saddam's departure was never a stated objective of our policy. We were always very careful to negate it as a war aim or political objective. At the same time, we never really expected him to survive a defeat of such magnitude."[13]

On the second point, plans for the regime change—both during and after the Gulf War—consisted of the following: the use of special operation forces to "assassinate Hussein," the employment of "special bunker buster" missiles to destroy hardened strategic command facilities frequented by the Iraqi leader, and an overt campaign on 15 February 1991 to enlist "the Iraqi military and the Iraqi people to take matters in their own hands, to force Saddam Hussein ... to step aside." The "Iraqi people" the President spoke of consisted of the Shiites and the Kurds.[14]

---

12   Baker, J.A., III (1995), *The Politics of Diplomacy: Revolution, War and Peace, 1989–1992*, New York: Putnam's, 442.

13   Ibid., 437–38.

14   On the plans to kill the Iraqi leader, see "The Plan to Kill Saddam Hussein," *Newsweek* (January 10, 1994), 4–5; Seymour, J. (2001), *Operation Provide Comfort,*

The impact of these strategies proved disastrous for Bush, and eventually redefined his legacy. The results of these endeavors represented "post-victory blues," the notion that in spite of high postwar approval ratings, the President's earlier triumph in the Gulf War was dubbed "operation desert shame," and the Administration's abandonment of the Shiites and the Kurds was considered reprehensible.[15] With respect to Iraq, two postscripts were influential in defining Bush's legacy. In the first instance, by defeating internal dissent, the Iraqi leader transformed himself from an "international outlaw into the champion of Iraq's survival as a state, goals to which the Bush Administration and most ... of the allies were also committed. It was the cruelest twist of the whole affair. Saddam had, in effect, joined the coalition."[16] Secretary Baker illustrated the significance of the second point: "I am reminded of something Tariq Aziz said to me in Geneva: We will be here long after you're gone. It was one of the few things he said that proved to be true."[17]

In the end while Bush's legacy took a major hit, there were other less obvious casualties: the President's test case for postwar stability, Iraq, had been derailed, and an Administration that earlier boasted of an era of new internationalism reversed course talking instead of isolationism as a means to recover from the post-Gulf War verities.

The Younger Bush

For the younger Bush Iraq represented both opportunities and challenges. The opportunities were rudimentary: end the regime of Saddam Hussein, and with the absence of Iraq, the Administration was positioned to enhance regional stability. However, initially the Administration publicly moved away from its original objective. Instead of opting for a multilateral approach to force Saddam to disarm, privately, the White House thought that Iraq would violate the UN Security Council Resolution (UNSCR) 1441 which required unfettered access to suspected Weapons of Mass Destruction (WMD). Recognizing that his Iraq policy lacked international support, the President prepared for the implementation of preventive war with Iraq. Second, Saddam's removal would represent a vindication for the Bush family and to those advisors who served with the senior Bush, namely Vice

---

Montgomery, AL: Maxwell Air Force Base. In another example of the efforts to kill Hussein in command bunkers, see Pincus, W. (1998), "Saddam Hussein's Death is a Goal Says Ex-CIA Chief; Bush Advisers Hoped that Collateral Damage Would Include Iraqi Leader," *Washington Post* (February 15).

15   For more on this point, see Talbot, S. (1991/1992), "Post-Victory Blues," *Foreign Affairs* 71/1 (Winter), 53–69; and Ledeen, M. (1991), "Operation Desert Shame," *American Spectator* 24/6 (June), 12.

16   Talbot, op. cit. fn. 15, 63.

17   Baker, op. cit. fn. 12, 442.

President Dick Cheney and Secretary of State Colin Powell. Other than Powell, few in the Administration concerned themselves with how the war would be conducted or the reaction to the "unilateralist impulse" or its rhetoric touting a "coalition of the willing." In the end the Bush Administration was more concerned about one critical aspect of its war aims—unseating Saddam Hussein—rather than with a clearly thought out plan for dealing with postwar realties in Iraq.

Returning to the second point, the Iraqi threat posed numerous challenges for the Bush Administration. In the preparation for the war against terrorism, bureaucratic rumblings indicated that no consensus existed on a series of critical issues. If the Administration intervened in Iraq, for example, Bush strategists were concerned with the timing of the invasion. Similarly, the President and his advisors had to access how the new phase of the War on Terror would affect the coalition, particularly Arab members, thus the Bush team would have to develop a strategy to manage the regional fallout.

To be specific, David Phillips, the only diplomat to participate in the Office of Reconstruction and Humanitarian Assistance (ORHA), warned the last minute bureaucratic replacement of the State Department directed "Future of Iraq Project" could lead to postwar chaos. Having been on the ground in Iraq, and attempting to implement the limited, and often unproductive objectives of the ORHA, Phillips made a bold prediction: President Bush may ultimately lose in Iraq.[18]

Another dilemma that awaited President Bush involved clarification on how and to what extent the Administration planned to utilize Iraqi opposition forces. To put this point in context, consider that the elder Bush rallied the "Iraqi people" to overthrow the Iraqi leader but, absent US military support, the opposition groups were in no position to defeat Saddam. In the final analysis, the end game was obvious: the Kurds and Shiites were slaughtered by remnants of Iraq's elite Republican Guard.

Certain of regime change, the younger Bush not only enlisted the Kurds and Shiites to rise up against Saddam, but the President was determined to ensure the united opposition following the transition to a post-Saddam regime. Consistent with this approach, strategists at the Pentagon opted to train elements of the opposition in preparation for any American-led invasion.[19] By taking this approach, the younger Bush silenced the criticism that preoccupied his father—that he would betray the Kurds and Shiites. Similarly, in Northern Iraq American Special Operation Forces not only trained but conducted offensive warfare alongside Kurdish militias determined to end Saddam's hold over that part of the country.

The second issue concerned doctrine. The President's "axis of evil" address dramatically altered Administration strategy and provided renewed impetus

---

18   Phillips, D. (2005), *Losing Iraq: Inside the Postwar Reconstruction Fiasco*, New York: Basic Books.

19   See Slevin, P. (2002), "US Pushes for Iraqi Opposition," *Washington Post* (August 9), A20.

to remove the Iraqi President.[20] Noting that Iraq's WMDs threatened world peace, Bush launched a new doctrine on terrorism and issued this caveat: the United States would not allow rogue states to hold the country hostage to "terror weapons." To protect the homeland against rogue states (Iraq, Iran and North Korea), Bush introduced a doctrine of "preemption" and "prevention."[21] According to the President, the United States would employ force to destroy WMDs in a "preemptive attack" or "preventative attack" in an attempt to protect the homeland. The doctrine immediately alienated alliance members in the Middle East and it caused considerable consternation among NATO allies concerned about American unilateralism.[22] In an effort to defuse the increasing apprehension regarding his Administration's intentions, Bush asserted the future of world peace rests with a victorious outcome in Iraq, "As for Mr. Saddam Hussein, he needs to let inspectors back into his country, to show us that he is not developing weapons of mass destruction."[23]

As for the second Bush–Hussein showdown, according to the President, "this is personal," noting the Iraqi leader attempted to assassinate his father. Thus, for Bush the stakes were raised considerably. Moreover, there is an important side note to this struggle: Bush intimated that his anger and frustration were direct not only at the Iraqi leader, but former President Bill Clinton who failed to "appropriately respond' to Iraq's assassination attempt of the elder Bush. To illustrate the President's point, in response to the assassination attempt in June of 1993, Clinton observed in a speech to the nation that: "The plan [was] devised by the Iraq Government ... As such the Iraqi attack against President Bush was an attack against our country and against all Americans."[24] In a counter attack, Clinton launched 23 cruise missiles that destroyed one of the four Iraqi intelligence facilities. For the younger Bush, Clinton's use of cruise missiles was unsettling and contributed to the perception of a weak America: "The antiseptic notion of launching a cruise missile into some guy's tent is a joke. I mean, people viewed that as the impotent America."[25]

---

20   US, White House (2001), "President Speaks on War Effort to Citadel Cadets," (December 11) online at www.whitehouse.gov/news/releases/2001/12/20011211-6.html.

21   Mikkelsen, R. (2002), "Bush Outlines Strategy of Preemptive Strikes," *Washington Post* (September 20).

22   Risks, T.E. and Loeb, V. (2002), "Bush Developing Military Policy of Striking First: New Doctrine Addresses Terrorism," *Washington Post* (June 10), A1.

23   Allen, M. (2001), "Iraq's Weapons Could Make it a Target, Bush Says," *Washington Post* (November 27).

24   Clinton, W.J. (1993), "Address to the Nation on the Attack on Iraqi Intelligence Headquarters," *Public Papers of the President, Administration of William J. Clinton* (June 26).

25   Woodward, B. and Bolz, D. (2002), "We Will Rally the World: Bush and His Advisers Set Objectives, But Struggle on How to Achieve Them," Part III, *Washington Post* (28 January), A1.

On another issue, the younger Bush utilized the UN as a means to take up the case against the Iraqi leader. Employing similar verbiage as his father, Bush argued the struggle against Iraq could define the future of the UN: "Will the United Nations serve the purpose of its founding, or will it be irrelevant?"[26] After making a prosecutorial case outlining Iraqi contravention of post-Gulf War Security Council agreements, the President offered this caveat: "The purpose of the United States should not be doubted. The Security Council resolutions will be enforced, or action will be unavoidable. And a regime that has lost its legitimacy will lose its power."[27]

Finally, in another paradox the younger Bush ignored advice that was presented by his father. For starters, George H.W. Bush acknowledged that any occupation of Iraq would result in "mission creep" and would produce "incalculable human and political costs." There would be other problems according to the elder Bush: "The coalition would instantly ... collapse, the Arabs deserting it in anger and other allies pulling out as well," and there was this additional dilemma, "the US could conceivably still be an occupying power in a bitterly hostile land."[28]

Finally, with the tenure of President Bush concluded a number of critical questions remain. Of immediate focus is how will the Iraq War assist in the evaluation of Bush's legacy? The rapid collapse of the regime of Saddam Hussein ended an old debate concerning his father's inability to "remove the Butcher of Baghdad." Thus the military victory in Iraq, in the eyes of many Republicans, permitted the younger Bush to rewrite the earlier negative history associated with the closing months of his father's tenure. Unfortunately, without clearly defined postwar objectives, along with the failure to secure the country, a pre-surge environment that is absent of security permitted insurgents to create chaos across Iraq. Equally troubling is this sobering reality: Bush had no answer to the ever-expanded pre-surge sectarian violence that further undermined US authority and the confidence of the Iraqi people. It is these issues, and others, that created a negative perception about the younger Bush's legacy.

The Third Linkage: The War on Terror

As with the former cases, the War on Terror offered another variable that indicated a connection between the father and son Presidents. For the elder Bush, during his tenure as the Vice President for Ronald Reagan, and then as President, the issue of terrorism represented a continuing and vexing aspect of his Administration's foreign policy. At issue then is the contribution of the elder Bush in confronting

---

26   US, White House, Office of the Press Secretary (2002), "Address by President Bush: Remarks at the United Nations General Assembly, 12 September 2002" (12 September).

27   Ibid.

28   Bush, G.H.W. and Scowcroft, B. (1998), *A World Transformed*, New York: Alfred A. Knopf, 489.

terrorism during a twelve year span in which he occupied the positions of Vice President and President of the United States.

During the Reagan Administration, the elder Bush's role was mixed, if not controversial. In confronting terrorism, Lebanon remained an area of concern for the Reagan Administration, particularly since the US embassy was destroyed, and six months later 241 US Marines were killed. In addition to these events, several US citizens were held hostage by Hezbollah, an Islamic extremist group allied with Iran and Syria.

As a member of the National Security Planning Group (NSPG), Vice President Bush participated in a number of critical decisions. That said, as a member of the faction that was averse to the use of force (Secretary of Defense Casper Weinberger also belonged to this faction), Bush found himself in the untenable position to recommend to Reagan that the US should not launch any military reprisals against Hezbollah for their attacks on US interests in spite of overwhelming evidence of their complicity in the 1983 "triple attacks." At the very least, these recommendations damaged Bush's standing among conservatives within the Administration and those in the Republican Party.

During his second term, Bush chaired the committee to combat terrorism. In a speech in February of 1986, Bush issued a report that noted: "We are prepared to act in concert or alone to prevent or respond to terrorist acts. *We will make no concessions to terrorists* [italics in original]." The problem for Bush and the Administration is that one month earlier (January 17, 1986), the Vice President, along with the national security advisor Admiral John Poindexter, in a meeting with the President, provided Reagan with a memo that outlined the proposed sale of weapons in exchange for US hostages in Lebanon.[29] The result of this meeting undermined the report of the counterterrorism task force and Administration policy, and laid the foundation for the Iran-Contra Scandal. In the fight against terrorism, the elder Bush, like many other participants in the scandal, appeased terrorists.

Beginning in 1989, Bush reduced terrorism to a low priority. Moreover, having been tainted by Iran-Contra, Bush made an astute decision: he had terrorism remanded to interagency deliberations where bureaucratic turf battles ensured the subject of terrorism would die a slow death, and cease to be a major foreign policy issue. According to Michael Ledeen, this attitude was kept in place during the Clinton Administration. The result was a "do-nothing approach" that culminated in the horrific events of September 11.[30]

The events of September 11 thrust the younger Bush into a historic position: in little over a year the War on Terror redefined American security interests and international relations. The creation of the Department of Homeland Security

---

29   Menges, C.C. (1988), *Inside the National Security Council: The True Story of the Making and Unmaking of Reagan's Foreign Policy*, New York: Touchstone Books, 274–75.

30   See Ledeen, M.A. (2002), *The War Against the Terror Masters: Why It Happened, Where We Are Now, How We Will Win*, New York: St. Martin's Press.

(DHS) represented the first of many initiatives that indicated that President Bush was serious about securing the United States against future terrorist attacks. Staying on the domestic side of the war on terrorism, the President created a special military command US Northern Command (USNORTHCOM) whose sole purpose was to provide military security for the defense of America.

These two initiatives represented the central domestic components of an extraordinary grand strategy in a concentrated campaign to defeat al-Qaeda. President Bush introduced the overall strategy and plans to prosecute the first war of the twenty-first century during a nationally televised address to the nation on September 20, 2001. In this speech, the President argued: "every means of diplomacy, every tool of intelligence, every instrument of law enforcement, every financial influence, and every necessary weapon of war [would be used for] ... the destruction and to the defeat of the global terror network."[31]

Nearly a month into the second year of the War on Terror President Bush scored significant victories. The Taliban had been routed in Afghanistan. In addition, al-Qaeda had been defeated and dispersed and was no longer utilizing Afghanistan as a staging area to export transnational terror. Consistent with Administration strategy, in 2002 the President deployed detachments of Special Forces to the Philippines, Yemen and Georgia in an effort to defeat al-Qaeda and its affiliates in those countries. In another example of the expansion of Administration counterterrorism efforts, a CIA-controlled unmanned Predator aircraft patrolling the skies over Yemen launched a Hellfire missile that killed six members of al-Qaeda. This attack demonstrated Bush's willingness to employ "any and all means" to achieve the President's objective: a post-September 11 world free from the threat of terrorism.[32] The rhetoric notwithstanding, the Administration success in the first term dissipated as al-Qaeda regrouped in Afghanistan. To confront cross border raids by Taliban and its growing strength in several areas of the country, President Bush was forced to increase the American military presence in Afghanistan. Thus a once promising legacy in Afghanistan became one that was decidedly mixed. On another front, in the beginning of the War on Terror Pakistan was dubbed "an indispensible ally"; however, prior to the close of the Bush Presidency the verities were far different. To qualify this statement, al-Qaeda established a new operational base in the Federally Administered Tribal Areas (FATA), which forced President Bush to increase US unmanned drone attacks on targets throughout the region. In another illustration of the changing realities, the Taliban controlled the Swat Valley, once a major source of tourism for the Pakistani Government, but now a place replete with chaos. In the end, an opportunity for a grand legacy in the War on Terror gave way to new realities which recognized that by shifting focus to Iraq both Pakistan and Afghanistan became conspicuous fronts that remain in flux.

---

31   Bush (2001b), op. cit. fn. 11.

32   Risen, J. and Miller, J. (2002), "CIA is Reported to Kill a Leader of Qaeda in Yemen," *The New York Times* (November 5).

Conclusion

In October of 2002 President Bush uttered the words "this is personal." Ultimately, these words symbolize several aspects of his legacy. Whether known or calculated, it is clear that since the commencement of the War on Terror—with respect to the three areas, stability in the international system, Iraq, and terrorism—a connection exists between the 41st and 43rd Presidents of the United States.

In lieu of the aforementioned connections, how then do we evaluate Bush's legacy? With the second Bush Presidency over, it is now appropriate to make a more definitive assessment. The assessments link stability in the international system, confronting Iraq and the War on Terror. The research has established a relationship between the two Presidencies and these factors, leaving the investigator with a quandary. On the one hand, with respect to the War on Terror, evidence supports the contention that the younger Bush had a proven strategy. Moreover, true to his word, the President conducted a campaign of global reach. However, there are a number of necessary qualifications that should be made. In the case of the search for stability within the post-September 11 international order, President Bush enlisted imagery in defining the parameters of the world that the Administration attempted to construct, absent the threat posed by international terrorism. As envisioned by the President, that world never materialized.

On the subject of Iraq, as the leading threat within the "axis of evil," the Administration focused global attention on ridding the world of Saddam and his alleged stockpile of WMDs. It is clear now that the center of gravity of the President's strategy was constructed on distortions of the truth and faulty intelligence. These failures produced two backlashes for the younger Bush. His credibility was forever questioned and the moral authority to conduct the War on Terror had dissipated.

With respect to the last area of focus, the War on Terror, the Administration, even with notable setbacks, exceeded expectations. Though the President spoke of a campaign of global reach, few took Bush at his word, or expected that terrorism would end. The introduction of US Special Forces in the Philippines, Georgia and Yemen produced the desired outcomes—the containment and dispersal of al-Qaeda and its affiliated organizations. Consistent with this point, the US President deployed SOFs to Africa and created two highly successful coalitions. The Combined Joint Task Force in the Horn of Africa (CJTF-HOA) and the Trans-Sahara Counterterrorism Initiative (TSCTI), along with a new regional command structure, Africa Command (AFRICOM), succeeded in ways unanticipated by Administration strategists.

Thinking globally, the "four pronged" strategy—the combined use of diplomacy, the requirement for global cooperation in intelligence and law enforcement, along with the sustained and purposeful use of force (except in the case of Iraq)—proved highly productive and resulted in an opportunity fulfilled.

Finally, the irony of this research endeavor is that in the final analysis, Bush's legacy is linked to that of his father. As the study identified, a clear linkage exists between the policies of the father and the son. In each area, the son benefited from the mistakes and successes of the father. This is true except in the case of the Iraq War, where Bush's inability to implement strategy that adapted to the admonitions of his father resulted in unnecessary US military and Iraqi civilian casualties. In the end, with success in two of the three areas discussed in this chapter, Bush redefined his father's legacy. This leads to a concluding paradox: the current results in the Iraq War serve as a barometer for the younger Bush's legacy. Certain of victory, Republicans inside and outside the Administration predicted approval ratings reminiscent of the elder Bush and that US forces would be welcomed as liberators. Unfortunately, many of the architects of the Iraq War strategy failed to understand the realistic situation on the ground in Iraq and they lacked an understanding of the impact that a US occupation of an Arab country would have within the region. Like his father, the younger Bush's approval ratings may have been high during the military phase of operations, but with the postwar realities, the rapid decline of the securing environment along with the increase in US and Iraqi casualties dramatically affected the President's approval ratings. According to a *CBS News/New York Times* poll, Mr. Bush's final approval rating had dropped to 22 percent. The poll results for President George W. Bush are among the worst in the history of American Presidents. In the end, an historic opportunity for young Bush was lost in Iraq. That is, the complete victory sought by Bush for his father and for himself is now a matter that will be determined by his successor President Obama.

Chapter 8

The Evolution of Homeland Security and the War on Terror

Neil Reedy and Justin Miller

Introduction

Two months after the September 11 attacks, Attorney General John Ashcroft asserted that, "The chief mission of US law enforcement … is to stop another attack and apprehend any accomplices or terrorists before they hit us again. If we can't bring them to trial, so be it."[1] Thus began the modern era of homeland security. Through all the reorganizations, criticisms, and late night jokes about colored alert levels, Ashcroft's November 2001 words to Federal Bureau of Investigation (FBI) Director Robert Mueller illustrate the post-9/11 domestic security environment. What a shock this must have been for Director Mueller to hear given his US Attorney background and the Bureau's culture of evidence collection for prosecution. Ashcroft's message was clear—the mission of US homeland security was the prevention of additional terrorist attacks at all costs.

The history of homeland security is surprisingly rich, spanning throughout the United States, which provides insight into its current structure. Similar to the post-9/11 reaction, most security strategies were shaped by events such as the movement for American Independence and the Second World War. Ironically, homeland security and defense have not always been strengthened by the concurrent US rise to primacy, which is demonstrated by US support of the mujahedeen in the 1980s to counter the Soviet invasion of Afghanistan, and the later al-Qaeda attacks against US interests. From an enemy standpoint, as US prominence and influence grows, so does its target.

Today, US homeland security policy is still largely focused on responding to terrorism, even after the failed response to Hurricane Katrina. The response to homeland threats planned after 9/11 reflects Ashcroft's philosophy of prevention at all costs. In battling enemies and organizational challenges, US homeland security efforts exemplify historical changes and shed light on the current state of America's War on Terror.

---

1   Woodward, B. (2002), *Bush At War*, New York: Simon & Schuster, 42–43.

Homeland Security and Terrorism

Assessments of homeland security and terrorism will vary based on numerous definitions. Nearly all scholarly works on these topics include sections entitled "What is Homeland Security?" and "What is Terrorism?" suggesting these terms are largely subjective, and no one definition will please every critic. Regarding terrorism, the "one man's terrorist is another man's freedom fighter" phrase, though vastly over-used, rings true. Definitions of terrorism also vary based on cultures, some of which do not recognize a distinction between terrorism and murder, and thus do not implement a specific mechanism to combat the terrorist threat at the state level while relying on methods used to apprehend the typical murderer. Military actions overseas are generally justified as defense of the homeland, but "homeland security" generally refers to domestic efforts to protect the homeland from attack.

For the purposes of this chapter, we will base our assessment of homeland security on US Government definitions, since it is the US Government we will be evaluating. Terrorism is defined as "violent acts designed to intimidate or coerce a government or civilian population in furtherance of political or social objectives."[2] Homeland security is defined as "a concerted national effort to prevent terrorist attacks within the United States, reduce America's vulnerability to terrorism, and minimize the damage and recover from attacks that do occur."[3] These definitions, though arguably incomplete, emphasize the US priority of preventing another attack similar to 9/11. Although Hurricane Katrina vastly contributed to a changed understanding of what homeland security should entail, terrorism is still the US Government's top focus. Our assessment will look at the evolution of homeland security throughout American history, the creation of the Department of Homeland Security (DHS), and those agencies charged with defense of the homeland.

The Evolution of American Homeland Security

Though not called "homeland security" until recently, America historically developed a diverse set of strategies and policies (both foreign and domestic) crafted to prevent and mitigate threats to the homeland relevant to certain time periods. The US often chose between two strategies: the actual defense and security of the homeland (that is, strengthening and protecting borders, ports, and territory within the US) and engaging its enemies abroad. As America grew, its security strategies were more often directed towards the latter, probably since external forces were responsible for two major attacks—the burning of the White House

---

2 Department of Justice, Federal Bureau of Investigation, *Terrorism 2002–2005*, [online]; available at http://www.fbi.gov/publications/terror/terrorism2002_2005.pdf.

3 Homeland Security Council, *National Strategy for Homeland Security*, October 2007, online at http://www.fbi.gov/publications/terror/terrorism2002_2005.pdf.

in 1814 and the attack on Pearl Harbor in 1941—while historically, America's foreign installations were threatened or attacked more frequently. The September 11 attack was the catalyst for an unparalleled security reorganization recognizing the necessity to synthesize and coordinate both of these strategies.

Notions of security in government were prevalent throughout writings of philosophers who influenced the American founding. According to Thomas Hobbes, security is the most fundamental good a state can provide.[4] Richard Ullman furthers Hobbes's conception of security arguing "a citizen looks to the state, therefore, for protection against [foreign and domestic] threat[s]."[5]

The federal framework outlined in the US Constitution assigns the Government the task of providing "for the common defense," meaning the actual defense from foreign invasion or aggression. The tenth amendment provides significant power to the states which is problematic due to the number of state and local actors involved in homeland security. Morton Grodzins indicates federalism "divide[s] decisions and functions of government" which "mixes" functions in the system, as designed by the American founding.[6] This leaves state and localities to "take important formal responsibilities in the development of national programs [such as] civil defence."[7] Each system component serves its own priorities which creates difficulty in implementing a coherent national homeland security strategy based upon national priorities.

Ultimately, three eras in American history helped shape homeland security into its current post-9/11 structure: Post-American Independence, events before and after the Second World War, and Post-Cold War America.

Post-American Independence

After the American War of Independence (1775–1783), fearing the centralized control favored by the British, the US elected to rule under a loose confederation of states created under the Articles of Confederation. This model enabled the US to maintain the authority and legitimacy of an autonomous state in foreign conflict while the individual states within had mechanisms to act independently and secure their own interests. As a result, threats to US homeland security at the time would likely come from within. From 1783 to 1789, the Articles of Confederation failed to ensure federal control over the states. Several states' economies went into decline, rebellion erupted in Massachusetts, and tensions grew between states as

---

4   Ullman, R.H. (1983), "Redefining Security," *International Security* 8/1 (Summer): 130.
5   Ibid.
6   Grodzins, M. (2000), "The Federal System," in O'Toole, L.J., Jr. (ed.), *American Intergovernmental Relations: Foundations, Perspectives, and Issues*, 3rd edn, Washington, DC: CQ Press.
7   Ibid.

the different tariff rules led to a reduction in trade.[8] Despite providing the authority to declare war, send and receive Ambassadors, and conclude treaties, the Articles of Confederation could do little else to curtail internal conflict, inevitably weakening homeland defense.

The Constitutional Convention (1787) established America's most fundamental security apparatus. Stephen Krasner refers to the Constitution as uniquely bridging sovereignty and security:

> The principles of justice, and especially order, so valued by Bodin and Hobbes, have best been provided by modern democratic states whose organizing principles are antithetical to the idea that sovereignty means uncontrolled domestic power.[9]

The Constitution sets the precedent that sovereignty could be achieved without a dictatorship. Separation of powers and the system of checks and balances gave the Government legitimate authority it needed to implement sovereign control. The new Government quickly achieved international credibility through this system. The experiment of the Articles of Confederation and the creation of the US Constitution laid the legal groundwork for homeland security in the US.

Pre- and Post-Second World War

The public attitude leading up to US involvement in the Second World War reflected apathy towards security debates and a preference for isolationism due in part to the concern over the Great Depression.[10] President Roosevelt remained neutral prior to the start of the Second World War stating the following in a letter to then German Chancellor Hitler:

> The Government of the US has no political involvements in Europe, and will assume no obligations in the conduct of present negotiations … The conscience and the impelling desire of the people of my country demand that the voice of their government be raised again and yet again to avert and to avoid war.[11]

---

8   Papp, D.S., Johnson, L.K. and Endicott, J.E. (2005), *American Foreign Policy: History, Politics, and Policy*, New York: Pearson Education, Inc., 72.

9   Krasner, S.D. (2001), "Sovereignty," *Foreign Policy* 122 (January–February), 21.

10   Sauter, M.A. and Carafano, J.J. (2005), *Homeland Security: A Complete Guide to Understanding, Preventing, and Surviving Terrorism*, New York: McGraw-Hill Companies, 13.

11   Franklin D. Roosevelt, Washington, DC, to Adolf Hitler, Berlin, Germany, September 27, 1938, "Letter to Adolf Hitler Seeking Peace," *The American Presidency Project* [online], University of California, online at http://www.Presidency.ucsb.edu/ws/index.php?pid=15544&st=&st1=.

The Japanese Navy's 1941 attack on Pearl Harbor quickly changed this perspective as geographic isolation was no longer an adequate strategy against foreign threats. Reassessing security, the US began a two-part strategy to protect the homeland. First, the US engaged the Axis powers militarily in Africa, Europe, and Asia from 1941 to 1945. Second, the US responded domestically, ordering the evacuation of over 100,000 persons of Japanese ancestry, purportedly to preclude acts of sabotage and spying. The FBI also played an active role in limiting domestic threats, including preventing sabotage by four German spies in New York and Florida.[12] Additionally, the FBI aided the newly formed Office of Strategic Services (OSS) by collecting intelligence on Axis powers in Latin America through their newly assembled group of Special Intelligence Service agents. This relationship between domestic and foreign agencies led to the creation of the Central Intelligence Agency (CIA) and encouraged similar collaboration throughout the beginning of the Cold War.[13]

Following the defeat of the Axis powers in the Second World War, the US was propelled into a conflict with the Soviet Union. Engaging their communist rival domestically and abroad, the US battled both ideology and the threat of nuclear war. American national security became preeminent, but also utilized homeland defensive measures to support its framework, shown by FBI investigations of alleged communist affiliates in the US balanced with the foreign-driven initiatives to curb communist expansion.[14] In the late 1950s, Soviet threats to US national interests, such as their first nuclear weapon test, their launching of Sputnik, and the Cuban Missile Crisis shifted America's security strategies. These became more concerned with foreign policy than domestic protection. United States diplomat George Kennan, in his famous "X Article," explained that the only way to limit or mitigate these threats was to apply counter–pressure where needed to contain Soviet interests.[15] American Presidents crafted numerous foreign policies during the Cold War era that overshadowed all other US security priorities. The containment strategy became the sole means of providing security for the US Every American President from Truman through George H.W. Bush followed Kennan's prescription.[16] Although there was never a direct conflict between the US and the Soviet Union, this immersion and focus into foreign affairs would further domestic vulnerability.

The immediate Second World War era saw a good amount of collaboration between foreign and domestic efforts to protect the homeland. As the Cold War emerged, foreign policy once again dominated as the primary strategy.

---

12   Lansford, T., Pauly, R.J., Jr. and Covarrubias, J. (2007), *To Protect and Defend: US Homeland Security Policy*, Aldershot: Ashgate Publishing, 47.
13   Ibid.
14   Ibid.
15   Papp, op. cit. fn. 8, 160.
16   Ibid.

Post-Cold War

Attacks on US domestic and foreign infrastructure during the turn of the twenty-first century rendered Cold War security doctrines of containment and deterrence obsolete. Presidents Bill Clinton and George W. Bush failed to develop coherent strategies countering these threats leading to the growth of international terrorist groups like al-Qaeda and the vulnerability of infrastructure and transportation systems. Reviewing the failures leading up to the attacks on 9/11 explains fundamental changes in the US homeland security approach.

President Clinton's approach preferred using law enforcement to combat international terrorism. After the 1993 bombing of the World Trade Center (WTC) in New York, the attack was treated as an isolated incident, strictly limiting the investigation to the FBI rather than allowing for collaboration with other intelligence agencies such as the CIA and Department of Defense (DoD).[17] While the prosecutorial efforts were highly successful in convicting multiple terrorists responsible for the attacks, they helped perpetuate the notion that law enforcement was the preferred method for handling all acts of international terrorism.[18] Perhaps the Clinton administration failed to capitalize on the opportunity to re–shape American public perception of terrorism after the prosecutions. Instead, Osama bin Laden's terrorist group, al-Qaeda, continued to grow and conduct a number of attacks against US foreign installations miles away from domestic law enforcement's domain, including embassy bombings in Nairobi, Kenya 1998; Dar-es-Salaam, Tanzania 1998; and the bombing of the USS *Cole* in 2000.[19]

Amidst these attacks, Clinton attempted to improve homeland security by forming the US Commission on National Security in the 21st Century (USCNS/21) (also called the Hart–Rudman Commission), which recommended the creation of a new independent National Homeland Security Agency to mitigate growing homeland vulnerabilities.[20] Much like earlier reports such as the Joint Chief of Staff's document, *Joint Vision 2020*, and the Quadrennial Defense Review (QDR), this effort was overlooked by the American public due to the focus on the 2000 Presidential election.[21] When President Bush took office in 2001, he also failed to act aggressively against terrorism in his first seven months in office, underestimating the value of former Director of Central Intelligence George Tenet's warning that al-Qaeda represented an "immediate" and "tremendous threat."[22] The failure to recognize these threats and encourage Government inter-agency

17　Lansford et al., op. cit. fn. 12, 50.
18　National Commission on Terrorist Attacks in the United States (2004), *The 9/11 Commission Report*, Washington, DC: GPO, 72.
19　Lansford, et al., op. cit. fn. 12, 52.
20　Papp, op. cit. fn. 8, 381.
21　Ibid.
22　Woodward, op. cit. fn. 1, 34–35. Reference made in Lansford et al., op. cit. fn. 12, 53.

cooperation set the stage for what would become the largest Governmental reorganization since 1947.[23]

Post-9/11 Response

The entire nation felt 9/11's ripple effects. The attacks opened the door to an old problem with a new name, homeland security, testing America's institutional capacity for prevention, protection, and response. A reactive system was necessary but assigning responsibility proved difficult.

The first strategy the US Government implemented was "executive order coordination"[24] allowing for more direct Presidential control and "rapid response and flexibility," that would not have been available through an initial approach of centrality.[25] On October 8, 2001, President George W. Bush signed Executive Order 13228 calling for a tremendous change in how those parties responsible for homeland defense and security collaborate, while avoiding the establishment of a centralized body. While its overall function was to coordinate the executive efforts in homeland security, the new Office of Homeland Security's strategy was to work with agencies, local governments, and private entities to combat terrorist threats and review strategies as necessary.[26] The establishment of this office signaled the beginnings of modern approaches to homeland security.

However, President Bush was unable to keep this new initiative as an exclusive executive office and about one year later Congress would gain more control when it forced the President into establishing the Department of Homeland Security (DHS). This new cabinet level department not only took over the former office but when it began its operations on January 24, 2003, it comprised 22 agencies and 170,000 people. The department included five directorates: Border and Transportation Security; Emergency Preparedness and Response; Science

---

23   Woodward, op. cit. fn. 1. National Commission on Terrorist Attacks in the United States, op. cit. fn. 18. Though Bush is believed to have criticized Clinton's terrorism strategy of aiming "cruise missiles into tents" and he was "tired of swatting flies," essentially a recognition that a broad terrorism strategy was required, his first few months in office was a basic continuation of Clinton's terrorism policy.

24   In Wise, C.R. (2002), "Organizing for Homeland Security," *Public Administration Review*, 62 (March/April), 131–44. Reference made in Perrow, C. (2006), "The Disaster after 9/11: The Department of Homeland Security and the Intelligence Reorganization," *Homeland Security Affairs* II/1 (April), 5.

25   As will be explained later one of the fundamental problems the system of homeland security is now experiencing is a delay in operations due to increased bureaucracy emanating from "centrality."

26   E.O.13228, October 2001, online at http://frwebgate.access.gpo.gov/cgibin/get doc.cgi?dbname=2001_register&docid=fr10oc01–144.pdf.

and Technology; Information Analysis and Infrastructure Protection; and the Management Directorate.[27]

The Department of Homeland Security is not the only agency responsible for providing security to the domestic homeland. In some respects, it is quite limited and takes a back seat to other more established organizations like the FBI and local law enforcement. Charles Perrow notes the initial fiscal limitations of DHS when he claims the following:

> Touted as receiving 40 billion dollars, DHS received far less in new money. One-third of the money went to other agencies such as the Pentagon, and most of the other twenty-seven billion was not new money. Five of the twenty-two agencies had a total budget of nineteen billion dollars which they brought with them, and this is counted in the 40 billion dollar figure.[28]

In commenting on other problems he also states:

> The department has had very limited success in making our vulnerable chemical and nuclear stockpiles more secure. Our borders are still so porous that it would be sheer luck if a guard happened on to a terrorist … DHS promulgates an "all-hazards" approach, hurricane Katrina in 2005 prompted inquiries that disclosed substantial funds were diverted from programs aimed at natural disasters to those focused upon terrorist attacks. First responder funds, for example, were cut.[29]

There are three other elements of the US Government that have played a role in homeland security post-9/11: the Department of Defense, the US Intelligence Community (USIC), and state and local governments. Communications between these entities and DHS is crucial. The Department of Defense has a homeland security role shown by the creation of the US Northern Command (NORTHCOM). Its creation on October 1, 2002 consolidated and implemented existing defense and civil support missions directly aimed at homeland defense. This strategy reflects the profound change in homeland security in that the US now had enacted a military combatant command to protect the territory of the US similar to the nine other commands that protect foreign interests (notably, European Command and Central Command), a clear sign that homeland defense is on par with foreign policy and international security.

---

27   "The Executive Branch," online at http://www.whitehouse.gov/our_government/executive_branch/. Further explaining DHS's growth over its short history is the fact that its personnel level has risen to 216,000. Albeit effective, another complicating aspect of DHS is that it continues to reorganize itself. As of 2009, the directorates include National Protection and Programs Directorate; Policy Directorate; Directorate of Management; and Science and Technology.

28   Perrow, op. cit. fn. 24, 11.

29   Ibid., 28.

Another issue with homeland security that received significant criticism following 9/11 was the lack of effective channels of communication among those agencies falling under the intelligence community. In order to improve this, Congress passed The Intelligence Reform and Terrorism Prevention Act of 2004. This Act's purpose was to improve communication between agencies such as the CIA and the FBI by creating an outside overseer to the intelligence community (Director of National Intelligence) and including provisions for the intelligence clearinghouse formally created within Executive Order 13354, known as the National Counterterrorism Center. The final contributor to homeland security is the state and local governments. Their diverse interests sometimes exacerbate attempts at coherent national standards; however, they are home to the emergency first responders that are tasked by the Homeland Security Act of 2002 with providing initial efforts to secure, protect, and assist at the scene.

Bureaucratic Realities

Ambitious homeland security plans, policies, and proposals are rarely implemented as intended. Despite the hyper-vigilant atmosphere and public demand for results in the post-9/11 era, a significant obstacle not linked to any terrorist organization remains: the bureaucracy. More often than not, the best intended policies fail once exposed to the administrative procedures and cultural realities entrenched in certain law enforcement and homeland security agencies. Any homeland security assessment must consider the bureaucracy as it permeates virtually everything.

Michael Kenney aptly describes the agencies responsible for implementing homeland security as "large and cumbersome, employing thousands of people organized in numerous divisions characterized by multiple management layers and Byzantine decision-making protocols."[30] Procedures, protocols, and traditional methods of doing things are all factors that can contribute to the inefficiency of bureaucratic organizations which make seemingly simple tasks daunting. The general public's positive (and often unrealistic) perception of law enforcement bears little resemblance to bureaucratic reality and also contributes to the failure to recognize the limits of certain agencies.[31] Policymakers rarely consider the ramifications of these bureaucratic entanglements when attempting to affect homeland security.

---

30   Kenney, M. (2007), *From Pablo to Osama: Trafficking and Terrorist Networks, Government Bureaucracies, and Competitive Adaptation*, University Park, PA: Pennsylvania State University, 176.

31   In recent years, the public perception and inability to understand bureaucratic procedures has had such an effect that several law enforcement officials have complained of a "CSI effect," after the popular television show, in recent court cases indicating juries routinely believe law enforcement agencies are capable of doing what they see on television. Further described in *East Valley Tribune* (Phoenix), July 1, 2005.

Kenney cites the implementation of the Foreign Intelligence Surveillance Act (FISA) as an example of bureaucracy's impact, "The judicial review process for terrorism-related electronic surveillance … remains cumbersome, requiring multiple levels of administrative review."[32] Conceding that most of these wiretap applications are eventually approved by the FISA court, Kenney argues the large numbers of requests have created logjams in the approval process that can potentially hinder counterterrorism investigations. As the example illustrates, FISA is an important tool for homeland security officials, and it remains affected by bureaucratic procedures.

Kenney's argument also applies to the various reorganizations of the FBI, in addition to the establishment of DHS. Among the factors Kenney cites as leading to bureaucratic entanglements are turf battles between agencies, and culture clashes.[33] Most notably, FBI and CIA culture clashes are most often cited as the most distinct as one agency is designed to collect, analyze, and evaluate intelligence and the other to investigate crimes which are detailed in the official 9/11 report. Since terrorism is an international enterprise, investigations inevitably cross agency lines, demanding a coherent and successful working relationship. Relations between the agencies are significantly improved since 9/11 but clashes are still apparent.

The FBI in particular has been under fire due to a lack of analytical capabilities pre- and post-9/11. These issues result in some calling for a new domestic intelligence agency modeled after the British MI5 since the FBI's law enforcement culture is ingrained so much so that it is not suited to pursue terrorist plots requiring patience and analysis. Current investigations tend to focus on collecting evidence for the purpose of admitting it in criminal trials, and law enforcement tends to prefer disruption and early preventative arrests contrasted with European counterparts who generally allow targets to come closer to operational capacity.[34] A study by the RAND Corporation indicated a new agency would include exploratory activities designed to produce new leads and tips to develop strategic understanding of threats.[35]

In response to the call for increased analytic capability, the FBI has undergone a series of organizational changes and realignments stressing comprehensive long–term analytical trends and information gathering to thwart attacks before

---

32   Kenney, op. cit. fn. 30, 186.

33   Ibid.

34   Greenberg, K.J. et al. (eds) (2006), *Terrorist Trial Report Card: US Edition*, New York: New York University Centeron Law and Security, online at http://www.lawandsecurity.org/publications/TTRCComplete.pdf.

35   Rand Corporation Research Brief, *Should the United States Establish a Dedicated Domestic Intelligence Agency for Counterterrorism?*, prepared by the RAND Corporation Homeland Security Program and the Intelligence Policy Center, online at http://www.rand.org/pubs/research_briefs/RB9369/index1.html.

they occur.[36] These reorganization efforts signal an intense long-term effort by the FBI to transform its deeply ingrained law enforcement culture into a more analytical focus. The impact on the bureau's culture is clearly a factor in the attempt to transform the focus of how FBI approaches homeland security.

The impact of culture on bureaucracy is also seen in the creation of DHS. One criticism of the proposed establishment of a US domestic MI5 is the time it would take to gain respect throughout the community. One concern of DHS is its infancy—since it does not have an established history, it has trouble gaining respect throughout the community. According to Congressional testimony, one official cited the department's "newness" as an explanation for its "lack of established relationships" and "[in] ability to quickly gain the trust and commitment of states and major cities" in implementing a project.[37]

Terrorism thrives on uncertainty and unpredictability.[38] As counterterrorism policy develops, bureaucratic realities make managing uncertainty challenging as it requires adaptation, quick thinking, and efficient processes, all anathema to bureaucracy. Kenney argues that despite a resource disadvantage, terrorists are not constrained by administrative layers and legal regulations which allow them freedom to adapt tactics, strategies, and operations giving them a sort of flexibility advantage over their pursuers. As a result, they become organizations that can rapidly exchange information and make quick decisions to effectively accomplish their goals.[39] These advantages make homeland security more challenging since officials are required to battle their own bureaucracy in addition to combating networks unaffected by an equally constraining element.

Homeland Security in the Modern Era

Bali, Riyadh, Casablanca, Jakarta, Istanbul, Madrid, London, and Islamabad have all suffered terrorist attacks on their soil since 9/11. Most of these attacks have been perpetrated by al-Qaeda or other like-minded Islamic terrorist groups. Notably, the US has not suffered a similar terrorist attack on its soil since the 9/11 attacks, begging the question, "why?" The answer may be impossible to prove with any certainty considering the following potential variables:

---

36   Jacobson, M. (2007), *Transforming US Efforts to Fight Transnational Terrorist Networks*, The Washington Institute for Near East Policy, October 24, 2007, online at http://www.washingtoninstitute.org/templateC05.php?CID=2671.

37   Congress, House, Committee on Homeland Security, Subcommittee on Intelligence, Information Sharing and Terrorism Risk Assessment, Frank Defer, Assistant Inspector General (2006), *The Homeland Security Information Network: An Update on DHS Information Sharing Network*, 109th Cong., 2nd sess., September 13, 2006, 5.

38   RAND Corporation Policy Brief, *Consequence Prevention: A New Model for Addressing Uncertainty About Terrorist Threats*, online at www.rand.org.

39   Kenney, op. cit. fn. 30, 176.

1. the successful invasion of Afghanistan could have so dismantled al-Qaeda rendering it unable to expand their reach to US soil;
2. the US invasion of Iraq could have changed the central focus of al-Qaeda's attack planning;
3. the al-Qaeda organization itself could have shifted planning to other targets for its own reasons; or
4. the hyper-vigilance of homeland security efforts could have rooted out and/ or discouraged further attacks on US soil.

Whatever the reason, the multiple attacks on global targets indicate a continued desire by al-Qaeda and like-minded organizations to conduct attacks against Western targets and their allies.

Despite no post-9/11 terrorist attack on US soil, some speculate the US is not immune from attack due to various systematic weaknesses.[40] Interestingly enough, the FBI report "Terrorism 2002–2005," indicates that *domestic* terrorism accounts for the majority of terrorist *incidents* during the period, what Sauter and Carafano call "the forgotten threat."[41] The FBI indicates that this is a longstanding trend with most attacks committed by animal rights and environmental activists. Distinguishing from international terrorism, domestic terrorism is based and operated entirely within the US or Puerto Rico, typically targeting materials and facilities rather than persons. Given the scale of 9/11, which targeted both facilities *and* civilians, it is understandable that the focus is more on international groups given their goals and trends of conducting significantly larger–scale attacks. In addition to the continued domestic terrorism threat, US security agencies actively work to prevent additional attacks on the homeland in the post-9/11 era.

Legal Tools

The hyper-vigilance post-9/11 has produced an interesting trend in the legal environment. An analysis of terrorism trials from 2001 through 2007 was conducted by NYU's Center on Law and Security which argues the trials show an emphasis on prevention and disruption on the part of the Government's homeland security efforts. They argue that despite President Bush's rhetoric that the courtroom is not where battles against terrorism should be fought, the Bush administration has used the Department of Justice (DOJ) effectively to prosecute suspects linked to terrorist activity. The DOJ has used more than 100 different federal laws, many of which were enacted before the USA PATRIOT act. The arrests examined were part of a terrorism–related investigation (that is, the defendants weren't necessarily initially charged with terrorism offenses). In fact, the Center indicates that in two thirds of the cases studied, terrorism charges were never brought. The reason for this varies, but can include secret plea agreements, defendants as cooperating

---

40   Meyer, J. (2007), "Post-9/11: We are Not Safe," *Los Angeles Times*, November 1.
41   Department of Justice, Federal Bureau of Investigation, op. cit. fn. 2.

witnesses or the Government's unwillingness to divulge an intelligence method at trial. The Government may argue for a terrorism sentencing enhancement after the facts are proven and a conviction has been given. This enhanced flexibility provides the most opportunities for creative convictions of terrorists based on the "get them at any costs" Ashcroft doctrine.

Prevention is the clear priority of the US as shown by the FBI preference to disrupt plots when suspects are far from achieving objectives. This strategy has drawn criticism from some, as European counterparts are more likely to let suspects run their plans to uncover previously unknown information.

International cooperation

New York University indicates the highest profile plots were not on US soil which suggests a need for US Government cooperation with foreign entities. Arguing military force alone is too "blunt" an instrument to fight terrorism, Seth Jones and Martin Libicki of the RAND Corporation argue for using "police intelligence" as a new strategy to fight terrorism.[42] Jones and Libicki argue local police elements are best suited to deal with terrorism issues since they know the culture, customs, and practices of the local population better than outsiders. They also cite that US Government successes against al-Qaeda were basically the result of good police work indicating how international police cooperation has been a crucial tool in combating terrorism post-9/11 including the capture of key leaders.[43] Increased cooperation and interaction with foreign countries also contributed to US Government success in terrorist financing which was one of the few areas deemed successful by the 9/11 Commission's 2005 report card. International cooperation between the US and allied governments has been a remarkable success in combating terrorist threats against the homeland since 9/11.

Are these tools effective? It is certainly difficult to tell due to the short and long–term implications of preemptive incarceration. Could US law enforcement's quick reactions hinder further intelligence collection? The debate between prevention and punishment is significant, and continues.

War on Terror Today

Increased vigilance post-9/11, creative use of the legal system, and international cooperation led to the detection of a number of attempts to attack the US homeland. The plots attempted shed light on the current state of the War on Terror and a shift from the threat in the immediate 9/11 aftermath.

---

42 Jones, S. and Libicki, M.C. (2008), *How Terrorist Groups End: Lessons for Countering Al Qa'ida*, Santa Monica: RAND Corporation, 125–139.
43 Ibid.

Plots

James Jay Carafano of the Heritage Foundation compiled a list of 19 terrorist attacks thwarted by the US since 9/11. These plots were attempts by individuals and/or groups to attack the US homeland and were identified by US law enforcement authorities and prosecuted (or are awaiting prosecution). Examining some of the plots and the law enforcement efforts to thwart and prosecute them provides insight into US homeland security efforts since 9/11. As one goal of the National Strategy for Combating Terrorism is to "prevent attacks by terrorist networks," looking at prevented attacks will judge how well the US Government accomplishes its stated objectives.

Carafano's plots were predominantly attempted by Islamic radicals, some of whom were convincingly linked to the al-Qaeda organization. Similar to the attacks in foreign capitals, these plot attempts show the continued desire by like-minded individuals, such as those who conducted the 9/11 attacks, to attack the West. Broadly speaking, the attacks can be divided into two categories: al-Qaeda planned and al-Qaeda inspired.

Al-Qaeda Planned Attack Attempts

The first category of thwarted attacks includes those perpetrated by individuals who had convincing links to the al-Qaeda organization.[44] Richard Reid's December 2001 attempt to explode an airplane with a shoe bomb, Jose Padilla's alleged attempt to use a "dirty bomb" in the US (arrested May 2002), the "Lackawanna Six" conspiring with terrorist organizations (arrested October 2002), Dhiren Barot's alleged attempt to attack the New York Stock Exchange and other financial targets (arrested August 2004), Hamid Hayat's alleged attempt to attack US supermarkets and hospitals (arrested June 2005), and the plot to explode multiple airplanes headed to the US from Europe in August 2006, are all examples of plots attempted by individuals with convincing links to the al-Qaeda organization.[45] In all of these instances, the plotter or a member of the group attended an al-Qaeda training camp, in some cases meeting with Osama Bin Laden himself.

These individuals attempted plots directed by, or were arrested for being members of and/or supporting the al-Qaeda organization. A top priority for

---

44   Defining an individual as "member" of al-Qaeda is a difficult enterprise. Experts feel the true measure is swearing a loyalty oath to Osama bin Laden usually, although many well-known al-Qaeda terrorists like Khalid Sheih Mohamed and Ramzi Yousef never did such, but their strong links would undeniably classify them as al-Qaeda. See Sageman op. cit. fn. 53; and Wright, R. (2001), *Sacred Rage: The Wrath of Militant Islam*, New York and London: Simon & Schuster for further discussion. For purposes of this chapter, those with strong links to al-Qaeda are called "al-Qaeda affiliates."

45   Profiles of these individuals available online at http://www.globalsecurity.org/security.htm.

homeland security after the 9/11 attacks was to pursue al-Qaeda affiliates, especially those who may be plotting attacks against the US homeland. Also a factor was the Government's aggressive (and later controversial) terrorism policy abroad which, according to former Bush Administration officials, was a significant factor in preventing future attacks.[46] The al-Qaeda affiliate plots indicate a preference for using planes and attacking high-profile targets on the US homeland, similar in philosophy to the 9/11 attack (which used both).

Al-Qaeda Inspired Attack Attempts

More recent attack plots and arrests in the al-Qaeda inspired category show a different trend. Syed Haris Ahmed and Ehsanul Islam Sadequee surveilled Washington, DC-area landmarks in April 2006,[47] the plot against Fort Dix in New Jersey involved youths training in the mountains with paintball guns, the plot to blow up a jet fuel artery at JFK airport in June 2007,[48] and the Sears Tower plot in June 2006,[49] all involve young individuals who were more inspired by al-Qaeda's ideology but who did not necessarily have connections to the organization. As indicated by the following Joint FBI–DHS Bulletin, these plots are uncoordinated acts by ideologically inspired groups:

> The arrests of [the Fort Dix plotters] illustrates the continuing threat posed by homegrown Islamic extremists that are inspired by global jihad to plan attacks, but do not necessarily receive direct guidance from any overseas terrorist organizations ... these cells [plotting recent attacks in the homeland] identify generally with the ideas and goals of the global jihadist movement led by Usama

---

46   This speech goes into surprising detail about techniques used by intelligence officials to thwart a number of attacks planned from overseas. Though clearly an element of homeland security, for purposes of this chapter, incidents like these and other similar actions (by the military for example) are not included in this analysis for space concerns. Also see writings of former Bush Administration official Marc Theissen (2009), "The CIA's Questioning Worked," *The Washington Post*, online at http://www.washingtonpost.com/wp-dyn/content/article/2009/04/20/AR2009042002818.html.

47   Becker, M. and Zremski, J. (2006), "Toronto Cell's Extended Internationally: Arrests in Britain Underlie Global Web," *Global Security*, June 8, online at http://www.globalsecurity.org/org/news/2006/060608-toronto-cell.htm.

48   Kruzel, J.J. (2007), "Six Arrested for Plotting to Kill Soldiers at Fort Dix, N.J.," *Global Security*, May 8, online at http://www.globalsecurity.org/security/library/news/2007/05/sec-070508-afps02.htm.

49   Mckeeby, D. (2006), "Seven US Terror Suspects Seeking al-Qaida Support Arrested," *Global Security*, June 23, online at http://www.globalsecurity.org/security/library/news/2006/06/sec-060623-usia02.htm.

bin laden, and draw inspiration from the al-Qai'da message, but there is no evidence they receive direct guidance or instructions from its leadership.[50]

These plots signal a new trend apparent in the war on terror that combines with the "traditional" al-Qaeda adding a new significant challenge to post-9/11 security efforts.

Al-Qaeda as a Movement

Demonstrated by the plots described, US homeland security today faces two primary challenges—identifying operatives connected to the al-Qaeda organization, and thwarting ideologically-inspired plots of like-minded actors. The difficulty of combating homegrown attack plots is similar to how former DCI James Woolsey put it after the Soviet Union collapsed, "we'd fought this dragon for 40 years and killed him, the Soviet Union, and now found ourselves in a jungle full of a lot of poisonous snakes, and the snakes could kill you, and they were very hard to keep track of, snakes like rogue regimes and weapons of mass destruction and terrorism."[51] Al-Qaeda is the dragon (though not slain) and the hard to keep track of snakes are the homegrown extremists. As FBI spokesman John Miller suggests, this is part of al-Qaeda's current strategy:

> Al Qaida has tried to put the message out to get others to step forward ... and do things in its name. I think what al-Qaida is counting on now ... is trying to develop and execute the major [attack] plan while at the same time putting out the propaganda fodder and hoping that others will take that ball and run with it.[52]

This trend shown by recent plot attempts adds another dynamic to the War on Terror today. Young Muslims throughout Western society have shown increased radicalization in recent years. Polling from the Pew Research Center indicates Muslims in Europe are more likely than Muslims in the US to support Islamic extremism and suicide bombings. The rates are even higher for European Muslim youths, who are the core of the al-Qaeda inspired group. This trend makes rooting out terrorism more difficult for homeland security officials since many of these

---

50   Joint DHS/FBI Security Assessment (2007), "Fort Dix Plot Illustrates Continuing Threat Posed By Homegrown Islamic Extremist," June 4, online at http://www.boma.org/Advocacy/SafetyAndEmergencyPlanning/Alerts/isac082907c.htm.

51   Woosley, J. (2003), interview by Brian Williams, "James Woosley Discusses CIA's Role in Fighting Terrorism," April 30, online at http://www.defenddemocracy.org/index.php?option=com_content&task=view&id=11772180&Itemid=346.

52   Meek, J. (2007), "FBI Claims 'High Tempo of Terrorist Activity'," *The Washington Bureau*, May 31, online at http://www.nydailynews.com/blogs/dc/2007/05/fbi-claims-high-tempo-of-terro.html.

radical youths are essentially freelancers not linked to an established terrorist network. Despite these findings, US homeland security priorities must still focus on extremism at home and abroad: both the 2006 Planes Plot and 9/11 were planned almost exclusively in overseas environments.

Marc Sageman argues in *Leaderless Jihad* that despite US-led efforts in Afghanistan, the "al-Qaeda central" organization which includes bin Laden and Zawahiri's terrorist organization, remains bruised but intact, but what has followed has been a global social movement, or rallying call around Islamic extremist identity.[53] As indicated by John Miller's quote, the suspects of the Fort Dix plot couldn't contact bin Laden if they wanted to, but they were still inspired by al-Qaeda ideology and acted to commit terrorist acts.

Sageman's argument is essentially the current state of the War on Terror—combating a global ideological movement from attacking Western interests. US homeland security has successfully combated "al-Qaeda central" in the initial invasion of Afghanistan, but they must now counter the threat of an attack planned by both the original organization (still clearly intent on inflicting more mass casualties on US soil), but also the homegrown, al-Qaeda-inspired groups which often are not part of any known terrorist network.[54] Since the US cannot prevent every form of terrorist attack from occurring, this poses a significant challenge which must include traditional law enforcement tools of information sharing with appropriate partners inside and outside the country but also crucial outreach efforts to diaspora communities within the US in order to gain cooperation and potentially root out future threats.

The Future of Homeland Security and the War on Terror

Former Secretary of State Condoleezza Rice has argued that the Bush Administration's foreign policy approach reflected a blend of realism and idealism, instead of choosing one philosophy over the other. Similarly, homeland security efforts after 9/11 suggest homeland defense and foreign policy should be intertwined and coordinated, not separate and distinct. The fact that distinguishing "homeland" security from foreign policy is difficult is perhaps a good thing because it is an implicit recognition that one cannot exist without the other.

As shown by the evolution of the al-Qaeda threat, US homeland security efforts would be wise to be flexible enough to adapt to ever-changing situations. In recent years the threat is likely to drastically change from the status quo to something perhaps unanticipated. Only a nimble effort free from bureaucratic entanglements, working together with its multiple partners, will succeed in giving the US true security of the homeland.

---

53   Sageman, op. cit. fn. 44, 29–46.
54   Ibid., 71–88.

PART 3
Foreign Policy Implications

Chapter 9

The Middle East Peace Process after 9/11

Vaughn P. Shannon

Introduction

In 2001, George W. Bush inherited a stalled peace process in the Arab–Israeli dispute, as well as related renewed violence in the area. For several months, the new US President did not appear interested in getting involved in the perennial Middle East dispute. Events on September 11 changed everything in US foreign policy, including its approach to the Arab–Israeli conflict. The priority of addressing global terror threats on the US and its assets forced a renewed effort to win regional allies to aid in such a mission. Many of those allies in the Arab world sought movement on the peace process in order to give aid in the US agenda. Under such strategic circumstances, the US had put the cause of a Palestinian state at the brink of reality—a phenomenal event in regional and world affairs, if it actually comes about.

But the same strategic circumstances prodding the US toward this position of sympathy for the Palestinians also served as a constraint. The amount of Palestinian violence toward Israeli targets that can be defined as terrorism—for our purposes, premeditated, politically motivated violence perpetrated against noncombatant targets by subnational groups or clandestine agents, usually intended to influence a target[1]—was quite high in the initial years of the newest intifada begun in September 2000. This fact makes it difficult for a President "fighting terrorism" to get too close to those in the cause. Though Arafat denied involvement or endorsement of terrorist activities, he was seen as either unable or unwilling to stop terrorism and thus part of the problem.

Yet even after Arafat, the US did not make a priority out of achieving a solution until the end of the Bush Presidency. From a "Road Map" to peace with insurmountable hurdles, to Bush's green light to a new Israeli vision for unilateral disengagement, the Bush Administration exhibited great empathy for Israel's own "War on Terror," which effectively stalled the momentum of any plan for a Palestinian state. Bush also permitted, if not encouraged, Israeli wars on neighboring Hezbollah and Hamas

---

1 This definition is that of the US government (see Pillar, P.R. (2001), *Terrorism and US Foreign Policy*, Washington, DC: Brookings Institute, 13). While terrorism is a contested concept, this definition focusing on terror as a method is a useful approach that I employ in this chapter.

forces in 2006 and 2008, partly out of concern that the post-Saddam Middle East tilted the balance of power toward Iran and its proxies.

This chapter analyzes Bush policy toward the Arab–Israeli conflict in relation to the American "War on Terror." In 2003, I argued that a "balancing act" was struck between strategic needs for Arab and Muslim support for the War on Terror and the strategic and domestic pressures to support Israel and avoid appearing supportive of terror.[2] This tension, which I had found pervasive in US policy toward the conflict for decades, perpetuates inaction but also permits the possibility of innovation. Yet it seems any semblance of balance gave way to an Israel-first approach from 2003 through the remainder of Bush's tenure in office. With domestic reasons to back Israel already firm in not only the "Jewish lobby" but Bush's own Christian evangelical base, Bush also found Israel to share the US worldview for the region. From Bush's plans to oust Saddam Hussein, and—once his regime was gone—for containing if not attacking Iran, Bush found little sympathy from regional neighbors, but a symmetry of vision with Israeli counterparts.

I first discuss the context of US policy toward the Arab–Israeli conflict, then examine how the Bush Administration balanced domestic and strategic considerations after the events of 9/11, from the campaign in Afghanistan to the war against Iraq in the spring of 2003. I then elaborate on the "end of balance" from 2003–2008, and conclude with a call to "restore the balance," discussing the implications of US policy for the Obama Administration as it contemplates the Arab–Israeli equation.

US Policy and the Arab–Israeli Dispute: Domestic and Strategic Balancing Act

The Arab–Israeli conflict has been summarized thus: "At the heart of the problem is the Jews' sense of insecurity and the Arabs' feeling of injustice and dispossession."[3] There are several components to the Arab–Israeli conflict—that of the Zionist effort to establish statehood in friction against competing Arab interests in the area of Palestine; that subsequent conflict between the state of Israel and the Palestinian nationalist movement; and that conflict between Israel and its Arab and Muslim neighbors in the region. Since achieving statehood in 1948, Israel faced immediate and enduring hostility that, in conjunction with a history of persecution, has bred intense feelings of insecurity about its existence and safety in the years since. To the degree that insecurity brings occupation (for

---

2   This term is the title of a book analyzing US policy toward the Arab–Israeli conflict over time. See Shannon, V. (2003), *Balancing Act: US Foreign Policy and the Arab–Israeli Conflict*, Aldershot: Ashgate Publishing. Some sections of that book have been reprinted here.

3   Ball, G.W. and Ball, D.B. (1992), *The Passionate Attachment: America's Involvement with Israel, 1947–Present*, New York: W.W. Norton, 11.

"buffer zones" or "strategic depth") of Palestinian-filled lands in the West Bank and Gaza, the result is increased resentment by those under the permanent military rule of Israel: the Palestinian people. Each side feels the other "started it," and each side feels they are merely responding to aggression with resistance.[4]

As a whole, the Arab–Israeli conflict is essentially the battle for legitimate control over the area known as Palestine, as defined by the current state of Israel, the city of Jerusalem, and the occupied territories. The 1948 War for Palestine, and subsequent wars and negotiations, are reduced to this fundamental issue: who rules which parts of this area known as Palestine? Do the Jews get it all? Do the Arabs get it all? Do they share, and if so in what proportion? Importantly, would the answer to these questions be accepted by relevant parties? Control without legitimacy is coercion or occupation, and is likely to perpetuate hostilities as we see in the Gaza Strip and the West Bank today. What role does the United States play in determining these other questions?

The US position on the conflict has been tugged and pulled by the strategic interest of regional oil access and the domestic interest in support for Israel, leading to decades of a balancing act between pro-Israel sympathies and sensitivity to Arab opinion.[5] The result has been an awkward, situationally-driven patchwork of actions that leaves frustrated observers on both sides to claim "the United States does not have a Middle East policy."[6] I next will elaborate on the strategic and domestic factors that influence US policy, and discuss the implications for policy that result.

Strategic Influences

From a theoretical standpoint of realism, the dominant approach to international relations analysis, states define threats to security and interests, and pursue power and policies aimed at increasing influence and reducing such threats.[7] There are

---

4 On these images, see Heradstveit, D. (1979), *The Arab–Israeli Conflict: Psychological Obstacles to Peace*, New York: Columbia University Press and Shipler, D.K. (1986), *Arab and Jew: Wounded Spirits in a Promised Land*, New York: Penguin Books. For a look at Arab views, see also Harkabi, Y. (1972), *Arab Attitudes to Israel*, New York: Hart Publishing and Daniel Pipes (1998), *The Hidden Hand: Middle East Fears of Conspiracy*, New York: St. Martin's, the latter of which goes so far to say that "conspiratorial anti-Semitism and overwrought fears of Israeli expansionism perpetuate the Arab–Israeli confrontation" (28).

5 The "national interest" versus domestic interest contrast is made by many works, including Spiegel, S. (1985), *The Other Arab–Israeli Conflict*, Chicago: University of Chicago Press; Ball and Ball, op. cit. fn. 3; and Ben-Zvi, A. (1993), *The United States and Israel: The Limits of the Special Relationship*, New York: Columbia University Press.

6 Young, R.J. (1986), *Missed Opportunities for Peace: US Middle East Policy*, Philadelphia: American Friends' Service Committee, 7.

7 For the seminal realist statement, see Morgenthau, H.J. (1978), *Politics Among Nations*, New York: Knopf. For a discussion of the "strategic" or "national interest" approach

two general US strategic concerns in the Middle East: geopolitical stability and terrorism. Perceived threats to vital regions, resources, allies—those things that sustain state power—are an important determinant of policy.[8] The "Great Game" has been well documented in history, as world powers vied for control of vital trade routes, sea lanes, and oilfields in the Middle East.[9] Out of concern for relative position and the security and prosperity of the state, the argument here is that the US and others would seek to confront threats and safeguard those material resources deemed vital. In the case of the Middle East, oil is that resource, and one constant of US policy underlying its approach to the Arab–Israeli conflict is the determination to maintain the stability of the region and promote the free flow of fair-priced oil from the Gulf.[10]

After 9/11 particularly, a second strategic priority has been the pursuit and disruption of terrorist networks with "global reach," especially but not exclusively al-Qaeda. Confronting the capabilities and causes of terror in the region presents the US with new motivation to bolster relationships in the region for intelligence, law enforcement and military action. Much of this chapter, then, is dedicated to that process.

Domestic Influences

Others have shown the power of domestic politics explaining US policy. The source of domestic political influence comes in many forms, but can be summarized by institutional and societal inputs: Congressional-Executive relations, interest groups, and broader electoral politics, as well as the decision-makers' perspectives and beliefs.

A running theme in the history of US policy in the Arab–Israeli conflict involves a pro-Zionist/pro-Israel Congress clashing with an Executive interested in balancing considerations. While Congress is subordinate to the President in power and decision-making, all executives have dealt with the reaction their

---

to the Arab–Israeli conflict, see Quandt, W.B. (1977), *Decade of Decisions: American Foreign Policy Toward the Arab–Israeli Conflict: 1967–1976*, Berkley: University of California Press, 4–15.

8   For an application of geopolitical analysis to the Middle East, see Kemp, G. and Harkavy, R.E. (1997), *Strategic Geography and the Changing Middle East*, New York: Carnegie Endowment for International Peace. See also Brzezinski, Z., Scowcroft, B. and Murphy, R.W. (1997), *Differentiated Containment*, Washington, DC: Council on Foreign Relations Press for a discussion of US enduring interests in the Middle East.

9   George Lenczowski (1980), *The Middle East in World Affairs*, Ithaca: Cornell University Press, is a classic sweeping history of international relations related to the Middle East.

10   Yergin, D. (1991), *The Prize: The Epic Quest for Oil, Money and Power*, New York: Simon & Schuster, traces the rise of oil as a vital resource from the perspective of military advantage, as well as the role of this fact in the World Wars of the twentieth century. See especially Chapters 8–10 and 16–19.

policies will have on the Hill. Most decisions about foreign relations are made in the Executive branch. Nonetheless, Congress has the will and ability to serve as a check on Presidential power on this particular issue. In lock-step behind Israel by huge margins on most any issue, the US Congress does not hesitate to produce resolutions of support and appropriations and legislation aimed at publicly declaring support for Israel and cautioning the sitting President not to stray too far from this course.

How the US Congress came to be so pro-Israel may have a lot to do with interest groups. The most noted interest group related to US foreign policy is AIPAC, the American Israel Public Affairs Committee. Its electoral connections and financial and organizational strength are unparalleled by anything constituting an "Arab" or "Palestinian" lobby. From 1978–2000, one study concludes, Israeli Political Action Committees (PACs) outspent Arab/Muslim PACs 99 to 1 in Congressional contributions.[11] The "Israel lobby" includes other groups, such as the Conference of Presidents of Major American Jewish Organizations, composed of 38 groups that formulate and express the "Jewish position" on foreign policy, including the Arab–Israeli conflict.[12]

There is a growing Arab lobby present in the United States as well, but nothing comparable. The National Association of Arab-Americans (NAAA) was founded in 1972, based on the AIPAC model.[13] Both the Council on American-Islamic Relations (CAIR) and the American Muslim Alliance (AMA) have emerged to raise awareness on issues relevant to the Islamic world. There are also related interest groups that factor in situationally-based or economic interests. Oil companies, such as the Arabian American Oil Company (ARAMCO), constitute among the earliest of formal lobbies regarding the Middle East, sympathetic to policies yielding regional stability. These different interest groups attempt to frame foreign policy in terms of American national interests when confronting US policy elites.

Beyond the formal groups, foreign policy is also influenced by the electoral politics surrounding the "informal" lobby defined as "pro-Israel" or "pro-Arab." The Jewish population in the US is about six million (roughly three percent of the total US population), for instance, and while few of these are members of formal interest groups the vast majority are considered pro-Israel in sympathies. Add to this that an estimated 90 percent of American Jews live in twelve key electoral states, such as Florida and New York, the status of pro-Israelis as a political force is consequential, with some considering it "one of the largest veto groups in the

---

11   Berggren, D.J. (2001), "The New Kid on the Bloc: Muslims Responsible for Bush Win in 2000", *Middle East Affairs Journal* 7/3–4, 155–77, 167.

12   Mearsheimer, J.J. and Walt, S.M. (2007), *The Israel Lobby and U.S. Foreign Policy*, New York: Farrar, Straus and Giroux; Bard, M. (1988), "The Influence of Ethnic Interest Groups on American Middle East Policy," in Kegley, C. and Wittkopf, E. (eds), *The Domestic Sources of American Foreign Policy*, New York: St. Martin's Press, 61.

13   Bard, ibid.

country."[14] This is particularly salient for Democrats, the traditional home of the Jewish vote. Nonetheless, candidates from both parties are susceptible to election-year concerns about courting, and not alienating, votes. As Berggren suggests, "When it comes to Israel, partisan politics stops at the water's edge. Both parties are unequivocally pro-Israel."[15]

The pro-Israel domestic influence extends past the Jewish lobby. There is a coalition of conservative Christians and neo-conservative policy-makers siding strongly with Israel on most any issue. On the religious Right, some 55 million evangelical Christians are claimed to support Israel due to a perceived "powerful spiritual connection between Israel and the Christian faith" and belief that Palestine constituted "covenant land" that God bestowed upon the Jews.[16] In response to two attacks in Tel Aviv by Palestinian terrorists in early 2003, the Christian Coalition of America (the largest Christian grassroots organization in the US) issued a statement saying "that the enemies of America and the enemies of Israel are one and the same and seek the wanton goal of killing Westerners for their twisted cause." They vowed to urge Americans "of all faiths to stand by Israel and urge our government to understand that the Palestinian Authority is devoted to the destruction of the State of Israel."[17]

No such parallel exists in the power of the Arab or Muslim voting community, where the vote is less potent or more diffuse. The four to six million estimated Muslims in the US have not had a cohesive, single-issue record on the Arab–Israeli conflict, for example. Nonetheless, one study suggests that George W. Bush's narrow Presidential victory in 2000 could be attributed to the increasingly organized, bloc-voting constituency of Muslim-Americans.[18] As a whole, however, the "balance of power" in the domestic arena has tilted toward Israel, with public opinion, the media, and formal as well as informal aspects of the Israel lobby providing pressure and cover for elected officials.

As for the American voting public, there has historically been support and sympathy for Israel over the years, and much more so than for the Palestinians. Though the numbers have fluctuated at times, in 2003 the overall favorable ratings of Israel were at a highpoint according to Gallup polling. Polls showed Israel's favorable rating at 64 percent, and 58 percent said their sympathies were more

14 Ibid., 58–59.
15 Berggren, op. cit. fn. 11, 165.
16 This land could be said to include Jordan and the Sinai, in addition to Israel, the West Bank and Gaza. Ahmad Faruqui (2002), "Bush Freezes Peace Process," July 5, online at http://www.counterpunch.org/faruqui0705.html.
17 "Christian Coalition of America Condemns Terror Attack in Tel Aviv," January 6 2003, online at http://www.cc.org/becomeinformed/pressreleases010603.html.
18 The American Muslim Political Coordinating Council PAC (AMPCC) promoted a bloc vote in 2000, and endorsed Bush (see Berggren, 160). Bush encountered a difficult issue after 9/11, as at least one of his supporters, Florida professor Sami al-Arian, was linked to support for Palestinian Islamic Jihad (*USA Today*, February 21, 2003, A1).

with the Israelis than the Palestinian Arabs, compared to 13 percent who said they had more sympathy toward the Palestinians.[19]

A final consideration influencing policy is the decision-makers themselves. Those in political psychology and constructivism emphasize the personal or shared "constructions of reality" that serve as a lens for viewing the foreign policy environment, and thus the need to know how decision-makers view the world.[20] From this perspective, each decision-maker's viewpoint may be unique, in terms of perceptions of actors, perceptions of US interests (definition of threats and strategic priorities), and values. While each decision-maker is constrained by the strategic and domestic parameters, there is room for free will and innovation in US policy that sometimes leads to new turns in policy based on the personality or perceptions of individual Presidents and their advisors.

Some say the Bush Administration has swung "to the right" under the influence of "neoconservatives" who support Israel as a democratic ally in a strategic and hostile region.[21] Stanley Hoffman refers to this "loose coalition of friends of Israel" as "well ensconced in the Pentagon," and a senior US official was quoted saying "for the first time a US administration and a Likud government are pursuing nearly identical policies."[22] The Bush Administration put Elliot Abrams in charge of US Mideast policy at the National Security Council, lending credence to the charge of neo-conservativist influence. Having publicly decried the Oslo process and "land for peace" scenarios, Abrams is strongly pro-Israel. He also was a staunch advocate for "regime change" in Iraq well before the events of 9/11. He has also been said to push for Arafat's ousting from power as part of Palestinian "reform,"

---

19   Jones, J. (2003), "Americans' Views of Israel More Positive than Last Year," *Gallup News Service*, February 19, online at http://www.gallup.com/poll/releases/pr030219.asp. See also "Foreign Policy: It works at home," *The Economist* (April 20, 2002), 27–8, which cites a Pew Poll citing similar sympathies and contrasts the numbers with other countries more sympathetic with the Palestinians.

20   On "perspective," see Monroe, K. (2001), "Paradigm Shift: From Rational Choice to Perspective," *International Political Studies Review* 22/2, 151–72; building off the early works of Snyder, R.C., Bruck, H.W. and Sapin, B. (eds) (1962), *Foreign Policy Decision-Making*, Glencoe, IL: The Free Press; Harold and Margaret Sprout (1956), *Man-milieu Relationship Hypotheses in the Context of International Politics*, Princeton, NJ: Center of International Studies, Princeton University; Steinbruner, J.D. (1974), *The Cybernetic Theory of Decision: New Dimensions of Political Analysis*, Princeton, NJ: Princeton University Press; and Jervis, R. (1976) *Perception and Misperception in International Politics*, Princeton, NJ: Princeton University Press. For an application of psychological decision-making theory to Israel, see Brecher, M. (1974), *Decisions in Israel's Foreign Policy*, London: Oxford University Press; for the "Presidential Leadership perspective" related to US policy toward the Arab–Israeli conflict, see Quandt, op. cit. fn. 7, 28–36.

21   Zunes, S. (2002), "The Swing to the Right in US Policy Toward Israel and Palestine," *Middle East Policy* 9/3, 45–64.

22   Buchanan, P.J. (2003), "Whose War?" *The American Conservative*, March 24, online at http://www.amconmag.com/03_24_03/cover.html.

a view backed by Rumsfeld and Cheney and eventually adopted by Bush as a condition for a Palestinian state.[23]

The result of these various influences depends on whether strategic and domestic factors reinforce or conflict with each other. Policy is contextual to the broader domestic and strategic situation, meaning that the US approach to the Arab–Israeli conflict is often a means to an end rather than an end in itself. I now turn to analyzing George W. Bush's policy toward the Arab–Israeli conflict, considering the strategic and domestic influences that at once pushed for innovation (calling for a Palestinian state) and constrained real movement toward implementing his declared vision.

The Bush Approach before 9/11

George W. Bush inherited a moribund peace process. His predecessor had worked furiously to negotiate a deal between Israel and the Palestinian Authority, headed by Yasir Arafat.[24] The heady optimism of the Oslo peace process begun with a handshake on the White House lawn in 1993, had by early 2001 given way to pessimism, distrust and violence. Peace talks gave way to a Palestinian uprising, the "al Aqsa intifada" of 2000, which included terrorism aimed at Israeli settlers, civilians and military targets in Israel and the occupied territories of the West Bank and Gaza Strip. Israel responded with violence and collective punishment, and the result was a mounting death toll on both sides. With the failure of the Clinton-led peace talks and the renewal of violence, each side was less willing and less politically able to make concessions in the face of each other's bloody killing of their own constituents.

In this climate, the new US President George W. Bush took office at about the same time that Israelis elected hardliner Ariel Sharon. Both incoming regimes would shape the conflict in their own way, at times at odds with each other, other times in conjunction. Sharon, like other leaders of the Likud Party, framed the conflict in terms of "peace with security," demanding an end to violence prior to talking about peace. It implied a large security perimeter, an expansive view of Israel's control of Jerusalem, continued security presence in Jewish settlements

---

23   Lobe, J. (2002), "Neoconservatives Consolidate Control over US Mideast Policy," *Foreign Policy in Focus*, December 6, online at http://www.bintjbeil.com/articles/en/021206 _lobe.html.

24   The Palestinian Authority was the designated representative body for Palestinians under an agreement with Israel in 1993, the Oslo Accords. Under the agreement, Arafat's Palestinian Authority would administer negotiated territories from Gaza and the West Bank. This provisional arrangement was intended to stay in effect while the two parties negotiated a "final status" agreement on all outstanding issues. See Bickerton, I. and Klausner, C. (2002), *A Concise History of the Arab–Israeli Conflict*, 4th edn, Upper Saddle River, NJ: Prentice Hall.

and, traditionally, opposition to any independent Palestinian state with its own army.[25] In the US political context, the rise of a conservative Administration has mixed implications. Less beholden to the Jewish lobby or Jewish vote, Republicans had been more willing and able to challenge Israel when interests dictated. Nonetheless, a conservative strain of American sympathy to Israel influenced decision-making.

Bush's early policies indicated pro-Israeli politics and lack of interest in the peace process and its aftermath. In one of his first actions as President, George W. Bush instructed aides to begin exploring the process of moving the US Embassy in Israel from Tel Aviv to Jerusalem. Bush's early policies indicated a continuation of pro-Israeli sentiments with balanced calls for negotiations. During his campaign, Bush vowed to "begin the process" of moving the US embassy to Jerusalem "as soon as I take office." But Bush postponed the move, even when "recommended" by congressional legislation, citing the delicate negotiations between Israel and Arafat over the status of the city.[26] There were also efforts to remove anti-Israel language from the draft declaration of the upcoming UN racism conference in 2001. The UN World Conference Against Racism, Racial Discrimination, Xenophobia and Related Intolerance (UNWCAR) preparatory committee included language equating Zionism with racism. Secretary of State Colin Powell strove to have the language removed and, failing this, decided not to attend the UN conference.[27]

In terms of the Israeli–Palestinian tinderbox, the Bush Administration was decidedly hands-off in the first several months. In May 2001, the Mitchell Report was released, with conclusions about the new conflict and recommendations for where to go next in terms of dialogue and confidence-building measures. The emphasis of the report was on encouraging the two parties to: 1) end the violence; 2) rebuild confidence; and 3) resume negotiations.[28]

After taking criticism for the hands-off approach to the conflict, Bush sent George Tenet to produce a signed agreement that would bring together the previous ceasefire agreements and set the stage for the implementation of the Mitchell Report. The resulting Tenet Plan, which Israel accepted "with some reservations" and to which the Palestinians gave "conditional approval,"[29] called for Israel and the Palestinian Authority to:

---

25 Khani, A. (2002), "Sharon as Prime Minister of Israel," *Middle East Affairs Journal* 7/1–2, 161–77, 171–3.

26 Broder, J., "Bush 'looks into' moving embassy to Jerusalem," online at www.jrep.com/Reporter/Article-38.html.

27 See "AIPAC Praises US Leadership on UN Racism Conference; Regrets UN Decision," August 28, 2001, online at http://www.aipac.org/documents/AIPACrelease 0828.html; see also La Guardia, A. (2002), *War Without End: Israelis, Palestinians, and the Struggle for a Promised Land*, New York: Thomas Dunned Books, 335.

28 See The Mitchell Plan, or *Sharm el-Sheikh Fact-Finding Committee Final Report*, online at http://usinfo.state.gov/regional/nea/mitchell.htm.

29 Bregman, A. (2002), *Israel's Wars: A History Since 1947*, 2nd edn, London and New York: Routledge, 231.

1. resume security cooperation, including eventual joint patrols, to replace the adversarial posture on the ground;
2. take immediate measures to enforce adherence to Israel's unilateral ceasefire, including Palestinian arrests of those committing acts of terrorism;
3. provide information on terrorist threats to each other and the US, and take measures to prevent attacks;
4. prevent persons from using areas "under their respective control to carry out acts of violence";
5. forge "an agreed-upon schedule to implement the complete redeployment of IDF forces to positions held before September 28, 2000"; and
6. develop a timeline for the "lifting of internal closures" and "reopening of internal roads," bridges, airports, and border crossings.[30]

Despite the agreement on the terms and the cease-fire, the violence persisted, and the Palestinian leadership seemed either unable or unwilling to stop it. Many groups and individuals in the occupied territories claimed a right to resistance, suggesting the Palestinian uprising to be "legitimate self defense" against Israeli military occupation since 1967.[31] On August 9, 2001, a Palestinian suicide bomber blew himself up in Jerusalem, killing fifteen and wounding 130. In response, Israel seized the Palestinian headquarters in Jerusalem while launching rocket attacks on Palestinian police stations in Gaza and Ramallah.[32] Sharon placed the blame on Arafat for any terrorism emerging out of the territories under the administration of the Palestinian Authority (PA). With each strike and counterstrike, the PA's capacity to administer was weakened and the trappings of statehood nurtured under Oslo crumbled, under the Israeli belief that Arafat was either unwilling or unable to stop the violence. The United States stayed on the sidelines.

9/11 and the War on Terror

The events of September 11, 2001, altered US thinking on the Arab–Israeli conflict as it did for most any policy issue. Hijackers tied to al-Qaeda forcibly gained control of four US passenger jets, running two of them into New York City's World Trade Center and one into the Pentagon.[33] The death toll for the day was estimated at about 3,000. Al-Qaeda had emerged in the late 1980s from the Islamic resistance

---

30   See *The Tenet Plan: Israeli-Palestinian Ceasefire and Security Plan*, online at http://www.yale.edu/lawweb/avalon/mideast/mid023.htm.

31   Appel, Y. (2002), "Palestinians Promise to Keep Peace," *Associated Press*, August 19, online at http://story.news.yahoo.com/news?tmpl=story&u=/ap/20020819/ap_on_re_mi_ea/israel_palestinians_629.

32   Bregman, op. cit. fn. 29, 231.

33   The fourth plane crashed in rural Pennsylvania after a struggle with passengers; its destination was unknown but it was suspected to be heading toward Washington, DC.

to the Soviets in Afghanistan. Its leader, wealthy Saudi Osama bin Laden, directed the organization's attention toward the United States for its support of the Saudi regime and stationing of American forces on Saudi soil since the Gulf War. An Islamic organization bent on installing its brand of fundamentalism in Saudi Arabia and elsewhere in the Middle East, al-Qaeda and its leader bin Laden increasingly saw the United States as an obstacle to its goals. A series of terrorist attacks on US bases and embassies from Saudi Arabia to Kenya and Tanzania were linked to bin Laden's umbrella network organization, and in 1998 bin Laden declared war on the US, calling for attacks on all Americans, military or civilian.

After the embassy bombings of 1998, which killed some 300 people and wounded another 5,000, the US turned up pressure on al-Qaeda and the Taliban who provided the group safe harbor to train and plan in Afghanistan. But aside from sanctions on the Taliban and a one-time strike against al-Qaeda camps in Afghanistan on August 20, 1998, the United States had not fundamentally reordered its foreign policy orientation—not until 9/11.

The American response after the events of September 11 was a reordering of foreign policy priorities to fight an extended War on Terror. This new war was defined by Bush in a couple of terms; namely that "either you are with us, or you are with the terrorists," and that the United States would not distinguish between those who carry out acts of terror and those who harbor them.[34] In terms of who the terrorists were, the first immediate answer was al-Qaeda, a transnational network purportedly operating in over 60 countries. Beyond bin Laden's group, it was murkier whether the war included all other terrorism, but US officials left it at the slightly narrowed but ambiguous notion of terrorist organizations with "global reach." The target list also would expand to include state sponsors of terror—first the Taliban of Afghanistan (who gave aid and comfort to bin Laden), but also in the Bush Administration's crosshairs was Iraq.[35]

Addressing a transnational network like al-Qaeda required cooperation on all facets of counter-terrorism: disrupting financial flows, intelligence gathering, criminal investigation, and the potential use of force. The strategic priority of the post-9/11 world necessitated a new coalition of countries in the Middle East and beyond to assist in military campaigns, intelligence, defense, and criminal investigation. Bush assembled regional support for use of airspace and bases to conduct operations to root out the Taliban and smash al-Qaeda bases, camps and

---

34 Hirsch, M. (2002), "Bush and the World," *Foreign Affairs* 81/5, 18–19.

35 There was almost immediate calls for attacking Iraq right after 9/11 from some in the Administration, particularly Defense Secretary Donald Rumsfeld and his Deputy, Paul Wolfowitz. There was no link to al-Qaeda nor evidence of Iraq's hand in the events of 9/11, but some suspected Saddam Hussein could be involved and, regardless, he was enough of a threat or nuisance that 9/11 could provide an impetus for support for regime change in Iraq. See Woodward, B. (2002), *Bush at War*, New York: Simon & Schuster, 49; Cass, C. (2003), "Sept. 11 Attacks put US on Path to War," *Associated Press*, March 19, online at http://www.indystar.com/print/articles/8/029946-5788-010.html.

operations in Afghanistan, which it did with surprising speed with the help of internal Afghan rivals to the Taliban, notably the Northern Alliance. But, with bin Laden having escaped capture, and al-Qaeda being dispersed globally, the US continued to need the help of other countries in pursuit of those the United States identified as a threat, or those who would harbor such elements.

What this meant for US policy toward the Arab–Israeli conflict was a newfound need to curry favor with the Arab and Muslim world, both for image management and to foster a new coalition. First, the US devoted great attention to winning over the "Arab street," to counter al-Qaeda's rhetoric about the US as an imperial infidel power insensitive to the plight of Muslims, including the Palestinians,[36] and both enabler and lapdog to the Zionists.[37] When US operations against al-Qaeda and the Taliban commenced on October 7, 2001, bin Laden tried to link the cause with Palestine, vowing "neither America nor the people who live in it will ever taste security or safety until we feel security and safety in our land *and Palestine*."[38] Any US movement on the issue of the Palestinians, then, would hope to quell al-Qaeda's recruitment and try to avoid a "clash of civilizations."[39] If the United States sought further action in the region, it was deemed important to garner regional support the likes of which Bush's father obtained for the Gulf War.

An "American Balfour Declaration"[40]: Calls for a Palestinian State

The new strategic priorities of the US in the region lent themselves to new policy thinking regarding the Arab–Israeli conflict. Jordan's Foreign Minister said plainly: "it will be difficult ... to line up Arab support without a commitment to solving the Israeli-Palestinian dispute once and for all."[41] This view was shared not just among the Arab states but European allies as well.

The initial US response to the need to cultivate support in the War on Terror and prospective action on Iraq was a true landmark in American policy: the first explicit acknowledgment that there should be a Palestinian state since the original

---

36   There is a substantial Christian Palestinian community as well.

37   See bin Laden interview transcript, reprinted as "American Policies in the Middle East Justify Islamic Terrorism," in Egendorf, L. (ed.) (2004), *Terrorism: Opposing Viewpoints*, San Diego, CA: Greenhaven Press, 123–30.

38   Wright, R. (2002), *Sacred Rage: The Wrath of Militant Islam*, New York: Touchstone, 268 (emphasis added).

39   Huntington's (1996) thesis that "the West" and "Islam" were culturally doomed to conflict is embraced by conservatives in each "civilization," thus Bush tried to deflate bin Laden's rhetoric pitting the world in terms of Islam versus infidel.

40   LaGuardia, op. cit. fn. 27, 335. This refers to the British public proclamation backing the creation of a Jewish state in Palestine in 1917.

41   Price, R. (2001), *Unholy War: America, Israel and Radical Islam*, Eugene, OR: Harvest House Publishers, 40.

debate over Palestine in 1947.[42] While claiming they had decided matters prior to "9/11,"[43] the decision was in part driven by the new imperatives, including the "battle for the hearts and minds" of the Middle East. It also followed Sharon's public warning that the US not "appease" the "terrorists" as Hitler was appeased, implicitly comparing Bush to Neville Chamberlain in a way that did not sit well with the American President.[44]

The idea of declaring support for the creation of a Palestinian state was floated first in early October, about the same time the United States began Operation Enduring Freedom, the military campaign against the Taliban and al-Qaeda in Afghanistan. Bush formally declared the US stance to the UN General Assembly on November 10, suggesting the US sought "a day when two states, Israel and Palestine, live peacefully together within secure and recognized borders."[45] The two-state idea was formalized on March 12, 2002, with the passage of UN Security Council Resolution 1397. This resolution, which passed 14–0 with one abstention, affirmed the two-state vision of Israel and Palestine living side by side "within secure and recognized borders."[46] It also demanded a cessation of all acts of violence, and called upon leaders to implement the Tenet Plan and the Mitchell Report, and resume negotiations.

All previous attempts to endorse a Palestinian state in the formal language of a Security Council resolution had been vetoed by the US, so this was a watershed event, however symbolic. Some observers suggested the move was taken in return for "good will" from Arab states ahead of Vice President Cheney's regional visit to push for support in taking action against Iraq.[47] The courtship of the Arab world for US plans included the need to "accelerate US pressure" on Israel for acquiescing to an independent Palestine.[48]

This departure in American policy rhetoric sparked controversy and political commotion from predictable quarters. After the UN speech, a US Senate delegation emerged from a meeting with leaders of the American Jewish community with a letter to the President that declared "our shared commitment for the enduring

42 Previous Administrations had varying opinions about a Palestinian state, but none had made such a public commitment to such an outcome. Clinton made an open advocacy for a Palestinian state in the waning days of his term, but not in such a heralded and pronounced statement of intent (La Guardia, op. cit. fn. 27, 335).

43 Perlez, J. and Tyler, P. (2001), "Before Attacks, US Was Ready to Say It Backed Palestinian State," *New York Times*, October 2, A1.

44 Woodward, op. cit. fn. 35, 197–98.

45 Speech reprinted in *Journal of Palestinian Studies* (Winter 2002), 164.

46 Online at http://www.un.org/News/Press/docs/2002/sc7326.doc.htm. Syria abstained, neither satisfied that the resolution went far enough for achieving a Palestinian state nor interested in voting against this symbolic statement.

47 MacAskill, E. (2002), *The Guardian*, March 14, online at www.guardian.co.uk/israel/story/0,2763,666909,00.html; see also UN Resolution 1397, online at http://ods-dds-ny.un.org/doc/UNDOC/GEN/N02/283/59/PDF/NO2289359.pdf?.

48 Price, op. cit. fn. 41, 10.

security of the state of Israel, our close ally in the fight against terrorism" and stating frankly their opinion that "no solution can be imposed upon the parties," finally urging the President to "remain steadfast in standing with our ally, Israel."[49] It is notable, then, that beyond rhetorical support, the United States had not departed from its "procedural bias" of implementing the two-state vision.[50] That is, the United States had not unilaterally recognized the Palestinian state, nor did it even lay a specific, explicit time-line for its creation. Instead, the United States returned to the old stance of suggesting that such details be negotiated. At this point, the symbolism of the new approach outstripped the substance, creating questions amidst the domestic backlash to Bush's proposal about the sincerity of the US to enforce this vision.

Another reason that the US approach to the issue of Palestine slowed was the War on Terror. Defining the world and the implications of the Bush Doctrine in zero-sum terms, the "with us or against us" approach tended to label all terrorism as equally bad or evil. The rhetoric of terrorism lumped together various conflicts and violence, including those by Palestinians fighting the Israeli occupation.[51] Too much sympathy and assistance to the Palestinians, who in the new uprising witnessed new levels of terror against Israeli civilians, would be awkward on the domestic front both in selling the War on Terrorism and in relation to Israel and its sympathizers. Bush became entangled in his own rhetorical webs, finding it difficult to work with Arafat so long as Arafat was perceived to be linked to terror, for fear of the domestic backlash of an apparent double standard.

Palestinian Terror and US Policy toward Arafat

To the extent that Arafat's Palestinian Authority was responsible for the protection of areas such as Jenin and Bethlehem, continued terrorism emanating from these areas was seen as a sign of either Arafat's inability or unwillingness to stop it. Either way, this was an awkward time for an American President rallying the world in a "War on Terror" to be embracing the Palestinian leader.

When Israel sent troops and tanks into Palestinian cities on March 29 after a suicide bombing that killed 27 people at the start of the Jewish Passover holiday, the initial US response was to support a UN resolution urging Israel to withdraw its troops, reaffirming his commitment to a Palestinian state on the same day that Israeli troops invaded more West Bank towns. Within days, however, Bush received domestic criticism for his actions, with one Congressman calling

49   Letter reprinted in *Journal of Palestinian Studies* (Winter 2002), 164–65.

50   Quandt, W.B. (1993), *Peace Process: American Diplomacy and the Arab–Israeli Conflict Since 1967*, Berkeley, CA: University of California Press refers to "procedural bias" as the US tendency to focus on the negotiation method rather than outcomes.

51   Mansour, C. (2002), "The Impact of 11 September on the Israeli–Palestinian Conflict," *Journal of Palestinian Studies* 31/2, 5–18, 13.

diplomatic missions to the Palestinians "a bow to the bombers."[52] Bush took pains to address the terror issue, suggesting "to those who would try to use the current crisis as an opportunity to widen the conflict: stay out." Meanwhile, Israeli collective punishment and killing of civilians escaped such labels, though Bush called on restraint and withdrawal. Bush sent Powell to urge Israel to stop building settlements in Palestinian areas, but did not mention a timetable for Israel's withdrawal or for an end to settlements.[53] Sharon defied the US President's urging to withdraw "without delay," claiming he had to address terrorism, accusing Arafat of establishing "a regime of terror in the territories under his control."[54]

Bush appeared to back away from his demand for an immediate Israeli withdrawal, claiming Sharon had met the US timetable by withdrawing from some Palestinian areas, and that Israel had the right to try to root out five Palestinians blamed for the murder of an Israeli cabinet minister. This was simultaneous with a speech by Vice-President Cheney at an Israeli Independence Day reception, saying "Our friendship is strong and enduring, and it can never be shaken."[55] The US Congress passed resolutions expressing solidarity with Israel and condemning Arafat. The resolutions reminded the President of the position of Congress, that— in the words of Democratic House Minority leader Richard Gephardt—"we stand with Israel historically and morally."[56]

After meeting with Saudi, Moroccan, Jordanian, and Israeli leaders, Bush declared that Israel must negotiate an end to its occupation of Palestinian areas in the West Bank. The Saudi Crown Prince Abdullah had presented a peace plan at the Arab Summit of March 2002, and sought to push the President to embrace it. The plan, however, was "totally unacceptable" to the Likud government, in that it provided for a Palestinian state with full sovereignty. Bush gave the plan some public support, without committing to it, suggesting to Sharon that Israel get used to the "new reality" of the legitimacy of the two-state option.[57] Sharon said

52   Fournier, R. (2002), "Bush Urges Israel to End Incursion," *Associated Press*, April 4, online at http://story.news.yahoo.com/news?tmpl=story&u=/ap/20020405/ap_on_re_mi_ea/us_mideast_1029&printer=1.

53   Fournier, op. cit. fn. 52; also Woodward, op. cit. fn. 35, 324–25. Powell was criticized by some insiders for "leaning too much" toward the Palestinians by suggesting an international conference, an idea he was ordered to retract.

54   Spetalnick, M. (2002), "Sharon Vows to Press on with Offensive, Defying US," *Reuters*, April 8, online at http://story.news.yahoo.com/news?tmpl=story&u=/nm/20020408/ts_nm /mideast_dc_1363&printer=1.

55   A pro-Palestinian rally held near the White House at the time did not receive US representation; see Holland, S. (2002), "Bush Steers Back to More Pro-Israeli Policy," *Reuters*, April 20.

56   Allen, V. (2002), "Congress to Take up Pro-Israel Resolutions," *Reuters*, May 2, online at http://story.news.yahoo.com/news?tmpl=story&ncid=584&e=3&cid=584&u=/nm/20020502/pl_nm/mideast_congress_israel_dc_3.

57   Fuller, G. (2002), "The Future of Political Islam," *Foreign Affairs* 81/2, 48–60, 28–9.

that under stringent conditions, he would agree to the creation of such a state, at one point calling it inevitable; but he insisted that Israel could not negotiate with Palestinians before the terror ended and their leadership underwent reforms.[58] This latter point suggested the view held by Sharon, and soon Bush, that Arafat had to go.

Administrative attention and frustration turned on Arafat, seen as an obstacle to ending tensions and violence in the area. Under pressure to control the terror, Arafat's Fatah group announced an urge to the end to suicide attacks, to distance themselves from the perpetrators behind Palestinian attacks, and to reassert the Palestinian Authority as the legitimate security force of the Palestinian people, as opposed to the "armed militias" of Hamas and the al-Aqsa Martyrs Brigades.[59]

On May 10, 2002 Israel ended the six-week offensive against Palestinian militants across the West Bank with claims of success. As Bush set to announce a plan for an interim Palestinian state, extremists set off two bloody bombings in two days, one killing 19 and another killing seven.[60] In response, Sharon decided to reoccupy all Palestinian Authority territory in an open-ended stay "as long as terrorism continues." Washington warned Israel against toppling Arafat but also sharpened criticism of him, calling him "ineffective and untrustworthy."[61]

The bombing had a profound impact on Bush's thinking, and changed the substance and tenor of his proposal. The proposal called for the establishment of an independent Palestinian state, but there was a catch. Bush urged the Palestinians to "elect new leaders not compromised by terror." Despite Arafat's condemnation of the attacks, the perception at the White House, as in Israel, was that Arafat had encouraged or permitted these activities.[62] What had changed was the emphasis on replacing Arafat. The suicide bombings the week prior confirmed to Bush a view of Arafat as unwilling or unable to control terrorism that some say dates back to 1998.[63] "The violence did change the character of this speech," one official said.

---

58   Weizman, S. (2002), "Likud Party Defies Sharon," *Associated Press*, May 12, online at http://story.news.yahoo.com/news?tmpl=story&cid=514&u=/ap/20020512/ap_on_re_mi_ea/israel_palestinians_4087.

59   al-Mughrabi, N. (2002), "Fatah Group Urges End to Suicide Attacks in Israel," *Reuters*, May 29, online at http://story.news.yahoo.com/news?tmpl=story&ncid=586&e=2&cid=586&u=/nm/20020529/wl_nm/mideast_palestinian_fatah_dc_1.

60   "Suicide Bomb Kills 19 as Bush Expected to Announce Peace Plan," online at http://www.jordantimes.com/Wed/news/news1.htm.

61   Assadi, M. (2002), "Israeli Army Launches Reprisal Raid on Arafat HQ," *Reuters*, June 6, online at http://story.news.yahoo.com/news?tmpl=story&ncid=586&e=2&cid=586&u=/nm/20020606/wl_nm/mideast_dc_2484.

62   Woodward, op. cit. fn. 35, 297, notes that Bush increasingly viewed Arafat as just "evil"; see also Zunes, op. cit. fn. 21, 54–55.

63   See Klaidman, D. and Hirsh, M. (2002), "He Knows It, He Feels It," *Newsweek*, April 8, 28–29.

"It also crystallized again the fact that the disappointments that we've had with the Palestinian leadership."[64]

While Bush clearly placed the onus on the Palestinians, he said that once security began returning to the region, Israel would have to withdraw its forces to the positions they held prior to the outbreak of violence in September 2001, and would ultimately have to end the occupation. "Occupation threatens Israel's identity and democracy," he said. Once violence subsided, Bush insisted Israel would also have to end all settlement activity, as discussed in the Mitchell Report. Israel would also have to allow Palestinians more "freedom of movement" and release frozen Palestinian assets.[65]

Bush sought to distinguish the plight of Palestinians from the view of the terrorism and the alleged link to Arafat. The proposal reflected the balance of appealing to Arab sympathies while taking a hard line on terrorism, consistent with the "War on Terror," and a hard line on Arafat, consistent with the Israeli view, and Bush's own beliefs, about the Palestinian leader's intentions. Bush's speech was seen by many as a retreat from the ambitious tones of prior months: all the sudden, Palestinian statehood came with many strings attached, to a degree that some questioned its tenability. Many in the Arab world were disappointed, and saw the new language of the US position consistent with the Israeli perspective. The call for new leaders, a functional democracy, constitution, and market economy—prior to statehood, mind you—was a tall order that, as one observer notes, had not been accomplished by any Arab state after a half-century of independence.[66]

The official Arab response to the Bush plan was ambiguous, but the reaction from the "Arab street" was hostile and skeptical.[67] Egypt, Saudi Arabia and Jordan had tried to persuade Bush to set a timescale for Palestinian statehood and an end to Israel's 35-year occupation and settlement of the West Bank and Gaza Strip, in return for full Arab ties with the Jewish state.[68] As for those directly affected, both Israel and the Palestinian leadership emphasized aspects that best matched their views. Israel praised the parts condemning Palestinian leadership and calling for change, but was silent on the issue of a sovereign or provisional Palestinian state. Having previously rejected the idea of Palestinian statehood, Sharon had been

---

64   Mikkelsen, R. (2002), "Suicide Bombings Hardened Bush Rejection of Arafat," *Reuters*, June 24, online at http://story.news.yahoo.com/news?tmpl=story&cid=615&615 &e=6&u=/nm/20020624/pl_nm/mideast_usa_decision_dc_1.

65   Guttman, N., "Solana: Palestinian People Must Choose Their Own Leader," *Ha'aretz Daily*, online at http://www.haaretzdaily.com/hasen/pages/ShArt.jhtml?itemNo1 79734&contrassID=1&subContrassID=0&sbSubContrassID=0.

66   Faruqui, A. (2002), "Bush Freezes Peace Process," July 5, online at http://www.counterpunch.org/faruqui0705.html.

67   Ibid.

68   Lyon, A. (2002), "Bush Fails to Lift Arab Despair Over US Policy," *Reuters*, June 25, online at http://www.unitedjerusalem.org/index2.asp?id=112957&Date=6/26/2002.

forced to consider the eventuality, should the US press the issue.[69] Arafat lauded Bush's speech, downplaying the call for "change" and noting Bush did not mention Arafat by name. He continued with reform and a call for elections, while rallying international support for his leadership as the elected President of the Palestinian Authority. Arafat's cabinet quit in September 2002 to avoid a no-confidence vote in the Palestinian National Assembly. Arafat appointed a new cabinet, endorsed by a "reform-seeking" Assembly, on October 29, to serve until elections were held.[70]

Further signs of a US hard line on Palestinian terror, and sympathy toward Israel, came on November 2, 2002, when the State Department added Hamas, Islamic Jihad, PFLP, and Hezbollah to the list of groups associated with bin Laden. This made the groups targets of an Executive Order directing the US Treasury Department to sanction foreign banks that fail to freeze assets of groups on the list.[71] Those raising monies for such groups and their causes came under new pressure, which culminated in eight arrests in February 2003, including a Florida professor charged with running the North American fundraising operation of Palestinian Islamic Jihad.[72] The targeting of terror groups focused on Israel signaled the "War on Terror" was wider than al-Qaeda, but also that the US and Israel had developed a relationship of mutual interest in the region. While Arab states balked, Israel was fast becoming a willing partner in the US agenda.

Sharon had thought 9/11 would bring the US more into the Israeli perspective regarding terrorism and the Palestinians. After a rocky start dating back to the reference to appeasement, there were signs that the US and Israel were converging in their views and priorities. Sharon sought to firm up the relationship and persuade the US about the terrorist links in the Palestinian territories. Israel asserted at one point that al-Qaeda operatives had established a presence in Palestinian-ruled areas of the Gaza Strip and in Lebanon.[73] They claimed senior al-Qaeda officials sought to enlist Palestinian support and membership, a charge admittedly not backed by evidence.[74]

But al-Qaeda fueled the fires by beginning to target Israeli and Jewish targets with terror. On November 28, a suicide bombing of a Kenyan hotel used by Israelis

69   Amayreh, K. (2002), "Assassins, bulldozers and human bombs," *Ahram*, online at http://www.ahram.org.eg/weekly/2002/591/re1.htm.

70   Amr, W. (2002), "Arafat Wins Cabinet Vote; Israel Coalition in Chaos," *Reuters*, October 29, online at http://story.news.yahoo.com/news?tmpl=story&ncid=586&e=3&cid =586&u=/nm/20021029/wl_nm/mideast_cabinet_dc.

71   Online at www.aipac.org/documents/stalwartner111802.html; http://usembassy. state.gov/posts/ja1/wwwhse1246.html.

72   Locy, T. (2003), "FBI Charges Fla. Professor as Terror Fundraiser," *USA Today*, February 21–23, 1A.

73   al-Mughrabi, N. (2002), "Israeli Forces Kill 10 Palestinians in Gaza," *Reuters*, December 6, online at http://story.news.yahoo.com/news?tmpl=story&cid=578&u=/ nm/20021206/ts_nm/mideast_dc_32.

74   Harel, A. (2003), "Senior Officer: Qaida Chief in Region to Recruit Palestinians," *Ha'aretz*, January 2, online at http://www.haaretzdaily.com/hasen/pages/ShArt.jhtml?item No=247563&contrassID=1&subContrass ID=0&sbSubContrassID=0.

killed eight and wounded 80 others.[75] At the same time, missiles were fired at an Israeli airliner nearby, missing their targets. The attacks were the first direct attack on Israelis by Osama bin Laden's network, and al-Qaeda vowed more attacks against Israel and the United States.

Arafat sought to refute the link to al-Qaeda, and publicly told Osama bin Laden to stop claiming he was fighting for the Palestinians. Saying bin Laden's agenda is "against our interests," Arafat's public disavowal hoped to reassure the US and avoid an Israeli pretext for more operations in the name of the War on Terror. In fact, Israel sought to frame its incursions in the occupied territories as a "second front" of a pending war on Iraq, seeking "proper resources" to confront terrorism in the area to ensure "decisive victory."[76] But Arafat had more concerns than the kiss of death from al-Qaeda; a looming American confrontation with Iraq would bring out anti-Americanism within the Palestinian population, risking further isolation by the US as it sought friendly assistance in its campaign.

As for progress in the implementation of a plan for a Palestinian state, little has changed since Bush's proclamation in June 2002. It may be because Bush's end game was not a peace settlement but regional stability for the Administration's agenda regarding terrorism and Iraq. Showing interest in the Arab–Israeli conflict was a means to these ends. But, as time and again before, the competing pressures and needs for Israeli and Arab support made US policy equivocate and drift for fear of alienating either side. The US, which has usually preferred moderate parties and candidates as more amenable to negotiating with the Palestinians, this time backed Sharon. Bush personally moved to postpone the publication of the "Road Map" to peace drafted by the so-called "Quartet" (US, EU, Russia and the UN) until after the Israeli elections in early 2003, as a favor to Sharon.[77] Pre-election violence by Hamas and others boosted Sharon to victory, rallying Israelis into a hard line against terrorism.[78]

The re-elected Sharon sounded much like Bush, open to a Palestinian state in theory, but not before the removal of "terrorist leadership" in the Palestinian Authority. Neither Bush nor Sharon would deal with Arafat politically, since he was considered an affiliate of terror.[79] This dragged out the process, as Arafat promised

---

75   Mwakughu, N. (2002), "Suicide Bomb Kills Israelis, Kenyans; Qaeda Blamed," November 28, online at http://dailynews.att.net/cgi-bin/news?e=pri&dt=021128&cat=new s&st=newskenyaattacksdc.

76   Williams, D. (2002), "Arafat Tells Al Qaeda Not to Use Palestinian Cause," *Reuters*, December 15, online at http://story.news.yahoo.com/news?tmpl=story&ncid= 586&e=1&cid=586&u=/nm/20021215/wl_nm/mideast_dc.

77   Eldar, A., "American intervention in Israel's elections," *Ha'aretz*, online at http:// www.haaretzdaily.com/hasen/pages/ShArt.jhtml?itemNo=241378&contrassID=2&subCo ntrassID=&sbSubContrassID=0&listSrc=Y.

78   al-Mughrabi, N. (2003), "Violence Surges Days Before Israeli Election," *Reuters*, January 24.

79   Heller, J. (2003), "Sharon to Form Israel Govt, Oust Top Palestinians," February 9, online at http://dailynews.att.net/cgi-bin/news?e=pri&dt=030209&cat=international&st =internation almideastdc.

to appoint a prime minister in accordance with the demands of the Quartet Road Map,[80] which was unveiled in March 2003 in an attempt to link the process to a post-Saddam vision of a new Middle East.

From Afghanistan to Iraq

Meanwhile, the United States had largely fought and won the first battle of the War on Terror, without much help from the Arab world. Operation Enduring Freedom, combining US air power and Special Forces with local armies in Afghanistan, ousted the Taliban from Kabul and set up an interim successor through a UN conference, all by the end of 2001. By the spring of 2002, the operation was one of "mopping up" and pursuing the still-elusive Osama bin Laden and his associates.

Increasingly, and emboldened by its success in Afghanistan, the United States turned to its next priority in its War on Terror: Iraq. Some in the US Administration were convinced that Saddam Hussein, as a sympathizer to some terrorism while allegedly possessing weapons of mass destruction, was an unacceptable combination. As early as February 2002, the Bush Administration made the decision to "oust Saddam Hussein."[81] The question of when and how to proceed divided the Administration between unilateralist hawks—Cheney and Rumsfeld—and internationalist Powell, who made the case for going to the UN for the legitimacy of the mission.[82]

The internationalists won for a time, with the United States taking the case to the UN demanding that Saddam be held accountable for his material breach of Security Council Resolutions pertaining to weapons of mass destruction. The Council passed Resolution 1441 ordering inspectors back into Iraq and threatening "serious consequences" if Iraq did not fully comply.

But the Bush Administration was skeptical that the inspections would yield genuine disarmament, and spent the fall of 2002 and winter of 2003 building forces and support for the eventual use of force. They had little success. Unlike his father, the junior Bush appeared to be hurtling toward confrontation with or without the region, the UN, or the world—all this with less legal justification than the elder Bush, who was responding to an Iraqi act of aggression.

The Bush Administration lobbied the region for help, and offered a major missile sale to Egypt and an increase in foreign assistance to Jordan, but the concern for the Palestinian issue would not go away, nor was an Arab state politically able to side with the US in a war on an Arab country while the "other war" (Palestinian) continued to be ignored by the US. Bush did as his father had done, promising

---

80   Stack, M. (2003), "Arafat Says He'll Appoint a Premier," *Los Angeles Times*, February 15.

81   "Report: Bush Decides to Oust Saddam Hussein," *Reuters*, February 13, 2002, online at http://dailynews.yahoo.com/htx/nm/20020213/ts/attack_iraq_dc_4.html.

82   Woodward, op. cit. fn. 35, 330–32, documents this debate.

action on the Arab–Israeli problem after dealing with Iraq, but this time the sale was not effective. Middle East states were reluctant to participate or endorse a war started by a Western superpower against a fellow Arab or Muslim state. Jordan's King Abdullah said that a US attack on Iraq would be catastrophic for the Middle East.[83] Thousands took to the streets in Arab capitals to protest against a possible US war on Iraq, and most Arab countries advocated a peaceful solution to the crisis over Iraq's alleged weapons of mass destruction.[84]

In addition to assistance from Kuwait, the US found Israel to be a regional friend on the matter of war with Iraq. Israel shared intelligence with the US, and Israeli Defense Force units and security officials trained and coordinated with US forces for the contingencies of war.[85] Sharon sought to exploit the circumstances to show Israel's support and the ring of terrorism allying against them. Sharon accused Iraq of transferring chemical and biological weapons to Syria to hide them from UN inspectors—though his comments were based on unconfirmed information and involved no evidence to support the allegation.[86] Hezbollah and al-Qaeda chimed in with anti-US and Israeli rhetoric claiming the attack against Iraq was aimed to "protect the Jewish occupiers and achieve their expansionist dream of setting up a (Jewish) state between the Nile and Euphrates."[87]

The Palestinian leadership sought to dampen the pro-Iraq sentiments of their populations, which had gone unabated during the 1991 Gulf War. While Hamas and Islamic Jihad continued vocal support for Saddam,[88] the Palestinian Authority sought a prudent course to downplay any link with Iraq that could sour US

---

83 "King: Mideast Peace Conference Should be Based on UN Resolutions," *Jordan Times*, May 7, 2002, online at http://www.jordanembassyus.org/05072002001.htm.

84 Ersan, I. (2003), "Arabs Take to Streets to Protest War against Iraq," *Reuters*, January 27, online at http://dailynews.att.net/cgi-bin/news?e=pri&dt=030127&cat=interna tional&st=internationaliraqprotestsdc.

85 Price, op. cit. fn. 41, 37. Israel's intelligence gathering capabilities have been called "vital" to overall US security, and there was some indication that Israel had forewarned 9/11 with its own intelligence information. See also Harel, A. and Guttman, N., "IDF quickens pace in its preparations for US war in Iraq," online at http://www. haaretzdaily.com/hasen/pages/ShArt.jhtml?itemNo=243490&contrassID=2&subContrass ID=1&sbSubContrassID=0.

86 "Sharon Says Iraq May be Hiding Weapons in Syria," *Reuters*, December 24, online at http://story.news.yahoo.com/news?tmpl=story&ncid=586&e=1&cid=586&u=/ nm/20021224/wl_nm/iraq_israel_dc.

87 Abdeidoh, R. (2002), "Al Qaeda Claims Kenya Attacks, Vows More," *Reuters*, December 8, online at http://dailynews.att.net/cgi-bin/news?e=pri&dt=021208&cat= international &st=international attackqaedajazeeradc; MacFarquhar, N. (2003), "Hezbollah Becomes Potent Anti-US Force," *The New York Times*, December 24, online at http://story. news.yahoo.com/news?tmpl=story&ncid=68&e=2&cid=68&u=/nyt/20021224/ts_nyt/ hezbollah_becomes_potent_anti_u_s__force.

88 "Hamas pledges support to Iraq," *USA Today*, January 10, 2003, online at http:// www.usatoday.com/news/world/2003-01-10-hamas-iraq_x.htm.

relations or invite Israeli action.[89] Nonetheless, there were some rallies linking support for Iraq by members of the Palestinian Authority, according to Israel's Ministry of Foreign Affairs. Israel focused on Iraq's ties to Palestinian terrorism against Israel, suggesting Iraq has given substantial financial and military aid to the Palestinian Liberation Front (PLF) and the Arab Liberation Front (ALF), both pro-Iraqi organizations. An article published in the *Al Quds* magazine in June 2002 stated that "Saddam Hussein's popularity is growing due to the millions of dollars he contributes to Palestinian families hurt by the Al Aqsa intifada."[90]

In its pressure to be consistent in the "War on Terror," Bush had begun to mute criticism of Israeli tactics against the *intifada*. Picking up on Arab resentment, and still wanting for international and regional legitimacy in the coming war with Iraq, the US came out in successive displays of concern for the Arab–Israeli conflict in early 2003. In February, Bush made a grandiose speech about the postwar vision for a new Middle East that would include an independent Palestinian state. "Success in Iraq," he offered, "could also begin a new stage for Middle Eastern peace, and set in motion progress towards a truly democratic Palestinian state."[91] Linking Iraq to Palestinian terror, the argument was that once the patron is gone, Palestinian terror would be reduced, and willing Palestinian moderates could rein an independent Palestine.

Perhaps attempting "balance," the US rebuked Israel for its tactics in its fight against the uprising. Still, the US could not muster Arab and Muslim support for the war against Iraq, with Saudi Arabia and NATO ally Turkey refusing to participate, leaving only Kuwait, Bahrain and Qatar for bases of operation. Numerous demonstrations in the Muslim world in opposition to the US and its plans to invade Iraq continued, and leaders from those countries warned that any attack would destabilize the region and fuel more anti-American terrorism and retaliation. The Arab League announced "the complete rejection of a strike against Iraq,"[92] though Kuwait provided US base support pivotal to a ground invasion. With little help from regional allies, in March 2003 Bush went to war anyway.

---

89   King, L. (2003), "Ties to Iraq Less Binding This Time," *Los Angeles Times*, February 7, online at http://latimes.infogate.com/content.php?page=AllArticleXml&feed=latimes&type=xml&catkey=latimes_world&uniqueID=1044627415077190&bid=trib.la.li te&sid=48d63bac1eca45f2e6978c6e99136010&context=lite&liteuser=trib.la.lite:vps71.

90   Israeli Ministry of Foreign Affairs (2003), "Iraq's Involvement in the Palestinian Terrorist Activity against Israel," January, online at http://www.mfa.gov.il/mfa/go.asp? MFAH0n2h0.

91   "President George W. Bush Speaks at AEI's Annual Dinner," February 28, 2003, online at http://www.aei.org/news/newsID.16197,filter./news_detail.asp.

92   Sobelman, D., "Arab League Members Oppose Iraq Attack," *Ha'aretz*, online at http://www.haaretzdaily.com/hasen/spages/267987.html.

The End of Balance: US Policy after Iraq and after Arafat

Under pressure from the US and other Quartet members, the Central Council of Arafat's PLO approved his nomination of moderate, Mahmoud Abbas, to the new post of Prime Minister. The Central Council also called on Palestinian militants "fighting Israeli occupation and settlement not to target Israeli civilians inside Israel" so as not to give Israel a reason "to continue its annihilation war against our people."[93] Arafat resisted forfeiting control over peace policies and security decisions, but the reform-minded Palestinian Parliament passed a measure that bestowed some such powers upon Abbas.[94] Bush held out the promise that "immediately upon confirmation, the Road Map for peace will be given to the Palestinians and the Israelis" for input. At once, this promised some advancement but also heralded another round of haggling, delay and obstruction by the parties involved.

Particularly problematic was the new power struggle between Arafat and the new Prime Minister. Despite public claims to settle their differences and work together, Palestinian politics were stalemated and eventually Abbas resigned.[95] Alone in power, Arafat ruled isolated in a compound surrounded by Israeli forces until, seeking treatment abroad for his failing health, Arafat died in November 2004.[96] This created new opportunities in the peace process in theory, as both Israel and the United States could work with a successor more easily than with Arafat, whom neither trusted nor could work with politically. That successor was Mahmoud Abbas.

Yet the Road Map for resumed peace talks was fraught with problems. As a "performance based" blueprint for staged progress toward a two-state solution, stage I required unrealistic and unquantifiable measures of compliance, such as Palestinians "acting decisively against terror" and building a "practicing democracy."[97] Either side could cite the other for non-compliance as with demands

---

93 Assadi, M. (2003), "Palestinian Legislature Approves Premiership," *Reuters*, March 10, online at http://story.news.yahoo.com/news?tmpl=story&u=/nm/20030310/wl_nm/mideast_dc_52.

94 Heller, J. (2003), "Israel Vows to Target More Hamas Leaders," *Reuters*, March 9, online at http://story.news.yahoo.com/news?tmpl=story&ncid=586&e=3&cid=586&u=/nm/20030309/wl_nm/mideast_dc.

95 Greenberg, J. (2003), "Palestinians caught in power struggle between Arafat, Abbas," Chicago Tribune, August 31, online at http://www.accessmylibrary.com/coms2/summary_0286-7508267_ITM; "Palestinian Prime Minister Mahmoud Abbas Resigns," VOA News, September 6, 2003, online at http://www.voanews.com/english/archive/2003-09/a-2003-09-06-12-Palestinian.cfm.

96 Ward Anderson, J. and Moore, M. (2004), "Palestinian Leader Arafat Dies in France," *The Washington Post*, November 11, online at http://www.washingtonpost.com/wp-dyn/articles/A41474-2004Nov10.html.

97 "Quartet Roadmap to Israeli-Palestinian Peace," online at http://www.mideastweb.org/quartetrm3.htm.

for Israel's settlements to halt, and each could then blame the other for why the Road Map did not progress to its ambitious conclusion by 2005.

Add to this recipe for inaction the domestic political fissures in both Israeli and Palestinian governance, and the resulting stalemate was perhaps predictable. Responding to direct pressure from the United States to democratize, the Palestinian territories arranged for elections in January 2006. Perhaps unexpectedly for the US, the winner of the parliamentary elections was Hamas, the radical Islamist group with ties to terror and ties to the US nemesis, Iran. With a parliamentary majority, Hamas claimed the right to form the next cabinet for the Palestinian Authority, undermining the power of Mahmoud Abbas and his Fatah party. The US response was to cut annual aid to the Palestinian Authority, refusing to recognize or assist the regime.[98] If Arafat was intolerably linked to terror, Hamas was beyond the pale from the US standpoint.

Israel was undergoing a political seismic shift of its own at this time. Sharon, distrustful of the Road Map or the Palestinians, offered a new vision of "disengagement" for dealing with the Palestinian question. This involved constructing a wall (or "fence") around much of the West Bank, largely along the "Blue Line" of the border prior to Israel's annexation in the Six Day War (1967). As a barrier to defend Israeli territory from terrorist infiltration, it had the effect of creating a de facto border unilaterally on Israeli terms, incorporating parts of West Bank in the process. Disengagement also included the removal of Israeli settlements and control of the Gaza Strip, another Palestinian territory occupied since 1967. Together with a handful of indefensible West Bank settlements, this move showed Sharon's emerging preference for "demography over geography," separating Israel from heavily Arab territories for the sake of a viable, secure Israeli state.

Sharon quit his own Likud party in 2005 and formed a new one, Kadima, on this platform of disengagement. While Sharon suffered a coma, his Kadima party was successful in the 2006 elections. Sharon's successor, Ehud Olmert, carried forth the disengagement plans with virtual carte-blanche approval from the Bush Administration, despite questionable legalities regarding the wall, and the unilateralism inherent in the decisions taken by Israel. Concluding that Hamas was a non-starter as a partner for peace, Bush and Olmert's views converged regarding the threat posed and the acceptable responses to it.[99]

Part of the reason for US–Israeli perceptions was not merely the position of Hamas itself but the group's ties to Iran. This became particularly significant for the allies in the post-Saddam regional balance of power, in which Iran emerged

---

98   Berger, R. (2006), "Hamas Describes US and European Sanctions as 'Blackmail'," VOA News, April 8, online at http://www.voanews.com/english/archive/2006-04/2006-04-08-voa14.cfm?CFID=120194870&CFTOKEN=69251687&jsessionid=8830eb9b837991d074e72c4a4968e361f687.

99   On the convergence of Israeli and US perceptions, see Shannon, V. (2007), "On the Same Page?" *White House Studies*.

more confident with its former enemy vanquished and with the US bogged down with counterinsurgency. American, Israeli and even Arab fears of a resurgent revolutionary Iran (which is Persian, not Arab, and Shi'a Muslim in a predominantly Sunni Muslim Middle East) were expressed in increased description of a "Shi'a Crescent" from the Persian Gulf to the Levant.[100] However well-founded the beliefs and no matter what the US role was in bringing on such a turn of events, the Bush Administration and Israel seemed alarmed about Iran's shady nuclear programs and its ties to Hamas and Hezbollah in Lebanon. These two groups would become targets of US-backed Israeli military action.

The first Kadima war was against Hezbollah in the summer of 2006. Responding to a border incident in which two Israeli soldiers were kidnapped and a couple others killed, Israel launched a heavy offensive against Hezbollah deep into Lebanon. Initial bombing was followed with an invasion. Much of the world called for Israel to cease what was seen as a disproportionate and violent response to the incident, but the US shielded Israel in the Security Council and offered Israel its full support. By some later accounts, the US may have encouraged the war as a way to drive out Iranian influence from Lebanon, and was disappointed by Israel's decision to halt the war without finishing off the group.[101]

A similar war erupted again in late December 2008, this time aimed at Hamas in the Gaza Strip. Having been isolated by Israel, the US and Europe, Hamas competed for power with Abbas' Fatah, ruling from the West Bank with Western aid and approval. A brief conflict between the factions gave Hamas total control of Gaza, from which it continued attacks (what it calls "resistance") on Israeli targets. Having negotiated a ceasefire with Israel, the ceasefire broke down in late 2008. Blaming Hamas for renewed violence, Olmert again responded with surprisingly heavy-handed military force that ended up killing over 1,300. The Bush Administration again sided with Israel, blamed its foe for the violence, and resisted Security Council resolutions calling for a ceasefire.[102] As another proxy for Iranian influence, perhaps the US hoped Hamas would be routed, but again Israel stopped abruptly.

Restoring the Balance? The Future of US Policy

Amidst these wars on Israel's borders, the United States did take a final renewed interest in trying to negotiate peace between Israel and Mahmoud Abbas's

---

100　See "The Emerging Shia Crescent Symposium," Council on Foreign Relations, June 5, 2006, online at http://www.cfr.org/publication/10866/emerging_shia_crescent_symposium.html.

101　Barbalat, A. (2008), "A Friend Like This: Re-evaluating Bush and Israel," *Middle East Policy* XV:4 (Winter), 91–111.

102　"Bush Blames Hamas for Gaza Conflict," *CNN*, January 2, 2009, online at http://www.cnn.com/2009/WORLD/meast/01/02/bush.gaza/index.html.

Palestinian Authority. A self-congratulatory conference at Annapolis in late 2007 revealed the skepticism countries had in the US posturing for peace. Bush had little leverage or credibility to bring states to the table, and little came from the final year of talks despite numerous shuttling visits by Secretary of State Condoleezza Rice.

With the end of the Bush Administration comes the opportunity for the US to reassess the policies and implications of the post-9/11 approach to the Arab–Israeli conflict. The incoming Obama Administration signaled early an interest in jump-starting a peace process, appointing George Mitchell as a special envoy to the region. But what should the US do when it reengages? What are the lessons of the past eight years, what policies need to be continued and what needs to be changed?

What does not need change is continued aid and support to moderate regimes in the Middle East. Countries like Egypt, Jordan, and Israel should continue to receive US aid and assistance in a larger framework of encouraging a "New Middle East" much different than that envisioned by bin Laden and others, but still one that transcends the status quo of perennial conflict and division. All sovereign states, including Israel, deserve the guaranteed protection against aggression that the US has long granted them.

Given the Islamic-based terror that threatens Israel, the US, Egypt, Saudi Arabia, among others, there is a consensus focal point for continued cooperation to prohibit the rise of such forces in the greater Middle East. These forces already deem the US and these aforementioned states to be evil and violently met. Sadat was assassinated by an Egyptian Islamic Jihad, who killed the leader for making peace with Israel but also in their desire for a fundamentalist regime in Cairo. Saudi Arabia, too, faces such internal threat, the likes of which came to power in Iran. These targeted states must meet this challenge directly and cooperatively.

This continuity of purpose requires a keen focus on the priorities the US espouses: regional stability and countering terrorism. Such a focus makes plain the need to rally the region to the US cause. Rather than taking for granted 300 million Arabs and some 900 Muslims in the world, who control 60 percent of world gas and oil reserves, these constituencies need to be heard.[103] The resentment against America is widespread beyond al-Qaeda, and provides fertile ground for recruiting terrorists while constraining regional states from providing greater support to the US.[104] The United States must expend resources to ensure that the violence against

---

103 Curtiss, R. (2001), "The Cost of Israel to the American People," *Middle East Affairs Journal* 7/3–4, 101–12, 110.

104 Hoge, W. (2001), "A Sense of American Unfairness Erodes Support in Gulf States," *New York Times*, October 2, A6; Richey, W. (2001), "Muslim Opinion Sees Conspiracy," *Christian Science Monitor*, November 6, online at www.Csmonitor.com/2001/1106/p1s1-wogi.html; see also "Poll: Muslims call US 'ruthless, arrogant'," *cnn.com*, February 26, 2002, online at www.cnn.com/2002/US/02/26/gallup.muslims.

America does not similarly grow to match that resentment.[105] A new approach to the Arab–Israeli conflict must be soon, significant, and sincere.

It is still my belief that the fate of Palestinians, Israel and the US would all be improved with the creation of a Palestinian state. The difficulties in negotiating under present circumstances, with Palestinians divided between Gaza's Hamas and West Bank's Abbas, coupled with Israel's system providing government-toppling political power in the hands of small, reactionary parties, suggests that negotiated settlement will not or is highly unlikely to occur. Two possible alternatives exist: as Tom Friedman suggests, two "civil wars" may be necessary, to root out extremists in the Palestinian and Israeli camps who pose a barrier to the two-state solution.[106] To some degree, these battles began in 2005–2007, with Fatah fighting Hamas in Gaza, and Kadima's break with Likud while Israeli soldiers wrested settlers from abandoned settlements. The feasibility of this plan is questionable, however, asking each side to battle their own for the sake of the other.

Alternatively, the United States and the international community could unilaterally recognize a state of Palestine under West Bank and Gaza. Abandoning the procedural bias, the US action would be virulently opposed by Israel,[107] and would sour relations between the two countries to a degree. Nonetheless, the unipolar US is in a position to take such actions, and Israel's dependency on US aid places it in a position difficult to challenge the superpower. Unlike the previous proposal, this one is practically easier but politically difficult for an American President to take.

Interest group theory suggests that special interests prevail when there is no powerful counterbalance and when the general public is disengaged. Israel's peril in relation to its patron is that the latter may be changing. Long have everyday Americans been largely unaware of the Arab–Israeli conflict beyond the news spots that treat it as an "ancient" ethnic conflict. But 9/11 has awakened them to the US role in the region and may spawn questions about the costs of that role. A Newsweek Poll on October 6, 2001, found 52 percent of Americans responded that aid to Israel was "too much," and a 2007 poll showed 58 percent of Republicans and 80 percent of Democrats arguing the US "should not take either side" in the Israeli-Palestinian conflict.[108] This may mean that the tilt toward Israel at the expense not just of Palestinians but of Americans too, without the Cold War

---

105   The US has beefed up programs in public diplomacy in the battle for the "hearts and minds" since "9/11." See Robert Kaiser, "Making Sure the US Message Gets Heard," *Washington Post National Weekly*.

106   Interview of Tom Friedman on National Public Radio, online at http://www.npr.org/ramfiles/fa/20020529.fa.ram or http://freshair.npr.org/dayFA.cfm?display=day&todayDate=05%2F29%2F2002.

107   For an argument against a unilaterally declared Palestinian state, see Becker, T. "International Recognition of a Unilaterally Declared Palestinian State," *Jerusalem Center for Public Affairs*, online at www.jcpa.org/art/becker1.htm.

108   See "Polling the Nation" online at http://poll.orspub.com; Barablat, 94.

strategic context to justify the relationship, may lead to a change of heart, and a change of policy.

This does not suggest abandoning Israel or throwing its fate to the winds. The United States should still support Israel and its security. Rather, the suggestions provided here reflect an outcome I believe would benefit Israel as much as it would the Palestinians and the US. It would clarify the distinctions between the nationalist resistance violence by everyday Palestinians from the fundamentalists bent on pushing Israel into the sea. A new Palestinian state would then have the power and responsibility to clamp down on the latter, to the PA's political benefit, since Hamas and others are political rivals to Fatah and other secular nationalists. The rejectionists would then face the combined will and resources of a supportive Israel, US, and other moderates in the region. Israeli security would be clarified by distinct borders, and it would be free to defend such borders as a sovereign state may, without the international stigma that has undermined Israel's reputation over the course of its existence.

A more long-term alternative "change" in the US approach to the Middle East and Arab–Israeli conflict would involve extricating itself from it altogether. This seems politically and strategically impossible at this point, nor is it desirable under the current state of US interests and affairs. But to the extent that the US has increasingly become entwined in the Middle East and its conflicts, the first and foremost reason has been the strategic value of oil and of the region as its fundamental source of supply and reserves. Many similar conflicts have transpired in, say, sub-Saharan Africa, that lacked practicality in terms of American resource investment and would have "cost" disproportionally more than the "benefit." This suggests that either by policy or nature, oil will someday come to matter less, and matter not, to the US and the industrial world. Whether alternative energy sources precede or follow the future end to the finite supply of oil, there will come a time where this chief pillar of US policy in the Middle East will dry up with it. By then, if the Arab–Israeli conflict has not been solved, the US may lose interest, as the broader population questions the value of entangling alliances in a region holding no more legitimate interest to the US. Reducing oil dependency, in short, is an inevitable future (be it 100 years or more) that both Israel and the oil-rich regional states may fear, loathe, and had best prepare for.

These are profound political, military, and moral considerations that have been wrestled with for years already. September 11 brought new impetus to the cause, and the Bush Administration has made indications that it indeed is a new day, calling for a Palestinian state "within three years" under certain conditions. Whether the US musters its influence to coax lasting change remains to be seen. The legacy of the United States President to end the Arab–Israeli conflict, even if it gives way to a moderate/fundamentalist conflict already afoot, would be historic— if the political will that this book demonstrates would be required is present in the decision-makers of US foreign policy.

Conclusion

United States policy toward the Arab–Israeli conflict after 9/11 reflects some change but mostly continuity. The events of September 11 undoubtedly reordered US priorities, motivating the superpower to fight terrorism and stabilize this region that is so vital to the US definition of national interests. Like the Gulf War a decade before, another President Bush sought to lead in the Arab–Israeli peace process not for its own sake, but in a broader strategic context of American actions against al-Qaeda, Afghanistan, and Iraq. This at first translated into a courtship of the Arab and Muslim world, with the momentous declaration of US support for an independent Palestine. But the War on Terror served simultaneously as a constraint on US relations toward the Palestinian cause. The pervasive terrorist violence by Palestinians forced Bush to take a hard line toward Arafat and perpetrating groups, in the name of consistency with the US principles in the "War on Terror." Palestinian statehood thus became conditional on reform in the Palestinian Authority and the promise to end the violence, much in line with the Sharon view.

United States policy also reflected continuity in that a balance of strategic and domestic influences characterized the American approach, leading once again to a slow, deliberate, stalling policy that is ambiguous enough that it may not lead to real change. The Bush Administration is pro-Israel for domestic and strategic reasons: Israel has cooperated with the US throughout the "War on Terror" to a greater extent than the Arabs Bush had courted. Bush was personally affronted by Arafat, a sentiment intensified by the context of terror precipitated by 9/11 and the continued terror acts in the occupied territories. Domestically, President Bush had a freer hand to create new policy tracks, but remained cognizant of the domestic pressures that confined his behavior so as not to alienate Israel or its supporters.

The promise of Palestinian statehood thus far has been rhetorical, and its realization is by no means secured. The war against Iraq and numerous confounding stumbling blocks in the peace process provide room to question whether the "Road Map" ever becomes reality. But what Bush accomplished rhetorically is a shift in the debate—de-legitimizing any one-state solutions or those not giving Palestinians independence. This is an historic shift with which even Sharon has had to reconcile. The implementation is in question and may take time. But it is a moment the Bush Administration let slip by. A two-state vision would help US image greatly, defusing a regional argument for anti-Americanism by leading the way to the creation of a homeland for Palestinians. This would ameliorate the violence and conflict based on nationalism and the scourge of oppression, which has taken a toll on Palestinians and Israelis alike. While it would not likely ameliorate more extremist terrorism, such as that of Hamas, a Palestinian state would be an empowered ally to join both the US and Israel against fundamentalist extremism.

Chapter 10

The Limits of Military Power: The United States in Iraq

Tom Lansford and Jack Covarrubias

Introduction

Military strategy and tactics evolved rapidly during the twentieth century to account for the new reality of a modern world that has grown increasingly smaller and connected. While new weapons and new methods of waging war forever changed the nature of combat, the advent of sub-national actors capable of waging campaigns against the most powerful nation-states heralded an era of military operations other than war. At various points in history, the United States military has pioneered a number of innovative weapons systems and tactics to counter traditional threats. However, the nation's defense establishment has at times been slow to adapt to changes and evolutions in warfare giving rise to the oft-cited admonishment that "the military is always preparing for the last war." The end of the Cold War initiated a period of uncertainty and new missions for the US military which culminated in the War on Terror launched in the aftermath of the terrorist attacks of September 11. This was done without a firm understanding of the more holistic nature of international relations and the need to account for non-state national threats. More specifically, US military prowess was applied unevenly in the new campaigns in Afghanistan and Iraq. This chapter explores the evolution of modern warfare and the application of new strategy and tactics within the Iraq conflict. Specifically, the essay examines the rise of asymmetric warfare within the broader scope of the emergence of fourth generation warfare and the impact of the Iraq War on American military planning and force structures.

Revolutions in Military Affairs

US military doctrine of the twentieth century was based on symmetric warfare. Noted security studies scholar Donald Snow asserts that symmetric warfare "occurs when both sides adopt and fight in the same basic ways and follow the same basic rules"; it is essentially "traditional western warfare."[1] Symmetric warfare involves

---

1 Snow, D. (2008), *National Security for a New Era: Globalization and Geopolitics After Iraq*, 3rd edn, New York: Pearson, 9.

large relatively professional, conventional armies that more or less follow similar customs and largely abide by international conventions on the conduct of war.[2] The First and Second World Wars typified traditional Western warfare, and planning for symmetric conflicts dominated US Cold War strategy.

Conversely, throughout its history, the United States has alternatively used, or been the target of, asymmetric warfare. Asymmetric warfare involves efforts by one side of a conflict to use relative advantages against the perceived weaknesses of an opposing force. It can ameliorate numeric or technological superiorities by concentrating power and forces against weak points or utilizing tactics that negate an opponent's advantages. Actors using asymmetric warfare may concentrate forces against a specific unit or target of a larger enemy, thereby achieving temporary or situational numeric superiority. Actors may also use weapons or tactics outside the normal operating procedures of their opponents. Asymmetric warfare may be undertaken by either nation-states or non-state actors. Snow defines asymmetric warfare as:

> ... the situation in which both (or all) sides do not accept or practice the same methods of warfare. Asymmetry can extend both to the methods opposing sides use to conduct military operations and to the rules of warfare to which they adhere. Guerilla warfare, which the United States encountered in Vietnam through the use of irregular enemy soldiers in tactics such as ambushes, is one form of asymmetrical warfare. Terrorism is another, as are the methods used by the various insurgent groups in Iraq. Those fighting asymmetrically may also reject the rules of war favored by their opponents; consciously targeting civilians as an example.[3]

Writing in *Military Review*, Clifton J. Anker III and Michael D. Burke argue that "[o]ne way to look at asymmetric warfare is to see it as a classic action-reaction-counteraction cycle. Our enemies study our doctrine and try to counter it. Any competent enemy will do the unexpected ... [w]hen we understand the asymmetry, we counter it, and so forth."[4] By the 1990s, the threat of asymmetric warfare became an increasing focus of US military strategy and was cited as a major threat in the 1997 *National Security Strategy* which declared that:

> ... the United States must plan and prepare to fight and win under conditions where an adversary may use asymmetric means against us unconventional approaches that avoid or undermine our strengths while exploiting our

---

2   For an overview of the rise of the Western style of warfare, see Black, J. (2001), *Western Warfare, 1775–1882*, Bloomington: Indiana; and its companion work (2002), *Warfare in the Western World, 1882–1975*, Bloomington: Indiana University Press.

3   Snow, op. cit. fn. 1, 8–9.

4   Ancker, C.J., III and Burke, M.D. (2003), "Doctrine for Asymmetric Warfare," *Military Review* 83/18 (25 July-August), 18.

vulnerabilities. This is of particular importance and a significant challenge. Because of our dominance in the conventional military arena, adversaries who challenge the United States are likely to do so using asymmetric means, such as WMD, information operations or terrorism.[5]

Although the decade of the 1990s began with a large conventional war, the 1990–1991 Persian Gulf conflict, the *National Security Strategy* reflected the growing involvement of the United States in asymmetric conflicts in areas such as Somalia and the Balkans, as well as the increased use of terrorism against US interests. For instance, during the October 1993 Battle of Mogadishu, militias were able to negate the technological superiority of coalition forces after they shot down first one and then a second Black Hawk helicopter forcing American Ranger and Special Operations Forces to fight in a dense urban setting. The Somali experience highlights another aspect of asymmetric warfare, its ability to undermine the resolve or will of opposing forces. Writing in the 1970s, Andrew Mack argued that power asymmetry actually made larger and more powerful states less likely to win asymmetric conflicts since these actors typically have diverse and multifaceted interests while their smaller opponents were often more resolute and focused. Within democracies, publics would grow tired of the casualties or the resources expended in these conflicts, while elites in authoritarian regimes would often force an end to fighting in order to protect the regime.[6] Other scholars argue it is the ability of smaller actors to be more flexible or "nimble in shifting ... strategic approach" that explains the ability of lesser powers to win asymmetric conflicts.[7]

The First Generations of Modern Warfare

Asymmetric warfare was one component of a broader trend in conflict, the emergence of fourth generation warfare as part of a continuing series of revolutions in military affairs. First articulated in the 1980s, fourth generation warfare was asserted to mark a broad transition from the traditional European system of warfare.[8] Proponents of fourth generation warfare argued that the revolution in military affairs that accompanied the rise of the smoothbore musket created the first generation of modern warfare. First generation warfare (1648–1860) was characterized by a

5   US, White House (1997), *National Security Strategy*, Washington, DC: GPO, online at http://clinton2.nara.gov/WH/EOP/NSC/Strategy/.

6   See Mack, A.J.R. (1975), "Why Big Nations Lose Small Wars: The Politics of Asymmetric Wars," *World Politics* 27/2 (January), 175–200.

7   Arreguin-Toft, I. (2001), "How the Weak Win Wars: A Theory of Asymmetric Conflict," *International Security* 26/93 (Summer), 120.

8   See Lind, W.S., Nightengale, K., Schmitt, J.F., Sutton, J.W. and Wilson, G.I. (1989), "The Changing Face of War: Into the Fourth Generation," *Marine Corps Gazette* (October), 22–26.

near monopoly on the use of force by the state. Operationally, it was marked by a dramatic increase in firepower, including muskets and artillery, massed lines and relatively simplistic tactics. Tactical success was achieved by breaking the enemy's lines. In addition, as William Lind points out "most of the things that distinguish military from civilian—uniforms, saluting, careful gradations of rank were products of the First Generation and were intended to reinforce the culture of order."[9] The second generation emerged with the development of the rifled barrel with its greater accuracy and ever-increasingly powerful and sophisticated weaponry, ranging from breechloading rifles to machine guns to heavy artillery. In addition, other technological advances in transportation and communication, including first the railway and then motorized vehicles, paralleled by the telegraph and then the radio, changed the speed with which maneuvers could be undertaken as well as the degree of command and control. Second generation warfare culminated in World War I which still emphasized mass firepower and linear attacks. However, attrition replaced penetration as the mark of battlefield success. Third generation warfare emerged after World War I and exemplified the strategies and tactics of World War II, as well as Cold War strategic planning. As noted in a seminal 1989 essay on third generation warfare, the new warfighting was "[b]ased on maneuver rather than attrition," and provided, "the first truly nonlinear tactics. The attack relied on infiltration to bypass and collapse the enemy's combat forces rather than seeking to close with and destroy them."[10] Lind contends that third generation warfare "seeks to get into the enemy's rear areas and collapse him from the rear forward. Instead of 'close with and destroy,' the motto is 'bypass and collapse'".[11] The armored thrust that was exemplified by the blitzkrieg tactics of speed and coordination of close air support utilized by Germany during World War II emerged as a central component of third generation warfare.

Fourth Generation Warfare

Elements of fourth generation warfare have existed for centuries and date at least to the writings of Sun Tzu and have their modern roots in the strategy and tactics of Mao Zedong. It is a form of asymmetric warfare that seeks to integrate the totality of a society or group and engage the enemy on multiple fronts to inflict enough damage to defeat them on the political front, while acknowledging that a traditional military victory may not be possible. Thomas X. Hammes, a fellow in the Institute for the National Strategic Studies at the US National Defense University, summarizes fourth generation warfare in the following manner:

---

9   Lind, W.S., "Understanding Fourth Generation Warfare," *Military Review* (September-October 2004), 12.

10   Lind et al., op. cit. fn. 8, 23.

11   Lind, op. cit. fn. 9, 13.

Fourth-generation warfare, which is now playing out in Iraq and Afghanistan, is a modern form of insurgency. Its practitioners seek to convince enemy political leaders that their strategic goals are either unachievable or too costly for the perceived benefit. The fundamental precept is that superior political will, when properly employed, can defeat greater economic and military power. Because it is organized to ensure political rather than military success, this type of warfare is difficult to defeat.[12]

Lind points out that fourth generation warfare is characterized by the loss of the state "monopoly on war" and that it marks the "most radical change since the Peace of Westphalia."[13] Fourth generation warfare recognizes the rise of non-state actors as first level security threats to nation-states, including powerful actors such as the United States. It also involves a diffusion of threats that extend beyond traditional notions of security. Societies will find themselves under attack both internally and externally from a smaller, less immediately potent enemy; but, it will be an opponent whose conflict horizon far exceeds that of the country under attack.[14]

At its core, fourth generation is the culmination of asymmetric warfare. Opponents utilize a variety of strategies and tactics to erode the will and defeat their enemy politically, rather than militarily. Hammes provides the following overview of how the various levels of fourth generation warfare extend beyond the Western European traditional notions of warfare:

> Strategically, fourth-generation warfare remains focused on changing the minds of decisionmakers. Politically, it involves transnational, national, and subnational organizations and networks. Operationally, it uses different messages for different audiences, all of which focus on breaking an opponent's political will. Tactically, it utilizes materials present in the society under attack—to include chemicals, liquefied natural gas, or fertilizers.[15]

The terrorist attacks against New York, London and Madrid, are demonstrative of the ability of non-state actors to inflict significant damage on modern societies through financial and other support from informal transnational networks. They also demonstrate the utility of the internet and other forms of digital communications to

---

12   Hammes, T.X. (2005), "Insurgency: Modern Warfare Evolves into a Fourth Generation," *Strategic Forum* 214 (January), 1.

13   Lind, op. cit. fn. 9, 13.

14   See, for instance, Barnett, R.W. (2003), *Asymmetrical Warfare: Today's Challenge to US Military Power*, Washington: Brassey's; or Bell, C. (2001), "The First War of the 21st Century: Asymmetric Hostilities and the Norms of Conduct," *Strategic and Defense Studies Centre Working Paper, no. 364*, Strategic and Defense Studies Centre, Australian National University.

15   Hammes, op. cit. fn. 12, 1.

develop and implement plans and to coordinate groups. The attacks also confirm an evolution of asymmetric conflicts wherein modern groups are "comprised of loose coalitions of the willing, human networks that range from local to global ..." and "operate across the spectrum from local to transnational organizations."[16] Such coalitions bring together diverse actors with a variety of goals. For instance, in Iraq, the insurgents range from Baathists who seek to restore the former regime (or at least their elite status) to Shi'ites seeking a theocracy to foreign fighters opposed to the United States.

Fourth generation warfare does continue trends of earlier eras, including the increased importance of tactical maneuvers and the ability of units to react quickly and employ overwhelming force. In addition, the emphasis on large deployments continues to wane. In their 1989 essay, Lind and his coauthors assert that "mass may become a disadvantage as it will be easy to target," instead "[s]mall, highly maneuverable, agile forces will tend to dominate."[17] This trend has been confirmed through the defeats suffered by the United States in Vietnam, Lebanon and Somalia and the succession of conflicts of 1990s and 2000s.

Fourth Generation Warfare and Iraq

Prior to the 2001 terrorist attacks on the United States, the Administration of George W. Bush initiated a review of US defense policy and force structure. Secretary of Defense Donald Rumsfeld was tasked to expand efforts to transform the US military into a more agile force that would be better suited to the smaller, regional conflicts that emerged in the 1990s. The new Secretary encountered significant resistance from both the civilian and military leadership within the Defense Department which supported the maintenance of a large, conventional force structure and third generation warfare weapons systems.[18] Nonetheless, there was a cadre of officials and officers who had advocated the need for a transformation of the nation's military to better address fourth generation warfare.

Rumsfeld emerged as a proponent of technology to counter asymmetric disadvantages. The 2001 *Quadrennial Defense Review* (issued less than a month after the September 11 strikes) calls for the nation to move away "from a 'threat-based' model that has dominated thinking in the past to a 'capabilities-based' model ..." that would allow the United States to "identify the capabilities required to deter and defeat adversaries who rely on surprise, deception and asymmetric warfare to achieve their objectives."[19] The report also called for the United States

---

16   Hammes, T.X. (2006), "Countering Evolved Insurgent Networks," *Military Review* (July-August), 19.

17   Lind et al., op. cit. fn. 8, 24.

18   Snow, op. cit. fn. 1, 110–112.

19   US, Department of Defense (2001), *Quadrennial Defense Review Report (QDR)*, Washington, DC: Department of Defense, September 30, 4.

to "maintain its military advantages in key areas while it develops new areas of military advantage and denies asymmetric advantages to adversaries" and undertake "the transformation of US forces, capabilities, and institutions to extend America's asymmetric advantages well into the future."[20] Hence, Rumsfeld sought to use asymmetric warfare to the advantage of the United States. For instance, the US military sought to take advantage of network-centric warfare,[21] a system that "broadly describes the combination of strategies, emerging tactics, techniques, and procedures, and organizations that a fully or even a partially networked force can employ to create a decisive warfighting advantage"[22] by integrating battlefield intelligence, communications, tactics and weapons so that everyone from commanders to the field soldiers has complete tactical awareness. Network-centric warfare was envisioned as a force multiplier that could mitigate asymmetric advantages of an enemy. If a patrol was ambushed, commanders in the rear would know immediately and could dispatch precision-guided weaponry and close air support to overcome any temporary numeric superiority of the enemy.[23]

Operation Enduring Freedom in 2001 provided the United States with the opportunity to utilize network-centric warfare during the coalition invasion of Afghanistan. Noted military scholar Stephen Biddle explained that "a novel combination of special operations forces (SOF), precision-guided munitions (PGMs), and an indigenous ally destroyed the Taliban's military, toppled their regime, and did so while neither exposing Americans to the risk of heavy casualties nor expanding the American presence in a way that might spur nationalist insurgency."[24] One analyst noted that "[s]trikes that took hours to coordinate in Desert Storm a decade earlier were carried out in Afghanistan and Iraq as quickly as 45 minutes from the time a target was identified."[25] Aerial support and intelligence were enhanced through the use of unmanned aerial vehicles (UAVs) which bolstered both the firepower and vision of the troops on the ground. The

---

20 Ibid.

21 The 2001 Quadrennial Defense Review Report notes that the Defense Department was in the midst of a "transition" to network-centric warfare; US, Department of Defense, op. cit. fn. 19, 37.

22 US, Department of Defense (2005), Office of Force Transformation, *The Implementation of Network-Centric Warfare*, Washington: US Government Printing Office, 3.

23 In one of the earliest essays on network-centric warfare, the authors note that the concept is "characterized by the ability of geographically dispersed forces to create a high level of shared battlespace awareness that can be exploited via self-synchronization and other network-centric operations to achieve commanders' intent"; Cebrowski, A.K. and Garstka, J.J. (1998), "Network-Centric Warfare: Its Origin and Future," *US Naval Institute Proceedings*, 124, 139.

24 Biddle, S. (2002), *Afghanistan and the Future of Warfare: Implications for Army and Defense Policy*, Carlisle Barracks, PA: Army War College, 1.

25 Luddy, J. (2005), *The Challenge and Promise of Network-Centric Warfare*, Arlington, VA: Lexington Institute, 4.

successful integration of technology and conventional force led Rumsfeld to create the Office of Force Transformation in order to apply the lessons learned to future conflicts.[26]

The Road to War

Operation Enduring Freedom encompassed more than the invasion of Afghanistan and included the deployment of US special operations forces and military training personnel in the Philippines, Central Asia and Africa. There was also increased cooperation between the United States and other nations in intelligence, law enforcement and in tracking financial networks. However, the next main front in the War on Terror was Iraq. Four factors were crucial in initiating the conflict. The first was the election of George W. Bush who had become convinced of the necessity of regime change even prior to the 2000 Presidential campaign. The second was the influence of pro-war advocates within the Administration, including Vice President Dick Cheney, Secretary of Defense Rumsfeld and Deputy Secretary of Defense Paul Wolfowitz. Most believed that Iraq could be transformed into a secular, democratic state that could, in turn, launch a wave of democracy in the region. In addition, as Jonathan Renshon notes, the "decision to invade Iraq did not take place in an historical or political vacuum."[27] Instead, the Iraqi patterns of defiance towards the succession of UN Security Council Resolutions lent credence to the proponents.

Third, the September 11 attacks provided a "bridge" between the War on Terror and a war with Iraq. The possibility that Iraq was pursuing weapons of mass destruction or supporting terrorism elevated the nation from a regional to an international threat to the Bush Administration.[28] Fourth, and finally, was the operational success of Operation Enduring Freedom in dislodging the Taliban regime. Despite the failure of the coalition to capture Osama bin Laden, Operation Enduring Freedom seemed to confirm the utility of network-centric warfare and the technological advantages of the US-led forces. In addition, one of the strategic components of the Afghan Model, that US forces would undertake the initial warfighting and then coalition members would provide the bulk of personnel for nation-building, seemed to offer the possibility of avoiding a long, drawn-out occupation by American troops.

While the United States enjoyed broad international support in Operation Enduring Freedom, efforts to develop a coalition of the willing to invade Iraq were limited. Some of the closest allies of the United States, including France and Germany, opposed the invasion, as did other major global powers such as

---

26   Moniz, D. (2002), "Afghanistan's Lessons Shaping New Military," *USA Today* (October 8), A13.

27   Renshon, J. (2006), *Why Leaders Choose War: The Psychology of Prevention*, Westport, CT: Praeger, 109.

28   Snow, op. cit. fn. 1, 260–61.

China and Russia. Turkey, a key regional ally, refused to allow the United States to use its territory to launch a second, northern front against Iraq. This forced Pentagon planners to redeploy the 4th Mechanized Infantry Division which had been scheduled to invade from Turkey.

Rumsfeld initially sought to overthrow the Iraqi regime of Saddam Hussein, utilizing the Afghan Model, through a combination of opposition groups and US special operations troops.[29] However, it became clear that the asymmetric advantages that the United States enjoyed in Afghanistan would be drastically reduced in Iraq which still maintained a significant, though degraded, conventional military and a much higher degree of control over its population and territory. There were also more urban areas. The planning for Iraq centered on a third-generation campaign that revolved around armored thrusts and encirclement, supported by massive firepower from the ground and air. Even though the invading force numbered only half of what had been deployed in 1991 during the first Persian Gulf War, US planners asserted publicly that the attack would produce "shock and awe" among the Iraqis. Unmanned Aerial Vehicles (UAVs) and Special Operations Forces would be force multipliers that compensated for the reduced numbers. The United States would engage in an asymmetric campaign that allowed it to utilize its technological advantages to offset Iraqi numeric superiority and negate the country's defensive advantages.

Concerns were raised about the number of troops involved in the invasion, most famously by then Army Chief of Staff, Eric Shinseki, who warned in February 2003 that the US would need more than an additional 100,000 troops to effectively oversee post-Saddam Iraq.[30] Other estimates were that an occupying force would need to include 500,000 or more troops.[31] In addition, regional allies, including Saudi Arabia, expressed concerns over the impact of an invasion on regional stability and the potential for increased terrorism in the Gulf Emirates. Nonetheless, the Bush Administration continued to prepare for war as the diplomatic wrangling continued through the winter of 2003.

The Invasion of Iraq

The United States and its allies issued an ultimatum to Iraq on March 17, 2003 that required Saddam and his sons to relinquish power and leave the country within 48 hours or face military action. On March 20, after Saddam failed to comply with the ultimatum, the coalition initiated airstrikes on command and control installations and air defense sites. Air superiority was quickly achieved and

---

29 Gordon, M. (2002), "Iraqis Seek to Oust Hussein with US Military Training," *The New York Times* (January 31), A10.

30 Schmitt, E. (2003), "Army Chief Raises Estimate of G.I.'s Needed in Postwar Iraq," *The New York Times* (February 25), A1.

31 Reported in Slavin, B. and Moniz, D. (2003), "How Peace in Iraq became So Elusive," *USA Today* (July 22), A1.

maintained throughout the campaign, as was control of Iraq's territorial waters. The invasion force for Operation Iraqi Freedom was a relatively light and agile force, with a significant Special Operations Force component. Total coalition forces included about 235,000 troops of which 168,000 were ground troops. The bulk was American forces, with about 46,000 British troops, 2,000 Australians, and small Special Operations Forces units from Poland and Denmark. Other coalition forces remained in Kuwait to provide logistical support. Officially, the coalition was named Combined and Joint Task Force 7 ("combined" meaning more than one nation and "joint" meaning more than one military service). Opposing the coalition were approximately 430,000 Iraqi forces that ranged from the elite Republican Guard armored and mechanized units to paramilitary security troops.

There were benefits to the small size of the coalition. First, there was high degree of interoperability among the allied nations, although the United States did provide some command and control gear to its allies to allow the forces to communicate and exchange information through satellites and secure internet connections. Second, the US was able to secure a unified command structure that avoided the problems of past coalitions, including the 1991 Persian Gulf War. The utility of a smaller coalition during a military campaign was one of the lessons taken by the United States from Operation Enduring Freedom.[32] The overall operational commander of the invasion was US General Tommy Franks, and the ground commander was US Lieutenant General David McKiernan. Third, and finally, the small force minimized logistical and supply requirements. This was especially important since the invading forces had a relatively small launching point from Kuwait.

The invading ground forces attacked on three fronts, a two-pronged pincer attack in the south, and a smaller campaign in the north. In the southwest, coalition Special Operations Forces, British commandos and US Marines undertook an amphibious operation to capture the Al-Faw Peninsula as part of an eastern prong led by the US 1st Marine Expeditionary Force. Coalition forces then secured Basra and moved north toward Baghdad. In northern Iraq, US and Polish Special Operations Forces worked with Kurdish militias to create a northern front in Operation Northern Delay. They were supported by the US 173rd Airborne Brigade. The main thrust of the campaign was an armored advance by the US V Corps, which formed the western prong of the pincer movement toward Baghdad. US forces reached Baghdad on April 4 in one of the fastest armored advances in modern warfare and had control of the city by April 12. On May 1, Bush declared that major combat operations were over. However, as Hammes points out: "While most Americans rejoiced at this announcement, students of history understood that it simply meant the easy part was over. In the following months, peace did not break out, and the troops did not come home."[33]

---

32 See Lansford, T. (2002), *All for One: Terrorism, NATO and the United States*, Aldershot: Ashgate Publishing.
33 Hammes, op. cit. fn. 12, 1.

The Insurgency

Even before organized resistance ceased, small bands of Saddam loyalists and foreign fighters began an insurgency against the coalition forces. The initial failure of the coalition to capture Saddam or his two sons motivated Baathists to continue fighting (the two sons were killed in fighting with coalition forces on July 22, 2003, and Saddam himself was subsequently captured on December 13). In addition to the Baathists insurgents, composed largely of former Baath officials and members of the former Iraqi military and security services, some 35–40 distinct insurgent groups are believed to exist within Iraq. These include Nationalists, the Iraqi Salafis, several Shi'a militias, al-Qaeda in Iraq as well as a number of other indigenous and foreign groups operating in the country. While their motivation for operating are as varied as the number of groups that exist, the return to power for Baathists, Islamic rule, nationalism, organized crime, tribal feuds, and so on, all have a common focus in desiring an end to American occupation.

The lack of a common strategy and motivation amongst the various factions involved in the insurgency is a major handicap for US forces that are used to, and have largely trained for, traditional military operations. With US experience in counter insurgency operations largely derived from its experience in Vietnam and other Cold War era examples, the Iraq insurgency does not fit the "classic" model of revolutionary warfare in which the goal is to seize power by a competing government. The agenda of the many often competing and disagreeing factions within the Iraqi insurgency means that there is no commonly recognized and understood "political, economic, and social agenda" outside the American foe.[34] Likewise:

> Modern insurgents operate more like a self-synchronizing swarm of independent but cooperating cells than like a formal organization. Even the fashionable cybernetic discourse of "networks" and "nodes" often implies more structure than exists.[35]

This implies, as has been pointed out in a number of places, that the insurgency is relatively immune to prediction and has no overarching authority with which to negotiate, remove, or otherwise directly attack.

The US military, according to Lind among others, is largely a product of the second generation of warfare—getting maximum firepower, quickly and on target.[36] While technology and tactics have changed since WWI, the threat has

---

34   Record, J. and Terrill, W.A. (2004), *Iraq and Vietnam: Differences, Similarities and Insights*, Carlisle, PA: Strategic Studies Institute.
35   Kilcullen, D. (2009), "Counter-insurgency Redux," in Art, R.J. and Waltz, K.N. (eds), *The Use of Force: Military Power and International Politics*, 7th edn, Plymouth, United Kingdom: Rowman & Littlefield.
36   Lind, op. cit. fn. 9.

also significantly changed. Even if the US successfully neutralizes command and control elements of the insurgency, the inherent autonomy that exists within the rank and file means continued resistance. With success being measured not in land and treasure, but instead in political pressure on the American Government to withdrawal from Iraq and the continued disruption of Iraqi civil authority, even military success locally can impose a loss for the US regionally and internationally. Lind points out in the same article that fourth generation warfare implies at its core "a universal crisis of legitimacy for the state." With political favor both domestic and abroad largely turned against US efforts in Iraq, it is easy to see that despite a military still very effective at neutralizing known enemies, it is largely ineffective at winning the modern political battlefield.

Conclusion

It is difficult to envision a future Iraq that is also viewed as a success of American planning and strategy. The sectarian conflict that grew in the post-war environment has successfully waged a war of politics against a US military that has proven slow to change to match the reality of a modern occupation against a modern insurgency. Since the end of major combat operations, occupation duties have cost the US well over the initial estimates of $50–60 billion.[37] By some estimates, the cost will rise over $3 trillion once efforts are concluded. Even if this figure is hyper-inflated, the more than 4,000 service members plus an unfathomable number of Iraqis killed in Iraq assure a high political and emotional cost for the US and the world.

It is important the US learn the "right" lessons from its experience in Iraq.[38] Friedman, Sapolsky and Preble point out that "Iraq is not an example of what not to do but of how not to do it." The US should rethink its national security strategies instead of debate comments about troop strengths, counter insurgency doctrine, and better planning. All of these debates fail to solve the fourth generation's attack on political legitimacy in a globalized world. While the February 2007 troop surge of 30,000 soldiers—down some 80 percent in 2008—as well as the meeting of 12 out of 18 major benchmarks set by the Bush Administration had an impact on security and stability within Iraq, the overall security and power of the US in the international community has suffered because of its involvement. These indicators of "success" serve to be little more than political excuses to allow a strategic withdrawal and possible opportunity to save face.

The unpopularity of the war has already damaged the immediate legacy of the Republican Administration of George W. Bush and long time public servant Donald Rumsfeld. Anti-war Democrats and Republicans staged a significant

---

37   Bimes, L.J. and Stiglitz, J.E. (2008), "The Iraq War Will Cost U $3 Trillion, and Much More," *The Washington Post* (9 March).

38   Friedman, B., Sapolsky, H. and Preble, C. (2008), "Learning the Right Lessons from Iraq," *Policy Analysis* 610, 13 February.

attack on Bush policies resulting in a 2006 loss of Republican control of Congress and the subsequent resignation of Secretary of Defense Rumsfeld on November 8, 2006—the day after the elections. This also set the stage for the 2008 election of Democratic President Barack Obama with a promise of significant change of US policies on the international stage and a promise for a timetable of withdrawal from Iraq—a position opposed by the Bush Administration.

The main advantage of the US military's way of "doing business," as envisioned by concepts such as network-centric warfare, is also the largest handicap the US has in shifting its strategic vision to fourth generational thinking. The ability to overwhelmingly and decisively destroy an enemy while reducing the number of troops required serves to handicap the ability to conduct "waging the peace" activities. Writing in *Wired*, Noah Shachtman summarized the problem in the following fashion:

> ... network-centric warfare, with its emphasis on fewer, faster-moving troops, turned out to be just about the last thing the US military needed when it came time to rebuild Iraq and Afghanistan. A small, wired force leaves generals with too few nodes on the military network to secure the peace. There aren't enough troops to go out and find informants, build barricades, rebuild a sewage treatment plant, and patrol a marketplace.[39]

United States strategic thinking remains stagnant, focusing on a past rooted in conventional warfare when it is increasingly apparent that future US military operations are likely to be Military Operations Other Than War (MOOTWs) and, more importantly, have an impact that reaches far outside geographic and military boundaries. The US strategic challenge is to protect and magnify the strengths of democracy and freedom while also maintaining decisive military advantage and capability. Current accepted doctrine seemingly allows only one or the other.

---

39 Shachtman, N. (2007), "How Technology Almost Lost the War: In Iraq, the Critical Networks are Social—Not Electronic" (15), online at http://www.wired.com/politics/security/magazine/15-12/ff_futurewar?currentPage=1.

Chapter 11

Three Dimensional Chess: An Analysis of the Circumstances of Terrorism in Central and South Asia[1]

Dirk C. van Raemdonck

Introduction

Most definitions of terrorism state in one way or another that terrorism is a means to a set of political ends. The means concern visiting destruction on representatives or institutions of a state, on infrastructure, or on random citizens. Blackmail, kidnapping, hijacking and fundraising through legal or illegal means are also common components of terrorism. Directly or indirectly, all of these create insecurity, manipulating the opponent's political actions.

Nowhere else is there such a complex tangle of actors and motives as in Afghanistan and neighboring Pakistan. The terrain on which these struggles are played out is physically vast and encompasses both Central and South Asia.[2] To make sense of the terrorisms confronting policymakers, this chapter will first present an analytical framework, consisting of what we term the Great Game, the Little Game, and the Domestic Game. Using this, we will explore the motives of the main players. Next, we will survey chronologically several of the most important event sequences that impact terrorism-related US foreign security policy in Central and South Asia, closing with some observations.

---

1 The author would like to thank Andrew Dowdle, Robert Maranto, and Bikash Roy for the many interesting conversations on the region and its inhabitants. We may not always agree, but disagreement and debate create new ideas and put old ones to the test. Thanks also to April Maranto for editorial suggestions and to Kim Torres and Jonathan Mills for assisting in research tasks.

2 South Asia can be defined as including Afghanistan, Bangladesh, Bhutan, Sri Lanka, India, the Maldives, Nepal, and Pakistan. Central Asia encompasses Afghanistan (again), Kazakhstan, Kyrgyzstan, Tajikistan, Turkmenistan, Uzbekistan, and the border regions of the neighboring countries of Russia, People's Republic of China, Pakistan, Iran, and India.

Three Dimensional Chess: Explaining Terrorism in a Complex Region

Politics as a Chess Game

The news we read about Pakistan and Afghanistan mentions great powers like the United States, small countries like Tajikistan, Pashtun tribes, religious groups like Shia Muslims, and political movements like the Taliban. They are all participants in politics. However, there is not one common political playing field or chess board for these actors. There are many. When we look at the players' goals and means, we notice that some make moves on only one chess board and others are present in other games too. So, terrorism and insurgency in Central and South Asia might be likened to a three dimensional chess game where the dimensions intersect.

The search for a remedy to control the terrorism and insurgency plaguing the region and spilling over into the rest of the world requires recognizing that there are mutually reinforcing causal linkages between the dimensions of the chess game. A successful policy therefore will include measures that address all levels of the game; otherwise any relief will prove to be temporary at best.

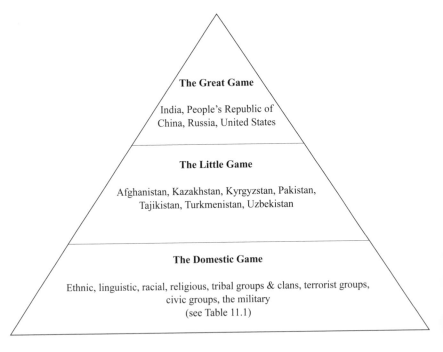

The Great Game

India, People's Republic of China, Russia, United States

The Little Game

Afghanistan, Kazakhstan, Kyrgyzstan, Pakistan, Tajikistan, Turkmenistan, Uzbekistan

The Domestic Game

Ethnic, linguistic, racial, religious, tribal groups & clans, terrorist groups, civic groups, the military
(see Table 11.1)

Figure 11.1 Three dimensional chess in Central and South Asia

The Great Game: Superpowers and their Global Concerns

The first dimension (or chess board) of the chess game is the global "Great Game" of geopolitical rivalry between the great powers for influence, dominance, and security for themselves and their allies. The Central and South Asian region sits astride four geopolitical fault lines, leaving a no-man's-land that is the subject of political maneuvering between the People's Republic of China (PRC), the Russian Federation, the United States, and the emerging player India.

The Great Game is a phrase popularized by English author Rudyard Kipling in his 1901 novel *Kim*. It refers to the strategic rivalry for dominance in Central Asia between the British Empire and Imperial as well as Soviet Russia from the early nineteenth century until the middle of the twentieth century. Each state perceived the other's expansionism in Asia as a danger to their own Asian interests and either conquered, dominated, threatened, spied on, bought, or allied themselves to the existing states or tribes in the region.

In the present day, the Great Game continues, albeit with different players. The causes are also somewhat different. Security is still achieved through dominance, but is defined more broadly. We go beyond the physical security of borders that must not be violated. Dependence on essential imports such as fossil fuels means that energy-hungry developed as well as developing countries seek secure sources and transportation routes for the petroleum and natural gas they need. Security may also be affected by transnational phenomena such as terrorism, trade, migration of people, and illicit drugs.

Recent discoveries of significant petroleum and/or natural gas reserves in Turkmenistan, Uzbekistan, and Kazakhstan have focused attention from all the great powers on these remote Central Asian states that emerged from the break-up of the Soviet Union. They have become the principal objects of the Great Game. The rise of globally active militant extremist Islamic movements and their activities in the same area have only increased interest in the region.

Great Powers and their Motives

The United States   A distinct dissimilarity between the US and the other major powers operating in Central Asia is that the former historically tended to play a short-term game. Following the final Soviet withdrawal from Afghanistan in 1989, a decade after the invasion that made the US provide support for an Afghan insurgency, the United States ended its involvement and lost interest. The threat to its influence in South Asia and the Middle East had abated. In the chaos that followed, the Taliban emerged as the dominant force in Afghanistan.

Perceiving the terrorist anti-Western al-Qaeda and Taliban as interdependent, the United States now seeks to destroy their infrastructure and capability to mount operations that threaten the US and its allies. The question which vexes the planning of every actor in the region is whether history will repeat itself and the

US walks into the sunset again after administering a beating to the Taliban and al-Qaeda that allows it the excuse to call the job finished.

Russia's recent return to assertiveness abroad, particularly its attempts to dominate the states that were formerly part of the Soviet Union, has raised worries abroad. US policymakers' first and foremost concern is for US and NATO supply lines through Central Asia to Afghanistan, as the land line through Pakistan is threatened by Taliban and al-Qaeda attacks just when President Obama has announced a massive increase in troop levels for Afghanistan. Central Asian states will also be strongly affected by the global economic downturn that started in 2008. These are poor countries with a proven potential for domestic insurgencies and political instability that can become another feeding ground for religious extremism and terrorism. They are governed by authoritarian presidents through weak governmental institutions and suffer from great income inequalities and high levels of official corruption. The area is a growing source of energy to allies and partners, while simultaneously close to interested rivals such as China and Russia, as well as regional opponents such as Iran. It is a major highway for narcotics smuggling, it is at risk for narcoterrorism, and its southernmost state, Afghanistan, is the world's primary producer of opium and a center of transnational terrorist training and activity.[3]

Russia   Russia's foreign policy under Presidents Vladimir Putin and Dmitry Medvedev clearly signals the end of the retreat that characterized the 1990s. The Kremlin is encouraging a resurgent, purely Russian nationalism that has reintroduced into public life pre-1917 Tsarist symbology and messianist imagery of a greater Russia.[4]

The goal of the foreign policy is familiar: security through domination of the "near-abroad" or the states that surround Russia, even though this conflicts with the second goal of ensuring that Russia has access to foreign markets for its energy

---

    3   Bissenova, A. (2009), "13 March 2009 Central Asia-Caucasus Analyst," *Central Asia-Caucasus Institute Analyst*, March 11, online at http://cacianalyst.org/?q=node/5065/print (accessed March 21, 2009); Blank, S. (2006), *Uzbek Foreign Policy, an Unexpected Crossroads*, September 25, online at http://www.isn.ethz.ch/isn/Current-Affairs/Security-Watch/Detail/?id=52510&lng=en (accessed March 16, 2009); Friesendorf, C. (2007), "The Difficult Stabilization of Afghanistan," *CSS Analyses in Security Policy* 2/11; Kucera, J. (2009a), "US: New Views on Central Asia," February 18, online at http://www.isn.ethz.ch/isn/Current-Affairs/Security-Watch/Detail/?id=96636&lng=en (accessed March 17, 2009); Omarow, N.M. (2009), "Kirgistan in der sozioökonomischen Dauerkrise – Wer ist 'schuld'?" *zentralasien-analysen* 14 (February), 2–5.

    4   One interesting aspect is the Kremlin creation of a nationalist, pro-Putin youth movement called Nashi ("ours"), which has been used to harass diplomats of countries considered unfriendly and has mounted provocative demonstrations outside Russia. Harding, L. (2008), "Back to the USSR," *The Guardian* (10 December), online at http://www.guardian.co.uk/world/2008/dec/10/russia.

and raw materials exports. The states that were part of the former Soviet Union[5] take a special place: Russian policymakers do not see them as truly independent countries, but, rather, publicly claim them as places of privileged interest for Russia.[6] A telling example is Russia's contempt for the territorial integrity of Georgia, which led to a mini-war in the summer of 2008 and the continuing partial occupation of the country.

Russian policymakers fear Islamic radicals and the spread of their ideologies to Muslim populations in Central Asia and Russia. This fear leaves them conflicted: On the one hand, they wish a defeat for the Taliban and al-Qaeda, but, on the other hand, they do not want the United States to gain a long-term foothold in the region, since that will come at the cost of Russian influence. So, Russia at first acquiesced in the US use of the airbases in Central Asia, because it was still was mired in its own internal war against Islamists inside Russia (in the breakaway region Chechnya) and was given an implicit carte blanche by the US in this notoriously brutal counterinsurgency. Russia's previous silence, however, did not signify agreement. Its foreign and security policy thinking uses a zero-sum game logic, in which the stationing of US or any other troops signifies a decline in the Russian position.[7]

Russia has turned its near-monopoly control of oil and gas pipelines to Europe into a weapon of diplomatic and economic extortion by cutting supplies from Russia, the Caucasus, and Central Asia to Ukraine and Belarus.[8] The purpose is not only to maximize revenues, but also to dominate the politics of these states. Russia seeks to preserve its dominance of energy markets in Europe by controlling the purchase and transportation of energy exports emanating from Central Asia and the Caucasus.[9] In short, Russia is involved in a long-term game for resource access and continental hegemony.

---

5 Estonia, Latvia, Lithuania, Belarus, Ukraine, Azerbaijan, Georgia, Armenia, Kazakhstan, Uzbekistan, Turkmenistan, Kyrgyzstan, and Tajikistan.

6 Antonenko, O. (2007), "Russia, Central Asia and the Shanghai Co-operation Organization," *Russian Analytical Digest* 25 (July), 7–11; Blank, S. (2009a), *Russia, India Row Over Tajik Base*, January 14, online at http://www.isn.ethz.ch/isn/Current-Affairs/Security-Watch/Detail/?id=54013&lng=en (accessed March 16, 2009); Toomas Hendrik Ilves (2009), "Rede auf der 45. Münchner Sicherheitskonferenz," *Munich Security Conference*, online at http://www.securityconference.de/konferenzen/rede.php?id=241&menu_2009=&sprache=de&.

7 McDermott, R.N. (2008), "NATO/USA und Usbekistan. Chancen und Probleme einer Wiederannäherung," *zentralasien-analysen* 09 (September), 2–5.

8 Blank, op. cit. fn. 3; Blank, S. (2007a), *Russia Moves Toward Natural Gas Cartel*, May 18, online at http://www.isn.ethz.ch/isn/Current-Affairs/Security-Watch/Detail/?id=53308&lng=en (accessed March 16, 2009).

9 Blank, S. (2007b), *SCO: Identity in Crisis*, August 13, online at http://www.isn.ethz.ch/isn/Current-Affairs/Security-Watch/Detail/?id=53626&lng=en (accessed March 16, 2009).; Blank, op. cit. fn. 6; Ilkhamov, A. (2007), "Russia Lures Uzbekistan as its Strategic Satellite in Central Asia," *Russian Analytical Digest* 29 (October), 8–10; Perovic, J. and

India and the People's Republic of China   The Chinese and Indian economies have grown rapidly in recent years and this has increased the need for reliable access to raw materials and especially energy supplies. China and India therefore seek more supplies and a greater variety of suppliers to shield themselves from disruptions and political strife in the Middle East and Indonesia. Current supply routes run through areas with severe security problems (Straits of Malacca and the Strait of Hormuz). The concern was so great that both sent warships to join the international naval patrol in 2008–2009 to control rampant piracy in the Arabian Sea and are stepping up the development of their navies to increase their ability to project power.[10] The discovery of large oil and/or gas reserves in Turkmenistan, Uzbekistan, Kazakhstan, and now even Afghanistan has raised the possibility of supplier diversification, and pipeline projects are being discussed.[11]

Since Russia is a rival great power in Asia and since Russia has not been shy to use (the denial of) energy supplies as a foreign policy weapon against states formerly in the Soviet orbit and, implicitly, even against Western Europe, the Chinese and Indians are increasingly reluctant to pursue strategic partnership with Russia. The interests conflict all too obviously. Hence, their strategic ambitions have begun to include Central Asia. India's drift away from Russia as its chief weapons supplier towards the United States and Europe is telling, and both China and India have begun to try to gain a military foothold in the region.

Physical security interests rank highly for both China and India in their relationship with Central Asia. China is confronting terrorist incidents involving Muslim-Turkic Uighurs in the western border province of Xinjiang and faces the risk of spillover to and from Kazakhstan, Kyrgyzstan, and Tajikistan. Like the United States and Russia, China and India are concerned that one or more of the states in the region could become a haven for Islamic radicals. The whole region has experienced domestic unrest and insurrection, sometimes with Islam as the governing principle, sometimes not. Both China and India see them as sources of terrorism that could draw in their domestic Muslim populations.[12] Further,

---

Orttung, R. (2007), "Russia's Energy Policy: Should Europe Worry?" *Russian Analytical Digest* 18 (April), 2–7; Overland, I. (2009), "Natural Gas and Russia–Turkmenistan Relations," *Russian Analytical Digest* 56 (March), 9–13.

10   Ramachandran, S. (2007), "India's Quiet Sea Power," *Asia Times Online*, August 2, online at http://atimes.com/atimes/South_Asia/IH02Df01.html (accessed March 22, 2009); Wallis, K. (2009), "Asia Held Hostage on the High Seas," *Asia Times Online*, November 20, online at http://www.atimes.com/atimes/Middle_East/JK20Ak04.html (accessed March 22, 2009).

11   Blank, op. cit. fn. 6; Blank, S. (2007), "SCO: Identity in Crisis," *International Relations and Security Network*, August 13, available online, http://www.isn.ethz.ch/isn/Current-Affairs/Security-Watch/Detail/?id=53626&lng=en (accessed March 16, 2009); Antonenko, op. cit. fn. 6.

12   Antonenko, op. cit. fn. 6; Blank, op. cit. fn. 8, and (2007), op. cit. fn. 11; Babakhanov, U. (2009), *Examining the Kyrgyz-Sino Relationship*, March 19, online at http://www.isn.ethz.ch/isn/Current-Affairs/Security-Watch/Detail/?id=97936&lng=en (accessed March 19, 2009).

the presence of ethnic Russian minorities in large numbers in the region should be disconcerting to all those involved in the region, given Russia's ruthless past expansionism. For example, Russia declared the inhabitants of the rebel South Ossetia region in Georgia in 2008 to be Russian citizens as a justification for its military occupation and virtual annexation of another sovereign country.

India's physical security is primarily related to Pakistan and their long-festering border dispute, primarily over the Kashmir region, which has led to several wars. Present Indian policy seeks rapprochement with Central Asian states and Afghanistan to outflank growing Chinese influence and present Pakistan with the nightmare of a two front war threat (the necessity of this is debatable, given that the balance of military and economic power is so overwhelmingly in India's favor). In addition, building Indian influence in Central Asia and Afghanistan makes it more difficult for Pakistan to use local conditions there to sponsor anti-Indian terrorism.[13]

Lastly, India has unresolved border disputes with China. This includes the little-mentioned occupation by China of Aksai Chin (North and East of Kashmir) and parts of Arunachal Pradesh (on the Sino-Indian border east of Bhutan). Both areas have been the subject of an undeclared war in 1962 and several other armed skirmishes. While these disputes have cooled, both countries perceive each other as rivals in Asia. India's interest in Central Asia therefore includes the desire not be outflanked, especially if the energy pipeline from Central Asia becomes an executable project.

Second Dimension: The Little Game

The Little Game of the regional powers constitutes the second level of our imaginary chess board. While power politics may seem the province of the great nation-states, it is a game which anyone may try to play. Of course, the Great Game creates restrictions on the freedom of the smaller states. Their power is more limited, but it does not mean that they do not have interests and concerns and will not seek to maximize their independence of action. Their basic interests are not all that different from those of the great powers: security and access to markets and resources. The greatest difference is the narrow geographic definition of their security interests and their inability to project power. Hence, they have to move more cautiously and more in concert and compromise with others. For the largest among them, there is the temptation to pursue regional power ambitions. Iran supports Shiite Muslims (and terrorism, the poor man's hard power) in Iraq, Lebanon, and Afghanistan as a means of dominating the course of events

---

13   Bajoria, J. (2008)a, "Pakistan's New Generation of Terrorists," *Council on Foreign Relations Backgrounder*, February 6, online at http://www.cfr.org/publication/15422/ (accessed November 30, 2008).

in neighboring countries. Pakistan does the same through its Taliban clients in Afghanistan.

The Little Game can be an uneven and strange experience due to the asymmetrical nature of the power distribution between the players. These range from impoverished Kyrgyzstan or Afghanistan to ambitious middle ranking players as Iran and Pakistan, who possess with some quantitative strengths (basic nuclear capability, resource wealth, and/or relatively professional armies), but who wrestle with conspicuous qualitative deficiencies. They are constrained in their game by the presence of the great powers on site or just over the horizon.

Five of the six Central Asian republics gained their independence as a result of the collapse of the Soviet Union in 1991, ironically retaining their repressive communist leadership that rebranded itself as nationalist and Muslim. They have sought to maintain their independence by playing the great powers against each other, trying to befriend everyone, while offending no-one. So, they seek Western economic assistance and have accepted Russian, Indian, and Chinese investment, loans, and cooperation, when these became available and safe to use in the context of the Great Game.

The Central Asian energy producers have an interest (but not the money or perhaps the political will) in pumping oil and gas east to China and India or to the Indian Ocean coastline, should this prove feasible, as a means to prevent Russia from having its finger on their economic jugular. They have much cause to distrust Russia. Among others, this is a response to Russian threats and tantrums when plans are fielded for pipelines that avoid Russian territory and thus Russian control.[14] Since Putin, Russian policy has been to exert state control over all strategic industries and none more so than the energy industry. Oil wealth and control of energy supplies and distribution systems have become one of the tools of choice in Moscow's foreign policy.[15]

Pakistan, on the border between Central and South Asia, is the locus of much of the instability in Central and Southern Asia. It sits astride the Kashmir triangle, where China, Pakistan, and India have for over 60 years been locked in a stalemated struggle over the allegiance of this region where some valleys are predominately Muslim and others Hindu or Buddhist. The Jammu and Kashmir

---

14   One such case is the Baku-Tblisi-Ceyhan pipeline. In August of 2008, during the Russian-Georgian war over Abkhazia and South Ossetia, Russian proxies directly threatened the pipeline with destruction. Robin Pagnamenta (2008) "Analysis: energy pipeline that supplies West threatened by war Georgia conflict," *Times Online* (8 August), online at http://www.timesonline.co.uk/tol/news/world/europe/article4484849.ece.

15   One notes the gas cut-offs to the Ukraine in 1992, 1993, 1994, 2005–2006, 2007–2008 and 2009 and Belarus in 2007. Similar disputes occurred with Moldova and Georgia in 2006. Ostensibly, the disputes were always over payment issues and term, though action always coincides with the presence in office of leaders that show independence from Moscow. Solutions in all cases gave Russia or its proxies such as the state-controlled Gazprom energy giant further control over distribution networks.

region is 75 percent Muslim (disregarding which state has de facto control over which valleys). Pakistan's northern border is the so-called Durand Line, disputed in its entirety by Afghanistan. The legacy of the British Indian Empire is by no means settled as yet. Neither is the idea of Pakistan.

The one constant in Pakistan's foreign policy since its painful birth out of British India in 1947 has been its antagonistic relationship with India. On the surface, this is due to unresolved border disputes, as the current border is largely a cease-fire line that is the consequence of major wars in 1947, 1965, 1971, a minor war in 1999, and various skirmishes in between.

The more basic reason for the trouble is that Pakistan is a country in search of a reason to exist. British India was an ethno-linguistic and religious crazy quilt. The political movements that pushed for independence could agree on the principle of independence, but not on how to implement that independence: One nation or two nations (one Hindu and one Muslim)? Even though they defined themselves explicitly as Indian, Muslim elites of British India believed themselves to be culturally, civilizationally, and historically so distinct (and more advanced) from Hindus that a one state solution could not work. Any remaining possibility of an undivided post-British India collapsed over the fear that Muslims would be marginalized in a majority Hindu India unable or uninterested to find compromise. Partitioning and the bloody immediate aftermath created an elite group (landowners, the state bureaucracy, and army) that blames India.[16]

Pakistan is effectively a garrison, dominated by a strong army, its only well-functioning institution, and burdened by a weak state, battered by provinces in near-continuous rebellion, and devoid of a rationale other than not to be India. Still, Pakistan has limped along, in large part due to its strategic location and consequential role in the Great Game. The US lavishly supported Pakistan during the early years of the Cold War as the eastern anchor of an alliance covering the Middle East. In the latter years, it benefited from serving as the funnel for aid to anti-Soviet guerillas in Afghanistan. While the US thought of Pakistan as a strategic ally in the Great Game, Pakistan saw the relationship as insurance in the Little Game with India. After the end of the Cold War, the United States lost interest in Pakistan, leaving it to develop self-insurance. This fundamental misalignment between the Little Game strategic interests of Pakistan and the global and regional strategic interests of the West continues to the present day.

Third Dimension: The Domestic Political Chess Games of Divided Societies

The myriad ethnic, religious, linguistic, cultural, tribal, clan, and other allegiances and fault lines which traverse the region's countries and borders deeply affect the internal politics of Central and South Asian countries. The contentious domestic

---

16   Cohen, S.P. (2004), *The Idea of Pakistan*, Washington, DC: Brookings Institution Press.

politics, driven by the heterogeneity of these societies and difficult to manage in states with weak institutions, form the last level of our chess game.

The distribution of various factions in society leads to both real and politically expedient frictions between and within various states as members of a tribe, ethnic group, religion, or linguistic group find themselves on the losing end in the domestic political process. Others live on opposite sides of international borders that are a reflection of the combined effects over time of the Great Game, the Little Game, and the Domestic Game, rather than the realities of habitation patterns on the ground. Co-religionists and co-tribalists with a long history of relationships find themselves separated and turned into minorities. The demographic patchwork severely stresses the already generally poor states in the region. The histories of authoritarian and totalitarian rule in these states—save for India—leave few mechanisms to mediate or resolve conflicting demands and grievances.

A red line of terrorism runs through all levels of the Central and South Asian chess boards. Conflicts (and past conflicts) at each level may lead to terrorism. Examining key events in this troubled region's history is the only way to fully understand the complex interrelationships and bitter rivalries forming the very dangerous game of three dimensional chess.

An Analysis of Central and South Asia after September 11, 2001

Collapse of the Taliban (Afghanistan, September-December, 2001)
Cast of Players: Great Game: United States, Russia
Little Game: Afghanistan, Pakistan
Domestic Game: al-Qaeda, Taliban, Pashtun and other tribes, Northern Alliance[17]

As irony would have it, General Tommy Franks, Commander-in-Chief of US Central Command[18] (CENTCOM) was on his way to Pakistan for consultations on security cooperation and terrorism as both lower Manhattan and the Pentagon were enveloped in the smoke and dust of terrorist attacks. On his return, he was

17   The actual name is: United Islamic Front for the Salvation of Afghanistan. Most observers consider there to be five factions: (1) Islamic Movement of Afghanistan (claims to represent Shias), led by Ayatollah Muhammad Asif Muhsini; (2) Islamic Party of Afghanistan (mostly ethnic Tajiks), led by figurehead Burhanuddin. Real powers were Ahmed Shah Massoud and Mohammed Fahim; (3) Islamic Union for the Liberation of Afghanistan—(Pashtun) led by Abdul Rasul Sayyaf; (4) Islamic Unity Party of Afghanistan (Shia Hazara ethnic group from Central Afghanistan) led by Mohammed Mohaqiq and Karim Khalili, supported by Iran; (5) National Islamic Movement of Afghanistan (ethnic Uzbeks and former communists), led by Abdul Rashid Dostum, supported by Turkey.

18   Central Command is one of six theater-level operational commands of the US armed forces. These joint forces commands direct forces of all branches of the US military in a particular geographical region, in this case, the Middle East, Egypt, and Central Asia (including Afghanistan and Pakistan).

charged with developing "credible military options." The concept developed was for CENTCOM "… to destroy the al-Qaeda network inside Afghanistan along with the illegitimate Taliban regime which was harboring and protecting the terrorists." The Bush Administration declared a global "War on Terrorism." It was expected that the effort would include allies and, by 2002, some 68 states had signed up ("Operation Enduring Freedom" 2008).

Operation Enduring Freedom included an unusual level of cooperation with other agencies in the US Government, driven by a shared sense of outrage and the difficulties of quickly mounting a response in a remote place. The goal was to take the initiative, avoid being perceived as the invader acting against the local population, and to win local cooperation. The Taliban was to be destroyed as a military force, using unconventional warfare forces alongside the existing anti-Taliban forces whose interests coincided with those of the US and who would get material support to enhance their fighting capability.[19] Special Operations Forces and CIA paramilitary units would provide reconnaissance, fight limited engagements and, where needed, fight in coordination with existing opposition militias. They would also make possible the introduction of conventional forces if the need arose. Specialists on horseback were to provide forward air controller services that called in and provided targeting for US Air Force and US Navy air assets.[20]

During the first days after the infamous September 11, Russian intelligence agencies and diplomacy moved to play the Great Game and tried to deny US access to Central Asia. They staged a meeting in Dushanbe (Tajikistan) with representatives of Indian, Iranian, and Uzbek intelligence agencies and the Northern Alliance. The ethnic Uzbek and Tajik components of the Northern Alliance had for years received assistance from Tajikistan and Uzbekistan due to their fear of domestic Islamist insurgency supported by the Taliban and likeminded others. Russia offered military assistance to the Northern Alliance and persuaded Tajikistan to state that it would not grant the US the use of its air space. Russia put the message out that the US would not be able to use Central Asian air space. However, the gambit failed as Uzbekistan broke ranks to offer the US bases, hoping that US power would be more likely to defeat the Taliban threat. Their front crumbling, the Kremlin quickly shifted gears and next held a meeting with all Central Asian governments to offer the US temporary bases in Central Asia. In return, among others, the US agreed not to criticize Russian actions in the rebellious Muslim Chechnya Republic in the Russian Federation and to consult Moscow regarding US actions in Central Asia.[21]

With access to the region resolved, apparent success came quickly for the United States. Combat operations began on October 7, 2001. Within two weeks, the

19   Rashid, A. (2008), *Descent Into Chaos: The United States and the Failure of Nation Building in Pakistan, Afghanistan, and Central Asia*, New York: Penguin.
20   "Operation Enduring Freedom," 2008.
21   Rashid, op. cit. fn. 19, 68–70.

aerial bombing destroyed what large targets the relatively unsophisticated Taliban military machine could present. The firepower mounted by US forces caused many Taliban units to suffer severe casualty rates. al-Qaeda training camps had already emptied on September 11 and the leadership scattered. That same October, Special Forces mounted a successful raid on the residence of Taliban leader Mullah Omar in Kandahar, birthplace and headquarters of the Taliban movement.[22] Other similar strikes in many different locations around Afghanistan served to unbalance and demoralize the Taliban rank and file.

The logistics, aerial firepower, and hope provided to opposition forces allowed these to advance on a battered Taliban army and the northern city of Mazar-i-Sharif fell on November 9. Within three weeks following, Kabul and other major cities changed hands with the Taliban melting away and significant resistance coming only from fanatical foreign fighters supplied by al-Qaeda. The Taliban retreated to Kunduz in the northeast and to their southwestern roots in the provincial capital of Kandahar. In Kandahar, they were isolated and pressured from three sides by 3,000 Pashtun fighters organized by Pashtun tribal leader Hamid Karzai, a contingent of 1,000 US Marines brought in by helicopter, and forces of the Northern Alliance. A surrender or battle never occurred, as an outnumbered and outgunned Taliban and its leaders melted away into the mountains of central Afghanistan or escaped to the border areas of Pakistan.[23]

In Kunduz, in mid-November, Pakistan's intelligence services organized an airlift operation with the secret knowledge and consent of a small circle at the White House, given directly to Pakistan's President Musharraf, and flew out of the country not only its own intelligence operatives that had been assisting the Taliban, but also close to one thousand Taliban leaders, foreign volunteers, and al-Qaeda operatives. Perhaps the White House was duped by Pakistan into believing that the cargo would be limited to Pakistani personnel, but Pakistan's long time support for the Taliban should have left little to the imagination. The United States made no attempt check the human cargo.[24] White House decision makers clearly feared that embarrassing Pakistan would jeopardize their paramount relationship with Musharraf and the latter's standing in his own army. Their failure to check should also be seen as a quid pro quo for allowing the US to secretly use a Pakistani air base and an indication that Central Asia and Middle East Great Game considerations were dominating. The support of Pakistan and Saudi Arabia (virtually the only countries to give formal recognition to the Taliban regime) were very valuable to

---

22   Ibid., 61.
23   "Operation Enduring Freedom – Afghanistan" (2008), *Global Security.org*, February 9, online at http://globalsecurity.org/military/ops/enduring-freedom-plan.htm (accessed March 8, 2009); Rashid 2008; Ashley J. Tellis (2008), "Pakistan and the War on Terror: Conflicted Goals, Compromised Performance," Carnegie Endowment for International Peace (24 January), online at http://www.humansecuritygateway.info/documents/CARNEGIE_pakistanwaronterrorconflictedgoals.pdf.
24   Rashid, op. cit. fn. 19, 91–93.

the US in their ever more likely attack on Iraq, even more important than ensuring that all enemy combatants and leaders were caught. After all, the war was virtually over.

On December 22, 2001, a provisional Afghan Government was inaugurated in Kabul. Operation Enduring Freedom had lasted 78 days.

The quick successes with minimal forces created a mirage which was called victory. Taliban achievements in battle and recruitment in previous years had resulted in their transformation into larger units that created the illusion of regular army battalions and regiments, especially to Westerners used to thinking in conventional warfare terms. At heart, they remained a guerilla movement and, when faced with overwhelming US firepower, simply dissolved back into their natural form of small insurgent bands that disappeared into the mountains to recover and reorganize.

A Janus-faced Foreign Policy (Pakistan, September 2001-December 2003)[25]

Cast of Players: Great Game: India, United States (and Allies)
Little Game: Pakistan, India
Domestic Game: Taliban, al-Qaeda, Pakistan Army, ISI, Pashtun and other tribes,
Islamic extremist groups (pro-government, anti-government)

Pakistan, militarily weaker than India and dogmatically fearful of Indian intentions,[26] has since the late 1980s pursued a double-pronged strategy: indirect attack and protecting the rear. The military intelligence service of Pakistan (the Inter-Services Intelligence Directorate or ISI) has encouraged rebellion by Muslims

---

25   The Janus image is borrowed from Amir Mir (2005), "Janus-faced counter-terrorism," *Asia Times Online* (21 September), online at http://www.atimes.com/atimes/South_Asia/GI21Df02.html.

26   "Vajpayee Govt Failed, Incompetent at Checking Terror: VHP" (2002), *Expressindia.com*, October 1, online at http://www.Expressindia.com/news/fullstory.php?newsid=15219 (accessed March 23, 2009). Though exaggerated, the Pakistani weariness isn't entirely unfounded. Militant Hindu extremists have made public calls for attacking Pakistan and have been a source of pogroms on Indian Muslims in India. They are quick to blame Pakistan for any act of terror inside India and employ that blame to suit their political goals. These militants also talk in terms of a war between civilizations, where Pakistan is the equivalent of Muslim invaders of yesteryear seeking to proselytize Hinduism out of existence (Cohen, op. cit. fn. 19, 31). Indian intelligence has in the past conducted violent covert action on Pakistani soil and is known to have supported separatist movements in such places as Balochistan and Sindh province. Bajoria, Jayshree (2008b), "Pakistan's New Generation of Terrorists," *Council on Foreign Relations Backgrounder*, February 6, online at http://www.cfr.org/publication/15422/ (accessed November 30, 2008). On the other hand, Indian policymakers would respond that these moves come in response to Pakistan's actions.

in Kashmir as a means of pressuring India. In addition, and because the local Kashmir rebellion never gathered the desired ideological strength, the ISI secretly sponsored or nurtured anti-India militant Islamist movements[27] in Pakistan. These movements were allowed to operate openly in Pakistan, solicit funds and recruit members. They created or used their existing armed wing to carry out attacks in Kashmir and India proper.[28]

The secrecy provided a fig leaf of deniability for the Pakistani leadership. The double advantage was that local rebellions kept considerable Indian forces busy with counterinsurgency work and unable to threaten Pakistan. Any harsh Indian policing measures would reinforce the insurgency and provide justification for Pakistan's self-appointed role as protector of apparently oppressed Muslims as well as its claim to Kashmir. However, Pakistan's approach was also dangerous: since the point was to pressure India, but not to provoke an open war, the recruits to these organizations would inevitably become disappointed when held back. Radicalized in order to perform the dangerous task of terror attacks, they would inevitably come to feel betrayed and turn on their masters in frustration.

Pakistan's great desire to protect the rear is founded in its fear of a two front war. An Afghanistan under Indian influence is a strategic nightmare. Pakistan looked with great wariness at any Indian contacts in that direction and needed to ensure that Afghanistan was either neutralized or reliably pro-Pakistan.[29] Pakistan's chosen solution was to use the contacts laid with Afghan tribes when the ISI was the instrument with which the US armed and assisted the anti-Soviet opposition in Afghanistan during the 1980s. These contacts were principally Pashtuns, who form a plurality of Afghanistan's population and are easy to communicate with, given that Pashtuns form a sizable minority in Pakistan.

In the aftermath of 9/11, the United States realized quickly that the source for the attack was in Afghanistan. An ultimatum was given to Pakistan: either us or the Taliban. The direct link between Pakistan's national security strategy and its support for groups espousing radical Islamist ideologies had created a nearly unsolvable dilemma: supporting the US would leave Pakistan's national security strategy in tatters, since that country wanted to destroy the Taliban client and the

---

27   Harakut ul-Mujahedeen (Islamic Freedom Fighters Group), Jaish-e-Muhammad (Army of Muhammad), Lashkar-e-Taiba (Army of the Pure). "Kashmir Militant Extremists," 2006.

28   Kaplan, E. and Bajoria, J. (2008), "Counterterrorism in India," Newsweek, Council on Foreign Relations (28 November), online at http://www.newsweek.com/id/17120. Bajoria (2008a), op. cit. fn. 13; Bajoria, J. (2008c), "Pakistan's New Generation of Terrorists," *Council on Foreign Relations Backgrounder* (February 6), online at http://www.cfr.org/publication/15422/ (accessed November 30, 2008).

29   Pakistan's distrust is fed in many ways. For example: A number of Afghan leaders, including President Hamid Karzai, have studied at Indian universities and maintain ties to India. India's main intelligence service, the Research and Analysis Wing (RAW), has maintained close links to Afghan intelligence agencies in the past, except under the Taliban (Bajoria, op. cit. fn. 26).

al-Qaeda group around Osama bin Laden. The members of the Northern Alliance had no love for Pakistan's policy in Afghanistan and pursued a friendly policy towards partial sponsor India. Cracking down on already disgruntled and unruly radical Islamist groups and political parties inside Pakistan, many of whom had contacts with the Taliban and al-Qaeda, could only result in domestic unrest in Pakistan, weakening it relative to India. On the other hand, not joining the United States meant the loss of any chance to influence its policies in the area and losing the financial and military benefits of being the US' regional strategic partner. Worse, the United States would likely turn to India as its principal regional ally.

The Pakistani military leadership, headed by President (and Chief of the Army Staff General) Pervez Musharraf, decided it could afford to neither lose its great power sponsor nor abandon its Taliban client in Afghanistan. So it chose to try and square the circle: denounce extremism, follow the United States, but attempt to salvage as much as possible of Pakistan's ability to influence events in Afghanistan and extract as much military and financial benefit from the alliance with the US.

Moving against al-Qaeda was easy and curried favor with the US Pakistan's military and civilian elite was genuinely appalled at the attacks on New York and Washington. Moreover, al-Qaeda served no meaningful strategic or tactical purpose to Pakistan's interests. If anything, its growing relationship with the Taliban had undermined Pakistani control over the latter. Pakistan provided the US with bases and other assistance in Operation Enduring Freedom. It pursued and arrested al-Qaeda terrorist operatives and handed them to the US. Significant Pakistani army forces moved into the inhospitable Federally Administered Tribal Areas (FATA)[30] on the border with Afghanistan for the first time in generations to trawl for al-Qaeda members crossing the border. While these operations were successful in capturing over 700 foot soldiers, they were costly in casualties and al-Qaeda leadership elements benefited from local tribal traditions regarding hospitality to find refuge with some of the local tribes that are very pro-Taliban (some of which supplied volunteers—so-called Pakistani Taliban—for the Afghani Taliban prior to 2001) and resent the incursions of the Pakistani Army.[31] Longer term, this result, however, created a backlash against Pakistan from the local tribes in combination with al-Qaeda cadres.

Not surprisingly, the treatment meted out to the Taliban was rather different. Pakistan tried to limit the damage to the Taliban as best it could. In secret, Pakistan's military facilitated or at least did nothing to stop the escape of Taliban leaders across the border into FATA and Balochistan province. There, they found refuge and rebuilt. The Taliban leadership is assembled in four major Pakistani cities: Quetta, Peshawar, Miran Shah, and Karachi. The first three function as

---

30 FATA has never been a place where the central government (whether Pakistani or British Indian) has been able to exert any significant influence. It should be considered as an area self-administered by local tribes.

31 Tellis, op. cit. fn. 23.

headquarters directing military operations in various regions of Afghanistan, and Karachi is the logistical unit for relations and supplies from the outside world.[32]

Pakistan confronted the many Islamist movements and militants within its borders, but did so in a very selective way. The policy choice of cultivating and co-opting Islamic militants and their political organizations meant that there could be serious trouble if arrests were too public or too numerous. Many militant groups (like the Taliban in Afghanistan) had organized around madrassas (religious schools) which—with Saudi money—had taken on the role of a parallel education system that principally focused on imprinting an ultra-conservative version of Islam. The radicalized groups were far from being a majority of the population, but they did form a potent political bloc easily roused quickly to frighten the bulk of a more moderate population. The terrorist clients of the Pakistani regime in its policy against Afghanistan and India were spared (save the odd symbolic arrest). They were deemed too valuable a weapon against India. This practice continued even after the attack on the Indian Parliament in December 2001. Their activities were toned down as needed, depending on the success of Musharraf's diplomatic initiatives with India on Kashmir.[33]

So in the short term, Pakistan was unable to moderate the assault and the damage to the Taliban. However, it was successful in extracting substantial benefits in terms of US assistance, such as $2.64 billion in direct aid in 2002–2005 and the dropping of US sanctions.[34]

Consequences of a Cheap War/Lost Chances of a Cheap Peace (Afghanistan, 2002-Present)

Cast of Players: Great Game: US (and NATO), Russia, China (via United Nations)
Little Game: Afghanistan, Pakistan, India
Domestic Players: Taliban, Pashtun and all other tribes, al-Qaeda, the national Government, warlords

The dismal history of Russian, Soviet, and British intervention did not make the Pentagon enthusiastic about invading Afghanistan. That General Franks had to develop a plan from scratch and limit himself to Special Operations troops and

---

32   Tellis, op. cit. fn. 23, 6–7.

33   See Tellis, op. cit. fn. 23, 4–6.

34   Jones, O.B. and Shaikh, F. (2006), "Pakistan's Foreign Policy Under Musharraf: Between a Rock and a Hard Place," *Chatham House Asia Programme Briefing Paper* 06/01. The inflow of US and other aid turned Pakistan's finances around: Between 1999 and 2004 Pakistan's foreign exchange reserves rose from an anemic $1.6 billion to a comfortable $12 billion. Government debt service declined from a crushing 50 percent of revenues to 25 percent. Economic growth doubled to 8.4 percent and the budget deficit halved to 3.2 percent. (Jones and Shaikh 2006, 2).

air forces suggests as much. Russian opposition, Pakistani and Central Asian reluctance to provide facilities for logistics and supply, as well as geographical realities of a mountainous, landlocked country argued against the feasibility of an invasion. So, what remained for use were Special Operations Forces from the United States and the United Kingdom, CIA paramilitary, the few (retired!) CIA covert operations officers with local linguistic skills, and the Northern Alliance (NA).

Central Intelligence Agency and MI6 (UK foreign intelligence) operatives entered Afghanistan within two weeks of September 11 and began handing out large amounts of cash to local tribesmen and warlords that possessed militias, encouraging them to fight against the Taliban. The distrust bred by the abandonment of the Afghan opposition after the end of the Cold War had to be overcome and the weakened state of the warlords that made up the Northern Alliance had to be reversed. Fahim (representing an ethnic Tajik group and leader of the strongest component), Rashid Dostum (Uzbeks and former communists), and Abdul Rasul Sayyaff (Anti-Taliban Pashtun group) each received about $1 million or more in cash as upfront goodwill money.[35] Promises were made of logistical assistance. For instance, General Franks personally handed over another $5 million to Fahim on October 30 in return for an agreement by the NA to attack in the north, stopping short of Kabul.[36] This request recognized the most important factors in the Domestic Game: Afghanistan's long history of tribal rivalry and the Taliban's almost exclusively Pashtun membership (though the Taliban are only a minority among Pashtuns). The capital city Kabul is on the northern edge of the traditionally Pashtun lands, which stretch in roughly a crescent shape towards the southwest (Kandahar) and then back up towards the northwest of Afghanistan past Farah. Any march beyond Kabul by the NA could have raised suspicions and the risk that anti-Taliban Pashtuns in the NA might disengage.

The strategy was both traditional and cheap. The US provided massive air power, some commandos, and logistical support, but the real fighting and bleeding on the ground was done by warlord militias. In the post-war environment, this trend persisted: no US or coalition occupation army arrived to fill the power vacuum left by the collapse of the Taliban. Unlike the occupations of Germany or Japan in 1945, there was no effort to consolidate, secure, and rebuild the country into a future ally. The limited forces that did arrive were employed in hunting down Taliban and al-Qaeda. There was no national governmental infrastructure in place. Some areas were left ignored and, elsewhere, warlords were paid to serve without much supervision as surrogate occupation troops. They were expected to maintain

---

35 All of these warlords were notorious for their human rights abuses. Sayyaf, for example, was known for massacres of Shias in the Kabul region during the 1990s (Human Rights Watch (2002), "Afghanistan: Return of the Warlords," Human Rights Watch Briefing Paper (June 6), online at http://www.hrw.org/legacy/backgrounder/asia/afghanistan/warlords.htm; Rashid, op. cit. fn. 19, 433).

36 Rashid, op. cit. fn. 19, 63.

public order and some form of local governance, at least until a reconstituted national government took over these tasks. The field was left open for them to carve up Afghanistan.[37]

Most top Bush Administration officials, with Secretary of Defense Rumsfeld as their most prominent exponent, opposed the idea of nation-building as a quagmire risk. Moreover, the quick defeat of the enemy created the illusion of weakness and the corollary that they could not rise again. Humanitarian aid was to be provided to the Afghan people, but only as long as the war lasted. The US Department of Defense (DoD) did not plan any post-war commitment for reconstruction, since that was a political, rather than a military issue, instead pushing it off on an overburdened United Nations and the allies.[38] As one DoD internal memo put it: "nation-building is *not* our key strategic goal."[39]

In the real world, this reliance on Afghan warlords had the side effect of entrenching regional military commanders in their ethnic or tribal homelands. They had no incentive to give up their extensive local power and sources of wealth (especially the drug trade). On the contrary, it was in their self interest to frustrate the creation of an effective national government or at least to ignore it. One perilous consequence was a loss of American ability to fight the drug trade. A byproduct of the lack of assistance, the absence of a functioning government, and the absence of boots on the ground, was the (re)turning of warlords and ordinary farmers to the highly profitable cash crop of opium poppies and the export of the hallucinogenic drugs that are made from opium. Afghanistan supplies 90 percent of the world's raw opium and much of its heroin. This would play a role later in the endemic corruption of the new government of Afghanistan and the return of the Taliban, funded by drug profits. At that time, US and UK Special Operations Forces and intelligence remained aloof and, in concert with paid warlord militias, focused on pursuing Taliban or (especially) al-Qaeda fighters, leaving the US blind as to what was actually going on elsewhere in the country.

The consequences became visible already in June of 2002, barely six months after the fall of the Taliban. Human Rights Watch (2002) reported that ordinary Afghans were being terrorized by these warlords. The cooperation and visible contacts with US and UK forces created the impression among the Afghan population that the warlords were endorsed by foreign powers. The misdeeds of the warlords were grafted onto the reputation of the foreign forces by incidents such as when warlords provided with US satellite telephone equipment waved it about while directly threatening to call American air strikes on recalcitrant local people and tribal leaders.[40]

37   Ibid., Feith, D.J. (2008), *War and Decision: Inside the Pentagon at the Dawn of the War on Terrorism*, New York: Harper.
38   Rashid, op. cit. fn. 91, 74–76.
39   Feith, op. cit. fn. 37.
40   Human Rights Watch, op. cit. fn. 35.

Among these handicaps, US and United Nations diplomats mounted a major effort and managed to cobble together an interim government headed by Hamid Karzai, a Pashtun tribal chieftain, with a cabinet that assembled all opposition groups. In June 2002, in line with tribal customs, a Loya Jirga or Grand Council of tribal leaders from all over Afghanistan met to select Hamid Karzai as interim Head of State until a constitution could be written and approved by the Loya Jirga and elections held. In December 2004, Hamid Karzai was duly elected as first President of the new Islamic Republic of Afghanistan.

The hope was that a quarter century of civil war would come to a close. However, the Afghan national government was a government in name only and therefore at a serious disadvantage in acquiring legitimacy and control, and commanding loyalty. Without forces and without a functioning administration (that had to be built from scratch), the warlords continued to enjoy their fiefdoms unchecked. The warlords, a number of whom were members of the interim government, could easily ignore or actively frustrate the nation building from the inside and the outside. Their unloved presence did nothing to increase the government's credibility in the eyes of suffering Afghanis, irrespective of tribe. When the national government began to attempt to enforce its will, Karzai and warlords clashed, yet the US refused to intervene to support the interim government. A May 6, 2002 Pentagon memo reads: "Make it clear we are not Karzai's enforcer ... If we do [intervene] ... once ... we will find ourselves doing it again and again ... will be a major expansion of the US mission ... Will create a dependency on the US, setting the US up for the blame if Afghanistan falls apart after we leave ... we will likely be viewed as an invading force ... find it more difficult to achieve our basic mission ... to root out remaining Taliban and al-Qaida forces ..."[41] Ordinary Afghanis had no choice but to submit to the local warlord. It was a matter of personal survival.

The international community was of little initial help. The rebuilding effort faltered because the promised assistance was never delivered and the national government had no substantial independent means of raising money. Many nations pledged funding via the United Nations agencies or directly to Afghanistan; actual monies spent were much smaller. For example, for the period 2002–2008, a total of $14.7 billion in aid was actually disbursed, but $9.7 billion committed to specific projects remains undisbursed. Nearly $14.8 billion pledged since 2002 does not even have a specific spending purpose and is therefore also undisbursed.

The United Nations, in response to US reluctance to engage in nation building also pursued a strategy of limited engagement (the so-called "light footprint"). Stabilization and reconstruction tasks were left to the Afghans to run, but there was virtually no institutional infrastructure in place to design or implement development projects. Experienced indigenous project managers were hard to find.[42] The US State Department did try to build up the various government departments in Kabul, but faltered due to poor management, opaque funding, and no strategy. The

---

41   Feith, op. cit. fn. 37, 532–34.
42   Friesendorf, op. cit. fn. 3, 2.

consequences for Afghanistan's ability to absorb aid were disastrous: as late as 2005, the government managed to spend only 44 percent of the money it received for development.[43] Therefore, although foreign aid increased substantially later on, the actual effect on the ground would be minimal. Aid inflows are now significantly higher, but pursuing reconstruction while simultaneously engaged in fighting an insurgency is a great challenge and requires close cooperation between militaries and development agencies and NGOs.

Table 11.1 Violence in Afghanistan

	2001	2002	2003	2004	2005	2006	2007	2008
Violent incidents (average per month)[1]	–	50	80	No data	150	425	566	–
Number of IEDs and roadside bombs	–	22	83	325	782	1,931	2,615	–
Suicide bombings	1	0	2	6	21	123	160	120 (Jan-Jun)
Number of foreign troops	–	4,988	5,500	8,500	8,934	33,460	41,741	43,250
Foreign aid (in USD billions)								
Funds committed								
Official development assistance	0.45	1.61	2.46	2.88	3.43	3.22	4.39	–
Other official flows	–	–	–	0.01	0.02	0.01	0.09	–
Funds disbursed								
Official development assistance	–	0.91	1.16	1.15	2.39	2.58	3.19	–
Other official flows	–	–	–	0.00	0.02	0.01	0.01	–

Sources: Cordesman, A.H. (2009), *The Afghan-Pakistan War: New NATO/ISF Reporting on Key Trend*, Washington, DC: Center for Strategic and International Studies, http://www.csis.org/media/csis/pubs/090326_afghannatoisaf.pdf (accessed April 2, 2009); Stockholm International Peace Research Institute, http://www.sipri.org/contents/webmaster/databases (accessed April 2, 2009); Organization for Economic Co-Operation and Development, http://stats.oecd.org/qwids/ (accessed April 2, 2009).

---

43   Rashid, op. cit. fn. 19, 194.

The international community was even more reluctant to put boots on the ground. The initial contingent of some 3,000 peacekeepers (the International Security Assistance Force-ISAF) arrived in January of 2002, but limited its assistance to Kabul and nearby Bagram air base, simplifying Taliban and al-Qaeda fighters' pullback into remote and inaccessible tribal areas. Even when the number of peacekeepers increased after the Taliban insurgence, many nations restricted the use of their troops to the safer areas of Afghanistan, diluting their effect and pumping water where there was no fire.[44] The main problem lies with governments, especially European ones, reluctant to make a forceful and clear case to their own publics for intervention in Afghanistan, even after agreeing to let NATO run ISAF. The Bush Administration's invasion of Iraq was deeply unpopular among Europeans and that complicated convincing a deeply skeptical European public. On the American side, the main problem resided with the botched occupation of Iraq, which drained away nearly all available units until late 2008.

The tribal nature of politics is yet another factor that encumbers the process of reviving Afghanistan. Historically, the Pashtun tribes have always been very prominent in the political life of Afghanistan. There are multiple Pashtun tribes and the same is true for other ethnic groups. Tribes may be divided into sub-tribes and clans. Therefore, much rivalry exists between leaders within tribes. The Taliban come from the poorest of the Pashtun tribes. Until the new constitution was enacted in 2004, Pashtuns felt that they were discriminated against by the international community in favor of the Tajiks and other northern tribes. Issues ranged from violent mass evictions of Pashtuns from northern areas of the country to disputes of whose language(s) would be used in the Afghan army.[45] Disaffection among Pashtuns likely played a role in the regeneration of the Taliban.

The politics of Afghanistan is still the politics of tribes and tribal leaders, where the focus is on the well-being of one's tribe—often seen as a zero-sum game. This culture differs greatly from the practice of Western democracies, where political parties tend to fight on the basis of ideology and policy. For example, some in the West have criticized Hamid Karzai for carrying a bag of cell phones and spending much time in conversation with tribesmen. As tribal leader in a tribal society, it is his role to be arbiter, petitionee, and dispenser of favors or money. He must successfully fill those roles in order to remain chieftain. The same is true for the other leaders in Afghanistan.

Table 11.1 indicates that in 2002, 2003, and 2004, there is a clear window of opportunity for success of nation-building Afghanistan: the security level is tolerable and there are major political advances in forming and constitution and government. Alas, the resources were inadequate to transform political success into actual improvement for the average individual Afghani. The lack of sufficient troops also means that very little land can actually be held permanently and the Taliban cannot be swept out or cornered.

44　Friesendorf, op. cit. fn. 3.
45　Rashid, op. cit. fn. 19, 215; Friesendorf, op. cit. fn. 3.

To make up for the shortage of troops, NATO and the US rely on aerial bombing, even though the targets are tiny and guerillas do not possess the high-value formations of military equipment like armor that justify hi-tech bombing. Since enemy and villager are nearly indistinguishable, this strategy leads to large civilian casualties, even when one relies on precision bombing, further disaffecting civilians and reducing support for the new Afghanistan. The air campaign has diminished to killing individual Taliban, but experience in Vietnam and Malaysia teaches that you cannot kill your way out of a guerilla war. The path to victory lies with giving the population a stake in the outcome you desire.

2009—A New Policy: Convincing all that America is in it for the Long Haul

On March 27, 2009, US President Barack Obama unveiled a new policy on Afghanistan and Pakistan:

- Objective: Disrupt, dismantle, and defeat al-Qaeda and its safe havens.
- Treat Afghanistan and Pakistan as two countries but one challenge.
- Significant increases in US and international support and resources, economic, civilian, and military, linked to Pakistani performance against terror.
- Involve the Afghan and Pakistani governments, partners and NATO allies, other donors.
- International organizations and regional governments.
- Intelligence sharing and military cooperation along the border.
- Address common issues like trade, energy, and economic development.
- Train the Afghan National Security Forces so that they can increasingly take responsibility.
- A new Contact Group for Afghanistan and Pakistan that brings together all who should have a stake in the security of the region—NATO allies and other partners, the Central Asian states, Gulf nations, Iran, Russia, India and China.[46]

The Obama Administration may be on the right course. They are working to pay attention to fixing the Domestic Level game in Pakistan and Afghanistan. In turn, that will make the Great Game and the Little Game level more tractable. All games are operating simultaneously and at cross-purposes. As long as there is no legitimate state in Afghanistan *and* Pakistan, each game level fuels the fire on the other levels. The goal must be to reverse the feedback loop between the games.

---

46   White House Press Office (2009), "What's New in the Strategy for Afghanistan and Pakistan" (March 27) *The Briefing Room*, online at http://www.whitehouse.gov/the_ press_office/Whats-New-in-the-Strategy-for-Afghanistan-and-Pakistan/ (accessed April 1, 2009).

So, building a legitimate state in Afghanistan will limit the utility and ability of Pakistan's gaming in Afghanistan. It will also limit India's ability to do the same. That, in turn, reduces the fuel to Pakistan's fears of India and will support the simultaneous effort to transform Pakistan into a legitimate state. A Pakistani state built on foundations more secure than being the *un*India will encourage India and further reduce its scheming against Pakistan.

For all of this to be possible, the Obama Administration has the crucial but difficult task of convincing all actors on the ground, whatever the level, that the US is in the region for the long haul. Only then will they change their own behavior. The same could be said for NATO. Demonstrating credibility and staying power will be the primary challenge and it will take years. What needs to be overcome is not the Taliban, but the reputation acquired from the history of US engagement in Vietnam, Somalia, and 1980s Afghanistan. This makes more sense than fruitlessly trying to kill your way out of an insurgency, something which rarely succeeds.

Chapter 12

The Effects of Globalization on Transnational Terrorism

Shahdad Naghshpour and J.J. St. Marie

Introduction

Globalization is multi-faceted phenomenon comprised of economic, political and cultural dimensions. In a like manner, transnational terrorism is a complex issue encompassing all the dimensions of globalization, plus religion. Given that both globalization and terrorism have some of the same dimensions it is only logical that some linkage should exist between the two. In this chapter we explore the relationship between globalization and terrorism. This chapter examines globalization and how it can affect terrorism in the political, economic and cultural realms. Furthermore, this chapter evaluates those factors that make some parts of the world inviting for terrorist groups to base their operations. Finally, an analysis of recent terrorist events, based upon severity, geographic region and target, highlights not only the methods and effectiveness of terror attacks but illuminates those aspects of globalization that either promote or retard the growth of terrorism on a global scale.

Globalization

Globalization is a multi-dimensional process as noted by Joseph Stiglitz who sees a:

> Closer integration of the countries and peoples of the world which has been brought about by the enormous reduction of costs of transportation and communication and the breaking down of artificial barriers to the flows of goods, services, capital, knowledge, and (to a lesser extent) people across borders.[1]

This sort of integration envisioned by Stiglitz has been a reality for many years in the developed world, but in the developing world much more integration must take place to catch up with the developed nations. The unique feature of globalization

---

1 Stiglitz, J. (2002), *Globalization and its Discontents*, New York: W.W. Norton and Company.

is the acceleration in the rate of globalization once the process is initiated. This acceleration may create social, economic and political stresses that underlie an individual's participation in political violence.

The link between globalization and poverty is complex and is seen as a cause of terrorism by some. The underlying logic is that underdevelopment and poverty can create conditions of relative deprivation in which the dissatisfied attempt to recover some share of the wealth through terrorist activities.[2] Thus globalization and its negative social consequences, namely increasing poverty, can be seen as creating "breeding grounds" for terrorists. When this sort of relative deprivation is combined with cultural globalization the resulting alienation may be sufficient to cause terrorism to be seen as a viable alternative to cooperation with either the government or the perceived perpetrators of cultural globalization. Weak states are particularly susceptible to terrorist organization as seen in parts of Africa.[3]

To be sure, culture is a feature of societies that individuals value highly. While culture is certainly changeable, the rate of change can be problematic for some groups. The malleability of a particular culture can determine the social response to change. For example American culture is highly malleable in so far as it incorporates ethnic foods quickly and easily. The acceptance of Mexican, Thai and Japanese food in a relatively short time demonstrates malleability in one respect. Conversely, a more rigid culture as in France has difficulties assimilating new non-European immigrants into greater French society, in much the same way as the French language is officially hostile to anglicized French words. For example, official government e-mail must now be called *courriel*, a derivation of *courrier electronique*. Such rigidity can lead to alienation as a rigid social culture is bombarded with new and perhaps culturally inappropriate or taboo ideas. Economic globalization can exacerbate culturally rigid societies while an accelerated rate of globalization can and will increase tensions even more.

The notion that globalization can create poverty and that poverty is a root cause of terrorism has been disputed by some.[4] This falls in line with recent research that postulates that globalization indeed reduces poverty. The poorest in society tend to see their incomes increased through globalization as they tend to fill mostly unskilled jobs that are the first created by trade. Later on, skilled positions

---

2   See Biden, J.R. (2001), *Toward Economic Growth in Africa: The Fifth Action in the War on Terrorism*, online at http://biden.senate.gov/press/speeches/economicgrowthinafrica. htm; Bush, G.W. (2002), *President Outlines Plan to Help World's Poor*, online at http:// www.whitehouse.gov/news/releases/2002/03/print/20020322-1.html; Tyson, L. (2001), "It's time to step up the global war on poverty," *Business Week*, December 3.

3   Jackson, R. and Rosberg, C. (1982), "Why Africa's Weak States Persist: The Empirical and the Juridical in Statehood," *World Politics* 35, October, 1–24.

4   Krueger, A.B. and Maleckova, J. (2002), *Education, Poverty, Political Violence and Terrorism: Is there a Causal connection?* NBER Working Paper No. 9074, Cambridge, MA: National Bureau of Economic Research.

see wage increases as more sophisticated items are exported.[5] Globalization in underdeveloped nations does tend to present one problem since very low income households have highly specialized incomes, such as certain types of farming or micro-retailers. These households tend to see incomes rise later in the globalization process.[6] Thus, while globalization tends to increase incomes the poorest will have to wait much longer to find themselves benefiting from increased integration into global markets, culture and politics. In the interregnum between subsistence living and increased income many may find solace in religion, traditional cultural expressions or, if alienated, political violence in the form of terrorism, especially transnational terrorism which seeks to strike at the source of the perceived injustice—namely the developed Western nations. One way governments can alleviate potential problems is to assist the poor with various subsidies aimed at increasing incomes through better jobs or increased education.[7]

The Political Economy of Terrorism

The heart of terrorism is the destruction of life, property and institutions. As defined by Enders and Sandler, terrorism is the premeditated use of or threatening the use of violence to coerce or gain various religious, political or ideological objectives through the intimidation of a specific audience.[8] Terrorism can cross state borders; thus terrorism can be transnational. In general, most recent terrorism can be classified as transnational terrorism.

The political economy of terrorism is a simple logic that not only constrains but enables terrorists to pursue their goals. Terrorists and their organizations can be viewed as rational actors who are subject to certain constraints. These constraints are analogous to budgetary constraints that limit the actions of individuals, firms and governments—assuming no lending.[9] While ideologically motivated terrorist acts receive the most media and academic attention, the role of economic goals of terrorists cannot be neglected. Thus, as rational actors terrorists must marshal their resources in such a way as to maintain operational viability. This includes

---

5   Heshmati, A. (2005), "The Relationship between Income Inequality, Poverty and Globalization," *World Institute for Development Economics Research Paper*, No. 2005/37, United National University.

6   Kenny, C. (2005), "Why are we Worried about Income? Nearly Everything that Matters is Converging," *World Development* 33/1, 1–19.

7   Harrison, A. (2005), "Globalization and Poverty," University of California and NBER paper.

8   See Enders, W. and Sandler, T. (1993), "The Effectiveness of Antiterrorism Policies: A Vector Auto-regression-intervention Analysis," *American Political Science Review* 87, 829–44; (1999), "Transnational Terrorism in the Post-cold War Era," *International Studies Quarterly* 43, 145–67; (2000), "Is Transnational Terrorism becoming More Threatening? A Time-series Investigation," *Journal of Conflict Resolution* 44, 307–32.

9   Crenshaw, M. (1981), "The Causes of Terrorism," *Comparative Politics* 13, 379–99.

such actions that may seem irrational to the average terrorist. For example, such an action might be limited negotiation with a government. This has been suggested by al-Qaeda on more than one occasion. Such "tactical retreats" may be used by the rational terrorist to replenish manpower, overcome operational problems, obtain weapons or increase financing. In such an interregnum resources may be replenished through either legal or illegal activities.

The war on terror and the foreign policy of various nations has been focused on rejecting any overtures by terrorist organizations while attempting to undermine them when they are in a period of "tactical retreat." While negotiations are seen by some as victories for terrorists, others see this tactic as a weakness in the terrorist organization, which may not be the case. Indeed, sometimes after terror attacks, negotiation initiated by the target has produced lulls in violence, only to return with increased frequency as terror organizations seek greater concessions.[10] In general tactics such as negotiation may be more beneficial to terrorist organizations in an increasingly globalized world as some nations decide to negotiate while others do not. The benefits of reduced hostility may bring electoral success to negotiating states while less intensive anti-terror operations will give groups the opportunity to rearm and refocus operations. In all, a coordinated policy by all nations is needed more urgently in a globalized world than was previously the case. Instantaneous global communication affords terrorists a venue to showcase their operations and move domestic and world opinion.

The constraints on terrorists fall into two major categories the specific and the structural constraints. Both forms of constraints are affected by globalization. First, specific constraints such as increased security—especially if implemented internationally—can constrain terrorist activities. When confronted by specific restrictions such as increased security or the denial of bases of operations, terror groups will cause substitution in tactics and operations. This is the same as the economic substitution effect seen in consumers. For example, with falling incomes or the expectation of falling incomes, consumers will substitute their first preference with their second or even third preference to save on overall expenditure. In many cases this involves switching from branded goods to generic or store brands. Specific constraints placed upon terrorist organizations since 2001 have been increased airport security, increased maritime security for container shipping and other measures. When sources of international funds dry up due to international police actions many groups turn to the drug trade to finance their terrorist operations.[11]

Structural constraints are part of the international system of state relations and affect the legal and illegal activities of terrorist groups, thus their preferences for each are affected. The Cold War effectively provided havens for some terrorist

---

10   See Pape, R., "The Strategic Logic of Suicide Terrorism," *American Political Science Review* 97/3.

11   Leader, S. and Wiencek, D. (2000), "Drug Money: The Fuel for Global Terrorism," *Jane's Intelligence Review*, February.

organizations while excluding others. For example, some found refuge in Arab nations, while left-wing organizations or those with a socialist ideology sought help and refuge in the Soviet Bloc. In short, your ideology determined your residence and the scope of your operations. With the end of the Cold War some terrorist organizations had to find new centers from which to operate, while new organizations like al-Qaeda found homes in failed states. Globalization has again reshuffled the structural deck for terrorist organizations. This has brought both increased and decreased marginal costs of operations for terrorists. Globalization in the form of increased travel has provided more opportunities for terrorist movement and thus increased the number of available targets that they may find attractive. Increased movement has allowed individuals or ethnic groups sympathetic to terrorists to provide safe havens and assistance at great distances from their operation base. In a similar manner, trade has provided opportunities for transporting personnel and materials for terrorist operations. Social globalization is one of the largest contributors to decreasing terrorists' marginal costs in spreading their message and gaining recruits. The cultural tsunami experienced by many countries with the importation of goods, combined with foreign media, have created conditions where disaffected individuals turn to terrorism as an outlet for their frustrations and in most cases their desire for a return to a purer culture devoid of external influences. Thus in some instances globalization may increase the ability of terrorists to organize, plan and execute terrorist attacks. However, on the other hand, globalization presents law enforcement agencies with some specific advantages in catching terrorist or preventing terrorist attacks. Increasing economic integration can decrease the cost of illegal activities relative to legal activities as more opportunities for illegal activities are available given the increased number of countries with increased trade. In short, globalization increases the number of entry points for terrorists. Moreover, these entry points or targets will, with increasing economic expansion, become more densely packed and thus easier to attack and harder to defend.

The growth in international trade has further integrated the economies of developed and developing nations. Increased trade can bring about higher incomes and alleviate some of the pressures that cause individuals to turn to terrorism. This may in turn make terrorist recruitment more difficult as young males and females see themselves as having more income opportunities. Reduction of poverty is a major reason for the decline in terrorism in some countries and globalization can contribute to the decline if the benefits of trade in particular are distributed within society.[12] Political globalization, or the increase in transnational diplomatic and consular ties, can help fight terrorism by means of increased law enforcement networking which allows information to be disseminated to potential target nations so appropriate action can be taken by authorities. Such cooperation has

---

12   Korteweg, R. and Ehrhardt, D. (2005), *Terrorist Black Holes: A Study into Terrorist Sanctuaries and Governmental Weakness*, The Hague: Clingendael Centre for Strategic Studies.

been effective in thwarting terrorist acts in some instances and as a confidence building measure between governments. It also assists in improving diplomatic ties, which in turn can lead to stronger trade ties. Social globalization, as discussed earlier, can be a double-edged sword for terrorists. It can potentially create false impressions that may contribute to alienation and help drive some to terrorist groups. It can also, if used wisely, be a vehicle for understanding and defusing social tensions. For example, while television news can be a vehicle used by terrorists for propaganda based upon negative stereotypes of foreigners, it can also be used to portray residents of other nations in a realistic manner as opposed to the skewed manner in which terrorists attempt to portray their enemies. Breaking down barriers and fostering cross-cultural understanding is one way in which globalization can mitigate the conditions that lead to terrorism and the acceptance of terrorist ideas among a population.

Globalization as a process of change can and does affect developing nations, where most terrorism takes place and has its ideological roots. Globalization touches the political, cultural and economic foundations of a society. In some instances the changes are beneficial, while in others stress is the result. On whole, globalization puts social systems in new and sometimes uncomfortable positions. The decision making process that leads a society to allow terrorist groups in its midst or to tilt towards radical ideologies is certainly influenced by the rate and extent of globalization. Yet for globalization to be a prime motivator certain factors inherent within the state or society must be present.

The Ungovernable and Terrorism

The link between terrorism and globalization can only be fully understood when the constraints on a potentially terrorist supporting society and culture are examined. The notion of ungoverned territories serves as a backdrop for an examination of the terrorism/globalization nexus. In short, ungoverned territories are those areas where state penetration in all forms is low.[13]

One aspect of both structural and specific constraints can be found in ungoverned territories where globalization has been absent and terrorist activity remains high.[14] According to the RAND Corporation an ungoverned territory is

---

13   Migdal, J. (1988), *Strong States and Weak Societies: State-Society Relations and State Capabilities in the Third World*, Princeton: Princeton University Press.

14   Esty, D.C., Goldstone, J., Gurr, T.R., Harff, B., Surko, P., Unger, A.N. and Chen, R.S. (1998), "The State Failure Project: Early Warning Research for US Foreign Policy Planning," in Davies, J.L. and Gurr, T.R. (eds), *Preventive Measures: Building Risk Assessment and Crisis Early Warning Systems*, Lanham, MD: Rowman & Littlefield Publishers, Inc.

one in which the state cannot establish effective control.[15] Factors that contribute to ungovernability include the lack of state penetration in the forms of state institutions, physical infrastructure and social and cultural resistance. Second, the state lacks a monopoly on the use of force and is almost powerless against armed gangs, criminal networks and armed populations. Lack of a defensible border to stem illegal migration is another factor leading to difficult governance. Finally, external interference—the ease of interference by another state—can be viewed as a factor in ungovernability. Ungovernable areas of the world include: the Pakistan–Afghan border region; the south-eastern part of the Arabian Peninsula; East Africa (particularly the area of and surrounding Somalia); West Africa; the north Caucasus; ports of Indonesia; the Columbia–Venezuela border and the Guatemala–Chiapas border.[16]

Can globalization ease the pressures that states face and strengthen governability? If the state can capture the positive and lasting effects of globalization perhaps a reduction in terrorism may occur. Several indicators of conduciveness to terrorism or insurgencies have been developed as they relate to ungoverned territories. These include infrastructure, communications, financial transactions, and transportation. Demographic indicators include the presence of extremist groups, supportive social norms of political violence, a preexisting state of violence and the presence of criminal syndicates. A source of legal income is also important in extending the state's power into various regions.[17] While all these indicators of conduciveness to terrorist ideology and recruitment are not equally weighted in many of the world's ungoverned regions, they do tend to be related to the indicators of ungovernability. Would globalization be able to reduce these indicators of terrorist conduciveness while increasing those factors that assist the state in creating governability?

Globalization can assist states in providing a state structure that will help weak states in gaining control over unmanageable territories. Globalization can assist states in creating the atmosphere where the state can strengthen itself and penetrate regions that previously were impervious to the central government. Economic globalization entailing foreign direct investment and trade can assist the government by increasing the tax base while also increasing the overall national income. Increased government revenue can be used to alleviate infrastructure problems in peripheral areas where governance is not as strong. One impediment to economic development in many underdeveloped nations is lack of infrastructure. Infrastructure improvements can bring the benefits of globalization to areas that would be considered ungoverned. Moreover, infrastructure facilitates the spread of state power by making the redeployment of law enforcement or military units

---

15   Rabasa, A., Boraz, S., Chalk, P., Cragin, K., Karasik, T.W., Moroney, J.D.P., O'Brien, K.A. and Peters, J.E. (2007), "Ungoverned Territories: Understanding and Reducing Terrorism Risks," *RAND Corporation*, online at http://www.rand.org/pubs/monographs/2007/RAND_MG561.pdf.

16   Ibid., Introduction and Cases.

17   Ibid., Table A.2, 309.

quicker and easier, thus providing an advantage to the government vis-à-vis armed groups that compete with the state for control of the regions. The problem of dispersed social control in peripheral regions can be overcome if the central government has the will to bring the region and its population into the state and its monopoly of coercive force. This simply means rule of law, law enforcement, and the ability to extract from society in the form of taxes. Such measures can be accomplished with increased economic globalization as trade increases incomes and government revenue allowing the government to extend its rule into rebellious areas. Political globalization in the form of increased diplomatic relations and engagement in international organizations can also assist the government in dealing with criminal networks and lack of border controls. More integration into the global political structure can assist nations struggling with rebellious areas of their territory through increased cooperation with international organizations like NATO, the EU, or ASEAN. Social globalization in the form of more cross cultural contact and increased media penetration, along with tourism, can bring about a change in provincial attitudes in developing nations. Taken together ,the various forms of globalization can assist developing nations in creating more wealth, spreading the power of the state and gaining sovereignty over its landmass and population.

Increased globalization can also affect specific constraints or those indicators of conduciveness to terrorism in peripheral areas. Increased communications can decrease the level of xenophobia some underdeveloped areas have with the developed world, while an increase in or the initial use of financial services can help in building trust in the modern and break down old parochial attitudes. Extremist groups can be disarmed by the central government if it has more resources, especially if foreign assistance is provided to help put down traditional rivalries or indigenous extremist groups. Criminal syndicates can be broken up with outside aid and increased law enforcement resources. Sources of income can be transferred from illegal activities to legal activities.[18] This is especially important with substance level farmers. If they can be convinced to grow crops for export they will be more willing to trade some independence for government protection and an assured income. On the other hand, if the farmers are producers of illegal drugs, government penetration may be more difficult as it is difficult to create the same value per kilogram of legal crop versus opium, cacao, marijuana or hashish. Globalization in its various forms can assist states in gaining control over their territory and extending the rule of law and the coercive power of the state to break traditional social bonds.

While globalization does have some negatives with regard to the ultimate governability of an area within nation-states or entire nations, it can and does have the power to mitigate many of the negative aspects of development and ungovernability. Ultimately foreign help in assisting nations with ungovernable

18   Galeotti, M. (2005), "Central Asian Republics Increase Cooperation on Organized Crime," *Jane's Intelligence Review*, February.

regions or ungoverned states will be necessary for integration into global markets which will assist the positive aspects of globalization in politically and economically underdeveloped areas.

Globalization and Conduciveness to Terrorism

Factors contributing to terrorism that are endemic to ungoverned nations and areas include the adequacy of infrastructure, income for terrorists, and favorable demographics. In much the same way that the factors of ungovernability are conducive to terrorism, so are the factors that are conducive to a terrorist presence in a state or region within a state.

The lack of infrastructure, while crucial for economic and political development, is also attractive to terrorists. Lack of roads and communications networks allows ungovernable regions to be run by traditional local elites who may or may not assist terror organizations. The calculus of local elites usually depends upon the degree of assistance they can receive from the terrorist in settling outside feuds, helping to run local and traditional cartels and reinforcing local mores in the region. Lack of a financial infrastructure, namely a credible banking system, adds to the overall conduciveness in regions without effective central control. Globalization can assist in reducing the attractiveness of a region to terrorists not only by strengthening governance but also strengthening transportation, communication and the introduction of modern banking. To be sure, such changes cannot occur overnight, but increased integration into the global system can only help in alleviating those factors conducive to a terrorist presence.

When an ungovernable area is presented in a nation-state, terrorists become interested in the area as a base of operations, that is, if they can integrate themselves into the local economy and fund their activities. Naturally, external funding is necessary in most cases; however with increased international pressure, local funding is gaining in importance. Local income tends to be similar to the traditional non-agricultural, and in general illegal, enterprises of the indigenous population into which the terrorists blend. Protection rackets, smuggling, and cultivation of opium poppies are the traditional activities that terrorist organizations tend to get involved with either through assisting local elites or joining the enterprise. For locals, an alliance with terrorist organizations brings a military arm, organization and networking, thus local elites cooperate. Participation in the drugs and arms trade is very common.[19] Clearly, the ability to support the terrorist organization locally is important and the presence of easily acquired resources is conducive to terrorists operating from ungoverned areas.[20]

---

19   Khan, M.S.A. (1999), "Linkages Between Arms Trafficking and the Drug Trade in South Asia," in Dhanapala, J. et al. (eds), *Small Arms Control: Old Weapons, New Issues*, Aldershot: Ashgate Publishing.

20   Ghafour, H. (2004), "Spicy Solution to the Afghan Poppy Problem," *Los Angeles Times*, April 5.

The demographic environment of the ungoverned regions also helps terrorists in establishing a base in these regions. Such factors as similar norms or religion may create conducive conditions for terrorist groups to operate. If coupled with a large population of young men, this factor becomes even more important. Moreover, if economic development is low, these three factors can create conditions where terrorist recruitment is easy. Instability in the economic, governance and demographic realms is particularly helpful for terrorist in creating sanctuaries where they become self-contained units able to conduct the necessary operations needed for full scale terrorist attacks.

Taken as a whole or in parts these factors allow terrorist organizations to infiltrate ungoverned regions and set up operations. The activities can include training, recruitment, resource gathering and all other necessary activities. Globalization can create stresses on the social and economic system that exacerbate these factors, yet with skillful governance these same factors can be turned into advantages for the central authorities. For example, the penetration of government into rural Peru was exceedingly helpful in the destruction of the Sendero Luminoso group. Government penetration and alternative income can lessen those factors conducive to terrorist activity in ungoverned regions. The balance of this chapter examines data on the frequency, type and target used by terrorists. Many of these groups operate from various ungoverned regions inside nation-states.

Terrorist Activity, Targeting and Region

Terrorist activity is not uniform across the globe. Many groups are clustered in a few regions. The specific targets and methods terror groups use in their attacks are used to highlight variations in strategy, finance and recruitment. The analysis demonstrates a clustering around several factors. By examining these factors policy makers can devise policies to counter the formation and existence of terrorist groups.

The main source of data for this chapter is the Global Terrorism Database II, by LaFree and Dugan (2004).[21] The data set is a massive collection of information deemed relevant to global terrorism. Many of the variables are qualitative in nature. For the analysis in this chapter we select 30 variables that provide what we consider a realistic picture of global terrorism. Table 12.1 provides types of acts of terror by region for 1998–2004. LaFree and Dugan divide the world into 11 regions. They group countries by geographical proximity as well as by politics, culture, and ethnicity. For example, "Russia and the newly independent states" consist of Russia, Armenia, Azerbaijan, Belarus, Estonia, Georgia, Latvia, Lithuania, and Moldova. The region does not include all the states newly formed after the collapse of the Soviet Union. It does not consist of all the countries that were part of the former

---

21   LaFree, G. and Dugan, L., "Global Terrorism Database II, 1998–2004," *Ann Arbor, MI: Inter-university Consortium for Political and Social Research*, 10–23.

Soviet Union; for example, none of the countries in central Asia are included. For a list of countries in each region see LaFree and Dugan (2004, 17–18).

Acts of terror are different by regions and fluctuate over time in response to changes in abilities and capabilities of terrorists and the governments that fight them. Therefore, in the following analysis all the facts are reported on the "average" basis. For sake of brevity this fact will not be repeated in each case. The most common category of acts of terror is Bombing. The Middle East and North Africa lead all other regions in this category. In fact, this region leads all regions in Basic Assault, Assassination, Armed Intrusion, Hijacking, and Armed Assault as well.

Each region seems to "specialize" in a particular type of terrorism. The Middle East and North Africa's specialty is Basic Assault and Bombing. In Sub-Saharan Africa, Basic Assault is preferred. In Western Europe the terror act of choice is Bombing, but the region leads the world in Arson. In fact 55 percent of the global arson occurs in this region. In almost every category, the lowest number of acts of terror take place in Australasia and Oceania. This is expected since the group consists of Australia, New Zealand, and 15 small islands, none of which is a major terrorism hotbed.

Table 12.1 Terrorism by the region by the year

Regions	Country	Basic Assault	Assassination	Maiming	Kidnapping	Hijacking	Armed Assault	Armed Intrusion	Bombing	Mass Disruption	Arson	Sabotage	CBRN Attack	Other	Unknown	Total
North America	1998	4	0	0	0	0	0	0	10	1	3	10	0	0	0	28
	1999	3	0	0	0	0	0	0	5	0	5	0	0	2	0	15
	2000	1	0	0	0	0	0	0	3	0	0	0	0	0	0	4
	2001	0	0	0	0	4	0	1	1	0	4	0	9	0	0	19
	2002	0	0	0	0	0	0	0	20	0	0	0	0	0	0	20
	2003	0	0	0	0	0	0	0	0	0	2	0	0	0	0	2
	2004	0	1	0	0	0	0	0	0	0	0	0	0	0	0	1
Central America	1998	0	0	0	0	0	0	0	2	0	0	0	0	0	0	2
	1999	4	0	0	1	0	0	0	1	1	0	0	0	0	0	7
	2000	2	2	0	1	0	0	0	2	1	0	0	0	0	0	8
	2001	0	0	0	0	0	0	0	0	0	0	0	0	0	0	0
	2002	0	1	0	0	0	0	0	0	0	1	0	0	0	0	2
	2003	1	1	0	0	0	0	0	0	3	0	0	0	0	0	5
	2004	2	0	0	0	0	0	1	0	0	0	0	0	0	0	3

Table 12.1 continued

Regions	Country	Basic Assault	Assassination	Maiming	Kidnapping	Hijacking	Armed Assault	Armed Intrusion	Bombing	Mass Disruption	Arson	Sabotage	CBRN Attack	Other	Unknown	Total
South America	1998	14	3	0	14	1	0	1	61	0	1	0	0	0	0	95
	1999	30	5	0	35	2	0	4	44	0	3	0	0	0	0	123
	2000	26	3	0	20	0	0	2	42	0	5	0	0	0	0	98
	2001	11	4	0	15	1	0	4	19	0	0	0	0	0	0	54
	2002	25	7	0	9	2	0	0	50	0	3	0	0	0	0	96
	2003	17	7	0	9	0	0	0	64	0	3	0	0	0	0	100
	2004	23	5	0	19	0	0	1	11	0	0	0	0	0	0	59
East Asia	1998	0	1	0	0	0	0	0	3	0	0	0	0	0	0	4
	1999	0	0	0	0	0	0	0	3	0	0	0	0	0	0	3
	2000	3	0	0	0	0	0	0	2	0	0	0	0	0	0	5
	2001	0	0	0	0	0	0	1	12	0	1	0	0	0	0	14
	2002	1	0	0	0	0	0	0	1	0	0	0	0	0	0	2
	2003	3	0	0	0	0	0	0	3	0	1	0	0	0	0	7
	2004	0	0	0	0	0	0	0	2	0	0	0	0	0	0	2
Southeast Asia	1998	8	1	0	5	0	2	4	12	0	0	0	0	0	0	32
	1999	60	1	0	14	0	0	7	20	0	6	1	0	1	0	110
	2000	72	7	0	13	1	0	6	97	0	3	0	0	1	0	200
	2001	26	3	0	5	1	0	6	28	0	0	0	0	0	0	69
	2002	33	9	0	7	0	0	1	26	1	5	0	0	0	0	82
	2003	75	6	0	3	2	0	2	42	0	8	1	0	0	0	139
	2004	30	5	0	1	0	0	0	23	0	1	1	0	0	0	61
Western Europe	1998	17	3	1	0	1	0	0	79	1	24	3	0	1	0	130
	1999	34	4	4	5	2	0	4	122	0	53	5	0	3	0	236
	2000	29	19	0	0	0	0	1	114	0	39	4	0	1	0	207
	2001	13	9	1	0	0	0	3	64	0	16	0	0	0	0	106
	2002	9	5	0	0	0	0	1	59	0	11	0	0	0	0	85
	2003	17	3	0	0	0	0	0	64	0	10	0	0	0	0	94
	2004	5	0	0	0	0	0	1	30	1	2	0	0	0	0	39

Table 12.1 continued

Regions	Country	Basic Assault	Assassination	Maiming	Kidnapping	Hijacking	Armed Assault	Armed Intrusion	Bombing	Mass Disruption	Arson	Sabotage	CBRN Attack	Other	Unknown	Total
Eastern Europe	1998	34	1	0	1	0	0	0	34	0	3	0	1	0	0	74
	1999	38	3	0	1	0	0	3	35	0	3	0	0	1	1	85
	2000	31	4	0	0	0	1	0	28	0	0	0	0	1	0	65
	2001	16	2	0	1	0	0	2	13	0	1	0	0	1	1	37
	2002	7	0	0	0	0	0	1	7	0	1	0	0	1	0	17
	2003	10	2	0	0	0	0	0	6	0	4	0	0	0	0	22
	2004	2	0	0	0	0	0	0	0	0	0	0	0	0	0	2
Middle East	1998	90	2	0	4	1	0	0	107	0	1	0	0	1	0	206
	1999	118	12	0	12	1	0	7	135	0	23	0	0	0	1	309
	2000	83	9	0	8	4	0	7	74	0	4	0	0	1	0	190
	2001	73	5	0	2	1	8	13	49	0	0	0	0	0	0	151
	2002	139	3	0	2	1	0	1	74	0	1	0	0	0	0	221
	2003	91	10	0	1	1	0	0	75	0	2	1	0	1	0	182
	2004	110	21	0	20	0	0	5	137	0	2	3	0	1	1	300
Sub-Saharan Africa	1998	46	1	0	8	0	0	6	17	0	0	0	0	2	0	80
	1999	62	5	0	27	0	0	17	31	1	1	0	0	0	1	145
	2000	68	6	0	20	0	0	25	20	1	3	0	0	0	0	143
	2001	45	1	0	4	0	6	11	10	0	4	1	0	0	0	82
	2002	50	0	0	9	0	0	2	16	1	1	1	0	0	0	80
	2003	45	2	0	5	0	0	0	5	0	2	0	0	0	0	59
	2004	17	3	0	1	0	0	5	1	0	0	0	0	0	0	27
Russia and NIS	1998	10	6	0	5	1	0	1	21	0	0	0	0	0	0	44
	1999	13	8	0	8	0	0	3	32	0	7	0	0	0	0	71
	2000	47	11	0	4	1	0	0	57	3	2	1	0	0	0	126
	2001	16	5	0	1	1	0	5	35	0	0	0	0	0	0	63
	2002	30	8	0	4	0	0	0	38	0	1	0	0	0	0	81
	2003	33	3	0	1	0	0	2	26	0	3	2	0	0	0	70
	2004	13	2	0	0	2	0	3	11	0	2	0	0	1	0	34

Table 12.1 continued

Regions	Country	Basic Assault	Assassination	Maiming	Kidnapping	Hijacking	Armed Assault	Armed Intrusion	Bombing	Mass Disruption	Arson	Sabotage	CBRN Attack	Other	Unknown	Total
Australasia	1998	1	0	0	0	0	0	0	5	0	0	0	0	0	0	6
	1999	1	0	0	0	0	0	0	3	0	0	0	0	0	0	4
	2000	1	0	0	0	1	0	0	0	0	0	0	0	0	0	2
	2001	0	0	0	0	0	0	0	0	0	2	0	1	0	0	3
	2002	1	0	0	0	0	0	0	0	0	0	0	0	0	0	1
	2003	0	1	0	0	0	0	0	1	0	0	0	1	0	0	3
	2004	0	0	0	0	0	0	0	0	0	0	0	0	0	0	0
Total		1939	251	6	325	32	17	170	2244	15	283	34	12	20	5	5353

Terrorism Targets

The next step is to determine terrorist targets. Table 12.1 shows major discrepancies within and between regions and types of acts of terrorism. Table 12.2 displays acts of terror based on the target entity in each of the 13 regions. There are wide discrepancies by region as well as by target. The most common act of terrorism is the "Indiscriminate Civilians/Non-Combatant" category, with 2,094 reported incidents between 1998 and 2004. In seven of the regions this category is the most frequent act of terrorism. Indiscriminate acts of terrorism against civilians in these seven regions account for almost 69, or a little more than 2 out of 3 cases globally. The Middle East and North Africa leads all regions in this target by 638 or 31 percent of the cases. The second most frequent act of terror is against "Police/Military" targets. There are 1,673 of acts of terrorism against police/military targets. In ten of the 13 regions this target is either first or second among all targets. The greatest number belongs to South Asia (513, or 31 percent). Globally, the "Indiscriminate Civilians/Non-Combatant" accounts for 29 percent of all acts of terror, while "Police/Military" targets account for 23 percent of global targets. The remaining 47 percent is aimed at the other 21 listed targets.

Government is the next most frequent target with 779 cases, which is not even half as many as the Police/Military targets. The ranking for the remaining top 8 targets are: Domestic Business (530), other non-US (377), Transportation (331), Political Party (258), and Religious Figures/Institutions (233). Note that the category "other non-US" is a catchall for many diverse targets.

Table 12.2 Terrorism targets by region over 1998–2004

Target entity	Southeast Asia	Middle East and North Africa	Eastern Europe	Sub-Saharan Africa	South America	South Asia	Central Asia	Russia and the Newly Independent States (NIS)	Western Europe	Central America and Caribbean	East Asia	North America	Australasia and Oceania	Total
Diplomat	3	11	1	2	2	5	1	3	12	1	0	0	0	41
Domestic business	52	71	24	31	75	45	3	15	204	0	4	5	1	530
Foreign business	9	25	2	21	11	11	1	1	26	0	2	0	0	109
Government	60	111	18	33	82	173	14	99	161	12	4	7	5	779
Indiscriminate civilians	210	638	83	294	172	369	9	73	197	4	15	27	1	2092
International	15	16	10	37	3	39	2	8	9	0	0	0	0	139
Media	8	17	14	9	12	20	0	9	22	0	0	1	0	112
Military/Police	7	13	10	2	6	7	0	5	1	0	0	0	2	53
Other/Non US	47	79	14	59	27	73	1	16	42	1	2	16	0	377
Police/Military	186	380	74	81	121	513	10	194	99	5	6	4	0	1673
Political Party	9	43	24	0	13	96	0	5	66	2	0	0	0	258
Religious figures/Inst.	28	31	14	20	8	72	2	17	35	0	0	4	2	233
Transportation	49	50	14	26	25	94	3	33	26	2	6	0	3	331
Unknown	1	22	0	1	2	5	2	12	10	0	0	0	0	55
Utilities	18	26	2	1	69	25	0	6	14	0	0	1	1	163
US Business	3	7	1	2	9	2	0	0	12	0	0	21	0	57
US Diplomat	0	1	2	0	2	3	0	0	1	0	0	0	1	10
US Embassy	0	1	0	0	0	0	0	0	0	0	0	0	0	1
US Government	1	6	1	0	0	2	0	2	1	0	0	2	1	16
US Indiscriminate civilians	1	11	0	0	3	0	0	0	0	0	0	0	0	15
US Other	0	2	0	2	0	4	0	0	1	0	0	0	0	9
US Police/US Military	0	56	1	0	1	22	0	0	0	0	2	0	0	82
US Religious figures/Inst.	0	1	0	1	5	0	0	0	0	0	0	0	0	7
Total	707	1618	309	622	648	1580	48	498	939	27	41	88	17	7142
Total US targets	5	85	5	5	20	33	0	2	15	0	2	23	2	197
US target as % of all	0.7	5.3	1.6	0.8	3.1	2.1	0.0	0.4	1.6	0.0	4.9	26.1	11.8	2.8

The most frequent US target is US Police/US Military (82) followed by US Business (57). In the case of the latter, 21 of the acts of terror against US businesses were carried out in North America, which consists of US and Canada, alone. Compared to the total acts of terror, those against the US are very few. In fact less than 2.8 percent of all acts of terror are against Americans or American interests.

A regional perspective of Table 12.2 reveals that most acts of terror occur in the Middle East and North Africa region (1,618). A close second is South Asia (1,580), followed by Western Europe (939). The remaining regions are all below 1,000 cases over the seven years of study. In the regional analysis one should disregard the North America region, which consists of two countries, the US and Canada. Consequently, most of the targets would be American targets. In fact this region reports 23 acts of terror against US targets. This accounts for 26.1 percent of all terror acts in the region. This is also equal to almost 12 percent of the 197 US terror targets worldwide, which is also the third highest among all regions after the Middle East (85 cases) and South Asia (33 cases). This is higher than the sum of the eight lowest regions combined. The bottom row of Table 12.2 provides the percentage of targets in each region that are US targets. In this row, 26 percent of the targets are US targets in North America, which is not a real global issue but a domestic issue. The data does not indicate the national origin of the terrorist, only the origin of the target. The next highest percentage belongs to Middle East and North Africa, where 5.3 percent of all acts of terror in the region are aimed at US citizens and interests. Since this region also has the most acts of terror the result is a high number of attacks against US in the region (85 of the 197 or 43 percent). If the North America data is excluded, the share of Middle East and North America of US target increases to almost 49 percent. The second highest ranking in terror acts against US interests belongs to South Asia with 33 cases or less than 17 percent.

Conclusions

The analysis of terrorist incidents, targets and region shows that those nations in developed and more globalized areas of the world tend to have significantly less overall terrorism. Regionally, targets vary, with assault being the primary form of violence in Africa compared to bombings being the norm in the Middle East. While the Middle East and Sub-Saharan Africa have the highest incidence of terrorism they are also the least economically developed and are the least globalized. While many nations in the Middle East are wealthy oil producers they do not tend to have globalized economies except for petroleum exports. Politically they are globalized in so far as they have diplomatic relations with many nations, yet they tend to be either authoritarian or monarchical in nature. Neither form of government is open to political criticism, nor are elections "free and fair" in the Western sense of the phrase. Is there a link between terrorism and form of government? The data here seems to indicate such a link; however, while there may be a link, the causal direction of the relationship cannot be established.

The high percentage of attacks on government officials and the police/military indicate that terrorist organizations uniformly attack those entities that are seen as representative of the state. However, depending upon the region, kidnappings and assaults are the most productive methods used by terrorists for the advancement of their agenda. Property damage in Western Europe is also high, indicating that relative wealth generates targets, while also indicating that Western terrorist groups tend to come from the left of the political spectrum.

The data supports the fact that more globalized portions of the world are less likely to suffer from terrorism, and if these regions do experience terrorism it is of a different form than less globalized and less developed nations. In particular, ungovernable regions seem to be especially difficult for globalization to penetrate. The conclusions indicate that globalization can help alleviate terrorism by creating unfavorable conditions for terrorists in various regions with less effective governance. Clearly, these regions need aid from NGOs, the UN and other entities that can assist in creating infrastructure and governance mechanisms that allow the benefits of globalization, mainly economic, to change initial conditions such that terrorists find a social, economic and political environment inhospitable to their ideology and tactics. The creation of hostile environments for terrorists through globalization would no doubt cause a significant reduction in global terrorist activities while spreading prosperity, and integrating states into a closer global nation-state culture.

PART 4
Future Challenges

Chapter 13

"Terrorism" in the Moral Discourse of Humanity

Mark Evans

"Terrorism" and Moral Conviction

It has often been said by commentators of many ideological hues that we are living in an age of moral "uncertainty". If (fittingly enough) it is hardly certain that they are all talking about exactly the same phenomenon, we can nevertheless formulate one very influential version of their proposition thus: a significant and perhaps growing number of us have experienced an erosion of belief relating to the sources of the objective authority which moral judgments claim for themselves (for example, "'murder is wrong' is a fact and those who disagree with it are objectively in error"). This development has actually stripped away much of our confidence that even our deepest moral convictions are anything more than subjective "matters of opinion", personal—if sometimes shared—feelings or predilections, with no more objective authority over other views than the statement "*I like* banana ice cream" has over your statement that *you like* chocolate ice cream (statements which are not venturing claims about any supposed objective superiority of either flavor, even when they are replies to the ostensibly objectivist question, "what is the best flavor of ice cream?").

Put another way: without a belief in, say, God or some equivalent basis to account for the possibility of objective validity in judgments about good and evil, and right and wrong, we have subjectivized our beliefs about morality's wellspring.[1] Further, this has had the consequence of *relativizing* our moral convictions, radically transforming our moral outlooks. This loss of confidence in *moral judgmentalism*—the practice of passing moral judgment on the beliefs and acts of others in terms of objective right and wrong—has, so the claim runs, prompted a reconfiguration of our moral convictions to suppress any suggestion of objective superiority over opposing views. The whole practice, indeed, of *moral*

---

1 Bafflingly, perhaps, this does not always entail an official commitment to secularism. Sometimes, the nature of belief in God changes in ways which lead to peculiarly incoherent assertions, such as: "God's existence itself is only a matter of my belief and I have no warrant to believe that those who deny it are wrong." Since when have true religious believers been able consistently to believe that their God was simply a creation of their own minds? See the discussion in the chapter's second section.

convictionism—very simply, the practice of having certain convictions about what is right and wrong—is thereby rendered deeply problematic (and/or trivial).

For some experiencing it, this loss has generated an exaggeratedly heightened sensitivity to others' opinions, an attitude of tolerance that makes it almost a matter of principle that one has no *right* to challenge the validity of any opposing judgments. The banal truisms that people think that their belief that "X is wrong" is valid or justified, and that people with different beliefs think that *those* beliefs are justified, slide (perhaps almost imperceptibly) into the very different (and much more controversial) claim that "the status of X *itself* is only a matter of my personal opinion and I therefore have no objective grounds to claim that X is valid and holds for anyone who doesn't share it (I have no grounds other than my own opinion on which to say they are wrong and I therefore cannot say so)".[2] This move is tantamount to an abstention from moral judgmentalism and it is unclear that it would any longer make sense to talk of one having moral "convictions" at all. We can call this the "abstentionist" position. For others, relativism is pushed to yield an altogether new conviction: each moral view can only be thought of as being "as good as any other" and no claims which state or imply the contrary can therefore be regarded as acceptable, or valid. We can call this the "equal validity" position.[3]

From my experiences both as a teacher and in private, informal debate on such matters, I am disposed to accept the contention that some such position does indeed have widespread currency in the West today, particularly but not exclusively among younger generations. What makes "uncertainty" such an appropriate term to characterize its mindset is not so much the philosophical confusions with which it is evidently beset (and which I shall briefly review shortly) but the fact that, when put under pressure, it so often rapidly collapses into untenability as a form of moral response, a way of actually living moral life. The events of September 11, though tragically not unique in this regard, helped to force a brutal realization of this fact. How can anyone think, we might ask, that no objective matters of good and evil—no matters of moral *truth*—were at stake in the calculated sacrifice of thousands of lives by the hijackers? No matter what you think about September 11, and its causes and aftermath, can you really characterize to yourself your reactions to the moral *enormity* of it all as *just* your opinion, unwilling to impugn and indeed incapable of impugning their polar opposites? How could anyone confront September 11 with such moral spinelessness?

---

2   In other words, on moral questions our opinions are no longer conceptualized as tracking the *facts* of the matter. There are no criteria external to them which could validate or falsify them; it is in that sense that they are "merely" opinions.

3   Two authors of strikingly different political persuasion who have interpreted significant trends of modern culture in such terms are A. Bloom (1987), *The Closing of the American Mind*, New York: Basic Books; and C. Taylor (1991), *The Ethics of Authenticity*, Cambridge, MA: Harvard University Press.

And yet … if events of such magnitude in our lives jolt us into appreciating that perhaps we have not so readily abandoned all the objective moral convictions of yore, some may still fear that they present themselves in our thoughts despite our doubts about them. We may still be at a loss to account for the grounds upon which we judge the motives and consequences of the hijackings, and consequently we may still feel the grip of the relativist view that we have no right to pretend that our morality is superior to our opponents' (that, for example, those appalled by the attacks should not think their views to be superior to the hijackers who evidently felt that *they* were morally justified in their actions).

Now, it might be thought that these musings of the moral philosopher and the cultural critic are somewhat tangential to an empirically-driven assessment of the post-September 11 "war on terror" conducted by the USA and its allies. In fact, however, they are absolutely germane for numerous reasons. For a start, "terrorism" and hence the "war on terror" are morally loaded terms and their very application implies the making of moral judgments. (By calling the events of September 11 "terrorism" to distinguish them from the violence subsequently unleashed on Afghanistan, for example, is to pass moral judgment on them.) Obviously, any analysis constructed around these terms will founder if we are afflicted by moral uncertainty. Such uncertainty may well have provided one of the motivations for a type of "realist" analysis which has much been much employed with regard to September 11 and its aftermath and which sets out deliberately to eschew the adoption or assumption of definite moral convictions and judgments on the events. This sets up a debate between the "moral-judgmentalist" versus what we can call the "historical-political understanding" approaches to studies of, and formulations of practical responses to, September 11. One of the challenges we must face, then, is the resolution of this debate in order to determine which methodology we ought to employ. Hence the concerns of the moral/political philosophers are far more central to this project in ways it is easy to overlook or dismiss, and any gulf currently separating them from it needs to be bridged.

The first task of this chapter is to propose that the reasons which typically give rise to moral uncertainty do not necessitate the abandonment of moral judgmentalism and should be resisted. Uncertainty's philosophical grounds, such as they are, are not enough by themselves to settle the debate between "moral judgment" and "historical-political understanding" and we should feel no embarrassment at approaching this whole issue with certain moral convictions, whatever they may be, to the fore. The chapter then turns to the debate itself and argues that historical-political understanding's attempted avoidance of moral judgmentalism fails on numerous scores. We can then begin to outline the basic elements of an appropriately attuned mindset for the analytical-prescriptive task at hand.

One thing this chapter will not do is to say in detail what is right and wrong concerning September 11. Its aim is only to vindicate the practice of entertaining and employing definite moral convictions, *whatever they may be*, in our analysis of it.[4] Nevertheless, this part of its argument might look decidedly hollow if no attempt was made to sketch how such convictions might be constructed. Accordingly, the chapter offers a conception of "terrorism" as an evaluative epithet—and herein lies an important future challenge for this line of inquiry. For I contend that the internationalization of the "war on terror" prompts us to incorporate important cosmopolitan elements into our thinking about terrorism and morality. In the same way that it is no longer a matter for individual states alone to deal with as matters of domestic politics, we should explore the ways in which we can posit terrorism as a concern for humanity such that we give this international concern a sound moral basis. In some ways, of course, the theory of the new, more morally sound international order promised in the wake of the Cold War remains almost as primordial as its evidently hesitant and fragmentary empirical realization. Much needs to be done even to theorize this particular utopia before it can hope to act as an inspiration in the reconfiguration of world politics.

Defending Moral Judgmentalism

Let me straightaway acknowledge the vastness and complexity of the issues surrounding what has here been sweepingly characterized as "the problem of moral uncertainty." In these few short pages such philosophical puzzles can only be addressed in a highly simplified and attenuated form, and to call the claims that follow "arguments" may well be to overly dignify them. Their defence of judgmentalism is little more than a polemical insistence upon it barely pausing over the subtle rejoinders that its opponents can undoubtedly offer. Nevertheless, hopefully enough can be said to uphold it.

In the last section, I began my characterization of moral uncertainty in terms of an initial doubt over morality's source and the consequent authority that it claims for itself. In a persuasive interpretation of Western moral culture, our basic moral principles are seen as having theistic origins: people initially treated them as God's commands and their objective authority, their *truth*, was guaranteed because His existence and His right to create our moral rules were taken as objective facts. We can therefore see how moral uncertainty might arise once the existence of God is doubted, denied altogether or otherwise sidelined from the business of grounding moral conviction. If, for example, we say that God does not exist, on what grounds

---

4   To demonstrate the good faith in which the argument is offered, I will nevertheless venture my view that, though some legitimate grievances might have motivated the attacks (though as the precise motivations of those concerned are hardly transparent, the relevance of these to any justification for the attacks must remain obscure), the attacks themselves were completely immoral. There is much, however, in the West's subsequent war on terror, both in international affairs and domestic politics, that also crosses the threshold of immorality. The arguments that may be given in favor of these propositions may be constructed from the considerations adduced in this chapter's section on the concept of terrorism.

might we still claim objective authority for the moral principles that religion has left behind?[5]

It would be wrong to dismiss altogether as obviously wrong-headed the metaphysical and epistemological worries which accompany our reflections on the nature of morality (for example,, and respectively, "does God exist?" and "how can we be sure that what we think we know He has willed is indeed what He has willed?": such questions in general are often called matters of "metaethics"). As the late John Rawls persuasively argued, we should expect the exercise of free thinking by rational and reasonable people in a democratic society to generate a conflicting diversity of views on this question.[6] There is "reasonable disagreement" over such matters because of their essential indeterminacy (it is not unreasonable to believe in God or in atheism or to be agnostic). In these conditions it cannot therefore be regarded as unreasonable for people, when they survey the conflicting range of metaethical views, to manifest uncertainty over the basis on which moral judgments can be made.

But it *is* unreasonable to think that metaethical uncertainty necessarily mandates a subjectivization/relativization of one's views because this move leads into obviously self-contradictory, or self-refuting, positions. If A believes in the objective existence of God and B is an unswerving atheist, then the truth of one of the views necessarily entails the falsehood of the other. The reasonable-disagreement thesis may mean it is reasonable for both views to be entertained by different people and that can be safely regarded as a strong reason for socially and politically tolerating both. But that thesis does not—indeed, cannot—mean that it is reasonable for a single person to think both are equally valid in the sense of being true. So we can acknowledge the metaethical reasons why moral uncertainty arises, but we ought not to think that this must necessarily uncouple us as individuals from any determinate, objectivized (that is, presented as objective truth) view of our own.

Consequently, if we do not have to relativize the validity of our views about the source of morality, then we do not have to relativize its content either. It is pertinent here to bear in mind that our moral arguments-the point of debating the rightness of something and the language we use in such debates-are generally structured in a way that assumes there is objective right and wrong, and conducted with a passion that does not seem properly accounted for by any anti-objectivist metaethic. We do not engage in a moral debate *merely* to state opinions and hear others' opinions, the kind of dialogue we might have if we all came together to learn about each other's favorite flavor of ice cream. There is no argument, no contestation, in such a process at all yet this is what the relativists would have us believe moral debate is about. The facts that this is (a) at odds with the general practice of moral debate and that (b) the latter is something in which we do, perhaps rather frequently,

---

5   See Anscombe, G.E.M. (1958), "Modern Moral Philosophy," *Philosophy* 33, 1–19.
6   Rawls, J. (1996), *Political Liberalism*, 2nd edn, New York: Columbia University Press.

engage (particularly when events such as September 11 jolt our consciences) once again show that relativism is an attitude which—despite the hold it may have over many—begins to flounder on inspection.

The relativist might respond by urging that we should consciously give up the practice of moral argument as a search for right, or at least better, answers to moral questions. But the equal-validity and abstinence positions they recommend as far as moral judgmentalism is concerned are too deeply flawed to provide satisfactory alternative stances. From the mere fact that different people with different beliefs *think* that they are justified in their beliefs (that they *think* their beliefs are right, or at least right for them) it does not logically follow that we should say that they *are* justified in believing them (that they *are* right, or at least right *for them*).[7] Who would really want to say that it was no more or less justifiable for Hitler to believe that the extermination of the Jews was morally justified than it is for us to believe that he was horrendously wrong? The equal-validity position is also simple-mindedly self-refuting. It ascribes equal validity on the basis that there is no objective yardstick external to people's opinions by which they can be objectively ranked for validity (defined as the accuracy by which they track what is actually morally true). But the very idea that each opinion *must* therefore be regarded to be as valid as every other has to rely upon precisely some such "external" yardstick itself, for how else is the comparative judgment of equal worth to be obtained? The equal-validity hypothesis is not one, after all, that you find *inside* very many of the moral outlooks under comparison. So on its own terms it paradoxically passes a judgment *against* the claims of views it says cannot be objectively impugned and cannot therefore be considered as any more respectful of rival views than the kind of judgmentalism it attacks.

The abstinence position may be a more coherent response to moral uncertainty. Nevertheless, I have already questioned whether it is really existentially tenable: the events of September 11 are among those which have such moral import and magnitude that it is really difficult to think that it is inappropriate to take a moral stand on them. (If one happens to be very morally ambivalent about these particular events, would one want to think that there is no limit to non-judgmentalism? Can, say, the Holocaust be contemplated without immediate moral judgment to the fore? Who would *want* to abstain from objectivizing judgmentalism on the paedophiliac pornographer who films the rape of babies for his sexual gratification?)

The claim about the ultimate indispensability of moral conviction and judgment in human experience dovetails with a claim that some definite moral convictions are

---

7   Another way of making this point. Consider this statement made *by* X: "I think Y is true," and this statement *about* X: "Y is true for X," posited as an account of what X believes to be true. Some would appear to be disposed to think that these are first- and third-person versions of the same claim, as if "what is true" can only be rendered in terms of "what you think is true." But I think that, typically, the first-person statement is *not* offered as a description of what one thinks, but a statement of belief of what is independently the "truth of the matter."

actually indispensable in the business of justifying morality. To explain: we might say that our metaethical doubt has left us lacking a *justifying* theory, producing the uncertainty in our moral convictions. Such a theory would be able to tell us what the principles of morality are and why we should follow them. Our civilization's thinkers have expended considerable effort to furnish us with just such a theory to try to dispel such uncertainty. But how do such justifications actually proceed?

Consider one such justificatory theory: utilitarianism, which purports to show that the right act is the one which can reasonably be expected to maximize the greatest happiness of the greatest number of people (that this is an unfairly antiquated formulation of the theory is not germane to the argument). Now when we ask ourselves whether this is the right justificatory theory, by what criterion do we typically seek to answer the question? I suggest that we do so by determining whether the theory generates the kind of principles we would be prepared to accept. So, for example, utilitarianism may be thought to justify the enslavement of a small minority of people to serve the majority, making their lives so much more happy—and hence maximizing total happiness more than would any other social arrangement. But if we grant that this is not something we believe an adequate account of morality would sanction (on the grounds that nothing, not even "total happiness", could justify slavery), we actually use this conviction to conclude that utilitarianism fails as a justificatory theory.

It may be immediately objected that this renders justification an entirely circular process: we are evaluating an account of how to generate principles of morality by testing whether it generates the principles we want it to. The tail is wagging the justificatory dog and, indeed, the whole business of justification looks entirely otiose: if we already have the principles we want to justify at hand and are giving them such decisive authority in determining the validity of a justificatory theory, why do we need anything else to "justify" them at all? (Must we not be implicitly assuming that they are already justified if we employ them to test the adequacy of a justificatory theory? What else could we want?)

Now for reasons that need not detain us here I do not think that what I call justificatory dog-wagging makes the justificatory enterprise wholly redundant.[8] But it does suggest that we probably ought to expect a lot less from justificatory theory than might be demanded, or that we typically assumed that it set out to deliver. Or, perhaps better, we need not expect much from it in that we do not have to *suspend* all of our moral convictions prior to the acceptance of such a theory. In other

---

8   Given that our overall moral outlooks may well be a rather ragbag collection of incomplete, inconsistent and/or *ad hoc* principles and judgements, a justificatory theory may have a genuinely reformative and creative function in helping to order them. Nevertheless, I think the account of dog-wagging is largely accurate with respect to the kind of very basic moral conviction which is at play in the present argument. For a more detailed account of my views on the matter, see Evans, M. (2006), "Thin Universalism and the 'Limits' of Justification" in Haddock, B., Roberts, P. and Sutch, P. (eds), *Principles and Political Order: The Challenge of Diversity*, London: Routledge, 76–96.

words, metaethical uncertainty should not lead to the abandonment of all moral convictions. To be sure, some of them might reasonably falter under uncertainty. If you accepted a moral principle *simply* because you were told that this is what was specified by the moral authority you accepted (if, say, you believed that sex before marriage was sinful simply because that was what your religion specified), and you then doubted the existence and/or veracity of that authority (if, say, you lost your faith), then it may be reasonable for you to reject the principle. The point, however, is that for most of us there are certain principles whose strength—the basis on which we hold them as our moral convictions—is greater, or deeper, than any account of the authority from which it springs. We believe that murder is wrong not simply because our religion says so; justificatory dog-wagging here would suggest that if we found our religion did not actually support this belief, it would be the religious faith and not our conviction about the rightness of the principle that would be impugned.[9]

To conclude this passage of argument, it should be stressed that nothing in what has been said implies the misguided idea that the businesses of moral conviction and judgment are always simple, straightforward, unreflectively dogmatic applications of principles that should be obvious to all. Of course we are typically faced with many very difficult moral questions and some sort of at least initial uncertainty here is not only unavoidable but quite desirable as we grapple with their complexity. Rawls's "reasonable-disagreement" thesis, after all, applies as much to substantive questions of right and wrong, and the like, as it does to metaethical beliefs. All that the present argument seeks to establish is that we should not think such difficulties warrant a complete suspension or relativization of all our convictions. At heart, or so I have proposed, and sometimes despite ourselves, we do entertain some basic convictions in answer to what we think are very *simple* moral questions: that ethnic cleansing, child abuse, rape, torture and so on are just plain wrong, for example. For many of us, September 11 and its consequences posed some very simple as well as difficult moral questions—and the considerations which give rise to moral uncertainty should not lead us to suppress what plain moral convictions we might deploy in analyzing them.

Moral Judgment versus Historical-political Understanding?

Vindicating the practices of moral conviction and judgment demonstrates that there is a real debate between the moral-judgmentalist and historical-political-understanding approaches to the kind of project undertaken in this book. The latter approach often informs the claim, frequently heard in the wake of September 11,

---

9   Apart from the task suggested in n. 8, it might be thought that justificatory dog-wagging leaves moral and political philosophers with precious little to do. In fact, there is much that they can achieve by attempting to deduce and/or infer *further* moral conclusions from the basic, "settled" convictions we assume as starting-points.

that the US and its allies "needed to understand" the grievances that brought al-Qaeda into being: the implication at least sometimes being that they would come to see that they bore a significant degree of responsibility themselves for the attacks due to their past and present behavior on the world stage. Such "understanding" has often been *counterposed* to moral judgmentalism over the justice of the attacks and the military response to them, despite the fact that the inquiries of those developing this supposedly non-moral-judgmental methodology typically amount to critiques (particularly of the West).[10] Indeed, the kind of moral judgmentalism that, for example, proceeds from the conviction that, say, the hijackings were absolutely wrong is sometimes held to be inimical to "understanding" and consequently to be a dangerously unthinking stimulant of (unwarranted) violence in response (for instance, the war in Afghanistan).

A representative example of this viewpoint is a piece by Andrew Chitty attacking an argument which proposed to evaluate the nature of the US-led response to September 11 according to certain moral criteria.[11] Chitty claims that such "moralism" has a devastating tendency to neglect historical context: "for the more we know about the historical antecedents of any act, the less easy it is to be satisfied with passing a moral judgment on it, and moralism demands such judgment."[12] Far from taking the attacks seriously, moral judgmentalism neglects their full political and historical significance. "The language of extreme moral condemnation is the standard precursor to violence"[13] yet it is not, so Chitty claims, really central to the decision-making concepts and processes of the American foreign policy establishment. Thus, "in the sphere of international relations, public moral discourse in the West is little more than a means of selling decisions that have already been arrived at by other means to the domestic population in a language they can understand."[14] As a representative of the anti-war movement, he claims that this cynical "instrumentalization" of moral discourse helps to explain why the movement "has been quite right to be wary of adding its voice to an already deafening public roar of moral condemnation of September 11".[15] But another reason for the rejection of moral judgmentalism is hinted at in his concluding remark that the anti-war movement should develop its intellectual response to the "war on terror" not by "a fruitless counterposition of moral judgments" but by

---

10   Hence 'critical realism' may be an appropriate alternative formal title for the approach.

11   See Chitty, A. (2002), "Moralism, Terrorism and War—Reply to Shaw," *Radical Philosophy* 111 (January/February), 16–19; the article is a response to Shaw, M. (2002), "Ten Challenges for 'Anti-War' Politics," *Radical Philosophy* 111 (January/February), 11–16.

12   Chitty, op. cit. fn. 11, 17.

13   Ibid.

14   Ibid., 18.

15   Ibid.

what he describes as "a patient collective effort to understand the basic roots of the war."[16]

Though in essence it is a polemical piece, it is perhaps unfair to subject this particular text to much conceptual scrutiny, but it is a usefully bald statement of the critique of moral judgmentalism. The critique can be broken up into the following claims:

1. moral judgmentalism encourages overly rapid and ill-informed analysis and decision-making;
2. the more that historical and political contextual factors are taken into account, the less easy it is to pass moral judgment (the implication being, it seems, that sensible, justified moral judgment becomes impossible at a certain point);
3. that the language of moral condemnation is cynically employed to justify decisions, such as the war in Afghanistan, which have not in fact been taken on the basis of moral considerations;
4. that moral judgmentalism in general tends to encourage violence;
5. that arguing about moral judgments is "fruitless."

If one or more of these claims are justified, then it seems clear that a serious analysis of September 11 and its aftermath ought to eschew moral judgmentalism which, among other things, would involve us either developing a value-neutral concept of "terrorism" or (if I am right that it can only be coherently understood as itself a morally judgmental concept) abandoning it altogether in our analysis. Fortunately, we need do neither for this assault on moral judgmentalism ultimately fails to convince.

Perhaps the central mistake in Chitty's argument is the unwarranted generalizations about moral judgmentalism it draws from problems associated only with specific instances of it. Reviewing the claims in order:

1. I have no quarrel with the claim that September 11 elicited some instantaneous moralizing responses which lacked the sensitivity to historical and political context that would have improved them. But not only would I oppose the idea that the immediate elicitation of such responses was wrong (as moral beings, this was a very human phenomenon), I also see no reason why moral judgmentalism cannot insist upon the acquisition of this sensitivity in a particular instance before a *settled* conviction is obtained as a necessary prerequisite for justified decision-making.
2. Acquiring contextual understanding may well make the business of passing moral judgment more complex in some cases, but this is not a necessary general truth and hence there is no reason to propose that

---

16   Ibid., 19.

an adequate understanding will always preclude sensible, justified moral judgment. The two do not necessarily exhibit this inverse connection: it is perfectly possible to understand fully the grievances behind al-Qaeda's actions whilst still coherently condemning the murderous destruction of the Twin Towers.

3. I do not deny the propensity of moral judgmentalism to be used cynically in the official justification of policy decisions which have not been taken on moral considerations alone. I would reject, but lack the space to substantiate, the sweeping assumption that moral considerations are entirely absent in the calculations and consultations which lead to all such decisions. But the fact that moral concepts and the practice of judgmentalism can be abused is absolutely no reason to jettison them. Rather, it should be a call to defend morality against such abuse. It is highly significant that politicians feel constrained to employ moral reasons in public justifications for their policies. We should acknowledge their protestations that it is morality that legitimizes their beliefs and actions here and, if we wish to oppose our political leaders, we should do so on the moral ground they are attempting to occupy for themselves. (Chitty's critique would, rather unfortunately, seem to undermine the substance of what the most impassioned of anti-war movements actually say.)

4. If a disposition to violence is often whipped up by moral condemnation and exhortation, it is again obvious that this is not a necessary consequence: pacifism, after all, can be as deep a moral conviction as any. (In the next section we will also see how even a moral justification for violence, far from being "knee-jerk" and indiscriminate, can in fact be a highly sensitive and nuanced affair.)

5. Finally, it is unclear in what sense Chitty thinks that the exchange of moral viewpoints would be "fruitless," although moral-uncertainty considerations may well be at work here. If he has indeed been led to this claim by some version of the "reasonable disagreement" hypothesis, it is pertinent to challenge the assumption that a non-moral-judgmentalizing contextual understanding will be any less susceptible to reasonable contestation.[17] Furthermore, most importantly and perhaps obviously, one might very well wonder how a critical posture is possible (in this case, an anti-war-on-terror position) without it being in some sense morally judgmentalist. The facts we garner as we deepen our contextual understanding do not "speak for themselves" in this regard—or at least not with one voice.

---

17   It seems highly probable that Chitty shares the Marxist assumption that an objective social-scientific (and critical) theory is possible, and can be qualitatively contrasted with the "obsolete verbal rubbish" (Marx's words) of morality as being nothing other than a mystified presentation of ruling-class self-interest.

Evaluative judgments are made both in the selection and interpretation of these facts, and the same broad events can consequently be rendered in very different ways (hence the possibility that historical-political understanding is also prone to reasonable disagreement). Having had to make evaluative judgments from the very start, why must we necessarily think that we should thereafter cease to make them—particularly when, in Chitty's case, the whole point of the exercise is to defend a specific evaluative standpoint?

It seems fair to say that Chitty's critique of moral judgmentalism is in fact an opposition to a *specific* set of moral judgments which conflicts with his own (the latter seemingly to be that the attacks were not unambiguously unjustified morally and that the war in Afghanistan is definitely unjust). If I am right that moral judgmentalism cannot be dispensed with and need not be suppressed, his critique can nevertheless help us to stress that responsible judgmentalism should be sensitive to context and to the possibility that rival views may incorporate considerations that ought to be taken seriously and which may prompt desirable revisions to current convictions. An excellent example of this stipulation is the application of the concept of terrorism: a normative concept which requires considerable analysis before it can be justifiably attached to an act of political violence.

Conceptualizing Terrorism

Human beings are political animals because they are social animals whose groupings diverge from each other in interests and outlooks within a world whose finitude makes it impossible for them all to fulfil those interests and live according to those outlooks to their complete satisfaction. The resulting conflicts between them must be managed somehow: people must confront each other, deal with another as a result—and politics is the process by which they do so, whether it be peacefully or violently (or, most likely, some combination of the two), or under just or unjust social arrangements and rules of engagement.

This quick and highly partial characterization of politics helps to introduce the concept of terrorism. For one claim which is generally accepted is that terrorism is one type of coercive political engagement: the use of violence to pursue a political end. And if we accept the claim that "terrorism" is a morally loaded term, we can see that we apply it to a particular type of immoral use of violence for a political end: it is not the way in which political interests should be advanced among the community of fellow human beings.

The relevance of introducing "terrorism" in this way will shortly become apparent. But let us recognize, before we proceed, that the term has been thought particularly vulnerable to moral uncertainty and relativism as encapsulated in the well-worn saying "one person's terrorist is another person's freedom-fighter." Now, if this utterance is simply a way of making the claim that "because one person calls 'just' what another person calls 'unjust' we cannot/should not say who is right and wrong in this regard," we have already dismissed that conclusion. I think we can and should use "terrorism" as an objectively, morally judgmental epithet using the considerations set out below (which, by the way, make it possible that one can be *both* a terrorist and someone who is sincerely fighting for "freedom"). Its evaluative character has unfortunately allowed it to be used overly promiscuously and polemically to cover just about any act of violence one wishes to condemn. If we wish to render the concept intelligible and useful, we should not expect it to be able to account for all of these various usages. In particular, we should not pretend that all acts of illegitimate political violence must be fitted into it.

As a preliminary, I think it is helpful to distinguish a terrorist campaign from war in the sense that the latter is conducted on a certain magnitude, with a relatively high degree of organization among the conflicting military forces and employing certain types of tactic that are not found in terrorism. (Admittedly the boundaries may be blurred between the two concepts in some circumstances but we would not, I take it, want to call the Nazi conquests, though clearly immoral, "terrorist acts.") But I think that an act of violence can be judged as terrorist and hence immoral on the basis of at least some of the criteria which are familiarly used to identify just and unjust wars. The criteria in full are as follows:[18]

[I] *Jus ad bellum*: to have the moral right to wage war, the following conditions must be respected:

(a) the cause is just;

(b) the justice of the cause is sufficiently great as to warrant warfare and does not negate countervailing values of equal or greater weight;

(c) on the basis of available knowledge and reasonable assessment of the situation, one must be as confident as one reasonably can be of achieving one's just objective without yielding longer-term consequences that are worse than the *status quo*;

(d) warfare is genuinely a last resort: all peaceful alternatives which may also secure justice to a reasonable and sufficient degree have been exhausted;

(e) one's own moral standing is not decisively compromised with respect to the waging of war in this instance;

(f) even if the cause is just, the resort to war is actually motivated by that cause and not some other (hidden) reason;

(g) one is a legitimate, duly constituted authority with respect to the waging of war: one has the *right* to wage it;

---

18 This statement is presented and discussed in my "Moral Theory and the Idea of a Just War," in Evans, M. (ed.) (2005), *Just War Theory: A Reappraisal*, Edinburgh: Edinburgh University Press, 1–21.

(h)   one must publicly declare war and publicly defend that declaration on the basis of (a)–(g), and subsequently be prepared to be politically accountable for the conduct and aftermath of the war, based on the criteria of *jus in bello* and *jus post bellum*.

[II] *Jus in bello*: to fight a war justly, one must employ:

(i)   *discrimination* in the selection of targets: avoiding the direct targeting of those not directly participating in the immediate conduct of war, and taking all reasonable measures possible to avoid casualties among such non-participants;

(i_2)   *Doctrine of double effect*: the foreseeable deaths of "innocents" do not render a war unjust so long as they are not directly intended as the object of policy but are the unavoidable side-effects of a use of force justified by the other criteria of the theory;

(j)   *proportionality* in the use of force required to secure the just objectives;

(k)   *just treatment of all non-combatants*: by which is intended prisoners of war as well as non-combatants in the wider arena of the war.

(l)   One must observe all national and international laws governing the conduct of war which do not fundamentally conflict with the theory's other moral requirements.

[III] *Jus post bellum*: to secure the justice sought in the resort to war, one must be prepared to:

(m)   help to establish peace terms which are proportionately determined to make that peace just and stable as well as to redress the injustice which prompted the conflict;

(n)   take full responsibility for one's fair share of the material burdens of the conflict's aftermath in constructing a just and stable peace;

(o)   take full and proactive part in the processes of forgiveness and reconciliation that are central to the construction of a just and stable peace.

We should of course expect difficulties in accurately and fairly applying these criteria, which are a mixture of the evaluative and the empirical. But if we remain emboldened to retain certain convictions about the nature of justice, we can also stay committed in principle to the idea that we can objectively discriminate between just and unjust uses of political violence. For anyone thinking, along with Chitty, that this kind of theory makes us overly disposed to violence in explicitly setting out the conditions under which it may be justified, it should be noted that the nature of the criteria strongly suggests that any moral justification for violence is to be regarded as the lesser of two evils. And as the lesser of two evils is still an evil, a just conflict must still be considered as one fought in a morally tragic situation, that is, one in which it is impossible to avoid doing something that comes at great moral cost, that in some sense is still wrong. The deep humility this ought to prompt should motivate one to a sincere and rigorous contemplation of the criteria, far removed from the wilfully blind rush-to-arms Chitty fears.

If we fear that the analytical distinction between acts of war and acts of terrorism may be too exculpatory of the former, we may reasonably gather from the stringency of the criteria that many wars have failed to qualify as just, and therefore as justified.[19] Indeed, it strikes me as a significant advantage of this approach that it brings wars and at least some other kinds of political violence under the one moral standard.[20] So in the same way that there could be a just war there could be a morally justified use of violence on a sub-war scale (a necessary revolutionary insurgency against an unjust regime, for example). The point about terrorist violence, however, is that it will by definition fail to be justified on one or more of the just-war counts. Very often (though this is a contingent and not a necessary feature), a terrorist act will fail on many of them. I certainly believe this applies to September 11. Even if one grants the claim that al-Qaeda emerged from some deep-seated grievance against the West and its impact upon the Islamic world and that the attackers were sincere in their devotion to their cause (criteria [a] and [f]) it seems extraordinarily difficult to think that the attacks could qualify as justified on other criteria (such as [b] and [d] to [o]).

Certain criteria are obviously more decisive than others. Without meeting (a), for example, an act of violence can never hope to pass as justified. Satisfying (a) alone, however, is clearly not enough: one might indeed be fighting for the freedom of one's community from oppression and yet be employing such indiscriminate and disproportionate violence for the cause that one deserves the terrorist label (hence the possibility of being both a freedom-fighter and a terrorist). Conversely, (g) does not appear to be as decisive a consideration as (a) in some circumstances. Legitimacy (as being anything other than "having right on one's side", which would seemingly be already established under [a]) can be a decidedly murky affair in certain situations. Moreover, a properly constituted authority such as a legitimate state (thereby meeting criterion [g]) may nevertheless use sub-war violence in ways which fail to be justified on other counts: hence I do think it makes sense to talk of "state terrorism."

One could doubtless go on along these lines with the rest of the criteria, well beyond the remaining space available here. What is in general clear is that any

---

19   Indeed, such is their stringency that it would be consistent and not implausible to argue that to all intents and purposes they lead to a virtual pacifism. Although I would not go this far, the moral reservations over the war on terror I expressed earlier arise from what I judge to be certain shortfalls with respect to these criteria.

20   This might suggest that the theory should be renamed, perhaps as "just violence theory." Its familiarity will, however, lead me to retain the traditional nomenclature for the time being.

presentation of just-war theory which insists that each and every criterion must be met is overly stringent. A certain leeway in the combination of criteria which suffice to label an act as terrorist may be unavoidable given the variety of acts which might fall into the category. But we now have a framework which allows us to use "terrorism" as an objective evaluative concept.

Terrorism as a Crime against Global Civil Society

To prepare for the final part of the present argument, let us return to the thumbnail sketch of the nature of politics offered at the start of the previous section. Terrorism, we can say, is an immoral, illegitimate means of pursuing a political end among other human beings. In order to claim this, we must have a conception of how politics *ought* to be done. My proposal is that we develop such a conception out of the fundamental notion that each human being is the bearer of a certain set of basic rights simply by virtue of being human. Here is where my argument expresses its own deepest moral convictions and displays the basis upon which its own judgmentalism rests: regardless of any difficulties we may face in trying to justify this ascription of human rights (and the philosophical controversies surrounding this issue indicate that it may be no easy task), we may nevertheless remain committed to the idea that humans do have human rights. (Any adequate justificatory argument for them would therefore exhibit the "dog-wagging" characteristic.) Those who disagree with this proposition will doubtlessly decline to follow the rest of the argument. If they do so, on moral uncertainty grounds, then we have already rejected the justification for such hesitancy. If their disagreement arises because they entertain alternative moral convictions, then we should consider whether any position which conflicts with the idea of human rights is one to which we would be prepared to grant any credence. I suspect few of us would.

Now, people are not said to possess human rights simply by virtue of belonging to a specific political community such as a state even though the institutions of such a community may have primary responsibility for protecting the rights of its members. Instead, we may make this claim when we condemn certain states who fail to respect the rights of their citizens: when we learn of rights-violations by states, we feel connected in our concern to the other human beings in question thus: "this is not how human beings, like us, should be treated." I think this allows us to propose the idea of a human moral community: a *global civil society*.[21] It is an *idea* in the sense that we do not pretend it has been fully realized in practice, but it is what is implicit in our human-rights-based moral thinking and in the principles that key artefacts of the existing international order embody (such as the Universal Declaration of Human Rights).

---

21   The following argument in part follows Frost, M. (2002), "Global Civil Society: An Ethical Profile," in Hovden, E. and Keene, E. (eds), *The Globalization of Liberalism*, Basingstoke: Palgrave, 152–72.

Global civil society has no specific ends of its own to pursue beyond the facilitation of its members' variegated ways of life in a manner which allows people to exercise their rights. But now recall the point that humans are political animals who are thereby compelled to make claims for their interests in the midst of other people making claims of their own. The moral logic of global civil society demands that the political process be conducted within its norms, by ways which—as far as is possible—respect the rights of the people who participate in it (which is *ipso facto* everybody). To cut the story sufficiently short, I believe that this implies a peaceful and participatory[22] form of politics, with recourse to violence only as a last resort to strengthen, not undermine, global civil society (the ultimate just cause). And on this basis, terrorism as a means of pursuing a political objective is one which fundamentally violates its norms: using force in violation of the rights of fellow human beings to achieve an objective by means that, if extended and generalized, would destroy global civil society and lead to a chaos in which social life (and hence, given our mutual interdependence, life itself) would ultimately become impossible.[23]

A lot more needs to be said if we are to complete the theory of global civil society and I will not be able to do so here. But I will highlight just a few of its features in support of the contention that it offers a fruitful way of thinking about and conceptualizing how we tackle terrorism in the future. First of all, it decenters the state in our moral viewpoint and hence in what practical measures may seem to follow from it. I do not wish to deny that membership of a state may have vital intrinsic value, but-as the evolving norm of humanitarian intervention has powerfully suggested[24]—the right of a state to exist and to exercise sovereign power over its citizens is not absolute. These institutional rights are conditional on the state doing as much as it reasonably can to facilitate the rights that its citizens have as members of global civil society, and on its ability to coexist on rights-respecting terms with other political communities. Put slightly differently, states—as the means by which politics is conducted within particular subsets of the human community—exist on the sufferance of that community.

We should not leap from this to the conclusion that intervention by some states in the affairs of other states on human-rights grounds is always and everywhere justified or obligatory. Many complex moral and practical considerations come

---

22   Which does not necessarily mean *democratic* politics.

23   For those familiar with Hobbes' *Leviathan*, we can put this proposition in terms of those who attempt to advance their ends by means which are ultimately destructive of global civil society are plunging us closer to an impossibly violent anarchic "state of nature."

24   This norm is most evident in the official acknowledgment of the "responsibility to protect" ("R2P") by world leaders at the 2005 summit marking the 60th anniversary of the United Nations.

into play in such circumstances.[25] All that I wish to stress for now is the point that the moral theory which condemns terrorism as a violation of the norms of global civil society can also condemn states. A state-centric view of the world naturally privileges the state as *"the* way of doing politics" and might resist the possibility of moral equivalence between certain states and terrorist organizations. In such circumstances, the danger of hypocrisy is heightened as occurs with, for example, the state which wantonly employs violence for its own ends and which tries to occupy a moral high ground by condemning its opponents as terrorist.

Thinking about terrorism in the context of crimes against global civil society also chimes with the greater internationalization of the fight against terrorism that has emerged since September 11. Previously terrorism had, by and large, been treated as a domestic policy matter. While I do not wish to deny that many terrorist campaigns should probably remain such on grounds of relevance and practicality, it is clear that the nature of many others demands international concern: the globally fragmented nature of al-Qaeda and its multinational targets, and the internationally destabilizing consequences of the Israeli–Palestinian conflict, for example. We need, and are beginning to develop, multinational policies and organizations to tackle these problems. Unilateral military action by states against others even on terrorism/aggression grounds is increasingly seen as illegitimate, as became evident in the pressure placed on the Bush Administration to seek UN approval for its 2003 campaign against Iraq. A cosmopolitan political morality such as that conceptualized in the theory of global civil society can provide the moral basis for these developments.

One might immediately object that the course of events initiated by September 11 was far removed from this tale of "global cooperation against an evil scourge in the name of a universal human morality." Many critics of the Bush Administration believed, for example, that the veneer of multilateralism thinly disguised an aggressive new unilateralism fuelled by an imperialistic arrogance borne of the US's status as the sole remaining superpower and shorn of any genuine consistent moral concern. (The explicit repudiation of his predecessor's policies by President Obama in his inaugural address on January 20, 2009 decisively validated much of what the critics had said all along.) Yet one need not disagree with this analysis to embrace the concepts of human rights and the global civil society as ideals which inform our aspirations for the world, which even the most cynical of political leaders feel constrained publicly to acknowledge and which can form the basis—should one wish to support it—of this critical viewpoint. As we saw in the discussion of historical-political understanding, it is highly mysterious as to how a critique can be mounted without entertaining moral ideals—and if the critique is meant to imply that things could and should be done differently, that surely indicates the ideals are ones that can be realistically harbored.

---

25   I discuss some of these in Evans (2002), "Selectivity, Imperfect Obligations and the Character of Humanitarian Morality," in Moseley, A. and Norman, R. (eds), *Human Rights and Military Intervention*, Aldershot: Ashgate, 132–49.

Some who have ready recourse to political violence might argue that the world is too far removed from such ideals to believe there is any point in entertaining them. They would thus see no point in thinking and acting politically in any terms other than those of raw power unadorned by moral constraint. In response, we have to say that, if it is going to be possible objectively to identify which acts of violence are just and unjust, and therefore when an act counts as a terrorist act, it is necessary to believe that the world is not so far away from realizing the ideals of justice that there is no point in making such judgments. We do not live in an utterly amoral or immoral world, in which moral ends are utterly futile and naïve. It may be stretching matters to say that we are in a "nearly just" world (not least because it might seriously mislead us into underestimating the scale of what needs to be done to secure justice as best as we can). It may well be the nature of moral ideals, as aspirations of humanity, that they can never be fully realized: there will always be moral shortfalls. But this has never been a good reason not to hold them, however, as regulative guides to present-day conduct. And it may not be unreasonable to think that there are few injustices remaining in the world whose rectification legitimately warrants the use of violence as the last reasonable means.

A final thought. The need for continued and concerted interrogation of the concept of terrorism is also evident in the vigilance we must maintain over how governments have responded to the perceived increased threat from terrorists. Many critics have argued that drastically illiberal legislation has been passed since 2001 which significantly damages citizens' civil liberties out of proportion to the menace which it is ostensibly designed to help governments to confront. If at least part of the opposition to terrorism is based upon the claim that the latter seeks fundamentally to disrupt liberal democracy, then governments are in grave danger of paradoxically undermining liberal democracy in their attempts to protect it. Only clear thinking about our moral principles can thus explain how this paradox is to be avoided, a perennially urgent task to which this chapter has merely sought to contribute.[26]

---

26   I was prompted to develop this defense of a moral approach in the analysis of September 11 and its consequences by stimulating discussions with colleagues in the Department of Politics and International Relations, Swansea University and with the members of its political theory workshop: for these, I am very grateful. I also thank Anne Evans for her customary help in removing errors from the typescript.

Chapter 14

Why Bush Should Have Explained September 11th

Kristin Andrews

Introduction

There were various initial reactions to the terrorist attacks of September 11, and among those reactions were some contradictions. There were those who demanded an explanation for the attacks, and others who condemned attempts to explain as immoral or unpatriotic. Though some of President George W. Bush's rhetoric and remarks masqueraded as explanatory, it appears that he too believed that the very attempt to explain the terrorists' actions would be unpatriotic, if not immoral.

The arguments against generating explanations are based on moral considerations. Those who are critical of explaining September 11 defend their position by pointing to the depraved character of those who offer explanations, or by declaring that it is unfair to criticize a victim. The tone of the discussion is explicitly moral. However, upon close examination we shall see that these moral arguments against explaining the terrorist attacks do not hold up, and that there are, in fact, no moral barriers to offering an explanation. In addition, there are good pragmatic reasons for explaining the terrorist attacks. Given that the President has a moral obligation to protect US citizens from outside forces, it turns out that President Bush was morally obligated to seek an explanation for the attacks. His failure to accept this moral imperative, I suggest, is part of the reason why Bush's Presidency has been deemed a disappointment, even by his prior fans.

Looking toward the remarks Bush made in the days following the terrorist attacks, we can see that he chose not to provide the country with the explanation many were asking for. The rhetorical remarks he did make, such as "America was targeted for attack because we are the brightest beacon for freedom and opportunity in the world"[1] were not in fact explanatory, as we will see. Rather, his statements suggested that the acts of terror were unimaginably evil, and since unimaginable, they must have been inexplicable as well. Instead of answering people's why-questions, Bush chose to answer how-questions: "Americans are asking, 'why do they hate us?' They hate what we see right here in this chamber— a democratically elected government. Their leaders are self-appointed. They hate

---

1   September 11, 2001. Quotes from Bush's speeches are taken from the official White House website, online at www.whitehouse.gov.

our freedoms—our freedom of religion, our freedom of speech, our freedom to vote and assemble and disagree with each other."[2] While many were looking for a reason that led people to feel such hatred of America and American freedoms, Bush only describes the nature of that hatred. An explanation of 9/11 should tell us why the US was the target of such horrific acts, and what drove people to choose a path of murder and suicide in the name of politics and religion.

Bush's statements, however, fail to do that. His remarks imply that there are no explanations for the attacks; he made no attempt to explain why we were targeted. Such a response is not unusual. Many people take comfort in the face of horrible events by thinking that they are inexplicable, and this temptation was evident in Bush's remarks when he suggested that the events of 9/11 cannot be accounted for, and can never be understood.

For one thing, if Bush's remarks had actually been explanatory, he would have included an explanation of why the terrorists would choose to attack the US rather than some other country with a democratically elected government, freedoms, and so forth. Arguably, there are countries that are more democratic than the US, or at least as democratic, and countries in which people have just as many freedoms. Bush's "explanation" makes no attempt to answer the question "Why us rather than them?" What is missing is the causal history that led to the attacks of 9/11.

This unwillingness to provide US citizens with an explanation for the worst terrorist attack on American soil is not warranted. Whereas many take the position that we ought not attempt to explain the acts of our enemy, it will be argued here that we have an obligation to do just that. An explanation of the events leading up to 9/11 will help us to better understand terrorism, and will better prepare us to reduce the levels of global terrorism. Discovering the causes of terrorism, and constructing an explanation which takes into account those causes will show us where the causal chain can most easily be broken, and this is essential to avoiding future acts of terrorism. Without understanding the reasons terrorists have for taking action, we will be doomed to fight a continuing battle, rather than achieving the decisive victory Bush claimed as his goal.

To make this case, we shall first look at the critics' positions. Several closely related arguments against explaining the terrorist attacks have been suggested. Some worry that a search for the root causes of terrorism would result in feelings of sympathy for the perpetrators and an inclination to blame the victim. Others seem to think that if we understand the motivations of terrorists we will be driven to forgive, or worse, to justify terrorist activities.

Whereas the arguments behind these worries are not strong, there are good pragmatic arguments in support of finding an explanation for 9/11. Before we can examine these, some groundwork on the nature of explanations must be done. Without understanding the nature of explanations, we will be unable to see the benefits that come with providing them.

---

2 September 20, 2001.

Explanation

There is a large philosophical literature dealing with explanation which can be traced back to the ancient Greeks. My analysis of Bush's need to explain 9/11 benefits from more recent work done on scientific[3] and psychological[4] explanation.

Before looking at what an explanation is, it will help to see what it is not. First, it is clear that an adequate explanation for an act cannot just cite the actor's attitude when that attitude is expressed in the act itself. To claim that the US was attacked "because they hate us" is unenlightening. Of course they hate us; people who like us do not try to kill our citizens. Claims that the terrorists are monsters or madmen or animals also fail to explain. Even madmen can have reasons for their actions. For example, it makes sense to ask why John Hinckley, Jr. tried to assassinate Reagan. The right response is not just that he was insane, but also that he believed that by killing Reagan he could win the heart of Jodie Foster, and he valued her love more than Reagan's life. This explanation is satisfactory because it provides an answer to our why-question.

When attempting to find an explanation for an agent's intentional actions, we are looking for a psychological explanation. Unlike scientific explanations, psychological explanations are often given in terms of an agent's belief states and desires, in which case they are called reason explanations. In addition, a reason explanation usually refers to a relevant psychological law that causally relates

---

3   Contemporary philosophical work on scientific explanation begins with Carl Gustav Hempel and Paul Oppenheim (1948), "Studies in the Logic of Explanation," *Philosophy of Science* 15, 135–75. The development of scientific explanation that followed is discussed by Salmon, W.C. (1989), *Four Decades of Scientific Explanation*, Minneapolis: University of Minnesota Press.

4   Current theories of psychological explanation emphasize the importance of belief and desire attribution. For example Fodor, J. (1991), "You Can Fool Some of the People All of the Time, Everything Else being Equal: Hedged Laws and Psychological Explanations," *Mind* 100, 19–34, and Dennett, D. (1987), *The International Stance*, Cambridge, MA: MIT Press, both argue that psychological explanation is theory based. To predict and explain human behavior we determine which belief, desire, and law would result in said behavior. See also Stich, S. and Nichols, S. (1996), "How Do Minds Understand Minds? Mental Stimulation Versus Tactic Theory," in Stich, S. (ed.), *Deconstructing the Mind*, Oxford: Oxford University Press. Others focus on the role of understanding when providing explanations. Rather than taking explanations as providing theories about human behavior, it is argued that we simulate being the person whose behavior is to be explained. The simulation allows us to see things from another's perspective. See Goldman, A. (1995), "Interpretation Psychologized," in Davies, M. and Stone, T. (eds), *Folk Psychology*, Oxford and Cambridge, UK: Blackwell Publishers, 74–99; Gordon, R. (1995), "The Stimulation Theory: Objections and Misconceptions," in Davies, M. and Stone, T., 100–22; reprinted from *Mind and Language* 7/1–2, 1992, 11–34; and Heal, J. (1996), "Stimulation, Theory, and Content," in Carruthers, P. and Smith, P.K. (eds), *Theories of Theories of Mind*, Cambridge: Cambridge University Press, 75–89.

beliefs and desires on the one hand, and behavior on the other.[5] Both beliefs and desires are thought necessary for a good reason explanation, because one without the other will not be sufficient for action. Suppose I believe that investing in a particular company would make me wealthy. Will I invest? Perhaps not; if I do not *want* to become wealthy, I will not act to become so. The particular beliefs I have allow me to satisfy the desires I have, and because I can't satisfy a desire if I do not know how to do so, both beliefs and desires are thought to be a necessary part of a reason explanation.

Another feature of psychological explanation that philosophers point to is the requirement that such explanations "make sense" of behavior.[6] A successful psychological explanation will make the action intelligible; we will be able to recognize the connection between the psychological state of actors and their behavior. This idea is connected to the view that we are able to explain others' actions by engaging in a mental simulation of them. We use our own practical reasoning mechanisms in order to pretend, imagine, or simulate being the other person, and ask ourselves which sets of beliefs and desires would lead to the target behavior.[7]

If we accept that a reason explanation must fulfill both these criteria, that it includes reference to a belief and a desire that together serve to make sense of the behavior to be explained, then it is clear that none of Bush's public remarks following the terrorist attacks came close to offering such an explanation. His explanation for the attacks was limited to the attribution of fairly general beliefs of the terrorists: they believe that we have a democratically elected government; they believe that we have the freedom of religion, speech, and so on. Additionally, he identified an attitude the terrorists had toward these ideals, namely hatred. These beliefs and the attitude do not provide us with the desire, nor do they alone serve to make sense of the behavior. Without these elements, we do not have an explanation. In his September 20 remarks Bush didn't provide an answer to the question "why do they hate us?" Rather, he chose to answer a different question: "how do they hate us?"

To give an explanation of the events would be to determine what the terrorists hoped to achieve by their actions. What are their desires, and what are their beliefs? Though Bush said that the terrorists hoped to frighten us, this does not make sense of their behavior, either. Rather, that answer leads us directly to a new "why" question: "why do they want to frighten us?" Bush's comments lead us to ask this question because his purported explanation does not make sense of the behavior; he does not make the behavior intelligible to us. When an answer to a why-question leads us immediately to ask another one, there is good reason to suspect that an explanation has not been proffered to begin with.

---

5   Fodor, op. cit. fn. 4; Dennett, op. cit. fn. 4.

6   Davies, M. and Stone, T. (eds) (1996), *Folk Psychology*, Oxford and Cambridge, UK: Blackwell Publishers. Heal, op. cit. fn. 4.

7   For example, Gordon, op. cit. fn. 4; Goldman, op. cit. fn. 4; Heal, op. cit. fn. 4.

Why Bush Should Not Have Explained 9/11

Though Bush's remarks after the attacks did not help to explain them, it could be argued that the White House had good reason to avoid offering an explanation. There are at least two types of reasons that could be given for the position that Bush should not have offered an explanation for the terrorist attacks. One harkens back to the position presented at the beginning of the paper: there is no further explanation, so Bush *could not* provide an explanation.

This claim is not very plausible. Though it might be nice to think that we live in a world in which horrible events do not belong and so are without reason, it just is not so. That sort of thinking ignores a fundamental feature of the world, namely that every event has a cause. If the terrorists acted intentionally, then there is a reason explanation for the attacks, and the explanation will refer to the beliefs and desires of those individuals, as immoral and as incorrect as those beliefs and desires may be.

The second concern is more credible. This is the moral argument that offering an explanation puts America in greater danger, and that we ought not offer an explanation because doing so would lead to greater harm. There are different ways of defending this view, which, though related, deserve mention in turn.

Sympathy

Since providing an explanation for 9/11 would require that we take into account the terrorists' beliefs and desires, giving an explanation might be viewed as showing sympathy towards the terrorists. One might argue that since we could not engage in a War on Terror and develop terrorist sympathies at the same time, we must not offer a psychological explanation of terrorist acts.

Following 9/11, some people tried to seek an explanation for the terrorists' hatred of the US and their willingness to die for their beliefs. These attempts to understand were largely condemned by conservative media outlets. For example, consider the response to Susan Sontag's essay of September 24th published in the *New Yorker*. Sontag criticized the mainstream media's lack of analysis of the attacks, and the refusal to acknowledge that American foreign policy with regard to Iraq might provide *part of* an explanation of the attacks. She writes, "A few shreds of historical awareness might help us understand what has just happened, and what may continue to happen."[8] Specifically, she took exception to the claim that the terrorists were cowardly, writing "Where is the acknowledgment that this was not a 'cowardly' attack on 'civilization' or 'liberty' or 'humanity' or 'the free world' but an attack on the world's self-proclaimed superpower, undertaken as a consequence of specific American alliances and actions?"[9]

---

8 Sontag, S. (2001), "The Talk of The Town," *New Yorker* (24 September), 28.
9 Ibid.

In response to this essay, Sontag was portrayed as no better than a terrorist by right-wing publications. For example, the New Republic published an article beginning "What do Osama bin Laden, Saddam Hussein and Susan Sontag have in common?"[10] And the Human Events Online offered their condemnation as well, saying "As we move further away from the horrors of September 11, the liberal cries about 'moral equivalence'—the idea that the United States shares the blame for the terrorist attacks—become more common and more explicit."[11]

The implication is that Sontag is so sympathetic with the terrorists that she herself is no better than one. Why is she seen as sympathetic? Because she articulates the motivations behind the terrorists' immoral actions. That response assumes both that Sontag herself accepts all the beliefs she attributes to the terrorists, as well as all the desires. The critics ignore the fact that one may attribute beliefs and desires to others without holding those beliefs or desires in oneself.

A moment of reflection will show that understanding someone's motivations does not necessitate a sympathetic response to that person. If we were to attempt to explain the terrorist attacks, one place to look would be toward Osama bin Laden's public statements. Though it is difficult to listen to his repeated condemnation of US culture, rights for women, and his rationalization for killing innocent civilians, his comments must be heard in order to formulate an explanation.[12] However, hearing bin Laden's diatribe would not generate sympathy for him in the West. It would take a heroic act of imagination for the average New Yorker, say, to see bin Laden's point of view and fully develop an explanation for his actions.

Understanding someone's motivations does not require being sympathetic to those goals. Sociologists, surely, should not be accused of endorsing murder, truancy, or drug abuse when they offer explanations of these activities. When a documentary filmmaker recreates the causes of horrific actions by explaining to the audience the motivations of the perpetrator, we do not respond with feelings of outrage. Nor do we accuse the filmmaker of immoral sympathies. Just as we can explain the causes of thunderstorms and landslides without having a normative

---

10   Kaplan, L. (2001), "No Choice: Foreign Policy After September 11," *The New Republic* (1 October), 21.

11   *Human Events On-line*, week of September 24, 2001, online at http://www. humaneventsonline.com/articles/09-24-01/briefs.html.

12   Given the statements from bin Laden, we cannot conclude that he has provided us with the thorough explanation for the attacks. Psychologists are documenting the many ways in which introspection is fallible, and the difficulty we have identifying the true causes of our actions. For example, if a person is perceived as kindly, we tend to see her as more intelligent, though we deny that the person's kindness affected our judgment of her intelligence. See Kunda, Z. (2002), *Social Cognition: Making Sense of People*, Cambridge, MA: MIT Press, for a discussion of these issues. Though people are notoriously bad at explaining their own actions, and giving accurate descriptions of their own mental states and reasons, the professed reasons for the attacks would be taken into account as part of the explanation. This might be what some people see as dangerous.

attitude toward them, we can also explain the actions of terrorists without feeling the slightest bit of sympathy.

Blaming the Victim

If part of the explanation for 9/11 includes reference to aspects of US foreign policy, perhaps there is a worry that offering an explanation that includes these facts would amount to a condemnation of the US. Some seem to think that identifying US foreign policy as part of the explanation for the terrorist attacks amounts to blaming the victim.

One need only look toward the response to activities on university campuses around the nation to see the controversy that rose from frankly discussing the possibility that the terrorists were motivated by US foreign policy. According to the Defense of Civilization Fund's report *Defending Civilization: How Our Universities are Failing America and What Can Be Done about It*:

> Polls across the country, coupled with statements from public officials and citizens, have been remarkably uniform in their condemnation of the terrorist attacks ... In contrast has been reaction from the Ivory Tower. While there are no doubt numerous exceptions, a vast number of colleges and universities—public and private, small and large, from all parts of the country—have sponsored teach-ins and other meetings which have been distinctly equivocal and often blaming America itself.[13]

What is interesting about this document is the lack of discrimination shown in choosing the examples. Sixteen pages of quotes, references to teach-ins, and administrative decisions are given in order to demonstrate the dangers that exist within US universities. Most of these cases involve looking toward US foreign policy for a cause of the terrorist attacks, and working from that assumption in an attempt to determine what to do next. Here are just two examples from the report:

> Professor of art, University of North Carolina-Chapel Hill, shows a slide show of her artwork, "Places the United States has Bombed" at a teach-in entitled: "What is war? What is peace?"[14]

> "[We should] build bridges and relationships, not simply bombs and walls." (Speaker at Harvard Law School)[15]

---

13   Martin, J.L. and Neal, A.D. (2002), *Defending Civilization: How our Universities Are Failing America and What Can Be Done About It*, revised edition, Cambridge, MA: MIT Press, 9.
14   Ibid., 23.
15   Ibid., 14.

The authors of the report make no distinction between those faculty members who sponsor teach-ins on US foreign policy and those who say they were cheering when the Pentagon was attacked. All are portrayed as enemies who claim that the US is complicit in the attacks.

To blame victims is to claim that they engaged in some behavior that not only caused them to be the subject of violence, but also that his behavior was itself unjustified or immoral. The idea is that victims could have avoided the attack were they to take certain precautions, and that they *ought* to have taken those precautions. It was once fairly usual to hear a woman's rape being blamed on her style of dress or behavior. The victim was blamed for wearing the short skirt, or acting flirtatiously. Today such claims would be soundly criticized by those who point out that *even if* the woman's short skirt caught the eye of a rapist, women are under no moral obligation to avoid dressing in a particular way. Though the short skirt may have been relevant to the subsequent rape, and played a role in the causal chain leading up to it, if the woman were raped on the way to work, her decision to work also played a role in the causal chain. No enlightened person ever suggested seriously that women should be blamed for their rape because they chose to leave their house and go to work, because women *ought* to be free to leave their houses, even though if all women stayed locked away the number of rapes would presumably drop.

The line of reasoning that leads one to conclude that we ought not to try to explain acts of terror is based on a confusion of these issues. The argument seems to go along these lines:

1. To explain the terrorist attacks is in part to identify the role played by US foreign policy.
2. Any act leading to an immoral act is morally blameworthy.
3. Therefore, to explain the terrorist attacks is to blame the US.

Assuming the truth of premise (1), this argument fails at premise (2). Just as we did not blame Jodie Foster for the assassination attempt on Reagan, even though her decision to act in *Taxi Driver* was part of the causal chain that led to Hinckley's crime, we need not blame the US for the terrorist attacks just because US foreign policy was part of the causal chain leading to 9/11. If we were right to withhold blame in the Foster/Hinckley case, then premise (2) is false, because we need only one counterexample to falsify a universal claim.

Though the above argument is clearly unsound, it is still widely accepted. However difficult it may be, it is important to distinguish between identifying US policy as playing a role in the attacks and blaming the US policy for the attacks. There is a huge difference between saying "the chickens have come home to roost" and that US foreign policy was part of the cause for the terrorist attacks. What's the difference? The later purports to be a factual claim that is purely descriptive, and the former is normative. In order to get from a description of events to claims about moral equivalence or complicity, an evaluative premise is needed to connect the facts to the values.

Not all causes of immoral acts are themselves wrong. Jodie Foster isn't responsible, because there is no way she could have predicted that a bizarre act would be the result of taking the role, and as far as I know she violated no moral principles in doing so. Likewise, if the US is identified as part of the explanation for the terrorist attacks, nothing follows from that about whether those US policies are immoral. Whether the US should be deemed culpable for its foreign policy is a completely different issue, and should be evaluated separately from the purely descriptive explanation that would include reference to past and present US policy.

The view that we ought not to explain the terrorist attacks, because an explanation of those attacks would be akin to blaming the victim, is thus misguided. The US would only be open to moral suspicion if those acts that entered into the causal chain leading to 9/11 are independently morally questionable. So, it may be that there is a danger in explaining 9/11 because the White House is afraid of its policies abroad coming under scrutiny, because the Administration believes its actions are morally questionable, or are seen as morally questionable by others. This worry could lead to the denial that US foreign policy has any role to play in setting the scene.

Explanation and Justification

The general problem seems to come from the widespread difficulty we have distinguishing between an explanation and a justification. Articles offering an explanation of the terrorist attacks based on US support of Israel, its stationing of troops in Saudi Arabia, or the US support of UN sanctions against Iraq were seen by many as tantamount to an endorsement of the attacks. This concern may have been on India's External Affairs Minister Yashwant Sinha's mind when he said, "India's view is that when you are fighting a war against terrorism, one should not weaken the cause by trying to get into the root causes or the underlying causes of terrorism."[16]

Even if US policy in these areas is immoral, an explanation citing these policies and describing their immorality would not be sufficient to justify the terrorist attacks. In order to argue that the attacks were morally justifiable, one would have to make an additional argument to the effect that the attacks were a just response to immoral US foreign policy, and there is no plausible way of defending that claim.

In other cases we can easily explain an event by citing the causes and mental states that led up to it without condoning those causes and mental states. For example, critics of capital punishment can explain why a criminal was executed

---

16   As reported in the *Toronto Star*, September 21, 2002 "Terrorism, poverty link called a mistake" by Allen Thompson, A8.

by citing as part of the explanation the criminal's own wrong-doing and the laws of the state. This explanation does not amount to an endorsement of capital punishment laws, nor does it serve to undermine the arguments they might have against the death penalty.

The terms "explanation" and "justification" are often used interchangeably in common parlance; indeed, some dictionaries define one in terms of the other. However, the sense of explanation with which we are concerned here is quite different from a justification. Before looking at the differences between the two, it is important to note that there are structural similarities between them, which may help account for the confusion. A justification, like a reason explanation, can include reference to one's belief and desire. I may justify my speeding to a police officer by saying that I believe my friend is about to give birth, and I want to get her to the hospital. This is an explanation for my speeding, but it becomes a justification given the unstated value claim also being asserted. That premise is that getting someone to the hospital in time for her to give birth is more valuable than driving at a legal speed. In casual conversation our arguments are often enthymematic; we tend to leave out the key premise in an informal argument, especially when that premise is widely accepted. Because the police officer probably also believes that there are cases in which it is acceptable to break traffic laws (and this is one of them) there is no need for me to make explicit the value premise of the argument. Whereas an explanation for an act might only refer to the laws, states of affairs, or beliefs and desires behind someone's action, a justification is given to defend those desires, and to support the truth of the beliefs. The reason to provide a justification for an action is to show that the action is morally permissible or pragmatically reasonable.

It is clear that there is quite a distance between an explanation and a justification of the attacks. In fact, there are two additional levels of argument one must give in order to reach a justification from an explanation of this sort: first it must be shown that the behavior that explains is immoral, and then it must be shown that the act to be justified constitutes an appropriate response to the immoral action.

Though there may be some danger in developing an explanation for 9/11, it is not because an explanation will serve to justify the attacks. This danger comes not from any intrinsic problem with offering explanations, but because of the widespread difficulty people have in distinguishing between an explanation and a justification. That is, people may see a US admission that its foreign policy was part of what motivated the attack against it as an admission of guilt, though of course it need not be.

We have seen that there are a cluster of worries one might have about explaining an immoral action. I hope to have shown that none of these concerns is warranted. If there exist strong arguments against explaining an event (other than the concern that your own immoral acts will come to light), I am not aware of them. What I have done so far is to show that the obvious arguments are unsound. But just because there is not an argument against Bush's providing an explanation for 9/11, it does not follow that he ought to have searched out an explanation after the attacks. In the remainder of the paper I will provide these positive arguments to show that Bush should have attempted to explain the terrorist attacks in order to determine an appropriate response to them.

Why Bush Should Have Explained 9/11

To defend the claim that Bush ought to have explained the events of 9/11, let us first return to the topic of scientific explanation. Traditionally, science is considered to be a body of explanations for natural phenomena, many of which can be used for prediction and control of the physical world. Scientific explanations are useful because they allow us to make the world more comfortable for the humans who live here. Knowing why rain falls allows us to seed clouds and keep our crops watered. And knowing how the body functions allows us to cure disease. Just as technology that allows us to control the physical world comes from scientific explanations, an explanation of horrific human behavior can help us learn how to prevent that behavior in the future.

If we come to understand the psychological and environmental causes of some behavior that we want to modify, then we will gain greater ability to control those behaviors. The normative aspects of the behavioral sciences are predicated on this thesis, as is medical science. Doctors, when given the option, would choose to treat the cause of a disease rather than merely deal with the symptoms. Treating symptoms is better than doing nothing, and in many cases it is the first response, but for long term treatment of chronic ailments, getting to the cause of the illness is essential to curing the patient.

However, knowing a cause does not by itself guarantee the elimination of the target behavior. We must also be able to eliminate that cause. For example, suppose it was discovered that truancy is caused in part by growing up in a single-parent family. In order to solve one problem, truancy, we would have to first solve another. If the secondary problem is too difficult to solve, then one should turn back to the original problem and look for a fuller explanation. Once we learn more about the myriad different elements that contribute to truancy, we could find alternative and potentially more successful methods for reducing the truancy rate. The more complete an explanation one has for some phenomenon, the more opportunities there are to eliminate that phenomenon by breaking the causal chain.

To fight terrorists without trying to determine the causes of terrorism is like going to a doctor who does not examine the patient for the etiology of their illness. The public actions taken by the Bush Administration as part of the War on Terror were, in the most charitable interpretation, focused merely on treating the symptoms. Heightening security at airports, imprisoning suspected terrorists indefinitely, increasing attention to immigrants from Muslim countries, wiretapping US citizens, using aggressive or torturous interrogation techniques, and even overthrowing governments were among the steps purportedly taken to avoid future terrorist attacks on US soil. Regardless of whether these actions offered some advantage in an attempt to alleviate the symptoms of terrorism, they certainly did nothing toward identifying or modifying the root cause.

Without understanding the motivations behind the terrorist attacks targeting the US, the act of hunting down individual terrorists does not guarantee that new terrorists will not step in to take the place of those caught or killed. If a War on Terror is framed as a war against people's motivations, rather than a war against people, then the endeavor may have a chance of succeeding. Success should be defined not as killing or capturing all terrorists (which would make success impossible), but by reducing the animosity toward the US by people around the world. As long as there is such extreme hatred toward the US, there will be terrorists who target the US.

There is a pragmatic argument for Bush to have explained the events of September 11, which involves defending the security of Americans in the US and around the world. Because an explanation of behavior will allow one to understand the motivations and environmental conditions that caused the behavior, and because the best way to eliminate a behavior is to sever the causal chain leading up to it, we ought to generate explanations for those behaviors we want to eliminate. Further, since the stated goal of the War on Terror was the elimination of terror in the world, and because Bush as President had an obligation to the American people, he was duty-bound to do what he could within the limits of morality to stop acts of terrorism. Given that there are no good arguments against explaining the terrorist attacks, it follows that the Bush Administration should have made it a priority to develop a thorough explanation for the attacks of 9/11. Bush's failure to do so damaged the reputation of the US around the world, and his unwillingness to consider root causes arguably led to greater threats against American lives.

It is important to realize that this argument is directed at the phenomenon of terrorism itself, rather than at the terrorist leanings of any one individual. This is not a proposal for a 12-step plan intended to rehabilitate terrorists. Rather it is an argument in defense of a method aimed at reducing the creation of new terrorists. Whereas it may be impossible to cure Osama bin Laden, we may still be able to reduce the number of people who are convinced by his rhetoric. Unless he is able to recruit new terrorists, his movement will not succeed. When young people cease regarding terrorist groups as an attractive life choice, then the terrorist leaders will lack the raw materials necessary for carrying out successful terrorist attacks.

If the US were to choose to fight terrorism in this fashion, it would be utilizing the explanatory methodology of the sciences. Doctors who want to cure a disease will attempt to stop it from spreading to healthy cells. When there are a finite number of diseased cells, it is possible to track them down and destroy them. However, when the number of diseased cells grows faster than the doctor's ability to eliminate them, the doctors conclude that the outlook for the patient is bleak indeed.

If Bush had chosen to seek an explanation for the terrorist attacks, he could have attempted to fight his War on Terror by stopping the creation of new terrorists in addition to seeking out those terrorists who already exist. Instead, Bush focused exclusively on the latter task, but both must be accomplished in order to achieve a positive outcome. The failure of Bush's War on Terror was in no small part due to this unwillingness to seek explanations.

Chapter 15

Rebalancing America's War on Terror: President Obama

Matthew A. Williams and Jack Covarrubias

Introduction

President Barack Obama has promised to rebalance America's War on Terror and general approach to foreign policy by shifting ideologies, approaches, and political alliances in an attempt to strengthen the United States' weakened international image and political legitimacy. He will attempt this—or so he and his cabinet have alluded—through a return to pragmatism. This "smart power" doctrine, as announced by Secretary of State Hillary Clinton, is conceptually based on successfully balancing soft and hard political tactics to achieve the most pragmatic outcome in a given situation. Given the history of his predecessor it is little wonder that Obama would choose to tackle America's image to the world. Still, with September 11 still fresh in American minds and with the lessons of Iran, North Korea and other known international disruptions present, the test for Obama is the need to address America's falling status against very pragmatic concerns related to pariah states, terrorism, and a troubled world economy.

The origin of terrorism points to vast complexity and a tendency to render implications both domestically and abroad as demonstrated by the multiple viewpoints presented in this book and within the larger body of literature that exists on the subject. Certainly, this fact makes rebalancing the War on Terror a difficult minefield for the Obama Administration to navigate. While it is still the dawn of 2009 and his Administration, this chapter will examine whether or not President Obama's initial actions are consistent with his Administration's stated intentions. Will a return to soft power constitute Obama's foreign policy priority? This chapter examines the games that executives must play to ensure success in current international negotiations[1] and examines the conflicts that arise in the interest of maintaining a global "Security Community."[2]

The Obama Administration has certainly deployed a number of soft power tactics thus far. For example, President Obama has made a personal appeal to the Muslim world on Al Jazeera, the predominant news network in the Middle

---

1   Putnam, R. (1988), "Diplomacy and Domestic Politics: The Logic of Two-Level Games," *International Organization* 42 (Summer), 427–460.

2   Jervis, R. (2005), *A New Era of American Foreign Policy*, New York: Routledge.

East. In addition, he has promised to close Guantánamo Bay Prison, he has denounced torture—a serious allegation popularly waged against the preceding Bush Administration—he has re-engaged diplomatic efforts with Iran, and invited further nuclear disarmament talks with Russia, while promising an end to American occupation in Iraq. At the same time however, Obama appointee, Secretary of Defense Robert Gates, has promised to continue American targeting in Pakistan. President Obama has promised increased troop deployments within Afghanistan and has urged closer cooperation with NATO and the broader EU to enhance international security—all actions clearly aimed at maintaining and enhancing US hard power.

The following section will provide an overview of the scholarly discourse presented in this reader, illustrating the political climate surrounding international terrorism and the United States.

Overview: Domestic, International, and Future Prospects

The history and politics of terrorism is multi-faceted and definitions vary greatly because of the evolutionary nature of the concept. Its constant process of change and adaptation is described in the introduction of this reader as an ongoing *metamorphosis*. There are numerous organizations largely motivated by a common factor of religious extremism and ethnic nationalism (other factors do motivate terrorism but this seems to be the common thread in the modern era).[3] Though the United States has focused its War on Terror to Islamic Fundamentalist groups, these make up only a segment of what is a very broad threat. The US, in its effort to contain Soviet expansion, armed and supported factions such as the Mujahedeen in Afghanistan and other Islamic terrorist organizations throughout the 1970s and 1980s.[4]

President Obama is coming into his Presidency facing an established foreign policy regime.[5] George W. Bush created new commitments for the US in a revision of American foreign policy to reflect the political circumstances of the post September 11 environment. The President traditionally has increased flexibility in this arena.[6] President Obama and his cabinet will have to determine whether the Bush Doctrine is suited to current threats and trends. The new Administration will attempt to bear out a modified foreign policy regime and re-evaluate international commitments—a process that is already initiated. Thus far President Obama's actions in Iraq and Afghanistan—decreasing troop levels in Iraq and increasing numbers in Afghanistan—are consistent with the exiting Bush foreign policy.

---

3   See Chapter 1.
4   See Chapter 2.
5   See Chapter 3.
6   Ibid.

The moral and philosophical implications of waging the War on Terror continue to be a challenge for thinkers. The legitimacy of US efforts in the fight against terrorists continues to be questioned. Does this constitute a "just use" of military force? Effective foreign policy formulation, according to an earlier chapter in this reader, relies on the justified use of military force and the conception of the national interest. Assessing the War on Terror against the criterion of just war theory lends insight as to whether the ends of the US-led war are the "... result of good or bad foreign policy."[7] This type of analysis is necessitated because US policies emanating from this military effort profoundly effect and "shape" our world. In waging a just war, the ends must necessitate the means and a state must consider how its actions affect its citizens as well as citizens from other states. States must respond to terrorism and *terrorist threats* on an individual basis. In the context of just war theory, counterterrorism is of most concern because of US use of military force. Operation Enduring Freedom, in both its cause and intent, can be understood as a just conflict. The Bush Doctrine, which provides a basis for the use of preemptive and preventative military force, pushes the bounds of what has traditionally been understood as a justifiable war. By traditional definitions and parameters, then, while the Afghanistan war is just, Operation Iraqi Freedom in terms of cause, intent, and proportionality is unjust. In a broader context, America's War on Terror may have exposed the fact that wars thought to be of "lesser evil" may not be justifiable.

Establishing a definitive and specific identity of terrorists, however, is essential to fight them justly. The concept of terrorism is shrouded with ambiguity and various perspectives, and the threat is broad. Thus, in order to wage "war" against it we must identify the enemy which embodies terrorism—whether it be state, individual or group.

Also of critical importance in the United States' continuing military and political effort to curtail the terrorist threat is the national budget and how emergent realities will inform President Obama's prioritizing of future US action. From an earlier chapter, it is clear that Presidents, especially in the national defense arena, are influential actors in general and shape the national budget in particular.[8] Measuring how influential an actor President Obama will be is crucial. One informative method is to compare how his language correlates with budgetary realities. If the language "survives" with environmental changes then the individual leader can be understood as an influential actor in setting priorities. The priorities expressed in the language by President Bush focused on domestic oriented imperatives, and this point is reiterated various times in Chapter 6 of this reader. Thus far, President Obama's language evidences a similar focus. This is discussed in later sections and is consistent with Robert Kuttner's assessment that the economic crisis will demand President Obama's focused attention, at least inasmuch as his language. In the area of national defense and homeland security spending, President Bush was

---

7   See Chapter 4.
8   See Chapter 6.

very influential. In general, Presidents are more influential on national defense and homeland security than in the domestic and economic spheres of American policy. However, the President's influence is uneven. Chapter 6 notes that given the 2009 economic environment, Obama will have more leeway in influencing the budget and economic priorities and goals.

As an earlier chapter provided, terrorism and America's efforts to combat it globally will have to find their place in the moral discourse of humanity.[9] Whether or not our efforts are morally conceivable is dependent on the particular outlook. One outlook offered in an earlier chapter presents the notion that there is no moral reason that terrorism cannot be defined, and it is, in fact, a moral obligation for the President to seek an explanation for citizens.[10] In direct relation to the focus of this chapter, it is explained that it is not only "morally imperative" but "pragmatic" to explain terrorist attacks which is something on which the prior President failed to adequately capitalize. To legitimize efforts such as the War on Terror they must be explained not only as moral, but pragmatic. Also discussed in an earlier chapter are the correlations between the foreign policy of George H.W. Bush (1987–1993) and George W. Bush (2001–2009). The opportunity for significant historical legacy was created with the events in New York City on September 11.[11] Such events heightened the awareness of US domestic citizens, and the need to identify an enemy seemed all the more apparent. Thus, another chapter in this reader explored the reasons underlying the identification of the "axis of evil," and though such a confrontation is not without great risk and detriment, it may have been inevitable. Re-investment in diplomacy will be needed to mitigate any negative drawbacks.

It seems clear that despite very real threats to the homeland, US efforts will continue to focus on curbing the threat abroad and achieving preventative success when or wherever possible.[12] Securing the homeland has certainly evolved, but will continue to change so long as the transnational threat still exists. Security threats and implications emerging from the Middle East Peace Process will also continue to evolve, and the importance of strategically balancing interests is necessary so that a more successful Arab–Israeli relationship can take form.[13] For Obama, this will strengthen the still weakening Middle East road to regional peace and stability. The US still retains strategic concerns in the Middle East, primarily in terms of geopolitical stability and the war against terrorism. A two-state solution to the Arab–Israeli conflict is not likely to satisfy all interests, but remains as a positive step in the process, according to many analysts.

Current operations in Iraq and Afghanistan represent the realities of fourth generation and asymmetric warfare, in terms of both the United States' associated

---

9   See Chapter 13.
10   See Chapter 14.
11   See Chapter 7.
12   See Chapter 8.
13   See Chapter 9.

failures and successes in responding to non-traditional enemies.[14] The broader reality is that transnational terrorism exists, and is currently evolving right along with processes and products of globalization. Emphasizing and assuring successful adaptation to economic globalization will likely improve conditions that are generally correlated or linked with the formation of terrorist groups.[15] This notion coincides with the crux of this chapter in suggesting that President Obama must rekindle American soft power to properly combat the current terrorist threat. Aiding underdeveloped countries in the development process is exercising soft power and is a tactical foreign policy strategy. This is the type of action that is in the current best interest of the US.

Current Threats and Approaches

President Obama will challenge and rebalance much of the Bush legacy. President Bush made several diplomatic efforts in his last two years[16] as President but exited leaving a turbulent global situation. According to Haass and Indyk, international security issues requiring the new President's immediate attention include "straining" circumstances in Iraq, a nuclear-capable Iran, a "faltering Israeli-Palestinian peace process," weak regional governance in the Middle East and Africa, and ultimately a diminished US status in the international community.[17] Haass and Indyk articulated what Dennis Blair recognized several months later at a recent Senate hearing:[18] these international issues are delicate and time is not working on President Obama's behalf.

Tailored deterrence is the conceptual framework that the outgoing Administration began to adopt which favors adapting deterrence approaches to specific threats as they emerge. President George W. Bush, however, has maintained aspects of the Bush Doctrine, such as preemptive and preventative action, throughout his tenure. His Presidency will, at least in the near future, be marked by staunch negative criticism. Another legacy of the last eight years, receiving less attention, is that no major terrorist attack has occurred on US territory since September 11. One of the goals for President Obama and his Administration is to maintain this precedent.

---

14   See Chapter 10.

15   See Chapter 12.

16   *Public Diplomacy*, United States Department of State (December 2007). This outlines an economic development plan to aid Palestinian Youth through a convergence of leaders in the private sector and the US government, online at http://www.state.gov/documents/organization/98454.pdf.

17   Haass, R.N. and Indyk, M. (2009), "Beyond Iraq: A New US Strategy for the Middle East," *Foreign Affairs* 88/1 (January), 41–58, 1.

18   *Associated Press* (2009), "Intelligence Czar: Economy is top threat to US," February 12.

The Bush Doctrine was promulgated in 2002 and marked the first significant change in US foreign and security policy since the end of the Cold War. It emphasizes, "… preemptive military action, unilateralism, increased military capabilities, and a renewed emphasis on the promotion of democracy."[19] The doctrine served as the basis for US efforts in the Middle East and the Iraq War. Some argue it can not be reconciled because it retains aggressive stances such as preemption yet also contains idealistic goals such as democratization and soft power. President Obama's Administration is clearly favoring one side of this policy spectrum.

From the beginning of this reader, it is made clear that "terrorism" is a concept dependent on perspective. As such, much of the literature discusses terrorism in abstract terms. In a post-9/11 environment, the terrorist threat is such that reacting to its individual characteristics is necessary in attempting to combat it. The threat and capability of modern terrorist groups has heightened with the advent of weapons technologies, communications and vast improvements in transportation which have rendered temporal and spatial complexities obsolete.[20] This reality demands answers across all disciplines, academic and otherwise.

Terrorism includes actions resulting in the targeted disruption of the status-quo which attacks a citizen's perception of individual security. Outright war or other forms of significant militarized conflict will likely remain "unthinkable" between the "most developed" international superpowers.[21] Whether America remains the predominant world power is largely contingent upon how the incoming Administration will confront threats from rogue nations and terrorist organizations while maintaining alliances with other great powers so that a "Security Community"[22] can be sustained.

Robert Jervis argues that the international system is currently characterized by an overarching "Security Community" consisting of the US, Western Europe, and Japan. Jervis emphasizes that the "community" is not made up of all the great powers as China and Russia are still significant militarily, however, they lack developmental attributes that are found with their global counterparts—"… their internal regimes are shaky, they are not at the forefront of any advanced forms of technology or economic organization, they can pose challenges only regionally, and they have no attraction as models for others."[23] The potential threat posed by Russia and China must never be completely ignored, but "great-powers" conflict on the scale of the World Wars is unlikely. Currently, conflict provoked by China or Russia will presumably reflect an attempt to gain what it considers a critical "sphere of influence." Even the War on Terror, as Jervis argues, is unlikely to be

---

19   Lansford, T. (2007), *Historical Dictionary of US Diplomacy Since the Cold War*, Lanham, MD: The Scarecrow Press.

20   Riedel, B. (2007), "Al Qaeda Strikes Back," *Foreign Affairs*, May/June.

21   Jervis, op. cit. fn. 2, 12–13

22   Ibid., 14.

23   Ibid., 13.

a primary motivating factor in global politics. The US no longer has a need to protect national interests, rather it must protect democratic values and the status quo referred to by Jervis as "milieu" goals. Existing in a community that has mutual security interests redefines approaches to national security. It can be surmised that contemporary threats will not come from traditional great powers, rather those groups which directly and acutely seek to agitate the status quo.

Tailored Deterrence

Adapting to the multi-contextual reality of the international system, the United States Government began to tout the policy of "Tailored Deterrence" which focuses on "who" the subject of deterrence is rather than on "how" deterrence is carried out.[24] This policy is neither assumptive nor motivated strictly by national interests, which reflects the reality that Jervis explains through a security-as-community framework—that the US no longer adopts policy that is solely conducive to fulfilling perceived strategic interests. Interests are still secured but strategy changes. "Tailored Deterrence" seeks to shift the perspective of what constitutes terrorists and terrorism in the sense that it is a response to the abstractness of terrorism as a concept and seeks to narrow the understanding of the actors and their actions by being specific. The policy considers the following: characteristics and sets of complexities associated with terrorist groups, delineations of which specific groups embody these threats, what their specific weaknesses are, if states sponsor them, what type of individuals constitute a "typical" member and which solution could provide the best potential results given these traits coupled with realities and implications that accompany great powers in the era of globalization. This approach to deterrence policy considers how terrorist groups conceptualize themselves, their ideology, and their own action giving consideration to the realties and limitations that each faces in terms of culture, economy, politics, infrastructure, and geography. "Tailoring" US deterrence approaches to be progressive and auto-adaptive to threats as they unfold rather than stagnant and assumingly universal is the accepted deterrence approach of the United States in the current War on Terror.

The most pertinent threat, then, will not manifest at the state level, but rather be undertaken by individual group or specific regime (often taking actions that are not directly associated with the state), thus US conflict is with the Taliban Regime

---

24 Woolf, A.F. (2008), "Nuclear Weapons in the US National Security Policy: Past, Present and Prospects," *Congressional Research Service*, January 28. This paper discusses the current US policy of "tailored deterrence" which rejects "strategic deterrence" theory and focuses on "who" is being deterred rather than "how" such deterrence is being carried out. With emerging terrorist threats, biological weapons, and other unconventional forms of warfare, how the US responds to security threats is more a matter of knowing the specifics and nature of the threat, and tailoring deterrence policy to answer directly to these threats, than an assumptive framework of asymmetry.

and al-Qaeda as separate factions, and not Afghanistan. Tailored deterrence seeks to shape deterrence practices to combat these sorts of localized threats as opposed to states. Though asymmetric deterrence accounts for US military and economic advantage, its focus remains on states rather than the threats emanating from within but separately. Tailored deterrence seeks to re-shift this focus to both asymmetric and fourth generation warfare, in which unconventional tactics of warfare characterize counterinsurgencies in Iraq and Afghanistan (discussed at more depth in Chapter 10 regarding Iraq and counterinsurgency).

The Obama Administration will have to evaluate the efficacy of Tailored Deterrence as it relates to current security threats such as the Iranian-Israeli relationship and the reality of non-traditional threats. This already volatile situation will prove burdensome during Obama's initial days in office. On January 13, 2009, a mass of Iranian demonstrators were photographed burning pictures and defacing material depicting then President-Elect Obama while showing support for Palestinians on the Gaza Strip as they had been in conflict with Israel starting on December 28, 2008.[25] Additionally, on November 16, 2008 Ayman al-Zawahiri, a top al-Qaeda leader, released a statement characterizing Obama as the antithesis of "honorable Black Americans" suggesting that the President broadcasts as undesirable an image in the perspective of terrorist organizations as his predecessor.[26] Following this, on January 6, 2009 Zawahiri framed the Gaza crisis as the "first link" in the continuous "chain" of US efforts to combat Muslims, an effort that is now led by President Obama.[27]

To be sure, President Obama has no pre-determined political credibility in Iran or any other countries in the Greater Middle East. Obama must alter perceptions such as those displayed by the Iranian protestors and to do this he must take definitive stances on important security issues while also restoring and reinvesting in diplomacy. By favorably reacting on the peril of the domestic economy, he avoids making clear to the global community where he stands on issues such as the current crisis in Gaza. This lack in response could be perceived by foreign audiences as President Obama disproportionately weighing international concerns with domestic, which only acts to increase tensions among the Iranian, Israeli, and American public. The pictures will continue to burn, so to speak, until President Obama reassures the foreign citizens that he is responsive to their interests and vulnerabilities. Overall stability is contingent on successfully balancing interests of all parties and reflecting this in foreign policy. According to Kuttner, President Obama's most daunting challenge will be the economy, but of equal weight will be what some like Haass and Indyk consider the issue that will expose his weakest vulnerabilities: America's role and status in the international community.

---

25   Blair, E. (2008), "Iranian Protestors Back Gaza and Burn Obama Picture," *Reuters*, January 13.
26   Warrick, J. (2009), "To Combat Obama Al Qaeda Hurls Insults," *Washington Post*, January 25.
27   Ibid.

Issues dealing with foreign policy and hegemonic power struggle will pervade and consume President Obama's international agenda. Additionally, America's effort to subdue domestic and international terrorism is of primary concern. As recognized by the United States Department of Defense and Intelligence Czar Dennis Blair, terrorist groups posing the most direct threat to US security interests are al-Qaeda and Taliban forces operating around the world but primarily in Pakistan, Afghanistan and to a lesser extent, Iraq. According to US Government officials and various news sources issues that will pose the most significant challenge to the United States War on Terror in the timeframe of the next five years are instability in the Middle East and Africa, ongoing challenges in adequately securing national borders, and emergent technologies that are being exploited by numerous terrorist organizations.[28] Consistent with Woolf's discourse on "tailored deterrence," these three challenges call for a targeted restructuring of how US policy makers will approach the current and foreseeable threats of terrorist groups. One such threat is biological warfare, which currently lacks adequate mechanisms of deterrence as the problem and its various implications are still unfolding to US officials. Attacks carried out via cyber technologies are also of primary concern. Both internet-based attacks and biological weapons capabilities are difficult to preemptively identify which makes successful deterrence all the more difficult. This illustrates the potential inadequacy of preemption (that is, the Bush Doctrine) in responding to all threats and could be diminished by "smart power" tactics.

Iran continues to agitate the already unstable relationship it has with the United States which poses a direct threat to the predominance of the "Security Community." In the first part of February 2009, the Iranian Government modified its weapons technology as they launched Omid, a space launch vehicle (SLV) that has US State Department officials "concerned" because it provides a "technical basis" for potential long-range weapons capabilities which includes the possibility of "long-range ballistic missile systems" (LRBMS).[29] The US Department of State's official position released to the public is as follows:

> Working with the United Nations, we have passed a number of UN Security Council Resolutions, including Resolution 1737, which require states to take the necessary measures to prevent the supply of, inter alia, specified equipment and technology that could contribute to Iran's development of nuclear weapons delivery systems. We will continue with our friends and allies in the region

---

28   Sullivan, E. (2008), "Homeland Security Forecasts 5 Year Terrorist Threats," *Associated Press*, December 25.

29   This message was delivered on February 3, 2009 by Robert Wood, who serves as Acting Spokesman of US Department of State, Public Affairs office in Washington, DC. *Iranian Launch of Satellite*, online at http://www.state.gov/r/pa/prs/ps/2009/02/115895. htm.

to address the threats posed by Iran, including those related to its missile and nuclear programs and its support of terrorism.[30]

Elections are approaching in the country and Ahmadinejad no doubt has supported these efforts in his own effort to rouse national pride in spite of President Obama expressing interest in open dialogue with Iran.[31] Also at the February 13 Senate hearing, Blair discussed how the current security cabinet perceives the US relationship with Iran. He affirmed the fact that Iran will continue its efforts in this arena, potentially having success in the near future.[32]

Even the traditional terrorist groups and rouge state threats discussed above may wane in 2009. On February 12, 2009, US Intelligence Czar Dennis Blair reported to a Senate panel that non-traditional threats to US security will likely emerge in a more direct way than in the past. In a written statement to the panel Blair said, "The primary near-term security concern of the United States is the global economic crisis and its geopolitical implications."[33] Economic instability on the global level will further stifle the progress of developing countries which, in turn, creates "breeding grounds" that are conducive for future terrorists. This is the logic to which President Obama and his security cabinet adhere. However, Blair did recognize the current terrorist threat characterizing al-Qaeda as "less capable" than one year earlier in Pakistan, while efforts to curtail the Taliban insurgency in Afghanistan are being undermined as their influence continues to "expand." Blair attributes this to a failure in regional governmental legitimacy resulting from unsuccessful economic development.

Rebalancing with Smart Power: A Re-assessment of Approach

President Obama will counterbalance the doctrine of preemption and unilateralism with soft power tactics and a push for collective action on the terrorist threat. Thus, previous foundational ideologies and approaches found in the Bush Doctrine will be significantly challenged. As of this writing, the Obama Administration has made only minimal impact on the international system, and consequently we can make our best assessment by the language he and his foreign policy team have used thus far.

Investing in soft power was something that was lacking during the tenure of George W. Bush. Inevitably, both hard and soft power interests will have to be considered, but uneven focus on one over the other is counterproductive to

---

30   Ibid.

31   News Hour (2009), "Iran Launches Satellite, Escalating Tensions with US," *Public Broadcasting Station Online* (accessed February 15, 2009).

32   *Associated Press* (2009), "Intelligence Czar: Economy is top threat to US," February 12.

33   Ibid.

US security interests and the deterrence of terrorism. Soft power is the ability to coerce other states by the attractiveness of the attributes of culture.[34] Joseph Nye introduced this concept and has since expounded upon it. In 2003, Nye wrote in *Foreign Policy*:

> The attractiveness of the United States rests on resources such as its culture (sometimes), its political values of democracy and human rights (when it lives up to them), and its policies (when they are framed with some humility and awareness of others' interests) ... The United States must adopt policies that appeal to moderates and must use public diplomacy more effectively to explain common interests to would-be allies in the Muslim world.[35]

While Nye urges investment in soft power, he recognizes that a balanced investment in hard power is necessary "... to defeat terrorism."[36] Speaking to the most acute US terrorist threat, Nye asserts, "The United States will win the War on Terror only if moderate Muslims win, and the United States' ability to attract moderates is critical to victory," but that the, "... United States must learn to combine soft and hard power more effectively."[37] Nye stresses collective action and multilateralism to combat the terrorist threat.

In 2004, Nye addressed what he took as an evident decline in American soft power asserting that "public diplomacy" needed more "support from the White House."[38] Then Secretary of Defense Rumsfeld gave no credence to the idea of soft power, and seemed sure America's predominance was not reliant on it. The Cold War, according to Nye, was won by effective balancing of soft and hard power tactics, and in reference to terrorism in the context of diminishing US soft power, he writes:

> The United States cannot confront the new threat of terrorism without the cooperation of other countries. Of course, other governments will often cooperate out of self-interest. But the extent of their cooperation often depends on the attractiveness of the United States. Soft power, therefore, is not just a matter of ephemeral popularity; it is a means of obtaining outcomes the United States wants.[39]

---

34 Nye, J., Jr. (1990), "Soft Power," *Foreign Policy* 80 (Autumn), 153–171.
35 Nye, J., Jr. (2003), "The Velvet Hegemon," *Foreign Policy* 136 (June), 74–75.
36 Ibid., 75.
37 Ibid.
38 Nye, J., Jr. (2004), "The Decline of America's Soft Power: Why Washington Should Worry," *Foreign Policy* 20, 16–20.
39 Ibid.

Thus, such an approach constitutes the most pragmatic political means to achieving foreign policy goals in the face of the current threats and expectations of both domestic and international audiences.

To be sure, the US domestic population scrutinizes their leaders based on how well their interests are served. The American Executive, however, is also held to the will of an attuned international audience. For instance, in early 2009 Secretary of State Hillary Clinton visited Turkey and appeared on a television chat show, *Hadi Gel Bizimle* (*Come and Join Us*), taking on some political questions but most were focused on her personal life.[40] This "sideshow to diplomacy" demonstrates that global audiences are increasingly aware of the influence that US political actors have on their own existence and will scrutinize accordingly. Answering to audience demand must be reflected in the US approach and is a pragmatic action aimed at strengthening American soft power.

Most of President Obama's actions regarding national security and foreign policy can best be rationalized and criticized through a framework of "smart power." In 2006, the Center for Strategic and International Studies (CSIS) launched a bipartisan Commission on Smart Power chaired by Richard Armitage and Joseph Nye to develop "... a vision to guide America's global engagement."[41] Under this doctrine, maintaining a primary role in global affairs depends on the US transition from policies of coercion and "fear" to those of "optimism."[42] In essence, smart power is achieved by investing in the "global good"—providing assets to individuals and governments around the world who are prevented from attaining such resources for either developmental or governmental constraints. Smart power can accomplish this by "complementing" or balancing US military and economic predominance (hard power) with investment in diplomacy (smart power). As a framework, this is meant to work through global challenges answering to their unpredictability.

Investing in both hard and soft power is inevitable, thus smart power will combine the two. The new President must balance interests and conform policy to a "smarter" approach. This concept was touted early on by Secretary of State Clinton and is consistent with satisfying levels I and II of Putnam's international negotiations which has the inherent benefit of promoting a "Security Community." Investment in soft power will also require investment in hard power. Most acutely, hard security measures will be implemented in the continued effort to deter international terrorism.

---

40   Pleming, S. (2009), "Clinton tells how she fell for Bill long ago," *Reuters*, March 7, online at http://www.reuters.com/article/vcCandidateFeed1/idUSTRE5261P720090307.

41   *Center for Strategic & International Studies (CSIS)*, CSIS Commission on Smart Power. Several reports were composed and published, the last was on November 6, 2007, onine at http://www.csis.org/index.php?option=com_csis_progj&task=view&id=904.

42   Ibid.

Measuring Up and Future Challenges

In a 2007 edition of *Foreign Affairs*, Barack Obama stated,

> To renew American leadership in the world, I will strengthen our common security by investing in our common humanity. Our global engagement cannot be defined by what we are against; it must be guided by a clear sense of what we stand for. We have a significant stake in ensuring that those who live in fear and want today can live with dignity and opportunity tomorrow.[43]

It seems clear that Obama recognizes a need to improve "common security" and that individuals around the world exist in a perpetual state of fear which is worsened by terrorists, hardship and failed government. Though, how Obama would define "global engagement" is not aligned with the necessity for executive powers to engage in two-level games, successfully weighing out interests of domestic and international audiences. Global engagement, contrary to what Obama has stated, must to some degree be "defined by what we are against," as this is reflective of "tailored deterrence." To define "global engagement" by "what we stand for" is to incorporate ideology with US policy around the globe. To successfully break from the Bush Doctrine, President Obama must reject such notions. Aligning to what his one-time campaign rival and now Secretary of State Hillary Clinton has stated—that new American foreign policy will mark a return to pragmatism through a doctrine of "smart power"—President Obama must rethink how he defines "global engagement" as well as how he conceptualizes America's role around the globe. One direction suggested by Obama is working on the challenge of poverty. Reducing poverty is deterrent to terrorism in that it transforms an environment that Obama refers to as "optimal breeding grounds for ... terrorism."

Robert Kuttner suggests that a President is successful on a given issue in relation to the extent that they capture the American public's interest on that issue—"Fine programmatic ideas often fail unless a President succeeds in capturing the public imagination."[44] President Obama must hone the public's image of foreign policy and terrorism. Kuttner argues that Obama possesses the tools in an environment where political circumstances are such that a transformative style of leadership is possible. Kuttner's assessment falls short, however, in assuming that to succeed as a "transformational" leader the only challenge that must be met is the crippled American economic system. While President Obama will most likely see his primary and immediate obligations directed to the economy, to live up to the standard that Kuttner and others set out for a transformational leader the challenges

---

43   Online at http://www.barackobama.com/pdf/issues/Fact_Sheet_Foreign_Policy_Democratization_and_Development_FINAL.pdf.

44   Kuttner, R. (2008), *Obama's Challenge: America's Economic Crisis and the Power of a Transformative Presidency*, White River Junction, Vermont: Chelsea Green Publishing, 6.

related to foreign policy and the War on Terror must be successfully handled in terms of diplomatic, political and economic implications.

America's War on Terror, too, is persistently scrutinized by not only the domestic but the larger international audience. Though some of the suggestions for President Obama put forth by Kuttner and others exclude adequate focus on terrorism and American foreign policy, they are correct in the assessment that the circumstances President Obama is facing as the US President in 2009 are rare and conducive for transformational leadership. There are certainly situations for Obama to transform for the better—the War on Terror being one that is critical to America's future. Likewise, the success of Obama as President will be determined to some degree by how well he mends severed relationships with other nations. "Transformational presidents, when they succeed, also transform political alignments."[45] President Obama will face multiple challenges and only when weighing international interests the same as domestic will strategic alignments, political and otherwise, be repaired.

In late 2008, a *Foreign Policy*[46] article criticized Obama on ten points using what the then-candidate had said publicly. Though obviously slanted at critical interpretation, the article provides some points for serious consideration. Two points of criticism leveled at Obama are worth noting in the context of foreign policy and combating terrorism: engaging in militarized action toward Pakistan and engaging in talks with Iran's Ahmadinejad with no preconditions. Clinton has continued to promise both "pragmatism" and "smart power" as frameworks through which to approach foreign affairs. This could signify a set-in foreign policy approach that reflects a return to pragmatism, common to European approaches and that of the Nixon-Kissinger Administration. Clinton has also stated that she desires to remove ideology from foreign policy agendas. Henry Kissinger supports Obama's conceptual approach to foreign policy including supporting open direct diplomatic relations with Iran excluding those at the Presidential level. Recently, President Obama's actions have included sending Henry Kissinger to Russia, where the former Secretary of State participated in discreet negotiations regarding nuclear arms policy with President Dmitry Medvedev.[47] Recently, Secretary of Defense Gates has affirmed that air assaults on insurgent forces in Pakistan would continue.

---

45   Ibid.

46   Montanaro, *Reuters*, online at http://uk.reuters.com/article/reutersComService_2_MOLT/idUKTRE51547Z20090206?sp=true.

47   Blomfield, A. (2009), "Cold warrior Henry Kissinger woos Russia for Barack Obama," *The Telegraph*, February 6.

Balancing Interests: Successfully Engaging Two-level Games

In 1988, Robert Putnam introduced the political model and conflict-resolution theory referred to as "two-level game theory."[48] Two-level game theory is used to analyze relationships and negotiations between international regimes, primarily focusing on how liberal democracies will behave.[49] In an assessment of Obama's action regarding foreign policy, the applicable underpinning of Putnam's theoretical framework is that it perceives international regimes as unavoidably engaging in continuous arbitration and reconciliation on both intra-national and international levels (domestic vs. foreign issues). Level I represents the international "set or negotiation" and Level II represents the domestic "constituency or negotiation."[50]

Because the US is still considered a prevalent international power, President Obama will have to take into account all interests at stake when implementing policy both domestically and abroad, while effectively addressing concerns at both levels. In the era of globalization in which interdependence is acknowledged as a reality, American Presidents are beholden to a domestic audience and also a broader international community. Like the domestic audience, this global society has numerous interests which hinge on their relationship to the United States and how the superpower manifests its international agenda and foreign policy concerns. Obama's actions as a US Senator and his early days as President most directly represented concerns for domestic issues, the most pertinent being the status of the US economy. President Obama has endured criticism for inadequately addressing international concerns.

Putnam's theory suggests that only when balance is struck between levels of interest and concern will executive powers be successful, because only then will international agreements and consequent peace between regimes likely exist. When engaged in "domestic negotiations" the American Executive constructs alliances with domestic societal actors building public trust through an effort to satisfy their concerns and interests. Internationally, in order to achieve "win-sets" the executive power must attempt to express these concerns without disrupting relationships with domestic actors while also meeting the concerns of international societal actors. When balance is reached, international stability and consensus will be the byproduct. This approach satisfies Jervis's "Security Community" and currently in the United States both levels of actors are reaching for a revitalization of US diplomacy, pragmatism, and "soft" relations. The domestic game is characterized by actors and their interests whereas the international by political incentivizing and negotiation[51]—a détente for a new era.

---

48 Putnam, R.D. (1988), "Diplomacy and Domestic Politics: The Logic of Two-Level Games," *International Organization* 42 (Summer), 427–460.
49 Ibid.
50 Ibid.
51 Ibid.

Ultimately, Obama's actions as President in the realm of foreign policy must represent both domestic concerns and those of the broader global community establishing "... a more sustainable balance between US interests and US values."[52] For instance, President Obama overturned the Mexico City policy which restricts US economic aid to overseas organizations that do not "perform" or "promote" abortions. The policy was enacted by President Reagan, sustained by President George H.W. Bush, overturned by President Clinton, enacted again by President George W. Bush, and now overturned by President Obama.[53] Such a move is meant to satisfy domestic constituents and interests of the Democratic Party. This break from the last Administration exemplifies conscious rejection of previous political and ideological standards as well as a rekindling of America's image in developing countries whose citizens will benefit most from lifting the Mexico City policy.

Current International and Domestic Games

Israeli–Palestinian Conflict

Israel conducted Operation Cast Lead (Gaza Crisis) in an effort to deter Hamas forces from firing rockets into southern Israel and to weaken the regime's hold on vital territory.[54] In terms of its stated goals, the operation has proved minimally successful. Palestinians are sympathetic to the Hamas-run territory and Israel, along with Egypt, sees the Gaza Strip as integral to their national security and economic strategy. Currently, a cease-fire agreement proposed by Egypt is awaiting compliance. Conflicts in the Middle East serve as Obama's caveat to successfully counter criticism leveled at his seeming deficiency and shortcoming in the realm of international affairs. Simply, the situation provides a ripe political opportunity for Obama to both transform an aspect of his own image as well as how the American Executive branch will approach international issues of a similar nature.

An earlier chapter discussed President Bush's difficulty in reconciling and balancing his approach to the Arab–Israeli relationship. Conflict in the Gaza region between Israeli and Hamas military forces is the immediate and pervading issue for US foreign policy in the Middle East. The outcome of the situation will have implications for America's progress in fighting terrorism globally, because it will prove difficult to arrange a negotiated peace between a US ally on one hand, and a "terrorist-harboring" regime on the other. Should the US not want to appear hypocritical, President Obama will be pushed into redefining the US

52   Haass and Indyk, op. cit. fn. 17.
53   Bettelheim, A. (2009), "Obama Overturns Ban on Funds for Groups Supporting Overseas Abortion," *CQ Politics Today Online News*, January 23.
54   *Times Online*, "Burn victim vows to be suicide bomber while Israelis ask: 'Was it all worth it?'," online at http://www.timesonline.co.uk/tol/news/world/middle_east/article5567396.ece.

approach to the conflict between the Israelis and Palestinians. Dealing with this and broader issues in the Middle East will be unavoidable for President Obama. It should and will be equally weighted with the global economic crisis. Haas and Indyk recognize that, "Some might argue that these efforts are not worth it, that the Bush Administration paid too much attention to and invested too much American blood and treasure in an ill-advised attempt to transform the Middle East and that the Obama Administration should focus its attention at home or elsewhere abroad. But such arguments underestimate the Middle East's ability to force itself onto the US President's agenda regardless of other plans ... From terrorism to nuclear proliferation ... contemporary global challenges requires managing the Middle East." These authors contend that Obama should "... extend Washington's vision beyond Iraq."[55]

The new President will be in the difficult position of balancing the potentially volatile Israeli-Palestinian situation with demand from the domestic audience to repair the perceived economic crisis. The extent to which President Obama will focus political and diplomatic efforts on current foreign relations should remain under close scrutiny as situations in the Middle East and other areas of the world intensify. Presently, Obama "... has said little specific about his foreign policy—in contrast to more expansive remarks about the economy."[56] A lack of specificity and depth, coupled with the consequent deferment of critical questions about the Gaza Crisis to political counterparts suggests at this point, though admittedly early, that President Obama is neglecting to make any definitive steps in America's general foreign affairs much less the Global War on Terror.

So far, Obama has failed to politically capitalize on the Gaza Crisis. The situation warrants a reactive and engaged response from President Obama—similar to that which he has given to the American economic crisis—because it is just as much in the US national interest. A critical miscalculation by President Obama was his insistent deferment of foreign policy questions to Bush in late December 2008. While eagerly willing to take on questions about the economy, Obama opted to pass those dealing with terrorism, Gaza, and Iran to the current "one President."[57] By doing so, Obama represented an imbalanced view of interests and a failure to at least speak toward the diplomatic concerns surrounding the most pertinent security issues.

Iran

The United States cannot afford to have an unstable relationship with Iran, primarily due to the long-term logistical entanglement that would accompany

---

55   Haass and Indyk, op. cit. fn. 17.

56   Meyers, S.L. and Cooper, H. (2008), "Obama Defers to Bush, for now, on Gaza Crisis," *New York Times Online*, December 28.

57   Ibid. Kampeas, R. (2008), "Is Gaza Conflict a Crisis or Opportunity for Obama?" *Jewish and Israel News*, December 28.

any large-scale militarized conflict.[58] Iranian leaders have interest in achieving regional hegemonic power, and in the perception of the US this threatens the "Security Community" that Jervis discusses. Ensuring a sound structure for this community of mutually secured interests and keeping it intact is necessary for the US to maintain its hegemonic status and sphere of influence, both corollaries to broader security interests. As of present, Iran seeks to undermine US efforts in the Middle East because such efforts act as the chief deterrents to securing what Iranian strategists perceive to be their traditional sphere of influence. Currently, the US has interest in maintaining its position as the dominant power in the Middle East, and, to an extent, this stance allows more flexibility in approaching some of the most pervasive terrorist threats as well as increased assurance in the perpetuation of a more "secure" international "community." At the state level, linkages between terrorist funding and Iran continue to surface. Iran has interest in seeing America further entangled with efforts in Iraq, Afghanistan, and Pakistan. American resources and image in the region will diminish the longer it is engaged, thus Iran will use the opportunity to establish its predominance in the region. As numerous examples indicate, "hard" military tactics do not strengthen America's weakness in the region—image and political legitimacy—thus diplomatic coercion and softening of image will directly answer to the US disadvantage in conflict with Tehran.

Soft power, suasion and diplomacy will not, however, suffice all situations and cannot be successful without hard power measures providing the groundwork and a more conducive environment. A measure of hard power initiatives is unavoidable since Obama's Administration seeks to adopt "smart power" and "diplomacy." To be sure, this can be considered "pragmatic." Haass and Indyck argue that:

> Preventive military action against Iran by either the United States or Israel is an unattractive option, given its risks and costs. But it needs to be examined carefully as a last-ditch alternative to the dangers of living with an Iranian bomb. To increase Israel's tolerance for extended diplomatic engagement, the US government should bolster Israel's deterrent capabilities by providing an enhanced anti-ballistic-missile defense capability and a nuclear guarantee.[59]

In other words, soft power can only work when hard security factors are taken into account. Actualizing an approach of "smart power" will satisfy the primary "strategic challenge" for the US—it must magnify democracy while keeping its military advantage intact.[60] In a broader context, such measures are aimed at

---

58   For more extensive discussion on this point, see chapters in this volume written by Vaughn Shannon and Robert Pauly, Jr.

59   Haass and Indyk, op. cit. fn. 17.

60   This point is also discussed in Chapter 10—see for more discussion on strategic challenges facing the US.

maintaining what strategic alliances the US does have, both inside and outside of the "Security Community."

Obama proposed in his campaign a promise of "change" and he has thus far remained true to this by his attempt to repair America's image around the world. Current situations that demand Obama's focus will test whether or not the new President can sustain this promise. A *New York Times* article starkly points out that:

> Even before the conflict flared again, India and Pakistan announced troop movements that have raised fears of a military confrontation following the terrorist attacks in Mumbai. North Korea scuttled a final agreement on verifying its nuclear dismantlement earlier this month, while Iran continues to stall the international effort to stop its nuclear programs. And there are still two American wars churning in Iraq and Afghanistan, ... which, ... All demand his [President Obama's] immediate attention.[61]

On January 9, 2009, when announcing a cabinet pick for a national security advisory position, Obama was asked questions about America's volatile relationship with Iran as the state continues to develop nuclear technologies in spite of international denouncement. At this announcement, then President-elect Obama again failed to sufficiently answer questions regarding his foreign policy, in this situation those specifically about his security cabinet choices and whether or not they represent a "softening of the US stance on Iran."[62] This was a no doubt ripe opportunity in which to advance an argument for "soft power" reforms, but Obama offered only what could be called a deficient response to what is a vital security question. He did not waste the opportunity to speak on the status of the US economy—at present considered priority to American citizens. "This morning, we received a stark reminder about how urgently action is needed," Obama remarked about the economy.

Additionally, he spoke on torture, referring to the mishandling of the Abu Ghraib situation (2003–2005) by the Bush Administration, asserting that his Administration would succeed where Bush's had failed when dealing with such issues. He also claimed his Administration would conform to the Geneva Conventions.[63]

Both of the aforementioned policy stances have international importance and are aligned with what is presently in the best interest of the United States. As was mentioned earlier, one of Obama's initial actions was to close the Guantánamo

---

61 Ibid.

62 Montanaro, D. (2009), "Obama Marks Break from Bush on Intel," *MSNBC*, January 9.

63 *Office of the High Commissioner for Human Rights*, "Geneva Convention Relative to the Treatment of Prisoners of War," online at http://www.unhchr.ch/html/menu3/b/91.htm.

Bay prison and denounce torture as an unacceptable practice for states to carry out. Clearly, this message was broadcast to an international audience and represents an initiative in the direction that US foreign policy should lean—one that is espoused in this and other chapters. The closure of Guantánamo Bay is a political move with the intention to satisfy a portion of the domestic audience as well as international critics. Obama's action, however, in this situation had limited bipartisan input and potential repercussions in terms of national security. The backlash has already commenced. Former prisoners who were released as a result of political pressure have realigned themselves with al-Qaeda and other terrorist groups. One former prisoner, now heading up the al-Qaeda faction in Yemen, boasts that his imprisonment only furthered his drive for jihad.[64] However, criticism that Obama has faced from terrorist groups will be dismantled to some degree with the closure of Guantánamo Bay.[65] Putting an end to the negative propaganda being directed at him and addressing critics of the US were President Obama's motives for closing the prison, and whether this was in the interest of broader US security remains to be seen. The Guantánamo Bay closure aligns with Obama's "softening" approach, with unfavorable hard security implications, that is, a potential impetus to, and increase in, terrorist acts.

At this same press conference, responding to direct questions from reporters about Iran, then President-elect Obama offered an explanation answering to criticism leveled at him for his deferment of what are considered critical foreign policy questions:

> With respect to Iran, I'll have more to say about Iran after January 20th. I have said in the past during the course of the campaign that Iran is a genuine threat to US national security. But I have also said that we should be willing to initiate diplomacy as a mechanism to achieve our national security goals. And my national security team, I think, is reflective of that practical, pragmatic approach to foreign policy. And when we have a policy towards Iran that has been shaped by my national security team, we will release it.[66]

In the above statement, Obama does give credence to multilateralism and collective action as he claims that "diplomacy" will be the "mechanism" to fulfill "pragmatic" national interests. The problem with this explanation is that it lacks the specificity that such immediate and potentially destructive situations demand—currently with Iran, Israel, and Hamas—where the US Government has

---

64   *Associated Press*, "Two ex-Guantánamo inmates appear in Al-Qaeda video," online at http://www.google.com/hostednews/afp/article/ALeqM5hZflcWnHqBz4kQR90lC_pXaHeW4Q.

65   *Associate Press*, January 24, 2009, "Guantánamo Closure a Blow to al-Qaeda: Analysts," online at http://www.google.com/hostednews/afp/article/ALeqM5goJTU6Kyp6CHBOOZye_V2qEAbXRg. Montanaro, op. cit. fn. 62.

66   Montanaro.

suggested specificity in response and "tailoring" of perspective.[67] Pragmatism as foreign policy will benefit international alliances but the domestic audience, as consistent with Putnam's theory, must also have their interests satisfied—at least to the extent that is necessary. Pragmatism does not equate to diplomacy for all situations, as some defensive posturing is in the interest of American citizens, at least to the extent of deterring an attack on the level of September 11. So long as hard security concerns are ameliorated, diplomacy and soft power are more likely to succeed. In order to exploit the unique situation for transformative leadership on both national and international levels, in the face of a domestic economic crisis with an audience demanding focus coupled with the reality of inevitable international military engagements, the incoming President must definitively bear out a renewed US response to terrorism and rogue nations so that a concurrent strengthening of American soft power can take place. President Obama has balanced, and will continue to balance, what needed to be rebalanced—the largely one-sided, "hard" US approach to transnational terrorism and other threats.

Conclusion

President Obama has already started to rebalance components of America's War on Terror with diplomacy and soft power. Our hope is that the new President will strengthen America's image in the world and implement mutually beneficial policies to actors at all levels. Terrorism remains a pervasive and evolving threat. President Obama must respond to international situations in such a way so as to reassure citizens and satisfy interests at all levels. Hard and soft power must be strategically balanced forming an approach of "smart power" as states operating in an anarchical international system (no "international" 9/11) will be obligated to invest in both. President Barack Obama has the ability to transform perceptions and alliances, but his ability to maintain a "Security Community" is also of critical importance. To make such a transformative difference, his vigorous passion and engaging rhetoric must transcend public addresses and contribute to a more successful and secure United States of America, which will necessitate the creation of a more stable global environment. President Obama will rebalance his approach to foreign policy, particularly the War on Terror, through a rekindling of soft power and pragmatism. We have demonstrated this through his initial actions, ideology, and public interaction.

---

67 Here, we refer to tailored deterrence.

Appendix A

List of Non US-based Terrorist Organizations

Abu Nidal Organization (ANO)
Abu Sayyaf Group
Al-Aqsa Martyrs Brigade
Al-Jihad (Egyptian Islamic Jihad)
al-Qaeda
al-Qaeda in the Islamic Maghreb (formerly GSPC)
Al-Shabaab
Ansar al-Islam
Armed Islamic Group (GIA)
Asbat al-Ansar
Aum Shinrikyo
Basque Fatherland and Liberty (ETA)
Communist Party of the Philippines/New People's Army (CPP/NPA)
Continuity Irish Republican Army
Gama'a al-Islamiyya (Islamic Group)
Hamas (Islamic Resistance Movement)
Harakat ul-Jihad-i-Islami/Bangladesh (HUJI-B)
Harakat ul-Mujahidin (HUM)
Hizballah (Party of God)
Islamic Jihad Group
Islamic Movement of Uzbekistan (IMU)
Jaish-e-Mohammed (JEM) (Army of Mohammed)
Jemaah Islamiya Organization (JI)
Kahane Chai (Kach)
Kongra-Gel (KGK, formerly Kurdistan Workers' Party, PKK, KADEK)
Lashkar-e Tayyiba (LT) (Army of the Righteous)
Lashkar i Jhangvi
Liberation Tigers of Tamil Eelam (LTTE)
Libyan Islamic Fighting Group (LIFG)
Moroccan Islamic Combatant Group (GICM)
Mujahedin-e Khalq Organization (MEK)
National Liberation Army (ELN)
Palestine Liberation Front (PLF)
Palestinian Islamic Jihad (PIJ)
PFLP-General Command (PFLP-GC)

Popular Front for the Liberation of Palestine (PFLF)
Tanzim Qa'idat al-Jihad fi Bilad al-Rafidayn (QJBR) (al-Qaida in Iraq) (formerly Jama'at al-Tawhid wa'al-Jihad, JTJ, al-Zarqawi Network)
Real IRA
Revolutionary Armed Forces of Colombia (FARC)
Revolutionary Nuclei (formerly ELA)
Revolutionary Organization 17 November
Revolutionary People's Liberation Party/Front (DHKP/C)
Shining Path (Sendero Luminoso, SL)
United Self-Defense Forces of Colombia (AUC)

Source: "Foreign Terrorist Organizations: Fact Sheet," Office of the Coordinator for Counterterrorism, US Department of State, April 8, 2008.

Appendix B

January 15, 1990
The Tupac Amaru Revolutionary Movement bombed the US Embassy in Lima.

May 13, 1990
The New People's Army killed two US Air Force personnel near Clark Air Base in the Philippines.

January 18–19, 1991
Iraqi agents planted bombs at the home of the US Ambassador to Indonesia and at the USIS library in Manila.

January 17–21, 1992
The Red Scorpion Group kidnapped a US businessman in Manila, Philippines and the National Liberation Army and the Revolutionary Armed Forces of Colombia (FARC) kidnapped two US businessmen in Colombia.

March 17, 1992
Hezbollah bombed the Israeli Embassy in Buenos Aires.

January 31, 1993
The Revolutionary Armed Forces of Colombia (FARC) kidnapped three US missionaries.

February 26, 1993
Islamic terrorists associated with Umar Abd al-Rahman and Osama bin Laden bombed the World Trade Center in New York City.

April 14, 1993
Iraqi intelligence agents attempted to assassinate former US President George Bush in Kuwait.

February 25, 1994
Jewish right-wing extremist machine-gunned Muslim worshippers in Hebron.

September 23, 1994
The Armed Forces of Colombia (FARC) kidnapped a US citizen in Colombia.

December 24, 1994
The Armed Islamic Group hijacked an Air France flight to Algeria.

March 8, 1995
Terrorists killed two US diplomats and wounded another in Karachi.

March 20, 1995
The Aum Shinri-kyu cult attacked a crowded subway station with Sarin nerve gas in Tokyo.

April 19, 1995
Right-wing extremists bombed the federal building in Oklahoma City.

July 4, 1995
The al-Faran Kashmiri separatist group kidnapped and killed US citizens and others in India.

August 21, 1995
Hamas bombed a bus in Jerusalem.

September 13, 1995
Terrorists bombed the window of the US Embassy in Moscow in response to US strikes against Serbs in Bosnia.

November 13, 1995
The Islamic Movement of Change bombed a military compound in Riyadh.

November 19, 1995
An Islamic terrorist bombed the Egyptian Embassy in Islamabad.

January 8, 1996
Guerrillas from the Free Papau Movement kidnapped 26 people in Indonesia.

January 19, 1996
The Revolutionary Armed Forces of Colombia (FARC) kidnapped a US citizen in Colombia.

January 31, 1996
The Liberation Tigers of Tamil Eelam bombed a bank in Sri Lanka.

February 9, 1996
The Irish Republican Army detonated a bomb in London.

February 15, 1996
Terrorists fired rockets at the US Embassy in Athens.

February 16, 1996
Guerrillas of the National Liberation Army kidnapped a US citizen in Colombia.

February 26, 1996
A suicide bomber blew up a bus in Jerusalem.

March 4, 1996
Hamas and the Palestinian Islamic Jihad bombed a shopping mall in Tel Aviv.

May 13, 1996
Arab gunmen opened fire on a bus carrying students in Bet El. Israel.

May 31, 1996
Former Contra guerrillas kidnapped a USAID relief worker in Nicaragua.

June 9, 1996
Terrorists killed a US citizen in Zekharya, Israel.

June 15, 1996
The IRA detonated a bomb at a shopping center in Manchester, England.

June 25, 1996
Radical Islamic terrorists bombed the US military's Khobar Towers housing facility in Dhahran.

July 20, 1996
The Basque Fatherland and Liberty organization detonated a bomb at the Tarragona International Airport in Spain.

August 1, 1996
The Algerian Armed Islamic Group exploded a bomb at the home of the French Archbishop of Oran.

August 17, 1996
The Sudanese People's Liberation Army kidnapped missionaries in Mapourdit.

September 13, 1996
The Patriotic Union of Kurdistan kidnapped French and Canadian relief workers in Iraq.

October 1, 1996
Assassins killed the South Korean Consul near his home in Vladivostok, Russia.

November 1, 1996
The Sudanese People's Liberation Army kidnapped International Red Cross workers in Sudan.

December 3, 1996
Algerian terrorists bombed a Paris subway train.

December 11, 1996
The Revolutionary Armed Forces of Colombia (FARC) kidnapped a US citizen.

December 17, 1996
The Tupac Amaru Revolutionary Movement took hundreds of people hostage at the Japanese Ambassador's residence in Lima.

January 2–13, 1997
Apparent Egyptian terrorists mailed letter bombs worldwide.

February 4–17, 1997
Paramilitary terrorists abducted UN staff in Tajikistan.

February 14, 1997
Armed guerrillas kidnapped a US oil engineer and Venezuelan pilot in Colombia.

February 23, 1997
A Palestinian gunman opened fire on tourists at the Empire State Building in New York City.

February 24, 1997
The National Liberation Army kidnapped a US citizen in Colombia.

March 7, 1997
FARC guerrillas kidnapped a US mining employee in Colombia.

July 12, 1997
The Military Liberation Union bombed a hotel in Havana.

September 4, 1997
Hamas suicide bombers denoted bombs in a shopping mall in Jerusalem.

October 23, 997
ELN rebels kidnapped employees of the Organization of American States in Colombia.

October 30, 1997
al-Sha'if rebels kidnapped a US businessman near Sanaa in Yemin.

November 12, 1997
The Islamic Inqilabi Council (Islamic Revolutionary Council) shot US businessmen at their hotel in Karachi.

November 17, 1997
al-Bama'at al-Islamiyya terrorists killed tourists at a temple near Luxor in Egypt.

February 19, 1998
Georgian rebels abducted UN military observers.

March 12–23, 1998
FARC rebels kidnapped a US citizen and killed others near Bogata.

April 15, 1998
Somali militiamen abducted Red Cross and other international relief workers in Mogadishu.

August 1, 1998
IRA detonated a bomb in Banbridge, Ireland.

August 7, 1998
Osama bin Laden's terrorist network bombed the US Embassy in Nairobi, Kenya and the US Embassy in Dar-es-Salaam, Tanzania.

August 15, 1998
IRA terrorists detonated a bomb outside a courthouse in Omagh, Ireland.

October 18, 1998
The National Liberation Army bombed the Ocensa pipeline in Colombia.

November 15, 1998
Terrorists robbed and kidnapped members of the family of a US businessman in Colombia.

January 2, 1999
National Union for Total Independence of Angola (UNITA) rebels shot down an Angolan aircraft.

February 14, 1999
The Allied Democratic Forces exploded a pipe bomb in a bar in Uganda.

February 16, 1999
The Kurdistan Workers' Party stormed and occupied the Greek Embassy in Vienna, taking the Greek Ambassador and others hostage, and storming other diplomatic posts in France, Holland, Switzerland, Britain and Germany.

February 25, 1999
FARC rebels kidnapped and killed US citizens working for an international conservation organization in Colombia and Venezuela.

March 1, 1999
Hutu rebels attacked, abducted and killed tourists in Uganda.

March 23, 1999
The National Liberation Army (ELN) kidnapped a US citizen in Colombia.

May 30, 1999
ELN terrorists attacked a church congregation and kidnapped US citizens and others in Colombia.

June 27, 1999
A terror group known as Enough is Enough in the Niger River attacked and kidnapped a team of international employees of Shell Oil in Nigeria.

August 4, 1999
The Armed Forces Revolutionary Council kidnapped UN representatives in Sierra Leone.

October 1, 1999
Burmese dissidents seized the Burmese Embassy in Bangkok, holding people hostage.

December 23, 1999
The People's Liberation Army kidnapped a US citizen in Colombia.

December 24, 1999
Terrorists hijacked an Indian Airlines plane from Kathmandu to New Delhi.

January 27, 2000
The Basque Fatherland and Liberty organization set fire to a car dealership in Spain.

May 1, 2000
The Revolutionary United Front attacked a UN facility, killed UN peacekeepers, and kidnapped members of UN relief mission in Sierra Leone.

June 8, 2000
Terrorists killed the British Defence Attaché in Athens.

June 27, 2000
ELN militants kidnapped a woman and her infant son, a US citizen in Colombia.

August 12, 2000
The Islamic Movement of Uzbekistan took US citizens hostage in Kyrgyzstan.

October 1, 2000
Terrorists bombed a church in Dushanbe, Tajikistan.

October 12, 2000
The Popular Liberation Army kidnapped Spanish oil workers in Ecuador.

October 12, 2000
Terrorists associated with Osama bin Laden bombed the *USS Cole* in Aden Harbor, Yemen.

December 30, 2000
The Moro Islamic Front detonated a bomb near the US Embassy in Manila.

January 17, 2001
Lashkar-e Tayybe militants attempted to seize an airport in India.

March 4, 2001
Terrorists exploded a bomb outside the British Broadcasting Corporation's studio in London.

March 9, 2001
ETA terrorists killed policemen with a bomb in Hernani, Spain.

April 22, 2001
Hamas detonated a bomb at a bus stop in Kfar Siva, Israel.

June 1, 2001
Hamas bombed a nightclub in Tel Aviv.

August 9, 2001
Hamas bombed a restaurant in Jerusalem.

September 11, 2001
Al-Qaeda terrorists hijacked four commercial airliners and crashed two into the twin towers of the World Trade Center, one into the Pentagon, and one crashed in a field in western Pennsylvania.

Source: Office of the Historian, US Department of State.

Bibliography

Ackerman, B. (1991), *We the People: Foundations*, Cambridge, MA: Belknap Press.

Ackerman, B. (1998), *We the People: Transformations*, Cambridge, MA: Belknap Press.

Ackerman, B. and Golove, D. (1995), *Is NAFTA Constitutional?*, Cambridge, MA: Harvard University Press.

Allison, G. and Zelikow, P. (1999), *Essence of Decision: Explaining the Cuban Missile Crisis*, 2nd edn, New York: Longman.

Arnold, A. (1983), *Afghanistan's Two-Party Communism: Parcham and Khalq*, Stanford, CA: Hoover Institution Press.

Art, R.J. and Waltz, K.N. (eds) (2009), *The Use of Force: Military Power and International Politics*, 7th edn, Plymouth, UK: Rowman & Littlefield.

Baker, J.A. III (1995), *The Politics of Diplomacy: Revolution, War and Peace, 1989–1992*, New York: Putnam's.

Baylis, J., Wirtz, J.J., Cohen, E. and Grey, C. (eds) (2002), *Strategy in the Contemporary World : An Introduction to Strategic Studies*, Oxford: Oxford University Press.

Bickerton, I. and Klausner, C. (2002), *A Concise History of the Arab–Israeli Conflict*, 4th edn, Upper Saddle River, NJ: Prentice Hall.

Biddle, S. (2002), *Afghanistan and the Future of Warfare: Implications for Army and Defense Policy*, Carlisle Barracks, PA: Army War College.

Bloom, A. (1987), *The Closing of the American Mind*, New York: Basic Books.

Bregman, A. (2002), *Israel's Wars: A History Since 1947*, 2nd edn, New York: Routledge.

Brooman, J. (1986), *The Reign of Terror in France: Jean-Baptiste Carrier and the Drownings at Nantes*, New York: Longman Publishers.

Burnham, W.D. (1970), *Critical Elections and the Mainspring of American Politics*, New York: W.W. Norton.

Carruthers, P. and Smith, P.K. (eds) (1996), *Theories of Theories of the Mind*, Cambridge: Cambridge University Press.

Chubb, J. and Peterson, P. (eds) (1985), *The New Direction in American Politics*, Washington, DC: Brookings Institution Press.

Cordovez, D. and Harrison, S.S. (1995), *Out of Afghanistan: The Inside Story of the Soviet Withdrawal*, New York: Oxford University Press.

Daalder, I.H. et al. (2002), *Protecting the American Homeland: One Year On*, Washington, DC: Brookings Institution Press.

Davies, M. and Stone, T. (eds) (1995), *Folk Psychology*, Oxford: Blackwell Publishers.

Dekmajian, R.H. (1995), *Islam in Revolution: Fundamentalism in the Arab World*, 2nd edn, New York: Syracuse University Press.

Dennett, D. (1987), *The Intentional Stance*, Cambridge, MA: MIT Press.

Detter, I. (2000), *The Laws of War*, 2nd edn, Cambridge: Cambridge University Press.

Elshtain, J.B. (ed.) (1994), *Just War Theory*, New York: New York University Press.

Falkowski, L.S. (ed.) (1979), *Psychological Models in International Politics*, Boulder: Westview Press.

Farnham, B.R. (1997), *Roosevelt and the Munich Crisis: A Study of Political Decision-Making*, Princeton, NJ: Princeton University Press.

Feith, D.J. (2008), *War and Decision: Inside the Pentagon at the Dawn of the War on Terrorism*, New York: Harper.

Fulbright, J. (1972), *The Crippled Giant*, New York: Random House.

Fuller, G.E. and Lesser, I.O. (1995), *A Sense of Siege: The Geopolitics of Islam and the West*, Boulder: Westview Press.

Gaddis, J.L. (1982), *Strategies of Containment: A Critical Appraisal of Postwar American National Security*, New York: Oxford University Press.

Garthoff, R. (1984), *Détente and Confrontation: American-Soviet Relations from Nixon to Reagan*, Washington, DC: Brookings Institution.

Gates, R. (1996), *The Ultimate Insider's Story of Five Presidents and How They Won the Cold War*, New York: Simon & Schuster.

Gohari, M.J. (2000), *The Taliban: Ascent to Power*, London: Oxford University Press.

Graubard, S.R. (1992), *Mr. Bush's War: Adventures in the Politics of Illusion*, New York: Hill and Wang.

Guelke, A. (1995), *The Age of Terrorism and the International Political System*, New York: St. Martin's Press.

Hammond, T.T. (1984), *Red Flag Over Afghanistan: The Communist Coup, the Soviet Invasion and the Consequences*, Boulder: Westview Press.

Hermann, M.G. (ed.) (1977), *A Psychological Examination of Political Leaders*, New York: The Free Press.

Hess, S. (2002), *Organizing the Presidency*, 3rd edn, Washington, DC: Brookings Institution Press.

Holmes, R.L. (1989), *On War and Morality*, Princeton, NJ: Princeton University Press.

Isikoff, M. (2007), *Hubris: The Inside Story of Spin, Scandal, and the Selling of the Iraq War*, Three Rivers Press.

Jervis, R. (2005), *American Foreign Policy in a New Era*, New York: Routledge.

Kaldor, M. (1999), *New and Old Wars: Organized Violence in a Global Era*, Stanford, CA: Stanford University Press.

Khan, R.M. (1991), *Untying the Afghan Knot: Negotiating Soviet Withdrawal*, Durham, NC: Duke University Press.

Korteweg, R. and Ehrhardt, D. (2005), *Terrorist Black Holes: A Study into Terrorist Sanctuaries and Governmental Weakness*, The Hague: Clingendael Centre for Strategic Studies.

Kunda, Z. (2002), *Social Cognition: Making Sense of People*, Cambridge, MA: MIT Press.

Kuttner, R. (2008), *Obama's Challenge: America's Economic Crisis and the Power of a Transformative Presidency*, White River Junction, Vermont: Chelsea Green Publishing.

Lackey, D. (1989), *The Ethics of War and Peace*, Englewood Cliffs, NJ: Prentice Hall.

LaFeber, W. (1995), *The American Age: US Foreign Policy at Home and Abroad*, 2nd edn, New York: W.W. Norton.

Lansford, T. (2002), *All for One: Terrorism, NATO and the United States*, Aldershot: Ashgate Publishing.

Lansford, T. and Pauly, R.J. (2004), *Strategic Preemption: U.S. Foreign Policy and the Second Iraq War*, Aldershot: Ashgate Publishing.

Ledeen, M.A. (2002), *The War Against the Terror Masters: Why It Happened, Where We Are Now, How We Will Win*, New York: St. Martin's Press.

Logevall, F. (ed.) (2002), *Terrorism and 9/11: A Reader*, Boston: Houghton Mifflin.

Luddy, J. (2005), *The Challenge and Promise of Network-Centric Warfare*, Arlington, VA: Lexington Institute.

Martin, J.L. and Neal, A.D. (2002), *Defending Civilization: How Our Universities Are Failing America and What Can Be Done About It*, Cambridge, MA: MIT Press.

McMichael. S.R. (1990), *Stumbling Bear: Soviet Military Performance in Afghanistan*, London: Brassey's.

Mearsheimer, J. and Walt, S. (2006), *The Israel Lobby and US Foreign Policy*, Farrar, Straus and Giroux: New York.

Menges, C.C. (1988), *Inside the National Security Council: The True Story of the Making and Unmaking of Reagan's Foreign Policy*, New York: Touchstone Books.

Migdal, J. (1988), *Strong States and Weak Societies: State-Society Relations and State Capabilities in the Third World*, Princeton: Princeton University Press.

Munson Jr., H. (1988), *Islam and Revolution in the Middle East*, New Haven: Yale University Press.

Nelson, M. (ed.) (2000), *The Presidency and the Political System*, Washington, DC: CQ Press.

Norman, R. (1995), *Ethics, Killing and War*, Cambridge: Cambridge University Press.

O'Toole, L.J. (2000), *American Intergovernmental Relations: Foundations, Perspectives, and Issues*, Washington, DC: CQ Press.

Papp, D.S., Johnson, L.K. and Endicott, J.E. (2005), *American Foreign Policy: History, Politics, and Policy*, New York: Pearson Education, Inc.

Patterson Jr., B.H. (2000), *The White House Staff: Inside the West Wing and Beyond*, Washington, DC: Brookings Institution Press.

Pauly, R.J. (2005), *U.S. Foreign Policy and the Persian Gulf: Safeguarding American Interests through Selective Multilateralism*, Aldershot: Ashgate Publishing.

Pollack, K.M. (2002), *The Threatening Storm: The Case to Invade Iraq*, New York: Random House.

Ramsey, P. (1968), *The Just War: Force and Political Responsibility*, Oxford: Rowman & Littlefield.

Rashid, A. (2008), *Descent into Chaos: The United States and the Failure of Nation Building in Pakistan, Afghanistan, and Central Asia*, New York: Penguin.

Rawls, J. (1996), *Political Liberalism*, 2nd edn, New York: Columbia University Press.

Record, J. and Terrill, A. (2004), *Iraq and Vietnam: Differences, Similarities and Insights*, Carlisle, PA: Strategic Studies Institute.

Regan, R.J. (1996), *Just War: Principles and Cases*, Washington, DC: Catholic University of America Press.

Renshon, J. (2006), *Why Leaders Choose War: The Psychology of Prevention*, Westport, CT: Praeger.

Ricks, T.E. (2007), *The American Military Adventure in Iraq, 2003–2005*, New York: Penguin Books.

Roberts, A. and Guelff, R. (eds) (1999), *Documents on the Laws of War*, 3rd edn, Oxford: Oxford University Press.

Rosenburg, E.S. (1982), *Spreading the American Dream: American Economic and Cultural Expansion*, New York: Hill and Wang.

Sageman, M. (2008), *Leaderless Jihad: Terror Networks in the Twenty-First Century*, Philadelphia: University of Pennsylvania Press.

Sivan, E. (1985), *Radical Islam*, New Haven: Yale University Press.

Skowronek, S. (1997), *The Politics Presidents Make: Leadership from John Adams to Bill Clinton*, Cambridge, MA: Belknap Press.

Smith, C.A. and Smith K.B. (1994), *The White House Speaks: Presidential Leadership as Persuasion*, Westport, CT: Praeger.

Snow, D. (2008), *National Security for a New Era: Globalization and Geopolitics After Iraq*, New York: Pearson.

Sprout, H. and Sprout, M. (1956), *Man-Milieu Relationship Hypothesis in the Context of International Politics*, Princeton, NJ: Princeton University Press.

Stich, S. (ed.) (1996), *Deconstructing the Mind*, Oxford: Oxford University Press.

Stiglitz, J. (2002), *Globalization and its Discontents*, New York: W.W. Norton and Company.

Taylor, C. (1991), *The Ethics of Authenticity*, Cambridge, MA: Harvard University Press.

Thomas, W. (2001), *The Ethics of Destruction: Arms and Force in International Relations*, London: Cornell University Press.

Tucker, R.W. and Hendrickson, D. (1992), *The Imperial Temptation: The New World Order and America's Promise*, New York: Council on Foreign Relations Press.

Walch, T. (ed.) (1997), *At the President's Side: The Vice Presidency in the Twentieth Century*, Columbia, MO: University of Missouri Press.

Waltz, K.N. (1957), *Man, the State, and War*, New York: W.W. Norton.

Walzer, M. (1977), *Just and Unjust Wars*, New York: Basic Books.

Wheeler, N. (2000), *Saving Strangers*, Oxford: Oxford University Press.

Whicker, M.L., Pfiffner, J.P. and Moore, R.A. (eds) (1993), *The Presidency and The Persian Gulf War*, Westport, CT: Praeger.

Wildavsky, A. (ed.) (1975), *Perspectives on the Presidency*, Boston: Little, Brown.

Woodward, B. (2002), *Bush at War*, New York: Simon & Schuster.

Yetiv, S. (2004), *Explaining Foreign Policy: The United States and the Persian Gulf War*, Baltimore: Johns Hopkins University Press.

Zakaria, F. (1998), *From Wealth to Power*, Princeton, NJ: Princeton University Press.

Index

References such as "178–9" indicate (not necessarily continuous) discussion of a topic across a range of pages. Wherever possible in the case of topics with many references, these have either been divided into sub-topics or only the most significant discussions of the topic are listed. Because the entire volume is about "terrorism," the "War on Terror" and the United States, the use of these elements (and certain others occurring throughout) as entry points has been minimized. Information will be found under the corresponding detailed topics.